GAUGING the RESILIENCE of CITY and TOWN GOVERNMENT:

A Manual for Strategists

Foreword by Dr Reuel J Khoza

C·I·L

CENTRE FOR INNOVATIVE LEADERSHIP

Dublin, Ireland
www.cil.net

Cover design by Colleen Mulrooney
Edited by Sheena Carnie
Typesetting by Wouter Reinders
Publishing management by Clare-Rose Julius

First edition, first impression 2021
ISBN: 978-0-620-94231-7
eISBN: 978-0-620-94232-4

Set in 11pt on 14pt Century Schoolbook

CONTENTS

ACKNOWLEDGEMENTS

To my beloved wife Marie for her unconditional support of the need for a single-minded focus, constant encouragement and belief in this work, and her help with technical challenges, thank you.

Rachel never ceases to surprise me with her acute intuition, emotional intelligence and learning sense. Thank you, Tyche, for your encouragement and enthusiasm for your Papa's work on this study, and for suggesting names for other writing still to come.

To the scholars and scholarly publications on whose contributions this study is based, thank you – you are all part of my journey. To Prof Brenda Gourley, Drs John and Kathryn Williams, as well as Dr Pat Irwin, thank you for your lifelong friendship, interest in this study, encouragement and support.

A study of this magnitude, on which this manual is based, is never the work of one individual working in isolation. This manual is the result of many helping hands in the service of the greater good in terms of scholarly inquiry and the compilation of a practical manual for strategists. My sincere appreciation goes to Dr Frans Cronje, who introduced me to North-West University where Professor Dr Gerrit van der Waldt, a rated researcher, supervised this study in his capacity as Research Professor: Public Governance. My great appreciation goes to Gerrit for his leadership, critical thinking, academic rigour, encouragement and guidance. As I learn about what other doctoral students may expect from a supervisor I appreciate ever more deeply the academic, intellectual and spiritual qualities that Gerrit van der Waldt has brought to this study. Thank you.

Finally, to Clare-Rose Julius, and Book Lingo thank you for your masterful editing and formatting contributions respectively.

FOREWORD

L ouis van der Merwe's manual/field book on effectively managed towns and cities could not have come at a more appropriate time, particularly for burgeoning urbanisation in developing political economies. The tide of urbanisation cannot be stemmed. It is as inexorable as it is, at times, desirable. It can only be guided, effectively managed and led with appropriate vision and action plan application. Efficacy and attendant resilience are a sine qua non; without these, slums will abound, congestion will intensify, and crime will be rampant.

This manual has been developed as a platform for creating a community of practice for resilience practitioners. The diagnostic instrument for gauging organisational resilience provides a robust basis for feedback to leaders across eight hierarchical levels, regarding the state of resilience in their organisations. The resilience strategy hierarchy offers a practical approach for building organisational resilience.

Many cities and towns are now growing faster than their national economies. Fast forward 20–25 years and we will probably witness resilient cities and towns becoming the flywheels for building economic momentum for resilient nation states. Resilient organisations are vital to springing back from challenges and shocks that now loom large on the horizon such as climate volatility, migration into cities and towns, another viral attack similar to Covid-19, digital convergence resulting in the Fourth Industrial Revolution (4IR), energy disruption and transportation disruption. These dynamics are among many that will challenge and test the resilience of the nation-state. Building resilient city, town and corporate organisations may be vital to our very existence as a species. An important lesson we have learnt from the Covid-19 pandemic is the widespread lack of resilience in most city and town governments, corporations, and also among national governments.

The foundation for resilience is based on organisational capability. Capability consists of effective leadership, scenario-based strategy and citizen/customer-centric service and product delivery. Regular capability review processes are recommended to identify priorities for capacity building in what might be called key strategy enabling processes, also called cross-cutting competencies. Capability provides the capacity to anticipate, adapt and recover from discontinuities in the contextual organisational environment. Sustainable development, green growth and smart cities harness the technology convergence in the Fourth Industrial Revolution to create the ability to improve in the face of adversity; this is called antifragility by Nassim Taleb of "black swan" fame.

Central to this manual for strategists is the resilience strategy hierarchy which signals logic, priority and a requisite sequence within a hierarchy of eight levels. Capability, capacity building, anticipation, adaptation, recovery, sustainable development, green growth and smart cities provide a practical systemic framework for resilience practitioners.

Louis van der Merwe has aggregated a lifetime of reflective practice into this manual for resilience practitioners. He integrates his successful experience in large-scale organisational renewal and change leadership, executive education across the world, postgraduate business school teaching and consulting support into this timely contribution. He provides a rich research-based combination of back-to-basics practical guidelines and an innovative process approach to state-of-the-art management and development practice. He is deeply invested in supporting leaders who wish to build organisations that learn. Organisations that learn are capable of extraordinary levels of performance while, at the same time, honouring the individuals in them. The sovereignty of the individual is embedded in the processes Louis designs and facilitates.

I have known Louis since 1985 when I led Coordinated Marketing and Management, a nascent Black consultancy which provided services in market research, corporate culture change, and management development. At the time Louis was leading a dynamic team of strategic change agents at Eskom, South Africa's then great power utility at the cutting edge of transformation. Sequent to two years of a mutually rewarding agency-client relationship, Louis orchestrated my unique positioning as a member of Eskom's Top 30 Executive Management Group. I was charged with the responsibility of providing an African market and strategy perspective to this corporation which had no senior Black executives then. Together Louis and I became a mighty transformative force catalysing change at Eskom. Ten years later I was to become Eskom's first Black chairman, following a rigorous selection process.

In 1990 Louis was instrumental in bringing Peter Senge to South Africa. He and I were the first facilitators to introduce the concept and model of the learning organisation, and Louis later championed scenario planning as a transformational strategic tool.

Louis and I stayed in contact, exchanging views at regular intervals on strategy, corporate governance and transformational leadership. Louis' diligent transformational work in South Africa's transition from apartheid to democracy was recognised as far afield as the United Kingdom, where it was applauded in the House of Lords by the late Lord Francis Thurlow. His expertise in scenario planning was recognised by Shell International Group Planning in 2003. During his consulting work with Shell, Louis designed and facilitated ultra-large strategy workshops of more than 300 participants. He has the rare ability to work effectively at C-suite and executive levels in corporations, city – and national governments.

Drawing on his extensive knowledge in organisational design and implementation, Louis established the Centre for Innovative Leadership (CIL), a brand he utilises in South Africa and internationally, which focuses on scenario-based strategic planning, systems thinking, leadership development, organisational effectiveness and change management.

Louis' commendable delivery in the disciplines sketched above is not without educational and academic grounding. He holds a Bachelor's Degree from the University of Pretoria, majoring in Economics, Psychology and Ethnology; a Master's Degree in Applied Behaviour and Leadership from City University, Seattle, USA and A PhD (Development and Management) from North-West University. He is also widely published.

Very significantly, Louis is passionate about developing organisational capability and capacity. His preferred approach is to engage with leaders and organisations as composite, complex systems and to operate at scale in corporations, city – and national governments. He is a man of great integrity – competent, dedicated, diligent, sagacious and visionary. I recommend this manual as essential reading for resilience practitioners and for building resilient city and town government organisations.

Dr Reuel J Khoza

PREFACE

This book addresses the issue of resilience in organisations – and especially resilience in those organisations that go to make up the government of a country, its towns and cities and other units employed in managing an increasingly complex world. It not only gives practical guidance on how to gauge the levels of resilience, but also ways of developing strategies to improve resilience.

The manual comes at a fortuitous time. We would have done well to pay more attention to resilience before the advent of the Covid-19 pandemic. Emerging economies, as well as developed economies, are all experiencing serious economic decline as they struggle to adjust to the realities of life in a pandemic. Their lack of readiness to withstand the challenges posed are being exposed in all areas of public life: health, transport, supply chains, education, human capacity management, and governance systems, to name but some. It is almost like the sticking plaster that was keeping things together has been ripped off and the wounds below are exposed. Some would argue that this pandemic and how we steer our way through it is just a "dress rehearsal" for the much larger disrupter that lies ahead: climate change. However one frames the issues, there can be no doubt that making sure we have resilient towns and cities is a significant way to rebuild economies and organisations and prepare ourselves for a future that is significantly different to the past.

This manual serves resilience strategists and practitioners as they engage in that rebuilding exercise – at all levels.

This manual consists of four parts. Part I enables the practitioner to embark on the journey of building a resilience strategy. It describes a capability review and clarifies how to build capacity where it is lacking or insufficient. Part II builds understanding by providing the theoretical underpinning for effective and competent resilience practice. Part III describes the critical competencies for effective resilience practice, highlighting the qualities of a useful strategic conversation as part of the scenario-based strategy process. Finally, Part IV lays out a diagnostic instrument as a method of gauging resilience and stimulating learning.

These four components are a step by step process in a resilience strategy hierarchy.

The author, Louis van der Merwe, is particularly well-qualified to advise on this process. He has a lifetime of consulting experience in successful organisation renewal, assisting large organisations in a variety of sectors to design scenario-based strategy processes and robust strategies. His experience includes many years in city government and 15 years leading an internal team of 60 change agents in a major corporation. He also has extensive experience in executive education, more especially building capacity at the postgraduate level. His consultancy, aptly named the Centre for Innovative Leadership (CIL), has an impressive list of clients in several countries where he was enlisted to help drive organisational change.

He brings all his extensive experience to bear in his doctoral thesis where he develops the diagnostic instrument to gauge organisational resilience – a thesis which forms the basis of this manual – and an instrument solidly grounded in theory as well as practice.

Strategists seeking to build resilience in any sector of an economy will welcome the practical advice – and organisations would do well to ensure their resilience in a world where it will surely be tested to the limits in the not too distant future.

Brenda M. Gourley

ABOUT THE AUTHOR

After six years in city government as an organisational effectiveness practitioner, the author spent a year as the National President of AIESEC South Africa. AIESEC is an incubator for social entrepreneurs and the largest student-run international organisation in the world. Its flagship programme is international student exchange. He then spent 15 years as a successful internal organisational development and renewal practitioner at Eskom in the 1980s. Eskom is the South African electricity utility, supplying more than 90% of the electricity in South Africa. At the time that was approximately equivalent to 60% of all electricity supplied on the African continent. Eskom then ranked fourth in the world in terms of staff numbers and installed generation capacity. The author built an internal community of practice which resulted in successful organisational turnaround, renewal and an AAA+ credit rating, which was awarded in the '90s during the leadership of chair Dr Reuel Khoza. An AAA+ credit rating was better than the sovereign credit rating at that time. This internal community of practice consisted of 60 professional organisational renewal agents at the corporate head office and more than 200 line managers in the regions and power stations, facilitating capacity building and championing specific processes that enable renewal.

As a result of the success of this large-scale organisational transformation work, the author was invited to join Dr Peter Senge's MIT-based community of Learning Organisation practitioners. This community of practice evolved to form the Society of Learning. At the time, corporate member Shell Oil had dropped from number 2 to number 60 on the league tables for "Best Companies to Work For" in the USA. At the end of this engagement, Shell Oil had risen to number 32 on the league tables under the visionary leadership of its president, the late Phillip Carroll. As a result of this contribution, the author was engaged in supporting the leadership of Philip Turberville, President of Shell Europe Oil Products (SEOP), across Western Europe. The author worked in this role for three years, supporting the building of SEOP organisational strategic alignment and capability across Europe.

After a brief spell in Taiwan Cellular Corporation developing decision scenarios, he joined Professor Brenda Gourley, then the CEO and president of The Open University (OU), and supported her visionary leadership in the successful turnaround strategy for The OU. This scenario-based strategy enabled The OU to rebuild its financial viability and enter the digital age with more than 80 000 hits a day on its digital platform.

Louis van der Merwe has a passion for developing capacity at scale for building resilience strategies in cities and towns, and has consolidated the successful management of large-scale change into this practical manual.

A WORD IN ADVANCE

This manual has been developed to enable city – and town governments to build resilience strategies. Resilience strategies enable cities and towns to successfully navigate impending shocks from discontinuities in their contextual environment. This manual will also enable the building of a community of practice to support developing resilience strategies at scale in large towns and metros in emerging economies. Practitioners may be full-time professional practitioners or line managers and executives who choose to join this community of practice.

This manual is built on the foundations of a PhD study titled *City government resilience: Towards a diagnostic instrument*. Specific chapters of the manual are based on popular publications in peer-reviewed journals, publications in the popular press and published conversations with the author. These publications have been edited and included to provide a comprehensive resource and foundation for resilience practitioners. The PhD study is the culmination of many years of successful experience by the author in providing both internal and external support for leadership in large organisations in the 10 000 to 65 000 staff complement range. These organisations can be described as knowledge-intensive, for example, organisations in the energy and telecoms industries, local government and higher education sector – organisations that are, generally speaking, competently and courageously led in volatile environments. The study is supplemented with publications from organisations such as the World Economic Forum (WEF) to form a holistic, practical basis for practitioner development. References to authorities have remained in the text so that practitioners who wish to expand their knowledge base may consult the bibliography and resources. Practitioners will benefit most in terms of learning by using this resource as a readily available field guide.

Successful resilience practice depends on the alignment of at least three levels of learning *(see Figure 1.3 in Chapter 1)*.

Level Three: What are the tools and techniques that practitioners use to develop a resilience strategy?

Level Two: Which competencies (knowledge, skills, attitudes and values) are required to master these tools and techniques?

Level One: What is the foundational philosophy/worldview that underpins competencies and tools/techniques? From which perspective do we view these levels of learning?

It may be tempting to reach for level three out of the best of intentions, without attending to levels two and one. However, lack of attention to all three levels will inevitably result in disappointment and possible failure.

This manual serves as a key resource for resilience practitioners and scenario-based strategy practitioners. One of the key challenges faced by city – and town governments is that developing a useful and robust resilience strategy requires a 20 – to 25 year perspective on the future. Specific processes are best suited to build a 20 – to 25 year perspective on future conditions. More about this later. According to Jaques[1], this 20 – to 25 year time horizon is the length of time it takes for a policy decision in a city to be shown to be correct or incorrect. He called this "the time span of discretion" and it is based on a correlation he established between the level of a decision maker in an organisational hierarchy and the time span into the future where a decision would be proven to be right or wrong. This relationship forms the basis of what became known as the Paterson Job Evaluation system in the South African mining industry. This system uses job analysis, job evaluation and job grading as the basis for pay scales. Job evaluation can also be used for personal development planning, and for building succession management systems in large organisations.

It is well known that policymakers judge their policies by their intentions while citizens judge a policy by its impact on their lives. Sound theoretical foundations and practical frameworks offer a bulwark against good policy intentions often informed by populism and other narrowly defined interests. Theory is defined here as what works best in practice and why. Sound theoretical foundations provide a reliable basis for an evidence-based approach to policy formulation. This manual provides a low threshold/high ceiling platform for learning. The early chapters enable

---

1   Jaques, E. 2013. *Requisite organisation: A total system for effective managerial organisation and management leadership for the 21st century.* Orlando, FL: Cason Hall.

immediate action and results, while later chapters provide a basis for advancing key competencies for successful resilience strategy practice.

The manual consists of four parts: Part I enables an early successful start by assessing capability and capacity building. Part II provides the theory that underpins competent organisational renewal, development and resilience strategies. Part III enables the development of key competencies for effective practice. Part IV provides the diagnostic instrument and Part IV offers a roadmap and frame of reference with which to contract with a client system. Normative proto-scenarios for the future of cities will challenge policymaking with the intention of improving the robustness of policy. The aspirational nature of the indicators in the diagnostic instrument items within the eight factors provide a benchmark against which to truthfully assess the current reality in any city or large town, thus providing a basis for developing the desired results (aka vision) for continuous improvement within a robust resilience strategy.

Any new insights, even a single novel insight, which executive leaders and executive managers gain and put into practice from the application of the diagnostic instrument should be considered a win for developing a more robust resilience strategy. The processual approach, which enables learning as its focus, has been adopted with the application of this diagnostic instrument. This approach is structured as a low threshold/high ceiling process of learning. As uncertainty rises, city and town governments should build more robust resilience strategies.

Futurist and visionary Stewart Brand[2] has marked the current migration into cities and towns across the world as *the defining dynamic of the 21st century*. This global dynamic, amongst other disruptive forces, poses a threat to humanity's existence. It will also test and challenge city and town government resilience strategies.

Be prepared!
Resilient cities and towns can act as flywheels for mitigating climate volatility. They can also act as accelerators for development and job creation and the reduction of inequality.

Cities and towns, and the communities in and around them, are in search of ways to develop their economies and create wealth and jobs, as well as ways to reduce inequality and poverty. Management processes that lead them to more effective and efficient organisations will enable both resilience strategies and development.

---

2   Brand, S. 2017b. What squatter cities can teach us/TED Talk/TED.com. https://www.ted.com/talks/stewart_brand_on_squatter_cities Date of access: 8 August 2017.

Amidst a plethora of fanciful ideological rhetoric promising to achieve these same ends, this writing provides a practical, evidence-based diagnostic instrument for gauging city government resilience. The research on which this book is based also describes a learning approach to gauging city government resilience. It includes social transformation through the engagement of citizens in rights-based methods of sustainable community investment processes (SCIP) for economic development. Communities that take responsibility for their development also take back their independence, dignity and self-worth for the citizens within them. This approach to development is preferred to creating undignified co-dependence with government agencies using taxpayers money under the pretext of investing in development. The approach in this book may go some way to correcting the widespread disenfranchisement and dispossession that followed the colonial era and avoiding recolonisation by well-intentioned national, regional and local governments.

This study has resulted in a diagnostic instrument from the Centre for Innovative Leadership (CIL) which is different from other such instruments among the emerging plethora of work on resilience since the New York City attack referred to as "9/11".

Key differentiators of the CIL instrument include but are not limited to the following:

- the diagnostic instrument for gauging city government resilience strategy is positioned as an organisational renewal and development intervention which therefore rests on a substantial body of scholarship, proven theory and guidelines for successful practice
- it engages and stimulates a strategic conversation amongst executive leaders and executive managers in city government as an organisation
- key enablers for successfully executing a resilience strategy – such as capability assessment and capacity building in cross-cutting competencies, aka key strategy enabling processes – are prominently featured
- scenario-based strategy and systems dynamics (SD) modelling enable the shifting of assumptions in the minds of policymakers on a 20 – to 25 year planning time horizon
- descriptors of factors and items in the diagnostic describe aspirations and thus provide the basis for a truthful indication of desired results (vision) and possible benchmarks as well as a peer review of a city government resilience strategy, and
- it advocates building organisational infrastructure for sustaining successful change management, which may enable a higher probability of successful change, assuming a continuous flow of challenges to city government resilience.

These differentiators are embedded in this diagnostic instrument and address shortcomings in similar approaches emanating from developed economies. The primary aim of this diagnostic instrument is to enable the development of a city – and town government resilience strategy in emerging economies such as in Africa, China, India and South America. However, the underlying principles of successful resilience strategies are equally valid for First World cities, large towns and organisations. The dynamics of social transformation and strategic responses to predetermined driving forces and disruptions, such as climate volatility and technology convergence, respectively, may result in the emergence of so-called smart cities and towns. Smart cities and towns are probably the economical and societal flywheels that will mitigate the impending impact of global climate change and technology disruptions.

In the face of these and other impending disruptive forces, well-formulated, practical city government resilience strategies may be an essential element of development and survival in the 21st century.

HOW BEST TO USE THIS MANUAL

This manual will support the development of resilience practitioners. **Part I:** Early Action Now – will enable them to make a start; this part consists of one chapter and contains all the essentials necessary for using the instrument factors as a gauge. The centrepiece of developing a resilience strategy is the framework for guiding resilience represented by a hierarchy indicating the best sequence. Chapter 1 also contains the basic principles and foundational philosophy and worldview on which the instrument is based.

Part II: Theory Underpinning Effective and Competent Resilience Practice – contains the essential theory required for resilience practice. Theory is defined here as what works best and why. This theory consists of chapters covering organisational dynamics, resilience models and strategy schools of thinking, and finally a description of modern government. This theory is considered important for competent resilience practitioners as they also need to understand the theory of practice in order to be capable of making informed choices along the way to developing a resilience strategy for a particular city or town.

Part III: Key Competencies for Effective Practice – contains the essential components needed for enabling learning and shifting the assumptions in the minds of organisational decision makers. Scenario planning includes the practical application of systems thinking.

Part IV: Diagnostic Instrument as Feedback and Stimulus for Learning – contains the full instrument, consisting of factors and items which can best be used in action research mode with the top team of organisational decision makers. The instrument is contained in the Resilience Strategy Hierarchy™, which is also the logical sequence for best practice proceeding from foundation-building as a basis for adaptation, recovery, sustainable development, green growth and smart cities.

ABSTRACT

This study and the manual focus on city – and town government *as organisations*. Capability can be found and developed in the organisational structure which, in the broadest sense, can be regarded as a *human activity system*. Capacity building in cross-cutting competencies, also known as key strategy enabling processes, will enhance capability, which is essential for the subsequent levels in the resilience strategy hierarchy (see Figure 1.1). Resilient city and town governments provide critical mass and momentum, which as flywheels in nation states enable national resilience. A number of existential threats such as climate volatility now face humanity; resilient cities and towns may together provide mitigation for these threats.

This study starts by exploring the evolution of thinking regarding organisations as open systems. It provides a perspective on a total systems approach to organisational design and organisational renewal and development. From previous successful, practical experience it identifies high leverage components in systems which enable organisational resilience, providing a holistic perspective on organisational resilience and sustainable economic development. This includes the paradigmatic developments, schools of thinking, theoretical principles, theories and models for organisational resilience. It identifies anticipation, adaptation and recovery (AAR) as a framework and starting point from which a diagnostic instrument was developed. It investigates trends, patterns of behaviour and systemic structures that influence resilience, with specific reference to city government, including high leverage areas within the extended AAR meta-framework. Factors and items, together with aspirational descriptors, are key components of the diagnostic instrument. The aspirational quality of descriptors provides a perspective on the desired results (aka vision) for particular aspects and may form the basis for linking factors and items to benchmarks. Capability assessment, capacity building in cross-cutting competencies, anticipation, adaptation, recovery, sustainable development, green growth and smart cities form the meta-framework of the diagnostic instrument with descriptions for each meta-category. Within each category are items and their descriptors which form the basis for gauging the relative level of resilience. The instrument is also referred to as the Resilience Strategy Hierarchy™ (RSH). Triangulation between the literature study, the instrument design, and cross-checking with a purposive sample of users has established its validity empirically within a pre-test and post-test framework to develop the final diagnostic instrument for gauging city government resilience.

KEYWORDS: Capability, capacity building, city government, city government resilience, organisational resilience, systems thinking, systems dynamics, resilience indicators, hierarchy, scenario-based strategy, futuring, learning, strategic conversation, organisation learning, change management, innovation, leverage, developmental cities, urban dynamics

LIST OF FIGURES

LIST OF TABLES

PART I

Early action now

This part, consisting of Chapter I, enables practitioners to start the process of building a city government resilience strategy based on assessing organisational capability.

"Live as if you were to die tomorrow, learn as if you were to live forever."

Mahatma Gandhi

Contents

CHAPTER 1

INTRODUCTION TO CAPABILITY REVIEW AND CAPACITY BUILDING

"Learning is the process whereby knowledge is created through the transformation of experience"[1]

1   INTRODUCTION

Amidst a plethora of approaches to ensuring resilience in cities, the Centre for Innovative Leadership (CIL) has developed a process-based learning approach to building a city government resilience strategy. CIL has positioned its resilience planning focus on city and town organisations in emerging economies, with South African cities and towns as proxies for developing economies. The same principles are also applicable to first economy cities, towns and corporations. The CIL diagnostic instrument provides a framework and metrics for gauging current reality in a city or town against best practice for resilience planning. The instrument that has been developed to gauge resilience may be regarded as a hierarchy. The hierarchical logic is reflected in Figure 1.1 – The Resilience Strategy Hierarchy (RSH)™.

The Resilience Strategy Hierarchy™ reflects the factors in this hierarchy which are organised in a logical sequence. It starts with building the foundations for resilience by assessing capability and building capacity, which enables anticipation, adaptation and recovery and so on. This creates the basis for sustainable development as set out in various multilateral agreements and protocols. Green growth reflects the dimensions of an innovative logic which retunes the human mind (Whybrow) to a circular production and economic cycle. Once this is achieved, smart cities may be built through the positive use of the technology convergence contained in the so-called 4IR. The assumption underpinning sustainable development, green growth and smart city factors is that predetermined climate change and the digital revolution require these three responses in order to avert these resilience threats along this hierarchy, thus implying a priority. The factors in the hierarchy provide a logical framework. Items within factors have been listed in the comprehensive instrument contained in Chapter 7. Their aspirational character will stimu-

---

[1]   Kolb, D.A. 1984. *Experiential Learning: Experience as the source of learning and development.* Prentice Hall.

late a creative, strategic conversation to develop a specific gauge for the situation under consideration.

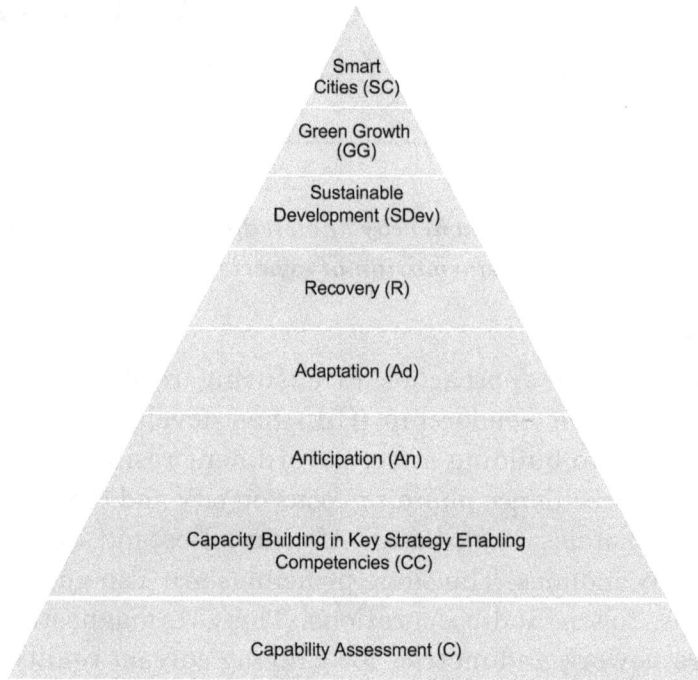

Figure 1.1: The resilience strategy hierarchy (RSH)™

Using the instrument as feedback to gauge organisational resilience will provide new insights which, when acted upon, will improve resilience as well as provide ideas and inspiration for further improvements. The CIL process approach aligns with the processual school of strategy which provides a scholarly framework for practitioners within which to develop their competencies and effective practice. CIL has a successful practice of change management in a Fortune 50 Corporation in the United States of America (USA) and Europe, a major university in the United Kingdom (UK) and a state-owned enterprise (SOE) in South Africa (SA). This successful experience forms the basis of the author's knowledge and practitioner support in building a resilience strategy in city and town governments. In the field of change management, more than 60% of efforts to change are fruitless.[2]

CIL has had success in large organisations such as Eskom, Shell Oil, Shell Europe Oil Products and The Open University, among others. CIL situates its systemic approach within the fields of leadership, organisation development

---

[2]   Kotter, J. 1995. Leading change: Why transformation efforts fail. *Harvard Business Review*, (March-April):59–67.

and scenario-based strategy. Resilience practitioners may draw on scholarly works from these fields and others to support their work as change agents in governing cities, towns and organisations in general. Predetermined dynamics such as massive urban migration, climate volatility, the digital convergence and other dynamics will confront and challenge organisational resilience in cities and towns. Developing cities and towns as sustainable economic entities can be based on circular economic principles, green growth and digitally-enabled smart cities. A process approach engaging systems thinking enables the addition of categories beyond the common frameworks for resilience planning to be found. Addressing these forces with a positive outcome in mind will require shifting assumptions that underpin policy in cities and towns.

David Kolb[3] defines learning as the process whereby knowledge is created through the transformation of experience. Building feedback loops as part of a process that enables influencing assumptions, and thereby changing behaviour, may be the key to enabling sustainable habitation on our planet. Species extinction, rising temperatures together with increasingly volatile weather means accepting that there may be an existential challenge to human habitation on the planet. It also raises the importance of finding a way to retune our thinking from its current unsustainable set of assumptions to a sustainable frame of reference. Quality communication is the vehicle for interpersonal and team learning. Critical thinking enables "seeing" clearly and formulating high leverage actions and interventions. Seeing wholes, patterns of behaviour over time and underlying structure, rather than parts, enables the creation of sustainable organisations, cities and national economies. The first step towards this outcome is assessing the capability of city- and town governments followed by capacity building based on self-assessment at organisational and individual levels using a personal development planning process (PDP).

1.1   Resilience matters

How resilient have metros/cities and towns been in the face of disruptions? The 9/11 attack, Hurricane Katrina or African cyclone Idai which devastated Mozambique, Zimbabwe and Malawi in 2019 have uncovered a lack of preparedness. Why were these regions not prepared? Were they able to spring back after these shocks? Leaders often seem to think that somehow a severe shock will never happen to their organisation. The latest shock, namely, the Covid-19 pandemic, has been no different. It remains to be seen how recovery will fare. The late Bill O'Brien, a leading corporate philosopher and past chair of Hanover Insurance Companies, a

---

[3]   Kolb, 1984.

prototype learning organisation, often remarked: "People only buy flood insurance after a flood." It may be a truism that leaders learn from their mistakes. Consider the costs of non-resilience in terms of loss of life and material wealth. In the domain of city- and town resilience planning, a wise investment may be to prepare a robust and strategic resilience plan in advance of a disaster. Anticipating discontinuities that may impact on cities and towns could deliver dividends to the citizens.

In this study SoA, and specifically SA, is treated as a proxy for testing resilience in emerging economies across Africa and globally. Emerging economies such as Brazil, Russia, India and China, as well as First World economies all have similar predetermined dynamics that will challenge the resilience of their cities. Migration to urban areas, climate volatility such as cyclones, a viral attack, prolonged drought and water shortages are just some of the dynamics that have an impact on them. It is unfortunately too late for cities and towns to develop a resilience strategy when a cyclone is bearing down on them.

The consequences of energy- and transport disruptions, and other disruptors such as the technology convergence referred to as the Fourth Industrial Revolution (4IR), are slowly but surely entering the consciousness of decision makers and leadership. Leadership is considering: What would life be like without electricity as we know it? A total blackout scenario requiring a black start would result in no electricity, no lights; after a couple of days generators would fall silent once the diesel has been exhausted, diesel deliveries would have ceased, resulting in no replacement diesel being available. There would be no deliveries of food and provisions to supermarkets. ATMs would stop working and no cash withdrawals would be available for buying essentials. Mobile phones would also fall silent once charges were exhausted and recharging had stopped. Water pumps would stop working, resulting in water shortages in cities and towns. In many cases there will initially be a run on these resources as they become scarce, then silence and immense suffering will occur together with economic catastrophe.

What would happen with crime? There would be chaos in communities. A *Lord of the Flies* scenario could prevail. Rural subsistence communities might be best off because of their independence from modern commodities such as electricity, piped water on demand and the like. In cities, camping stoves and other associated equipment would rapidly take the place of modern commodities. Camping-competent families might even abandon the facilities in their urban homes and permanently camp out using portable lighting, cooking and other facilities as their new normal.

One of the key variables in building resilience is the quality of leadership. Cities and towns where the leadership has thought through potential resilience challenges in advance will probably be better off. Where a robust resilience strategy and adaptive responses are routinely practised and embedded in the city- and town community, citizens know in advance of any shock what they are to do in the event of such an occurrence. This preparedness provides a safety net to cushion the most severe impacts and avert immediate disaster. Others may be caught off-guard because they had been hoping for the best and trusting that the tragedy would not occur. Unfortunately, hope is not a good strategy!

Both city- and national governments have learnt from the Oklahoma bombing in the USA, and later the attack on World Trade Center's twin towers in New York City which is often referred to simply as "9/11". That anticipation may be a fruitful strategy. Organisations that had thought through these eventualities before they took place fared better; prepared plans and emergency routines resulted in an entirely different response compared to organisations that had not thought through how they might best recover.

Cities and towns across the globe are facing a number of predetermined dynamics and discontinuities in their contextual environment, with climate volatility, migration, a viral attack, disruption to transport and energy being just a few that may be on governments' mental radar. These dynamics will challenge resilience. The most important of these dynamics is the massive global migration to cities and towns. Estimates are that by 2035, a mere 14 years from now, more than 50% of people in Africa will be living in cities or towns, with Lagos, Cairo, Johannesburg, Kinshasa and Dar es Salaam being among the emerging megacities in Africa that will result from this migration. Climate volatility, digital convergence, also known as "4IR", a viral attack on the human species similar to the so-called Spanish flu in 1918 where 20 to 50 million lives were lost, cyberattacks and even a nuclear attack are other forces which seem predetermined to impact populations.

Futurist Stewart Brand describes the massive urbanisation on a global scale as "the dynamic that will define the 21st century". City government resilience and how it deals with these patterns, discontinuities and disruptive dynamics may play a significant role in enhancing the resilience of nation states. The demographic profile of SA, for instance, is such that of a total population of 54 million, 26 million are below the age of 24.[4] At the same time, the total African population of 468 million will grow to more than 800 million, almost doubling by 2035 when more than 50% will have moved to cities and towns.[5]

[4] StatsSA. 2014. Statistics South Africa http://www.statssa.gov.za/?m=2014&gclid= EAIaIQobChMI2tWHooCj7QIVCU4YCh39xwPiEAAYASAAEgLiWfD_BwE Date of Access: 23 June 2017.

[5] Institute for Security Studies (ISS). 2016. *Africa's future is urban.* https://issafrica.org/events/africas-future-is-urban Date of access: 27 April 2017.

Cities may form the backbone of national resilience and sustainable economic development policies, as well as policy execution, such as supporting the emergence of the so-called developmental state. This is occurring in a century during which, according to Katz and Bradley,[6] a network of so-called sovereign "trading cities" with a potential federation of cities is in the ascendant. They posit that this dynamic may begin to rival the influence of the nation-state in crucial areas such as adapting to and recovering from climate volatility, cyberattacks and disruptive 4IR technological convergence, as well as energy and transport disruption.

Executive leadership and executive management in cities and towns may be the primary beneficiaries of a clear perspective on enabling city government resilience. The diagnostic instrument detailed in this manual also provides a basis for comparison, benchmarking and learning between members of a network of cities and towns.

Enabling city- and town government resilience may be associated with cities' economic performance and governance, which, depending on their economic policy, could increase cities' attractiveness for foreign direct investment (FDI), which in turn may result in greater economic development and job creation. Greater industrial development and job creation within cities and towns can be aggregated to improve the terms of trade on a national level. Resilient cities and towns may become the flywheels or catalysts for generating momentum for national development and resilience.

Diagnosis, and through it an assessment of the capability, capacity building and competence development for enabling city government resilience, may also lead to an expansion of the pool of competent executive leadership and executive management talent in cities and towns, and therefore enhance the leadership talent pool nationally.

In 2019 Cyclone Idai severely tested the resilience of cities and towns in its destructive pathway through Mozambique, Zimbabwe and Malawi. The rate of recovery of affected cities and towns in these countries will reflect their level of resilience.

The terror attacks on the city of New York on 9/11 severely tested the resilience of the government of this megacity. This event also stimulated research interest in the nature of resilience, as part of the management of risk. This throws into stark relief the interconnectedness and complexity of

---

[6]   Katz, B. & Bradley, J. 2013. *The Metropolitan revolution: How cities and metros are fixing our broken politics and fragile economy*. Washington, DC: The Brookings Institution.

the modern world.[7] In this regard, scholars such as Smuts,[8] Von Bertalanffy[9] and Forrester[10] offer a radical new way of looking at complex systems. They argue that any complex system analysed by uncovering and understanding the causal relationships and interconnections between its constituent parts offers novel insights and learning. This systemic perspective enables the *uncovering of the underlying structure of a system*. Looking at the parts of a complex system in isolation, often more visible, may not be the most useful perspective for sense-making endeavours. This perspective of uncovering structure and identifying areas of greatest leverage is referred to as a "systemic perspective". Thinking in systemic terms is still uncommon among decision makers.

Smuts's[11] and Von Bertalanffy's[12] contributions to holistic thinking and the theory of systemic interconnectedness, known as holism and general systems theory (GST) respectively, provide scholars and professional practitioners with an essential and revolutionary worldview. This worldview is useful for making sense of global interconnectedness. It is also useful for making sense of organisational dynamics.

Jervis[13] describes a system as a set of units or elements interconnected so that changes to some elements or their relations produce changes in other parts of the system. Meadows[14] describes a system as an interconnected set of elements that is coherently organised in such a way as to achieve something. She adds that it must consist of three kinds of things: elements, interconnections and a function or purpose. The distinguishing feature of an open or dynamic adaptive system is the presence of so-called "feedback loops", as described by Senge, Kleiner, Roberts, Ross and Smith,[15] Sterman[16] and Meadows.[17] City government resilience planning consists of rebuilding

[7] Wheatley, M.J. 2002. *It's an interconnected world*. Shambhala Sun. http://margaretwheatley.com/wp-content/uploads/2014/12/Its-An-Interconnected-World.pdf Date of access: 3 August 2015.

[8] Smuts, J.C. 1925. *Holism and evolution*. 3rd ed. London: Macmillan.

[9] Von Bertalanffy, L. 1968. *General systems theory: Foundation development and applications*. New York, NY: George Braziller

[10] Forrester, J.W. 1969. *Urban dynamics*. Cambridge, MA: MIT Press.

[11] Smuts, 1925.

[12] Von Bertalanffy, 1968.

[13] Jervis, R. 1997. *System effects*. Princeton, NJ: Princeton University Press

[14] Meadows, D. 2008. *Thinking in systems*. White River Junction, VT: Chelsea Green.

[15] Senge, P.M., Kleiner, A., Roberts, C., Ross, R.B. & Smith, B. 1994. *The fifth discipline fieldbook*. London: Nicholas Brealey, p. 89.

[16] Sterman, J. 2000. *Business dynamics: Systems thinking and modelling for a complex world*. Boston, MA: McGraw Hill Higher Education. p. 16.

[17] Meadows, 2008, p. 187.

feedback loops that enable the cities and towns to learn and self-organise to adapt to the discontinuities arising from their environment.

> "At its broadest level, systems thinking encompassed a large and fairly amorphous body of methods, tools and principles, all oriented to looking at the interrelatedness of forces and seeing them holistically as part of connected processes. The field includes cybernetics and chaos theory, gestalt psychology, the work of Gregory Bateson, Jay Forrester, Russel Ackoff, Peter Senge, Eric Trist, Ludwig von Bertalanffy and the Santa Fe Institute; and the dozen or so practical techniques for 'process mapping' of flows of activity. All of these diverse approaches have one guiding idea in common: that the behaviour of all systems follows certain common systems-based principles, the nature of which are being discovered and articulated as part of the literature on so-called learning organisations (Senge et al.)."[18]

In a democratic system of governance, feedback and learning may be triggered by media reporting, commissions of enquiry, citizen input and voter behaviour. These feedback loops, when they are critical, are generally the cues for city government to become more responsive. Senge[19] frames systems thinking as one of the five disciplines of a learning organisation. Disciplines point towards what it would take to become conversant in one of the disciplines. As a key to "team learning", Senge[20] identifies the process of double-loop learning, originally developed by Argyris,[21] with its effect on the minds of leaders and managers, and the shift it leads to in the assumptions they make. From a learning perspective, it is ultimately this change in thinking and in assumptions at scale that Whybrow[22] identifies when referring to re-tuning the human mind as the key to enabling global resilience, global sustainability and global survival. He advocates re-tuning the human mind from a mindset that extracts, beneficiates, uses and discards to a mentality of sustainable use through recycling in a circular economic cycle where the output of one cycle is the feedstock of another.

Forrester[23] invented systems dynamics (SD) modelling based on systems thinking, which uses causal loops and feedback loops to study urban dynamics.

---

[18] Senge et al., 1994, p. 89.

[19] Senge et al., 1994.

[20] Senge et al., 1994.

[21] Argyris, C. 1982. *Reasoning, learning and action individual and organisational.* San Francisco, CA: Jossey-Bass.

[22] Whybrow, P.C. 2015. *The well-tuned brain: Neuroscience and the life well-lived.* London: Norton.

[23] Forrester, 1969.

Later he used SD to study the global dynamics of supply and demand and the limits to growth for the world. The dynamics and elements he identified in an urban setting may be useful in developing an instrument for gauging city government resilience. Uncovering the interconnectedness of these dynamic elements leads to an understanding of how a system such as a city might behave when one or more of its constituent parts changes. This leads to the identification of the most effective point of intervention within a system. This point of intervention is known as "leverage".[24] Identifying leverage within a city government system provides the basis for a useful diagnostic instrument for a process of gauging city government resilience.

In the resilience equation, the level of trust is fundamental; some say it is everything! Amongst individuals in a community, trust functions like the operating system in a computer – it enables learning, responsiveness, alignment, agility and accountability to the rule of law.

1.2 Anticipating the need for essential reserves

When an organisation experiences a shock, the most immediate need is essential reserves which have to be on hand and available until the initial adaptation has taken place and stability is re-established. These reserves may include water, food, energy, medical and sanitary services and efficient communications. An essential reserve may also be the embedded emergency preparedness patterns of behaviour among the key role players. Knowing what to do in the event of a shock enables the immediate recognition of the situation followed by action. This reserve may be built up by routinely rehearsing emergency preparedness drills and processes until they are well known and can be automatically executed in the event of a shock. Anticipating the nature of potential shocks beyond the initial impact requires sense-making and appreciation of the systemic nature of a specific dynamic. Anticipating beyond the short term may require having state-of-the-art methodological processes in place with which to enable the correct mindset for the anticipation process itself.

1.3 Enabling fit with the future environment(s)

An effective resilience strategy may contain both short-term components and medium and longer-term elements. The purpose of a robust resilience strategy is to ensure that an organisation, in this case, a city government organisation, survives beyond the shock or the discontinuity in its environment. When there is a correspondence or fit between its resilience strategy and the challenge to its resilience, the organisation can conclude

---

[24] Senge, P.M. 1990. *The fifth discipline: The art and practice of the learning organisation.* London: Random House, p.64.

that its strategy is robust. During a shock, there may be specific needs that in any event must be anticipated and available in the form of essential reserves. These reserves may be both tangible and intangible. Tangible reserves include emergency supplies of water, food, blankets and medicines while intangible resources include attitudes and embedded resilient responses. One of the reasons that the future is so difficult to anticipate is because of the complexity embedded in the unfolding future.

According to Wack,[25] the purpose of a scenario-based strategy is "to shift assumptions and thinking in the minds of decision makers inside the organisation about what might happen in future outside the organisation".[26] Scenarios describe future conditions in the contextual environment, in the form of two or three or four internally consistent stories or narratives, supported by deep research.[27]

Van der Merwe[28] goes on to provide tests for the quality of scenarios:
- "relevant to decision makers using them;
- challenging existing thinking;
- plausibility based on deep, rigorous systemic research and analysis; and
- when an organisation has lived through the future described in scenarios no important dynamic has been overlooked."

Van der Merwe[29] points out that the dynamics contained in scenarios may be drawn from the following generic categories: politics, economics, societal dynamics, technology, regulations, ecology and history. He posits that "the greatest learning accrues amongst the people who research the behaviour of specific dynamics in the environment" and goes on to add that "further deep learning takes place when using scenarios to stress-test or wind tunnel strategy and policy".[30] Stress-testing, also known as wind-tunnelling, a resilience strategy for robustness, fit or correspondence in future conditions (scenarios), is analogous to testing an aircraft design in a wind tunnel.

1.4   Robust resilience strategy as fit
Figure 1.2 illustrates the principle of "fit", also referred to as correspondence, robustness, congruence or conformity with the future environment,

---

[25]   Wack, P. 1985a. Scenarios: Uncharted waters ahead. *Harvard Business Review,* September-October: 73–89

[26]   Van der Merwe, 2008, p. 219.

[27]   Van der Merwe, 2008, p. 232.

[28]   Van der Merwe, 2008, p. 232.

[29]   Van der Merwe, 2008, p. 232.

[30]   Van der Merwe, 2008, p. 227.

which is reflected in scenarios 1, 2, 3 and 4. Fit is required in order for an organisation to survive and thrive.

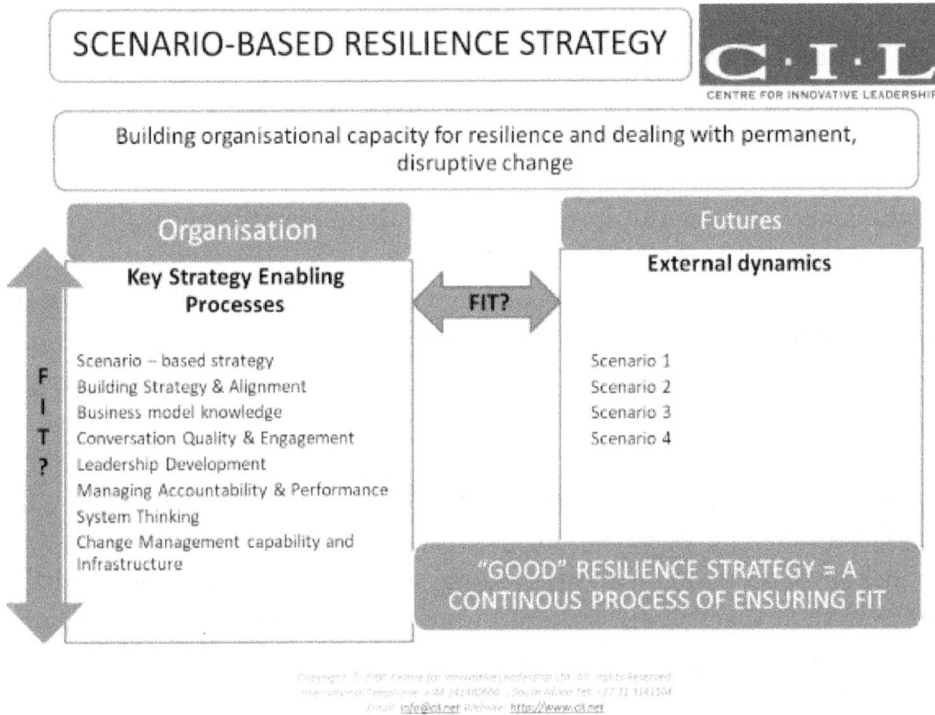

Figure 1.2: Scenario-based Resilience Strategy as Fit

Ensuring fit is described in Figure 1.2 as "the first-order fit", referring to the organisation's fit with futures (future environment scenarios 1, 2, 3 and 4) and "second-order fit" as the fit between the various "key strategy enabling processes" described in the diagnostic instrument as cross-cutting competencies, including amongst others specific management subsystems such as goal setting or "building strategy and alignment (BSA)" and "managing accountability and performance (MAP)" in an organisation. [31]

A scenario-based strategy may be regarded as both an individual and an organisational learning process which is enabled by the strategic conversation. Learning about how the external environment may unfold and adapting to enable fit with the various conditions in the environment can challenge the un-resilient organisation. There are many subtle processes, assumptions, ideologies and attitudes that disable learning; of these, mistrust ranks among the most important. Inappropriate competition for resources, factional divisions and other split loyalties which serve specific, narrow interests activate distrust and disable learning. Mistrust raises the transactional

---

[31] Van der Merwe, 2008, p. 222.

costs of decisions and actions, creating delays in adaptive behaviour. When this persists, the effective functioning and even the survival of the affected organisation are potentially threatened.

1.5   Significance of a resilience strategy for cities and towns

Katz and Bradley[32] have described the significance of rapid urbanisation and the growing importance of cities in the United States of America (USA) and elsewhere. Awareness is growing among futurists that migration to cities across the globe may be the most important dynamic influencing society in the 21st century.

City government is conceptualised by Glaeser[33] as a metropolitan municipality, mandated in terms of a constitution, which enables the planning and administration of the local affairs of a city in an inclusive, democratic, ethical, efficient, productive, economic, resilient and sustainable manner.

The *Oxford Concise Dictionary*[34] defines resilience in general terms as meaning "recoiling", "springing back", "resuming original shape after bending", "stretching", "compression", and also (of a person) readily recovering from shock or depression. Walker, Holling, Carpenter and Kinzig[35] add that resilience is the capacity of a system to absorb disturbances and reorganise while undergoing change, and at the same time retain essentially the same function, structure, identity and feedback.

In the context of city government, Duit[36] regards the rising interest in resilience as a need among scholars and practitioners to better understand the conditions for effective governance in a complex, interconnected and volatile world, fraught with a new class of poorly understood systemic risks flowing from turbulence in the environment. Orr[37] describes cities in general as "organised complexity where a half dozen or more quantities are all varying simultaneously and in subtly interconnected ways". De Weijer[38] states in summary that city and town resilience is rooted in understanding complexity,

---

[32]   Katz & Bradley, 2013.

[33]   Glaeser, E. 2011. *Triumph of the city*. New York, NY: Penguin Press.

[34]   *Oxford Concise Dictionary*. 1982. 7th ed. Oxford: Oxford University Press, p. 886, 1024.

[35]   Walker, B., Holling, C.S., Carpenter, S.R. & Kinzig, A. 2004. *Resilience, adaptability and transformability in social-ecological systems.* http://www.ecologyandsociety.org/vol9/iss2/art5 Date of access: 24 October 2017.

[36]   Duit, A. 2015. Resilience thinking: Lessons for public administration. *Public Administration*, 1–17. doi:101111/padm.12182

[37]   Orr, D. 2014. Systems thinking and the future of cities. *Solutions*, 5(1):54–61, p. 5.

[38]   De Weijer, F. 2013. *Resilience: A Trojan horse for a new way of thinking?* (Discussion Paper 139). European Centre for Development Policy Management. https://ecdpm.org/wp-content/uploads/2013/10/DP-139-Resilience-Trojan-Horse-New-Way-of-Thinking-2013.pdf Date of access: 20 November 2015, p. iii.

and that "when viewed as socio-ecological systems, cities are not deterministic, predictable and mechanistic". She adds that cities and towns are "organic in nature and [their] structures are intricately connected with each other".

It is important to draw a distinction between city resilience and city government resilience. City resilience is a broad concept incorporating the total environmental, social and economic dimensions of the urban setting. City government resilience refers to the organisational, administrative, developmental, managerial and leadership dimensions of a metropolitan municipality as a complex organisation. In other words, it focuses on the structural, systemic and administrative responses as the processes of a city in dealing with all areas that may influence and challenge its resilience. It engages organisational development (OD) as a perspective for gauging aspects of organisational resilience.

Duit[39] cites Hood (1991) and Duit and Galaz (2008), pointing out that previous discussions on how to design public (municipal/city) administrations often focused on values such as efficiency and equity; however, contemporary debates display an increasing concern for the "robustness", flexibility and adaptability of public governance. Glaeser[40] furthermore offers an overview of the aspects that make cities successful, resilient and sustainable. He places resilience in the context of both short-term crises and long-term sustainability. He also provides guidance on those aspects that can cause their downfall, that is, the non-resilience of cities. Glaeser[41] asserts that the primary function of a city is to bring people and their needs closer together in a more cost-effective and convenient manner. In this regard, Katz and Bradley[42] demonstrate the growing capacity for resilience by city government compared to declining national government responsiveness. They explain that this is because of the city's relative proximity to its citizens and the feedback received from them and their interaction with the city.

Flannery[43] analyses city resilience from an ecosystem perspective, positing that global climate change may severely test the ability of city governments to adapt and recover. He argues that cities are the most vulnerable ecosystem in the context of global climate change. This, according to him, is because of their complexity, as well as the many invisible interdependencies within

---

[39] Duit, 2015.

[40] Glaeser, 2011.

[41] Glaeser, 2011.

[42] Katz & Bradley, 2013.

[43] Flannery, T. 2005. *The weather makers: How man is changing the weather and what that means for life on earth.* New York, NY: Atlantic Monthly Press.

cities themselves and between cities and their external environments. Wack[44] and De Geus[45] accentuate the strategic planning and policy formulation dimensions which may affect strategy making per se and city government resilience strategy particularly. Wack[46] emphasises the role that scenario planning should play in enabling learning about the dynamics in the contextual environment that may have an impact on organisations. He describes scenario-based strategy as a learning process in the minds of decision makers, at the level of influencing assumptions about the future. In the context of city governments, learning may be important, especially when it takes place among policymakers, that is, executive leaders and executive managers. At the assumptions level, there may be the basis of deeper learning in all three of the initial AAR meta-categories – anticipation, adaptation and recovery.[47] [48] [49] [50] [51] Resilient cities and towns may form flywheels for propelling and maintaining momentum for national resilience.

A global, evolutionary perspective on sustainability and resilience is provided by Whybrow,[52] who points out that "within an evolutionary framework, our circumstances may be described as a decline in adaptive fit – a growing mismatch between what we do as humans and the sustainable well-being of ourselves and the planet". He goes on to argue that it is this shift in adaptive behaviour *at scale*, which he calls "re-tuning the human mind", which stands between generally accepted present behaviour and global resilience and a sustainable future. He refers to this process as "re-tuning our brains for a sustainable future".[53] The various dimensions highlighted above also illustrate the multidimensional nature of city government resilience and the need for a holistic and systemic approach to gauging resilience.

The complexity that cities face in ensuring resilience is reflected in the Ten Essentials pilot study carried out by the United Nations International Strategy for Disaster Reduction.[54]

---

[44]   Wack, P. 1985a. Scenarios: Uncharted waters ahead. *Harvard Business Review,* September-October: 73–89.

[45]   De Geus, A. 1988. Planning as learning. *Harvard Business Review,* March–April: 2–6.

[46]   Wack, P. 1985a

[47]   Wack, P. 1985a.

[48]   De Geus, 1988.

[49]   De Geus, 1997. *The living company.* Boston, MA: Harvard Business School Press.

[50]   Glaeser, 2011.

[51]   Katz & Bradley, 2013.

[52]   Whybrow, 2015, p. 301.

[53]   Whybrow, 2015, p. 293.

[54]   United Nations International Strategy for Disaster Reduction (UNISDR). 2012a. *City resilience in Africa: The Ten Essentials Pilot.* http://www.unisdr.org/we/inform/ publications/29935 Date of access: 27 October 2015.

Ten of the essential issues identified in this pilot study are:
- "Institutional and administrative frameworks;
- Financial and other resources;
- Multi-hazard risk assessment;
- Infrastructure protection, upgrading and resilience;
- Protection of vital facilities and supplies (e.g. education, health, food and water);
- Building regulations and land-use planning;
- Training, education and public awareness;
- Environmental protection and strengthening of ecosystems;
- Effective preparedness, early warning response; and
- Recovery and rebuilding communities".[55]

This writing places the dynamics of city government resilience in the context of systemic thinking and areas of high leverage, as a framework for a diagnostic instrument that gauges the level of city government resilience. Systems thinking will be applied to the anticipation of both external dynamics that affect city government and internal organisational dynamics that affect the adaptive capacity, in the short- and medium term, up to and including the 20- to 25-year time horizon. Examples of *external* dynamics at work include, but are not limited to:
- migration to cities across the globe
- population and demographic aberrations such as the so-called youth bulge
- property price fluctuation – the result of market supply and demand
- security of water supply and other natural resources
- demands by city officials and workers, through organised labour structures, for higher wages and so-called decent work
- levels of citizens' dissatisfaction with delivery of services, and
- stewardship of the so-called commons, including the need for effective waste management and pollution control (author's own research).

Examples of so-called "predetermined" dynamics include:
- human population beyond the limits and carrying capacity of planet earth
- rapid urbanisation
- terror attacks – nuclear detonation in a metropolis and cyberattacks on IT infrastructure
- the youth bulge and demands for inclusion, and

---

[55] United Nations International Strategy for Disaster Reduction (UNISDR). 2012a.

- increases in climate volatility as climate change breaches critical thresholds, resulting in prolonged drought(s) with fire threats and threats to water and food security (author's research).

Predetermined dynamics, by their very nature, are highly likely to confront organisations and challenge their resilience. It may be assumed that these dynamics will test the level of resilience and, therefore, be used as a benchmark or so-called "acid test" for testing resilience.

Examples of *internal* dynamics that have an impact on organisational responsiveness include:
- level of compliance with the rule of law embodied in a constitution and the municipal mandate
- level of *accountability* to the constitution
- lack of *capability* to execute the constitutional mandate for municipalities
- short-term (less than 15 years) strategic perspectives and assumptions about the future environment that may confront cities
- lack of capability to formulate strategy and policy that is robust against future conditions in the contextual environment
- lack of capability to execute strategy and policy on time, on budget and on quality
- the fit between the various organisational subsystems that affect organisational responsiveness
- low levels of community health and safety
- low levels of political and administrative leadership capability
- low levels of leadership and management capacity and competence
- high levels of corruption, maladministration and nepotism
- political factionalism
- low levels of organisational trust
- unrealistic levels of staff expectations
- under-investment in personal growth opportunities
- low individual and team motivational and commitment levels, and
- lack of understanding of the principles and practice of sustainable and circular economic development (author's research).

Both external and internal dynamics influence city resilience and, as such, have been considered in the diagnostic instrument. A systemic perspective also includes the interdependence of city government resilience with national, regional/continental and global resilience. This perspective uncovers important interconnections between the various levels and provides useful insights for the executive, political and administrative leadership in improving overall city government resilience.

According to the Global Reporting Initiative (GRI),[56] there are mandatory audited dimensions which are essential for robust, sustainable development. These dimensions are financial health, care of the environment and investment in the development of people. The GRI thus provides further indicators of city government resilience for a useful instrument to gauge this, using AAR as its frame of reference.

Among these initial dimensions and elements of the meta-framework are what are regarded as cross-cutting, enabling competencies which support organisational capability. Capability is conceptualised as the ability to formulate robust strategy and policy and to execute them on time, on budget and on quality. A checklist for capacity assessment is included in Table 1.1, and readers are invited to assess their capacity individually or collectively as an organisation. An initial list contains cross-cutting competencies such as knowledge of the Constitution and the rule of law, scenario-based strategy, systems thinking, effective servant leadership, goal setting and performance review processes, personal development planning, strategic conversation quality and engagement, cross-cultural competence, literacy in technology convergence and disruptions, innovation, e-governance competence, successful change management practice, good governance and financial literacy. Owing to the relative importance of developing organisational trust as an enabler of responsiveness, as pointed out by Stephenson[57] and Shockley-Zalabak, Morreale and Hackman,[58] competence in building organisation trust has been included in this list of cross-cutting competencies.

Capacity among executive leadership and executive management regarding the above competencies may be the foundation of and the primary enabler for developing capability and ensuring city government resilience. Capacity building to building capability may, therefore, precede other factors in a diagnostic instrument and may emerge as the priority for ensuring resilience.[59]

---

[56] Global Reporting Initiative (GRI). 2013. *Global Reporting Initiative: G4 Sustainability Reporting Guidelines.* Amsterdam: Global Reporting Initiative.

[57] Stephenson, K. 2005b. Trafficking in trust: The art and science of human knowledge networks. (*In* Coughlin, L., Wingard, E. and Hollihan, K. *Ed. Enlightened power*). San Francisco, CA: Jossey-Bass, pp. 242-264.

[58] Shockley-Zalabak, P.S., Morreale, S.P. and Hackman, M.Z. 2010. *Building the high-trust organisation.* San Francisco, CA: Jossey-Bass.

[59] Australian Public Service Commission (APSC). 2017a. *Organisational capability.* http://www.apsc.gov.au/about-the-apsc/parliamentary/state-of-the-service/state-of-the-service-2010/chapter-10-organisational-capability. Date of access: 19 August 2017.

Based on the AAR framework, the theory of system dynamics and resilience thinking, the respective dimensions of city government and the "ten essentials", the proposed diagnostic instrument displays a number of these properties.

The diagnostic instrument has been designed and developed so that it

- is systemic and holistic
- enables learning
- uses a meta-structure to provide an overview according to which the user can diagnose where individual or organisational strengths and weaknesses lie, thus providing context
- points towards high leverage areas, as well as scholarly resources which can be used by practitioners
- has a diagnostic instrument for assessing city government capability and enabling capacity building for specific cross-cutting enabling competency areas such as, amongst others, systems thinking, servant leadership, goal setting and review processes, good governance practice, sustainable economic development, conversation quality and engagement
- is designed as feedback and as a basis for reflection, strategic conversation, learning and action planning individually, in a team context and at scale
- may be used as a benchmark and index for comparing participants
- develops the quality of resilience thinking
- enables leadership to anticipate the future using a scenario-based approach
- enables successful complex and adaptive organisational behaviour
- includes recovering a prior position, and then leveraging growth beyond that to enable sustainable economic development, green growth and smart cities
- enables city government organisations to gain from disorder or what has been referred to as so-called "antifragility" by Taleb (2012), and
- provides for processes of continuous service quality improvement through structured innovation using total quality management principles.

According to Duit,[60] most definitions of resilience currently in circulation among practitioners in the social sciences refer to the ability to handle shocks and surprises. He goes on to add that "beyond that, there are a plethora of varieties of this basic conceptualisation". The implication of his assertion is

---

[60]   Duit, 2015.

that scholars and research institutions from across the world have responded with a matching "plethora" of solutions, frameworks and capacity-building programmes to address the capacities and competencies of cities to become more resilient. Among the "plethora" Duit[61] refers to, are a number of research institutes and networks which have resilience as their core activity and research focus. These institutions track the rapidly evolving field and usually focus their research on the needs of a local geographic area or a specific constituency.

A further problem is what Van der Heijden[62] and Jaques[63] refer to as the pervasiveness of "short-termism" inherent in organisational decision making. Resilience thinking and systems thinking require both a short term *and* a medium- and long term horizon. A typical planning time horizon for executive managers in a metro should be 20- to 25 years.[64] Jaques goes on to point out that this is the time it takes for a policy from this organisational level to be shown to be correct or wanting. Stimulating economic growth and creating jobs is one of the areas of great misunderstanding in emerging economies. In this regard, Johnson[65] in his work *How long will South Africa survive?* points out that governments do not create jobs, companies do. The implication is that the attractiveness of cities to investors via FDI is one of the keys to stimulating economic growth and creating jobs as part of the developmental role of metros and towns. Among the key conditions that attract investors are the rule of law, accountability, lack of corruption, low levels of crime and secure property rights, including intellectual property. In China, these are similar to those conditions for attracting FDI that can be found in the special economic zones (SEZs) and cities such as Hong Kong. Hong Kong is ranked as one of the most economically free cities in the world and has, together with other designated SEZs, given rise to the so-called "one country two systems" policy in China.

The primary purpose of a scenario-based strategy is to stretch and widen assumptions in the minds of decision makers in an organisation about what might happen in future in the external environment.[66] Competent practitioners of this process technology use a variety of processes to anticipate the range of

[61]   Duit, 2015.

[62]   Van der Heijden, K. 1996. *Scenarios: The art of strategic conversation.* London: Wiley, p. 93.

[63]   Jaques, E. 2013. *Requisite organisation: A total system for effective managerial organisation and management leadership for the 21st century.* Orlando, FL: Cason Hall, p. 37.

[64]   Jaques, 2013.

[65]   Johnson, R.W. 2015. *How long will South Africa survive? The looming crisis.* Jeppestown: Jonathan Ball.

[66]   Wack, 1985a.

future dynamics relevant to decision makers by embedding these dynamics in a portfolio of narratives, also referred to as scenarios. Scenario narratives are based on a rigorous systemic analysis of forces that may have an impact on city government resilience over the next 20- to 25 years. Testing a resilience strategy for robustness across the portfolio of scenarios provides a powerful basis for organisational learning, anticipating discontinuities and eliminating blind spots in the thinking of executives. The process of developing scenarios and testing for robustness enriches and widens assumptions about future dynamics and also creates selective awareness of forces that may have an impact on resilience. This selective awareness enables early recognition, sense-making and rapid adaptation to unfolding dynamics.

Figure 1.2 provides a framework for the principle of fit between an organisation and its future environments, referred to as "first-order fit". It also shows a "second-order fit"; that is, the fit between the various key strategy enabling processes. These processes, together, enable strategy making and execution. Current competency in these strategy enabling processes within an organisation will determine, amongst other things, its resilience capability. The direct link between capability and capacity building to raise capability is foundational for developing a robust resilience strategy and is reflected as the first steps in the diagnostic instrument in the process of developing a robust resilience strategy.

Chapter 6 describes a framework for a scenario-based strategy and has been included to give aspirant professional practitioners an introductory framework for developing and using a scenario-based resilience strategy. A systemic perspective and the techniques that accompany it provide a revolutionary way for practitioners to uncover the causal relationships that drive a particular dynamic. Systems thinking is central to sense-making and developing quality scenario narratives. Practitioners need to understand both practice and the foundations of their practice. Systems thinking and its founding father are therefore quoted at length from authoritative sources.

General systems theory (GST) was developed by Von Bertalanffy,[67] who is acknowledged by scholars for uncovering the foundations of systems thinking. Davidson[68] points out:

"Ludwig von Bertalanffy may well be the least known intellectual titan of the twentieth century. As the father of the interdisciplinary school of thought known as general systems theory, he made important contributions to

---

[67]   Von Bertalanffy, 1968.

[68]   Davidson, M. 1983. *Uncommon sense: The life and thought of Ludwig von Bertalanffy father of general system theory.* Los Angeles, CA: Tarcher, p. 9–12.

biology, medicine, psychiatry, psychology, sociology, history, education and philosophy. Yet he spent his life in semi-obscurity, and he survives today mostly in footnotes. I discovered that Bertalanffy's scientific contribution had been encyclopedic. For Bertalanffy, a wrongful act was equally wrong whether it was perpetrated by capitalist or communist, archbishop or atheist, professor or pipe-fitter, friend or foe ... he was a scientist who repudiated the arrogance of scientism, a biologist who rejected the heredity-is-everything dogma of biologism, a laboratory researcher who questioned the absolute value of empiricism, an agnostic who denounced materialism, an advocate of social planning and championed individualism, and a systems science pioneer who warned that systems science could be used for totalitarianism. With that much intellectual independence, the wonder is not that Bertalanffy was rather obscure but that he was permitted to leave any mark on the world at all. He further contributed to his obscurity by failing to organise his literary output. As he wryly acknowledged, his body of thought was 'dispersed in many places and therefore not easy to see as an organised system'. Bertalanffy's legacy is an imposing monument of contemporary thought, not just because of its extraordinary diversity, but also for its insight into an organising force that links us all to a cosmic unity. *It is the universal force that arranges the elements of reality into entities called systems.* It is a force, Bertalanffy warned, that we must no longer take for granted if we are to solve the uniquely complex and perilous problems of today's world. Philosopher John Stuart Mill observed that 'no great improvements in the lot of man are possible until a great change takes place in the fundamental constitution of our mode of thought'. Albert Einstein declared that 'we shall require a substantially new manner of thinking if mankind is to survive'. I believe that new manner of thinking was developed by Ludwig von Bertalanffy".[69]

The *holistic* approach, as described by Smuts,[70] preceded GST by more than 40 years. Systems thinking, and a holistic perspective, may be essential for making sense of complex interconnected social and economic systems. This perspective may also be useful specifically for gauging city government resilience. These perspectives uncover what Senge[71] and Meadows[72] describe as a systemic, structural (generative) level of observation, learning and intervention.

The dynamic nature of cities seen as an ecology is described by Forrester[73]

---

[69] Davidson, 1983, p. 9–12.

[70] Smuts, 1925.

[71] Senge, 1990, p. 52.

[72] Meadows, 2008, p. 145.

[73] Forrester, 1969.

in his SD modelling. In an urban setting, SD modelling forms the basis of robust policies and interventions in city government. SD also extends thinking beyond the short term to the required 20–25 year planning time horizon. SD modelling relies on causal relationships, feedback loops and logic between key variables rather than a database and trends within these data. A feedback process in general and feedback loops specifically, as described by Sterman[74] and Senge et al.[75] may be included to ensure the effectiveness and productive use of the diagnostic instrument. Together with skilful conversation and engagement, scenario-based strategy enables a city's executive leadership, executive management and other organisational levels to become more open to shifting assumptions and their behaviour, and therefore more responsive to shocks.

To build internal organisational capability among professional practitioners and organisational management in a sustainable manner, learning should, according to Senge,[76] take place on three levels (see Figure 1.3).

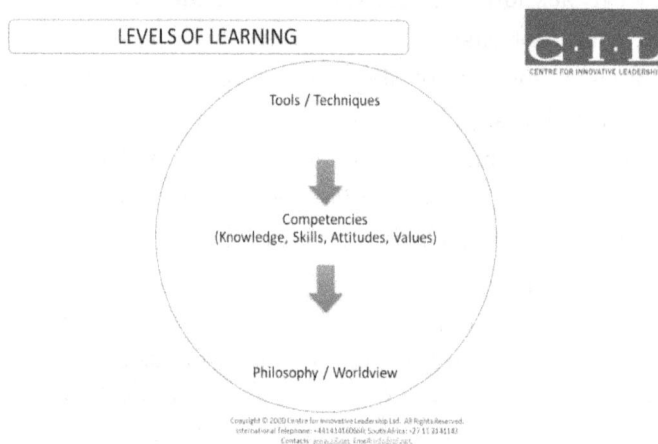

Figure 1.3: Levels of learning
Source: Senge[77]

"Tools and techniques" need to be underpinned by relevant "competencies" which in turn need to be underpinned by a relevant "philosophy or worldview". The first problem is that there is a tendency to reach for a tool or technique before investing in the other two levels which provide a platform for the sustainable use of tools and techniques. For example, scenario-based strategy requires one to first appreciate the underlying

---

[74]   Sterman, 2000.

[75]   Senge, P.M., Kleiner, A., Roberts, C., Ross, R.B. and Smith, B. 1994. *The fifth discipline fieldbook*. London: Nicholas Brealey.

[76]   Senge, P.M. 1995. Conversation with Peter Senge

[77]   Senge, P.M. 1995. Conversation with Peter Senge

philosophy and worldview that it is part of and typically view the world as fragmented. A holistic or systemic perspective will change this fragmented perspective. The second problem is we often treat assumptions as facts. The purpose of scenario-based strategy is to target the assumptions in the minds of decision makers and to confront these assumptions with narratives about the future that have been developed using a systemic perspective. This perspective will uncover interconnections and causal relationships, which are often hidden from view. With this understanding, a practitioner may start to develop appropriate competencies. Finally, the tools and techniques of scenario-based strategy may be applied based on these levels of learning. Without an investment in the first two levels of learning the use of tools and techniques will not produce optimal results.

In the current age of disruption, relevant scenario questions may be what learning will endure in the uncertain future we are now entering. The knowledge that has served us well in the past may no longer be useful in the face of artificial intelligence, machine learning, the use of big data and the like and the disruptive forces being unleashed by what is known as the Fourth Industrial Revolution or simply 4IR. Current estimates predict that more than 50% of current jobs will no longer exist as this digital future unfolds. Computers will do these better than humans and disrupt jobs by offering a simpler and better solution. As we know, computers do not strike or disrupt the workplace. In addition, over the past millennia, we have been well-served by the so-called "3Rs", reading, writing and arithmetic. In addition to the tried and tested 3Rs there are the so-called 4Cs which will become critical for navigating the future.[78]

The 4Cs are critical thinking, communication, collaboration and creativity.

The 4Cs provide a generic lifeboat to navigate and stay afloat, keeping our heads above the "white water" of continuous disruptive change. Practising and learning these valuable skills is embedded in the key strategy enabling processes.

The key strategy enabling processes reflected in Figure 1.2 are essential to responsiveness and organisational resilience. Capacity building should start with an assessment of capability at the individual level. This individual capability will naturally aggregate within intact teams and management groupings, thus providing a metric for organisational capability and priorities for capacity building.

To start this process, a framework is provided in Table 1.1 for the assessment of individual competencies. It is recommended that all members of the organisation develop a personal development plan (PDP) using the

---

[78]   Harari, Y.N. 2018. *21 Lessons for the 21st Century*. Spiegel & Grau.

framework in Table 1.1. This table contains a list of the strategy enabling processes from Figure 1.2. Behaviour descriptions at the basic, competent and advanced levels provide a gauge for the current level that a specific individual occupies. In order to bootstrap building capacity from within the organisation, individuals who score at an advanced level may engage in teaching others in their organisation using existing learning material for each competency.

You are invited to complete this assessment and identify your learning priorities for capacity building. Note that this self-assessment tool is also available online at www.cil.net. Once priorities have been established, learning resources can be identified and engaged. Notice that a number of additional competencies have been included (see Ai, Aj and Ak). These are considered essential to modern organisations. An example of coding is reflected in the table. Coding provided can be used to enable automating and tracking of PDPs.

Table 1.1: Self-assessment and learning priorities – key strategy enabling processes

Code:	Aa
General description:	Scenario-based Strategy (TAS)
Level:	
None (0)	
Basic (1)	Three or four of the following aspects done proficiently: Grounding scenario is the concerns of decision makers, ranking key driving forces (KDFs), rigorous systemic analysis, challenging assumptions, stretching thinking developing two, three or four internally consistent narratives (scenarios) on a 20-year planning time horizon, stress-testing strategy and decisions for robustness across the portfolio of scenarios
Competent (2)	Six or eight of the following aspects done proficiently: Grounding scenario is the concerns of decision makers, ranking key driving forces (KDFs), rigorous systemic analysis, challenging assumptions, stretching thinking developing two, three or four internally consistent narratives (scenarios) on a 20-year planning time horizon, stress-testing strategy and decisions for robustness across the portfolio of scenarios
Advanced (3)	All of the following aspects done proficiently: Grounding scenario is the concerns of decision makers, ranking key driving forces (KDFs), rigorous systemic analysis, challenging assumptions, stretching thinking developing two, three or four internally consistent narratives (scenarios) on a 20-year planning time horizon, stress-testing strategy and decisions for robustness across the portfolio of scenarios, multimedia dissemination and embedding of scenario narratives, multigenerational deployment of scenario-based strategy
Code:	Ab
General description:	Building Strategy and Alignment (BSA)

Level:	
None (0)	
Basic (1)	Goal setting in intact teams in alignment with strategic organisational priorities
Competent (2)	Goal setting in intact teams by determining desired results, purpose and strategic priorities, proto-scenarios, and rich, robust action plans in alignment with strategic organisational priorities
Advanced (3)	Goal setting in intact teams by determining desired results, purpose and strategic priorities, proto-scenarios, and rich, robust action plans to embed all action plans in individual jobs in alignment with strategic organisational priorities
Code:	Ac
General description:	Business Model Knowledge (BMD)
Level:	
None (0)	
Basic (1)	Basic overview of BMD as a system and an ability to identify critical components. Systems loops and links for limits to success. Mapping causal relationships, identifying distinctive competency, competitive advantage, new entrants, offerings, competitor dynamics
Competent (2)	Proficient in causal loop diagrams, mapping causal relationships, challenging thinking for distinctiveness, cost leadership, channel management, new entrants, offerings and competitor dynamics
Advanced (3)	Skilled in causal loop diagramming. Challenge creatively. Think about distinctive competency, product differentiation, cost leadership, channel management, new entrants, offerings and competitor dynamics, stress-testing across scenarios for robustness
Code:	Ad
General description:	Conversation Quality and Engagement (CQE)
Level:	
None (0)	
Basic (1)	Can conduct a necessary interactive one-on-one or one-on-many conversation responding to the thread and direction of the conversation to build a relationship and to develop trust and openness
Competent (2)	Facilitates a conversation in groups to level I skills (CIL checklist). Using 'I' statements balancing advocacy and inquiry. Intervenes effectively to correct imbalances
Advanced (3)	Facilitates a conversation with large groups to a Level II skills level (CIL checklist). Models taking a stand and intervenes, "in the moment", with dysfunctional conversations to produce individual and collective learning
Code:	Ae
General description:	Leadership for Results (LfR)
Level:	

None (0)	
Basic (1)	Taking a stand for the delivery of specifically agreed results
Competent (2)	Taking a stand for the organisational purpose, desired results, strategic priorities and delivery of specifically agreed team and individual results in terms of governing values of the organisation. Holding that stand until the system aligns with that stand
Advanced (3)	Taking a stand for the organisational purpose, desired results, strategic priorities and delivery of specifically agreed team and individual results in terms of governing values of the organisation. Holding that stand in a non anxious manner while staying in touch with the system using skilful conversation until the system aligns with that stand
Code:	Af
General description:	Managing Accountability and Performance (MAP)
Level:	
None (0)	
Basic (1)	Role clarity, using purpose and deliverable results, and competency development, performance assessment processes
Competent (2)	Role clarification using purpose, deliverable results, performance standards (evidence), conversational skills to Level I (see CIL checklist). Linkage to strategy, rewards, recognition and seen to be fair
Advanced (3)	Role clarification linked to strategy, priorities and plans, robust across scenarios. Competency development using personal development planning (PDP), conversation skills to Level II (CIL checklist) motivation and related theory. Seen and felt to be fair by members of the organisation
Code:	Ag
General description:	Systems Thinking for Sustainable Leadership and Transformation (STSLT)
Level:	
None (0)	
Basic (1)	Using the iceberg analogy to observe events-level information, patterns of behaviour over time below the waterline and structural causal relationships which hold patterns in place. Seeing interconnections and unintended outcomes. Boundaries, simple cause and effect relationships between two or more key variables
Competent (2)	Thinks and intervenes in a systemic way. Pinpoints capacity limits, unintended consequences and high leverage areas for interventions. Maps complex systems using more than one systems-based technique

Advanced (3)	Practises a systems worldview which is the leading guide in use for learning and contributing. Can map complex structures using causal loops, systems archetypes and can use other recognised techniques as well, such as influence diagrams and soft systems methodology (SSM)
Code:	Ah
General description:	Organisational Change and Renewal (OCR)
Level:	
None (0)	
Basic (1)	Feedback creates a sense of urgency for individual and organisational behaviour change
Competent (2)	Organisational infrastructure in a stakeholder forum enables data gathering, structuring, feedback and joint action planning for specific, strategic areas of inquiry and renewal for the organisation, intact teams and individuals
Advanced (3)	Organisational infrastructure in a stakeholder forum enables a strategic conversation for the prioritisation of high leverage areas, data gathering, structuring, feedback and joint action planning for specific, strategic areas of inquiry and renewal for the organisation, intact teams and individuals. Partnering to enhance organisational capability with capacity building in key strategy enabling competencies
Code:	Ai
General description:	Strategic Partnering (SP)
Level:	
None (0)	
Basic (1)	Partnering to enhance capability by supplementing key competencies which provide a competitive advantage
Competent (2)	Partnering to improve the capability for achieving strategic goals including disciplined, diligent, joint management of partnerships to achieve strategic results as agreed
Advanced (3)	Partnering to enhance capability for achieving strategic goals including diligent joint management of partnerships to achieve strategic results as agreed that are robust across the various scenarios
Code:	Aj
General description:	Building a service culture (BSC)
Level:	
None (0)	
Basic (1)	Routine goal setting and rigorous review of delivered results as agreed
Competent (2)	Embedded routines of goal setting and rigorous review with the organisation as a whole, within divisions, teams and between individuals in alignment with the organisational Purpose

Advanced (3)	Embedded routines of goal setting and rigorous review with the organisation as a whole, within divisions, teams and between individuals in alignment with the organisational purpose. Elimination of wastage and continuous improvement of total quality and productivity
Code:	Ak
General description:	Continuous improvement of total productivity and quality (TPQ)
Level:	
None (0)	
Basic (1)	Elimination of wastage and specification of jobs within teams, problem solving within teams to meet customer quality requirements
Competent (2)	Elimination of wastage and specification of jobs within teams, creative problem solving using proven techniques within teams to meet and exceed customer quality requirements
Advanced (3)	Elimination of wastage and specification of jobs within teams, creative problem solving using proven techniques within teams, benchmark against best practice to meet and exceed customer quality requirements

1.6 Determining capacity-building priorities
Learning priorities:

Priority	Individual priorities	Organisational priorities
1.		
2.		
3.		

Also see www.cil.net for descriptions of offerings available.
Contact Centre for Innovative Leadership (CIL) at info@CIL.net

2 CORNERSTONES FOR MODERN CITY GOVERNMENT
2.1 The New Urban Agenda

A gathering of world leaders has defined what is being referred to as a new urban agenda for city leaders. This agenda has particular relevance in light of the migration to urban areas. The dialogue (conversation-driven) approach adopted as the process for cementing agreement on "the new urban agenda"[79] [80] has resulted in both a wider and a deeper agreement on the specifics of this agenda. This has led to deeper commitment, where "world leaders

---

[79] Habitat3. 2016a. *The new urban agenda: Key commitments.* https://habitat3.org/the-new-urban-agenda/Florencia Soto Nino2016-10-26T16:44:36+00:00October 20th, 2016 | Cities, News Date of access: 20 July 2017.

[80] Habitat3. 2016b. *Urban dialogues.* http://habitat3.org/the-new-urban-agenda/preparatory-process/urban-dialogues/ Date of access: 20 July 2017.

have adopted the New Urban Agenda which sets a new global standard for sustainable development and may help us rethink how we plan, manage and live in cities".[81]

This agreement and commitment by world leaders includes to:

- "provide basic services for all citizens;
- ensure that all citizens have access to equal opportunities and face no discrimination;
- promote measures that support cleaner cities;
- strengthen resilience in cities to reduce the risk and impact of disasters;
- take action to address climate change by reducing their greenhouse gas emissions;
- fully respect the rights of refugees, migrants and internally displaced persons regardless of their migration status;
- improve connectivity and support innovative and green initiatives; and
- promote safe, accessible and green public spaces".[82]

This ability to self-correct through a process of dialogue underlines the value of strategic conversation and due process in formulating city policies and legislation. These conversations enable adapting and recovering and demonstrate the building of a resilience strategy inclusively.

Building a resilience strategy may be viewed as a learning process. Applying double-loop learning, described initially by Argyris,[83] [84] at executive leadership and executive management and other organisational levels, may enable the shift in assumptions and "mental models" that Sterman[85] refers to. These shifts may lead to more resilient policy decisions and, in the context of metros, to greater city government resilience.

Planning and learning in an organisational context engage knowledge-creating processes such as planning as learning,[86] [87] knowledge creation [88] and disciplines that enable learning.[89] Enabling learning is a vital aspect for

---

[81] Habitat3, 2016a.

[82] Habitat3, 2016a.

[83] Argyris, 1982.

[84] Argyris, 1993. *Knowledge for action: A guide for overcoming barriers to organisational change.* San Francisco, MA: Jossey-Bass.

[85] Sterman, 2000, p. 16.

[86] De Geus,1988.

[87] De Geus, 1997.

[88] Nonaka, I. & Takeuchi, H. 1995. *The knowledge creating company.* Oxford: Oxford University Press.

[89] Senge, 1990.

creating competitive advantage in an organisational context may be applicable to organisations in general and to city governments specifically.

Organisational resilience, according to Marcos and Macauley[90] has as a starting point been mapped onto a meta-framework including anticipation, adaptation and recovery (AAR). In the context of emergent and predetermined dynamics in the environment that may have an impact on cities in the future, this proto-framework has been extended based on research to include capability, capacity building, sustainable development, green growth and smart cities.

Essential perspectives reflect the foundations of this diagnostic instrument. Jaques[91] used a unifying theory and practice for developing a holistic approach to organisational design and organisational development. He pinpoints executive leadership and executive management as the unit of observation for organisations including government. Jaques[92] refers to his unifying theory as a *total systems approach*. He suggests this perspective may be an organisational necessity and a requirement for eliciting trust and organisational responsiveness, and through this resilience and sustainability.

According to Putnam,[93] engaging in regular, inclusive and quality strategic conversations builds alignment, as well as *social capital* – also known as *trust capital*, which enhances leadership capability and accountability in city government organisations.

Stephenson[94] and Shockley-Zalabak et al.[95] argue that organisational trust as social capital is the most critical and essential element for enabling collaborative work across divisions in diverse populations.

Modern city government capability and capacity building

Fukuyama[96] [97] reminds us that most nation states have their origins in a sovereign, trading city-state. Scholars posit that rapid urbanisation across the

---

[90] Marcos, J. & Macaulay, S. 2008. *Organisation resilience: The key to anticipation, adaptation and recovery*. Cranfield School of Management http://www.som.cranfield.ac.uk/som/dinamic-content/cced/documents/org.pdf Date of access: 26 March 2015.

[91] Jaques, 2013.

[92] Jaques, 2013.

[93] Putnam, R. 1993. *Making democracy work: Civic traditions in modern Italy*. Princeton, NJ: Princeton University Press.

[94] Stephenson, K. 2005a. *Quantum theory of trust*. New York, NY: Financial Times.

[95] Shockley-Zalabak et al., 2010.

[96] Fukuyama, F. 2011a. *The origins of political order: From pre-human times to the French Revolution*. New York, NY: FSG.

[97] Fukuyama, F. 2011b. *Political order and political decay: From the Industrial Revolution to the globalisation of democracy*. New York, NY: FSG.

globe,[98] together with technological advances and technological convergence,[99] as well as sustainability strategies and new economic development models, will have an impact on city resilience, including city government resilience. Over time, these dynamics may enable cities to recover from these shocks by displaying properties of strengthening and improving performance under conditions of adversity, called *antifragility*.[100] Cities will probably evolve to become, once again, sovereign, globally networked, trading cities.[101] This could be one plausible scenario for the future of cities. Bartlett[102] argues that "nation states came late in history and there is evidence to suggest they may not make it to the end of the century".

Fukuyama describes Chinese tribal society from its origins in 5000 BCE, when there were approximately 3000 polities, to 221 BCE, when there was just one polity, namely, the Qin Dynasty. He goes on to state that "progress in China from tribal to state-level society took place gradually with state institutions layered on top of kinship-based social structures".[103]

Fukuyama traces the emergence and evolution of the modern nation-state from its origin in trading city-states.[104] [105] He identifies the requirements for modern government as the *rule of law, accountability and capability*. These requirements also apply to city government and are the foundations of good governance, investment in development and wealth creation. According to Fukuyama,[106] political accountability in a modern government means that in an "accountable government the rulers believe that they are responsible to the people they govern and put the people's interests above their own". He goes on to state that

> "… accountability can be achieved in a number of ways. It can arise from moral education, which is the form it took place in China and countries influenced by Confucianism. Princes were educated to feel a sense of responsibility to their society and were counselled by a sophisticated bureaucracy in the art of good statecraft".[107]

---

[98]   Katz & Bradley, 2013.

[99]   Schwab, K. 2016b. *The Fourth Industrial Revolution*. Geneva: World Economic Forum.

[100] Taleb, N.N. 2012. *Antifragile*. New York, NY: Random House.

[101] Katz & Bradley, 2013.

[102] Bartlett, J. 2017. Return of the city-state. https://aeon.co/essays/the-end-of-a-world-of-nation-states-may-be-upon-us Date of access: 15 September 2017.

[103] Fukuyama, 2011a.

[104] Fukuyama, 2011b.

[105] Fukuyama, 2011a.

[106] Fukuyama, 2011b.

[107] Fukuyama, 2011b, p. 321.

Ultimately, the purpose of a government is limited to specific responsibilities which may best be discharged on behalf of its citizens and funded by taxes. These responsibilities are determined by the context and legislative frameworks within which a specific government functions and may be limited by what it is capable of executing.

Limits of government – new realities

The dilemma inherent in centrally directed policy as opposed to the delegated authority to act locally contains within it two extremes between, on the one hand, enforcing control from the apex or centre of an organisation to, on the other hand, enabling self-control locally or on the boundary of an organisation. In terms of resolving such dilemmas effectively, lopsided thinking may result if either extreme on this continuum is favoured to the exclusion of the other. In their contingency theory, Lawrence and Lorch[108] posit that the greater the volatility in the context, the more flexible the organisational structure may have to be and, by implication, the less volatile a context, the more rigid the structure. In the context of enabling city government resilience, the current volatile context, specifically in the service delivery area, may point to greater organisational flexibility and locally based self-control at city government level, while maintaining a measure of appropriate central control at the national level to discharge the minimum obligations of a modern government. In the African context, the so-called "big man" political leadership reflects a lopsided resolution of this dilemma by control from the centre with the "big man" at the apex. Mnguni[109] argues that the electoral and political structures and systems of many African states give a significant amount of power to the leader, and elect governments with large majorities, with few checks and balances. Mnguni argues that "[t]his prevalence of big man politics in Africa is not only structural but also due to a defect in character among the Africa leaders who think that no other person can lead their countries".[110] There are indications that both elements play a role in Africa's continued tendency towards "big man" politics. This tendency results in trying to extend the stay in power for the big man and also a tendency towards centrally directed governance.

Drucker[111] argues that "[t]he essence of totalitarianism is the assertion that the collective is the absolute. The party, the state, the Aryan race, the

---

[108] Lawrence, P. & Lorsch, J.W. 1967. Differentiation and integration in complex organisation. *Administration Science Quarterly*, 1(12):1–30.

[109] *In* Good Governance Africa (GGA). 2017. The presidential issue. *The Journal of Good Governance*, (42), July–September. https://gga.org/ Date of access: 10 November 2017, p. 12.

[110] Good Governance Africa (GGA). 2017, p. 13.

[111] Drucker, P.F. 1994. *The new realities: In government and politics/In economics and business/in society and worldview.* New York, NY: Harper Business, p. 6.

ethnic group (and their 'big man') are all variations of this dynamic. It is also the definition on which totalitarian regimes have been based: Lenin's own party, Mussolini's, Hitler's and Mao's".[112] Drucker goes on to argue that one of the recent dominant political debates has been between "the believers in a 'welfare state' on the one hand, in which there are democratic restraints on government. Specifically, on its control of the economy and society, and on the other hand the believers in totalitarianism either of the Marxist or the Anti-Semitic persuasion, who preached and practised absolute, unrestricted government power".[113] He goes on to state that "the political doctrines which the slogans of the welfare state or communism reflect have ceased to have much relevance or reality, politically, socially, even economically".[114]

This ideological discourse may be reflected in the economic discourse in many emerging economies and also in South Africa and its neighbours. As a contribution to this discourse few books in history have had a greater impact on society and economics than Adam Smith's *Wealth of Nations* (1776). Smith had little love for businessmen and even less for self-interest. Smith argued that government, by its very nature, *cannot* run the economy, not even poorly. Drucker[115] adds that "soon the argument turned from what government *can* do to what government *should* do". Hayek,[116] in his anti-government tract *The Road to Serfdom*, a discourse on the relationship between individual liberty and government authority, did not argue government incompetence, but came to the conclusion that the nature of information "makes it impossible both in theory and practice for the government to manage or even to control the economy".[117] Hayek was the first scholar to raise the question of the limits of government. When Margaret Thatcher became prime minister of Great Britain, she started to privatise amongst others many of the state-owned enterprises. After her successful transformation of the UK economy, privatisation not only became the programme of conservatives like Thatcher of Great Britain and Chirac in France; "[i]t has also become the official policy of Communist China".[118] The Special Economic Zones (SEZs) in China and cities such as Hong Kong reflect this economic freedom which has attracted foreign direct investment flows and has, through rapid economic growth based on export markets, lifted more than 600 million of its citizens out of poverty in the recent past. Former Chinese President Deng Xiaoping successfully

---

[112] Drucker, 1994, p. 7.

[113] Drucker, 1994, p. 8.

[114] Drucker, 1994, p. 9.

[115] Drucker, 1994, p. 59.

[116] Hayek, F.A. 1944. *Road to serfdom*. Chicago, IL: University of Chicago Press.

[117] *In* Drucker, 1994, p. 59, 60.

[118] Drucker, 1994, p. 61.

explained his liberalisation of the centrally controlled communist Chinese economy when he famously stated that he does not care if a cat is black or, white, if it catches mice it is a good cat. This dual economic system gave rise to a pragmatic economic philosophy that is also referred to by the current Chinese president, Xi Jinping, as one country two systems. Another form of privatisation is moving faster still: letting private contractors take over public service delivery on a competitive bid basis. In light of this trend, there may no longer be any doubt that there are limits to what government can do and alternative methods for delivering services. According to Drucker,[119] there are three reasons for this dramatic change:

- "The failure of government programmes and government operations since the second world war;
- there are limits to what taxation and spending can achieve; and
- there are limits to government's ability to raise revenue".[120]

Drucker points out that "[a] government activity can only work if it is a monopoly. It cannot function if there are other ways to do that same job, in other words, if there is competition".[121] He argues that whatever non-governmental organisations in the broadest sense (including the so-called private sector) can do better or do just as well should be not be done by government. In the context of emergent economies, constitutional democracy, a range of ideologies, principles and concepts and their consequences are in the process of being clarified. It may, therefore, be useful to further clarify the context in which governments may find themselves as well as the principles of modern government, as a guide to modern city government.

Emerging government – contextual and conceptual framework
According to Fukuyama,[122] "patrimonialism characterises many of the (post-colonial) African states". He goes on to state that these are "governments which are staffed by the family and friends of the ruler and run for the benefit of the ruler. Modern governments, by contrast, are supposed to be staffed by officials chosen on merit and expertise and run for the benefit of the broad public interest". With the outward form of a modern state, a neo-patrimonial government sometimes has a constitution, presidents and prime ministers, as well as a legal system and pretentions of impersonality. Nevertheless, the actual operation of the government remains at the core, a matter of sharing state

---

[119] Drucker, 1994, p. 63.
[120] Drucker, 1994, p. 63.
[121] Drucker, 1994, p. 67, 68.
[122] Fukuyama, 2011b, p. 287.

resources with friends and family. He terms this "neo-patrimonial". According to Fukuyama[123] the characteristics of African neo-patrimonial rule are:

- "personalism – the figure of the president or big man to whom all individuals owed loyalty (virtually all African post-colonial political systems were presidential rather than parliamentary, and all presidents were male); and
- the use of state resources to cultivate political support, which resulted in pervasive clientelism".[124]

Fukuyama[125] points out that in modern government "accountable government means that the rulers believe that they are, in terms of a constitution, responsible to the people they govern and put the people's interests above their own". Formal accountability is procedural. The government agrees to submit itself to specific mechanisms that limit its power to do as it pleases – so-called checks and balances. Ultimately, these procedures (which are usually spelt out in constitutions) "allow citizens to replace the government entirely for malfeasance, incompetence or abuse of power".[126] The South African Constitution was widely hailed as the most advanced constitution in the world at the time of its acceptance in 1996. It also contains in it a mandate for municipalities, defining their mandate as the vanguard of the so-called developmental state.

Fukuyama provides an overview of the emergence of the modern state.[127] [128] It can be said that city government per se and city government resilience in particular may also rest on the premises of modern government, namely, the rule of law, accountability and capability, and by building on these foundations an effective resilience strategy may be developed.

2.2 Capability in government

According to Osborne,[129] "reinventing government" has erroneously been seen as referring to reinventing federal government. The solutions to problems in government have been emerging from local state government and local government. He points out that in America, many dedicated people in government are trapped in ineffective government systems that

---

[123] Fukuyama, 2011b, p. 287.

[124] Fukuyama, 2011b, p. 257.

[125] Fukuyama, 2011b, p. 321.

[126] Fukuyama, 2011b, p. 322.

[127] Fukuyama, 2011a.

[128] Fukuyama, 2011b.

[129] Osborne, D. 1993. Public productivity: Fiscal pressures and productive solutions. *Management Review,* 16(4):349–356, p. 349.

are cumbersome and provide little incentive for improving performance. He pinpoints that "doing business in an outmoded way"[130] seems to be the fundamental problem with government. As society is transformed by both technology and social changes, the public sector should be widening its choice of service providers in line with the wide choice offered by a business.

According to Osborne, the move in business "to empower employees, introduce worker engagement in improving productivity and quality of services with quality circles, measure performance and focus on improving quality should also be applied in the public sector".[131] In fieldwork with Gaebler, Osborne uncovered "ten principles that underscore how public entrepreneurial government organisations structure themselves. They pinpointed the points of leverage that move them from centralisation to decentralisation, from monopolies to competition, from bureaucratic mechanisms to market mechanisms, from funding inputs to funding outcomes or results".[132] Osborne and Gaebler[133] found that entrepreneurial local governments are:

- "catalytic governments, steering by using contracts, vouchers, grants and tax incentives;
- community-owned, empowering by pushing control out of the bureaucracy into the community;
- competitive, injecting competition into service delivery;
- mission-driven governments, transforming rules-driven organisations thus enabling managers to find the best way to accomplish that mission;
- results-driven governments, funding outcomes, not inputs;
- customer-driven governments, meeting the needs of customers not the needs of the bureaucracy;
- enterprising governments focussed on earning rather than spending;
- anticipatory governments preventing problems rather than curing problems with services;
- decentralised governments moving from hierarchy to participation and teamwork;
- market-orientated governments leveraging change through the market rather than administrative systems".[134]

---

130   Osborne, 1993.
131   Osborne, 1993, p. 351.
132   Osborne, 1993, pp. 352–356.
133   Osborne, D. & Gaebler, T. 1992. *Reinventing government: How the entrepreneurial spirit is transforming the public sector.* Reading, MA: Addison-Wesley.
134   Osborne & Gaebler, 1992, pp. ix, x.

Osborne and Gaebler[135] go on to point out [that] "the impulse to control is embedded in almost every set of rules by which government operates: the budget system, the personnel system, the procurement system and the accounting system. The rule-driven government may prevent some corruption but at a price of monumental waste". Osborne and Gaebler's[136] findings with entrepreneurial local governments point towards an inclusive, holistic approach to reinventing government. In the UK Public Service, "capability reviews" were conceived in 2005 as a way to reinvent government in the UK and were launched by the Cabinet Secretary as a way "to hold government department leaders to account for improving their departments' capability to deliver".[137] In an evaluation of the capability reviews programme, it received mixed reviews among senior civil servants in a survey of 219 directors and deputy directors. These were reported as follows, "8% responded: Very effective, 56% responded: Quite effective, 25% responded: Not very effective, 3% responded: Not at all effective and 4% responded: No changes implemented yet".[138] In 2009, the UK House of Commons Public Accounts Committee published an assessment which concluded that "the introduction of capability reviews is a significant advance in bringing transparency and comparability to how government departments are assessed". It goes on to recommend that, if capability reviews are to secure sustainable improvements, there needs to be

- "improved metrics;
- external benchmarks against which to compare;
- a much stronger culture of individual performance linked to overall delivery metrics;
- higher confidence levels;
- strong, strategically focused senior management; and
- improved insight into service delivery partners similar to private sector organisations."[139]

---

[135]   Osborne & Gaebler, 1992, p. 112.

[136]   Osborne & Gaebler, 1992.

[137]   *Institute for Government UK. 2005. Capability reviews: A case study by Panchamia, N. and Thomas, P. London: Institute of Government.*

[138]   Sunningdale Institute 2007. *Take-off or tail-off? An evolution of the Capability Reviews Programme.* www.nationalschool.gov.uk Date of access: 14 October 2017, p. 19.

[139]   United Kingdom (UK) House of Commons. 2009. *Assessment of the Capability Review Programme: Forty-Fifth Report of Session 2008–2009.* London: The Stationery Office Limited, p. 5, 6.

The Australian Public Service (APS) follows and improves on the UK Capability Assessment by focusing on and defining capability. The APS positions its capability framework at the centre of its initiative to reinvent government which may provide an organisational focus in city government and a holistic frame of reference for enabling capability through capacity building. The Australian Public Service Commission's (APSC) description of capability has been useful in a diagnostic instrument for gauging city government resilience.

The APS and specifically the APSC have, as a priority, to build and sustain organisational capability in order to respond effectively (and at pace) to the contemporary needs of modern government and the dynamics in the environment, and to build capability in advance of these needs. Emerging needs can be reasonably anticipated and resilience established to cope well with unexpected shocks.[140] The APSC points out that organisational capability extends beyond the capability of employees, and combines people skills with the organisation's processes, systems, culture and structures to deliver outcomes. People and systems need to be consciously aligned to overall organisational outcomes and priorities with lines of accountability that are clear to ensure optimum performance of systems. Governance systems should ensure that large projects and contractors are managed with a strong emphasis on effective risk management. There should also be a focus on project implementation, supported by coordinated implementation strategies and the development of project management capability.

According to the APSC, "it has developed this capability framework (see Figure 1.4) as a basis for its capability assessment process". The APSC goes on to state that "[i]t is deliberately selective and focuses on the most crucial [high leverage] areas of capability and key enablers of successful performance namely leadership, strategy and delivery".[141] The APSC describes these aspects of its capability assessment framework as follows:

- "leadership: the critical juncture between government policy and strategy execution and delivery;
- strategy: the high level strategy developed by public service agencies to meet the government's policy directions; and
- delivery: the capability that agencies need to deliver on time and on budget the government's policy through high quality programs and services".[142]

---

[140]   Australian Public Service Commission (APSC), 2017a.

[141]   Australian Public Service Commission (APSC), 2017a.

[142]   Australian Public Service Commission (APSC). 2017b. *Capability assessment.* http://www. apsc.gov.au/priorities/capability-reviews. Date of access: 21 September 2017.

2.3 Execution of plans

The execution of strategy and plans, according to Bossidy et al.,[143] depends upon what they refer to as the missing link and the main reason why organisations and leadership fall short on their promises. According to Bossidy et al.,[144] to understand execution, three important points must be accepted:

- "execution is a discipline and integral to strategy;
- execution is the major job of organisational leadership; and
- execution must be a core element of an organisation's culture".[145]

Bossidy et al.,[146] assert that there needs to be a system for getting things done through questioning, analysis and follow-through. Also, there needs to be an embedded discipline of comparing intent, strategy and policy with an honest and truthful assessment of current reality and aligning people's energy with desired policy and goals. They go on to describe the building blocks for execution by citing leadership, building capability, culture change, choosing the right people, as well as a line-of-sight connection between divisions, departments and jobs with their role in executing policy. Regular reviews of current reality provide feedback on progress against goals.

2.4 The Resilience Strategy Hierarchy (RSH)™: A process perspective

The ability to anticipate, adapt and recover from shocks is based on the foundations of capability and, in the absence or partial absence of capability, building capacity. Individual learning forms the basis of collective capability. The best way to enable this is through individual assessment and planning, usually expressed in a personal development plan or PDP. Anticipation for a city should be on a 20- to 25 year planning time horizon.[147] Adaptation and recovery processes are situated in the domain of organisational development which provides a professional frame of reference for practitioners. Weisbord[148] reminds us that successful change management depends on getting the whole system in the room. Imperatives of climate volatility are described by the global guidelines for sustainable development and enabled through new economic models under the heading of green growth. Technology convergence in the 4IR, including impending disruptive technologies in transport and energy,

---

[143] Bossidy, L., Charan, R. and Burck, C. 2002. *Execution the discipline of getting things done.* New York: Crown Business.

[144] Bossidy et al., 2002.

[145] Bossidy et al., 2002, p. 21.

[146] Bossidy et al., 2002.

[147] Jaques, 2013.

[148] Weisbord, M.R. 1992. *Discovering common ground.* San Francisco, CA: Berrett-Koehler.

will enable the so-called smart city. The dynamics of building sustainable, green and smart cities as a way of extending recovery to encompass several predetermined dynamics into an antifragile domain provide an optimistic scenario for resilience planning. These interlinked processes comprise the Resilience Strategy Hierarchy (RSH)™.

2.5 Using the Resilience Strategy Hierarchy (RSH)™: A process perspective

Scoring using the Resilience Strategy Hierarchy (RSH)™ using the diagnostic process

Note: All scores registered on the diagnostic instrument must be truthful about current reality. The desired results for a resilience strategy should be recorded separately as an aspiration that is in tension with current reality.

The city government resilience diagnostic instrument consists of two levels of assessment and scoring, namely, **factors and items.**

Factors provide an overarching meta-perspective for determining a resilience strategy. They include
- Capability (C)
- Cross-cutting Competencies (CC)
- Anticipation (A)
- Adaptation (A)
- Recovery (R)
- Sustainable Development (SDev)
- Green Growth (GG), and
- Smart Cities (SC).

The second level of assessment and scoring can be found at the item level within the factors.

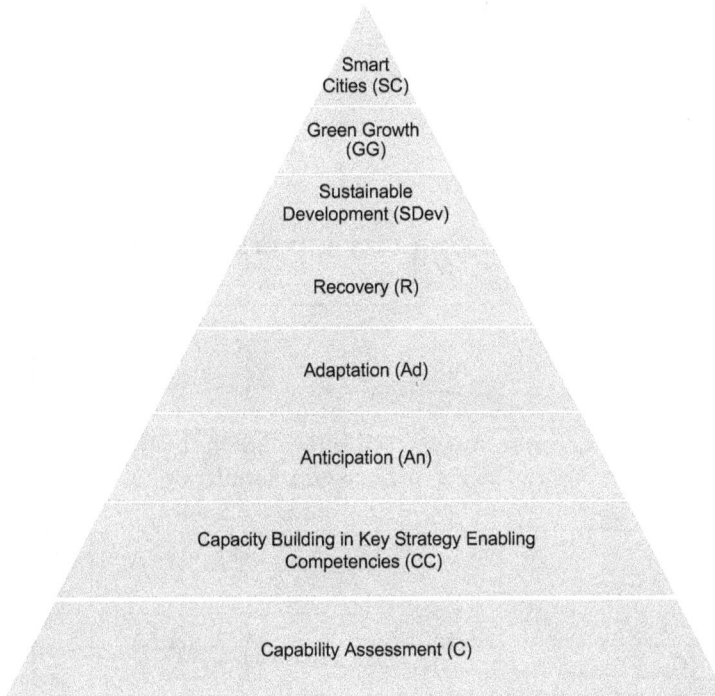

Figure 1.4: The resilience strategy hierarchy (RSH)™: A process framework

Assessing and scoring factors in the diagnostic instrument

Respondents are invited to respond to the descriptive statements for the factors *as a whole*, as the descriptors contain more than one element. The purpose of a composite measure consisting of many items is to provide a gauge and also to stimulate new thinking for developing a robust resilience strategy.

Score all factors by registering the level of agreement or disagreement on a *descending* Likert scale:

- "Agree Completely": Score 4
- "Agree Somewhat": Score 3
- "Disagree Somewhat": Score 2
- "Disagree Completely": Score 1

Note: When questions of clarification arise from technical descriptions and metrics such as "Networked Readiness Index (NRI) or Sendai framework" and "The new urban agenda (Habitat3)", a low score should be indicated for that factor or item.

Factors:

Table 1.2: Factors for gauging city government resilience C, CC, An, Ad, R, SDev, GG, SC

Factors for gauging city government resilience – meta-level. Score each factor as a whole, as a synthesis of its multiple dimensions.	Score			
	Agree completely (4)	Agree somewhat (3)	Disagree somewhat (2)	Disagree completely (1)
1. Capability (C) Capability may be evidenced by leadership, strategy and service delivery. City government capability may also be summarised as the ability to formulate robust strategy, policy, plans and budgets and execute these on time, on budget and on quality. Regular biannual reviews of capability take place to enable continuous overall improvement in the city government resilience strategy.	4	3	2	1
2. Cross-cutting Competence (CC) Cross-cutting competencies that enable capability. These include essential competencies that support intervening in high leverage points across factors that inform and enable a resilience strategy. City government has built capacity among executive leadership, executive management and middle managers based on competency assessment in teams and individually, which is included in a personal development plan (PDP) as part of their performance contract.	4	3	2	1

Factors for gauging city government resilience – meta-level. Score each factor as a whole, as a synthesis of its multiple dimensions.	Score			
	Agree completely (4)	Agree somewhat (3)	Disagree somewhat (2)	Disagree completely (1)
3. Anticipation (An) City government anticipates immediate short-term shocks, as well as medium- and long-term discontinuities in its contextual environment on a 20- to 25 year planning time horizon. The city engages state-of-the-art process methodologies and technologies such as scenario-based strategy and systems dynamics (SD) modelling to shift and broaden assumptions in the minds of executive leadership, executive managers and decision makers. SD modelling may be used to understand key dynamics systemically when building scenarios beyond the ten-year planning horizon. Emergency and state-of-the-art risk-management processes are in place, regularly practised and ready to be activated. Scenarios are used as a set to stress-test strategies, policies, plans and budgets for robustness across future conditions described in these scenarios.	4	3	2	1
4. Adaptation (Ad) City government absorbs short-term shocks by ensuring that emergency water, food and first aid are readily available. Effective communications and cyberinfrastructure to support coordinated adaptation activities have been operationalised. The city has built capabilities and competencies for adapting to shocks that may persist in the medium-term and long-term. Leadership is capable of resolving the tensions between performance and action, and has considered an evidence-based strategic direction along the path of the adaptation process. Leadership takes a stand for a policy that will support recovery, sustainable development, green growth and smart cities.	4	3	2	1
5. Recovery (R) City government is capable of springing back to a better position than that prevailing prior to the shock and also improve on it. Established change management infrastructure exists such as a forum which links to the whole organisation. The forum is building a shared vision and a sense of urgency and provides organisation-wide leadership by means of its powerful, inclusive coalition which regularly engages via the forum in strategic conversation. The forum enables the delivery of short-term wins in the city government resilience strategy and has built an institutional capability to sustain recovery and embark on sustainable development initiatives. High organisational trust facilitated by quality strategic conversations and regular leadership engagement enables responsiveness, agility and resilience.	4	3	2	1

Factors for gauging city government resilience – meta-level. Score each factor as a whole, as a synthesis of its multiple dimensions.	Score			
	Agree completely (4)	Agree somewhat (3)	Disagree somewhat (2)	Disagree completely (1)
6. Sustainable Development (SDev) City government complies with the Sustainable Development Goals (SDGs), Paris Agreement 2015 and the Sendai Framework for disaster risk reduction 2015–2030 and is enrolled in the global city mayoral parliament resolutions in the New Urban Agenda (Habitat3). It focuses on engagement with a national development plan and municipal mandate for economic development. Small, micro and medium enterprise (SMME) development is being stimulated. It is invested in community engagement in rights-based sustainable community investment programme (SCIP) development initiatives, including youth in service delivery. National government is engaged in enhancing education and learning quality through teacher development support. The city human resources planning focuses on attracting and nurturing talent.	4	3	2	1
7. Green Growth (GG) The city government resilience strategy extends beyond sustainable development, enabling the recycling of more than 50% of waste using waste as a feedstock for other processes and sectors in the economy. Utilisation of natural resources is improved through beneficiation processes, continuously measuring and reducing the city's carbon footprint through elimination of wastage, continuously innovating and identifying areas for improvement of quality of services.	4	3	2	1
8. Smart Cities (SC) City government has invested in the cyberinfrastructure to support sensors and connectedness and gauges its networked readiness using the WEF Network Readiness Index (NRI). It emphasises e-governance competencies and technology-enabled coordination and information sharing. It anticipates and leverages disruptions in transportation and energy to enable improved quality of city living. IMD Smart City Index 2019 reflects how citizens see their city.	4	3	2	1
Subtotal				
Score				
Grade %				

3 A CAPABILITY REVIEW PROCESS AND CAPACITY BUILDING USING A FEEDBACK-BASED APPROACH

CAPABILITY DEFINED: Government *leadership* with the ability to formulate *strategy* and policies that are robust across future conditions (scenarios) and perform *service delivery* on time, on budget and on quality (fit for purpose).

LEADERSHIP

- Organisational learning – learning limitations; distrust, arrogance, exceptionalism, equality of outcomes ideology
- Servant leadership as the preferred style of leadership
- Change competence (building infrastructure for leading disruptive discontinuities)
- Merit and openness in all decisions
- Setting direction-determining priorities
- Infrastructure for a regular strategic conversation, leadership and engagement of the whole organisation (strategic conversation of the whole organisation in the strategy, leadership and engagement forum)
- Maintaining momentum and focus
- Building trust
- Motivating people (using Herzberg's true motivators)
- Developing people using personal development planning (PDP) as part of the performance contract
- Taking a leadership stand.

3.1 Scenario-based strategy

City executives need to have a planning time horizon of 20–25 years to anticipate discontinuities in the contextual environment. This relatively long time horizon reflects the *time span of discretion,*[149] the length of time that it takes for a decision at director level to be seen as correct. A shorter planning time horizon will result in decisions that do not fit with the organisational context 25 years hence. Scenario-based strategy was developed by its founders to do precisely that – enable thinking that is comprehensive and which provides insights into the future that are novel compared to commonly held assumptions about the future. Modelling using the SD methodology is applied to develop a causal loop diagram which reflects the critical causal relationships within specific dynamics. SD models complement scenarios and assist in forming an idea of the future organisational context. SD modelling can support decision makers to penetrate this planning time horizon. A systemic

---

[149] Jacques 2013

study can also eliminate unintended consequences following policy decisions. Stress-testing strategic priorities for robustness across well-researched scenarios will remove most unintended consequences of the risks that surface during the stress-testing process, aka wind-tunnelling.

Scenario-based strategy tests strategy across the scenarios for robustness *before* committing resources to the plans. Evidence-based choices are preferred as they prevent plans and strategies which are not proven, based on outcomes, from being put in place.

The unfortunate truth is that policymakers formulate policy based on their intentions while citizens judge a policy by the results it delivers in their day-to-day lives. The foundation of policy and politics has to be economics. Unless policy is based on evidence-based economic sense, it should not be adopted.

Collaborating and building common purpose provides an anchor and *true north* for policy implementation. The national shared vision is usually contained in the agreed national or federal constitution, and for cities and towns the law can be found in the legislation guiding city and town government.

3.2 Service delivery

Service delivery best practice closely follows the industrial principles for customer-centric industrial strategy. Total Quality Control (TQC), Kaizen, Six Sigma and Total Productivity and Quality (TPQ) are similar proven methodologies. These are used for mobilising every ounce of organisational intelligence in the service of eliminating all forms of wastage, working smarter to reduce costs, and the continuous innovative improvement of quality of products and services.

The key to raising productivity and quality is in routine goal setting and review processes which create a line-of-sight connection to the purpose and desired results (vision) of the organisation followed by accountability for delivering on agreed commitments. Shared commitment and sound delivery models ensure that all significant people are involved and proven delivery models are used based on evidence and benchmarks from other settings. A back-to-basics approach and value-for-money services can be achieved through an approach of competitive merit-based bidding and tenders for external suppliers.

Embedding carefully structured organisational routines aligned with the overall corporate strategy is the preferred method of ensuring a sustainable service delivery culture. There are emergent rights-based alternative delivery structures suitable for specific applications and constituencies where rights are important, such as youth engagement in delivery and educational interventions. The Sustainable Community Investment Programme (SCIP) model has economics as a basis.

4 CAPABILITY REVIEW PROCESS – SELF-ASSESSMENT

A self-assessment checklist follows below:

Guideline: Capability assessment may best be done by executive leadership and executive management. Informal leadership may also participate to provide a perspective from the middle levels in the organisation. Select a colleague whose opinions and judgement you trust. Complete the checklist independently and then compare and have a skilful conversation to reach an agreement and proposed action in high leverage areas to shift scores. This checklist may also be completed amongst an intact team.

Table 1.3: Capability Assessment Category/Dimension

	Disagree completely	Disagree somewhat	Agree somewhat	Agree completely
LEADERSHIP:				
We take a stand for compliance with the Constitution	1	2	3	4
We take a stand for compliance with the municipal mandate	1	2	3	4
We take a stand for accountability and the rule of law	1	2	3	4
We take a stand for good governance practice	1	2	3	4
Regular goal setting and review forms the basis for team and individual accountability in the performance management system (PMS)	1	2	3	4
We take a stand for elimination of all wastage	1	2	3	4
We take a stand for continuous improvement of quality and value-for-money services	1	2	3	4
A regular strategic conversation among people with links to the whole organisation determines robust strategic priorities and goals, and monitors results	1	2	3	4
Organisational infrastructure has been built to determine strategy in a strategic conversation among leadership and to engage the whole organisation in a strategy, leadership and engagement (SLE) forum	1	2	3	4
Organisational trust is built through competence, openness and honesty, concerns for employees/stakeholders, reliability, job satisfaction and team and individual effectiveness	1	2	3	4
We motivate people by fostering a sense of achievement, recognition, and the work itself, including regular feedback, advancement on merit and personal growth of competencies	1	2	3	4

	Disagree completely	Disagree somewhat	Agree somewhat	Agree completely
Intact team competence profile identifies strengths and challenges	1	2	3	4
Individual personal development planning (PDP) forms part of the performance contract	1	2	3	4
Subtotal:				
SCENARIO-BASED STRATEGY:				
We collaborate and engage for building common purpose	1	2	3	4
We experience strategic planning as a learning process uses scenario-based strategy processes	1	2	3	4
We stress-test options and strategic priorities for robustness	1	2	3	4
We make evidence-based policy choices only	1	2	3	4
We conduct regular strategy reviews based on outcomes-focused strategic priorities	1	2	3	4
Subtotal:				
SERVICE DELIVERY:				
We regularly set goals and review performance of intact teams and individuals, for effective service delivery and alignment of performance with strategy	1	2	3	4
We build shared commitment and sound evidence-based delivery models	1	2	3	4
We plan, prioritise and resource delivery and include alternate delivery models	1	2	3	4
We use competitive bidding among subcontractors for service delivery contracts	1	2	3	4
Sustainable community investment programmes (SCIP) include human rights-based programmes, for example youth engagement in service delivery	1	2	3	4
We use joint ventures and partnerships for quality service delivery	1	2	3	4
Back-to-basics and value-for-money services to citizens	1	2	3	4
We embed organisational goal setting and review routines for ensuring a service delivery culture	1	2	3	4
Subtotal:				
LEADERSHIP:				
Leadership grade %:				

	Disagree completely	Disagree somewhat	Agree somewhat	Agree completely
STRATEGY:				
Strategy grade %:				
SERVICE DELIVERY:				
Service delivery grade %:				
GRAND TOTAL:				
Raw score:				
Overall capability grade %				

Overall capability score	Grade assessment				
0–25	POOR – look for successful models to learn from				
26–50	BELOW AVERAGE – keep learning				
51–75	CAPABLE – document successful processes and share				
76–100	EXCELLENT – share successes and provide mentoring support to other leaders				

PART II

Theory underpinning effective and competent resilience practice

Contents

CHAPTER 2

ORGANISATIONAL DYNAMICS: A SYSTEMS PERSPECTIVE

1 INTRODUCTION

In an organisation, the success of an effective resilience strategy may depend upon an understanding of the underlying organisational structure and leveraging this understanding of structure to enable responsiveness. The term "structure" is taken here to refer not only to the physical organisational structure (i.e. organogram), but also in the broadest sense to the systemic components of structure such as the interactivity with the contextual environment, compliance with the rule of law, leadership, goal setting and review processes, accountability, policy, ability to execute strategy and policy, norms, values and culture. These components of structure in the broadest sense constitute viewing an organisation as a dynamic, complex ecology. Organisational adaptation and responsiveness may ultimately determine the effectiveness of a resilience strategy.

The purpose of this chapter is to explore the evolution of thinking regarding organisations as open systems. This includes an analysis of the paradigmatic developments, schools of thinking, theoretical principles, theories and models of organisations. This analysis includes organisational design and development that are directly interconnected with responsiveness and general organisational resilience. It also explores the origins of organisations as well as subsystems within organisations. As such, the chapter intends to uncover the fundamental tenets and principles of organisational resilience. It will serve as a comprehensive systems approach to organisational resilience by pinpointing the influence of underlying structure, design and organisational development. It will also reveal the high leverage components of a systems approach which allow for large-scale adjustment, restructuring and change to foster organisational resilience.

2   ORGANISATIONS AND THEIR CONTEXTUAL ENVIRONMENT

Lawrence and Lorsch[1] argue that individuals operate in a social context that has a powerful influence on their behaviour. When this idea is applied to organisations, an analysis of its context uncovers external forces and inter-organisational relations that influence organisational structure and operations. Lawrence and Lorsch[2] continue by reflecting that "significant scholarly attention has been devoted to theories at the intra-organisational level that focus primarily on the internal structures, processes and dynamics of organisations. However, all of these internal elements can be influenced and shaped by forces operating outside the organisation".[3] They further assert that

> "... if there is a general theory under which environmental theories can be placed, it is the 'open systems model.' In this view organisational systems and structures are penetrated by and subject to a wide variety of external influences. The particular way in which these external influences shape an organisation is what distinguishes the various theories that fall under the rubric of the open the systems model."[4]

Lawrence and Lorsch[5] continue by suggesting that contingency theory is a relevant means to assess environmental dynamics and their potential influence on organisations. As it applies to organisations, contingency means that the effectiveness of a specific organisational structure or strategy depends upon the presence or absence of other environmental factors. According to Lawrence and Lorsch,[6] "one especially important dimension of an organisation's environment is the degree of certainty or uncertainty, defined by the levels of competition (for resources), changes in service innovation, the predictability of the supply of and demand for inputs and outputs". Lawrence and Lorsch[7] posit that the greater the uncertainty in the environment the more flexible and informal the internal organisational structure and, conversely, the greater the stability and certainty in the environment the more rigid and formal the internal

---

[1]   Lawrence, P. & Lorsch, J.W. 1986. *Organisational environment*. Boston, MA: Harvard Business School Press, p. 208.

[2]   Lawrence & Lorsch, 1986, p. 208.

[3]   Lawrence, & Lorsch, 1986, p. 208.

[4]   Lawrence & Lorsch, 1986, p. 209.

[5]   Lawrence & Lorsch, 1986, p. 209.

[6]   Lawrence & Lorsch, 1986, p. 209.

[7]   Lawrence & Lorsch, 1986.

organisational structure typically becomes. Table 2.1 reflects these contingency relationships.

Table 2.1:Lawrence and Lorsch's contingency relationships

Type of organisation	Environmental characteristics	Internal structure
Municipality/metro	Highly stable and certain	Rigid/formal
Provincial government	Highly stable and certain	Rigid/formal
National government	Highly stable and certain	Rigid/formal
Organisational sub-units in municipalities/metros		
Service delivery	Highly unstable and uncertain	Flexible and informal
Transportation	Moderately unstable and uncertain	Moderately flexible/ informal
Energy	Moderately unstable and uncertain	Moderately flexible/ informal

Source: After Lawrence and Lorsch[8]

Since this theory on the influence of the external environment on organisational structures in 1986 was posited, organisations globally have experienced increasing uncertainty, evidenced by factors such as global recession, climate volatility, fundamentalism, technological convergence and disruptions. Organisations, in general, need to be more flexible and informal. For national government, and city government particularly, there is increasingly the need to become more agile and to develop appropriate, more flexible structures. The appreciation of the interdependence between an organisation and the dynamics in its environment points to an emerging paradigm shift towards a systemic view, as implied by Lawrence and Lorsch's contingency theory.

3   PARADIGMS AND PARADIGM SHIFTS

Capra and Luisi[9] point out that–

> "during the first half of the twentieth century, philosophers and historians of science generally believed that progress in science was a smooth process in which scientific models and theories were continually refined and replaced by new and more accurate versions" this view of continuous progress was

---

[8]   Lawrence & Lorsch, 1986, p. 211

[9]   Capra, F. & Luisi, P.L. 2016. *The systems view of life.* Cambridge, UK: Cambridge University Press.

radically challenged by the physicist and philosopher of science, Thomas Kuhn[10] when he described the underlying "structure of scientific revolutions". Kuhn argued that, while continuous progress is characteristic of long periods of "normal science" these periods are interrupted by periods of "revolutionary science" in which not only a scientific theory but also the entire conceptual framework in which it is embedded undergoes rapid change.

To describe this underlying framework, Kuhn introduced the concept of "paradigm", which he defined as "a constellation of achievements, concepts, values, techniques, shared within a scientific community and used by the community to define legitimate problems and solutions[11] Changes of paradigms, according to Kuhn, occur in discontinuous, revolutionary breaks he called paradigm shifts. Perhaps the most important aspect of his definition of a scientific paradigm is the fact that it includes not only concepts and techniques but also values.

A systemic perspective, where one looks at the whole and interconnections, instead of the parts in isolation, may constitute a paradigm shift. Systems thinking may still be uncommon among executive leadership and executive management in organisations. Meadows[12] describes paradigms as "[t]he source of systems, the assumptions that govern our behaviour. The mindset out of which the system – as goals, structure, rules, delays, parameters – arises". To illustrate the power of paradigms, Meadows[13] cites Forrester as saying that –

"… it doesn't matter how the tax law of a country (or metro) is written. There is a shared idea in the minds of the society about what a 'fair' distribution of the tax load is. Whatever the law says by fair means or foul, by complications, cheating, exemptions or deductions, by constant sniping at the rules, external tax payments will push right up against the accepted idea of fairness. The shared ideas in the minds of society, the great unstated assumptions constitute that society's paradigms, or deepest set of beliefs about how the world works. These beliefs are unstated because it's unnecessary to state them – everyone already knows them."

---

[10] Kuhn, T. 1996. The structure of scientific revolution. 3rd ed. Chicago, IL: University of Chicago.

[11] Kuhn, 1996.

[12] Meadows, D.H. 1999. *Leverage points: Places to intervene in a system.* Hartland, VT: Chelsea Green, p. 162.

[13] Meadows, 1999, p. 163.

3.1 Evolution of systems thinking as a worldview

The ideas of contingency theory and the fact that paradigms are in constant flux can, in the context of organisational resilience, probably be best analysed by comprehending and applying systems thinking. The purpose of this section is to uncover the paradigmatic development of systems thinking as applied to the fields of system dynamics and organisational structures and functions.

3.2 General systems theory

Von Bertalanffy[14] is generally regarded as the father of general systems theory (GST). He described and formally initiated the development of the scientifically rigorous systemic perspective situated within a systems worldview. Fuller in Davidson[15] points out that "Ludwig von Bertalanffy and other physiological pioneers have yet to be rewarded with the finite system clarity attained by Euclid, Newton and others. This in no way diminishes the brilliance of Von Bertalanffy's conceptualizing nor the contribution that his general systems theory has made to vast fields of scientific enquiry and the scientific organisation of human efforts in general".

Davidson[16] describes Von Bertalanffy's GST as "a prescription for survival. Common sense which once assured humanity the world was flat, now assures us the world is the sum of its parts". Davidson goes on to draw attention to the fact that GST introduced a new perspective that is variously described as "holistic, ecological, *gestalt*, global, molar, integrative, organismic, synergistic, synergetical, synholistic and systemic … though this fundamental shift in outlook has been advocated by numerous twentieth-century thinkers-including Alfred North Whitehead, Jan Christiaan Smuts and Buckminster Fuller". Von Bertalanffy's GST is much broader than the systems approach usually associated with engineering, corporate management and public administration. GST applies the principle of integrated thinking to all areas of human experience. Von Bertalanffy conceptualised a system as –

"… any entity maintained by the mutual interaction of its parts, from the atom to the cosmos, and including such mundane examples as telephone, postal and rapid transit systems … it can be physical like

[14] Von Bertalanffy, L. 1968. *General systems theory: Foundation development and applications.* New York, NY: George Braziller.

[15] Davidson, M. 1983. *Uncommon sense: The life and thought of Ludwig von Bertalanffy father of general system theory.* Los Angeles, CA: Tarcher, p. 15.

[16] Davidson, 1983, p. 21–55.

a television set, biological like a cocker spaniel, psychological like a personality, sociological like a labour union, or symbolic like a set of laws. A system can also be a categorical combination, like the man-machine system that composes a factory. A system can be static like a crystal, mechanical like a clock, mechanically self-regulating like a thermostat, and organically interactive with the environment like plants, people and populations."[17]

The common denominator of the various definitions of a system is the idea of interaction and interdependence. Systems thinking demands what Von Bertalanffy called "a change in basic categories of thought".[18] Von Bertalanffy believed that the overall fate of the world depends upon the adoption by humanity of a new set of values based on GST, which he called a *Weltanschauung* (worldview). In the cultural sphere, Von Bertalanffy commended Whorf's hypothesis that "a person's worldview is largely determined by the assumptions that are implicit in that person's native language".[19] Von Bertalanffy's conceptual model of the living organism as an *open system* [my emphasis], as an entity continuously interacting with its environment, contained revolutionary implications for behavioural and social science".[20] The implication is that we as humans per se and as humans in organisations are active as well as interactive with our environment.

3.3 Towards a systems view

Capra and Luisi,[21] in their systems view of life in general, describe the mechanistic worldview as the worldview that *precedes* the rise of the systems worldview. Capra and Luisi[22] regard the evolution from "seeing the part to seeing the whole", as a result of growing tension between mechanism and holism in the history of western science. In twentieth-century science, the holistic perspective became known as "systems thinking". The main characteristics of systems thinking emerged during the 1920s in several disciplines in Europe (and in Africa with Smuts' writing on holism and evolution[23]). It was further enriched by Gestalt psychology and the new science of ecology. It probably had the most dramatic effect in quantum

---

[17] Davidson, 1983, p. 26.

[18] Davidson, 1983, p. 30.

[19] Davidson, 1983, p. 216.

[20] Davidson, 1983, p. 23.

[21] Capra & Luisi, 2016.

[22] Capra & Luisi, 2016, p. 63.

[23] Smuts, J.C. 1925. *Holism and evolution*. 3rd ed. London: Macmillan.

physics: the behaviour of a living organism as an integrated whole cannot be understood from the study of its parts alone. As the systems theorists would put it "the whole is more than the sum of the parts". Systems thinking is about thinking in terms of connectedness, relationships, patterns and context.

Capra and Luisi[24] offer the following clarification of a systems perspective:

"According to the systems view, the essential properties of an organism, or living system, are properties of the whole, which none of the parts have. They arise from the interaction and relationships between the parts. These properties are destroyed when the system is dissected, either physically or theoretically, into isolated elements … The emergence of systems thinking was a profound revolution in the history of western scientific thought … The great shock of twentieth-century science that living systems cannot be understood by analysis. The properties of the parts are not intrinsic properties but can only be understood within the context of the larger whole. Thus, the relationship between the parts and the whole have been reversed. In the systems approach, the properties of the parts can only be understood from the properties of the whole. Accordingly, systems thinking does not concentrate on basic building blocks but rather on basic principles of organisation."

They go on to explain that systems thinking is contextual, which is the opposite of analytical thinking. Analytical thinking requires considering the details of sub-elements by taking sub-elements apart, while systems thinking requires placing sub-elements into the context of and interconnectedness with the larger whole. In this regard, Ackoff[25] describes a system as a "whole consisting of two or more parts, each of which can affect the performance or properties of the whole, none of which can have an independent effect on the whole, and no subgroup of which can have an independent effect on the whole". In brief, then, a system is a whole that cannot be divided into independent parts or subgroups of parts.

---

[24] Capra & Luisi, 2016, p. 65.

[25] Ackoff, R.L. 1994. Systems thinking and thinking systems. *Systems Dynamics Review,* 10(23):175–188.

Closed and open systems

A closed system (see Figure 2.1) can be described as processes in a linear relationship i.e. INPUT(S) → PROCESSES → OUTPUT(S).

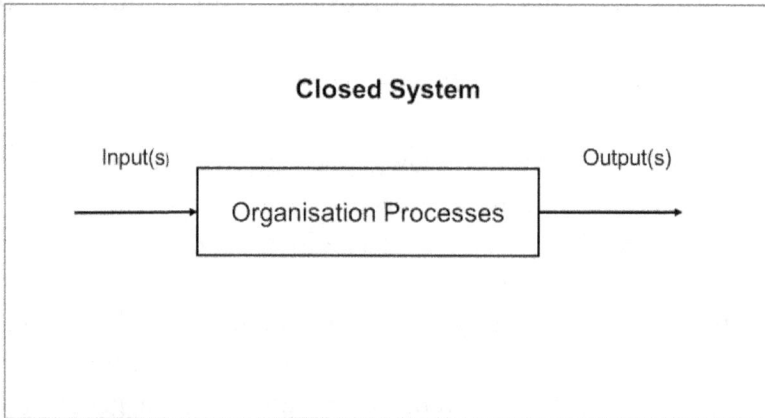

Closed System

Input(s)   Output(s)

Organisation Processes

Figure 2.1:   Closed system
Source: Centre for Innovative Leadership[26]

A closed system, because of the absence of feedback, is static and does not have the ability to respond or adapt to stimuli such as environmental changes.

In contrast, an open system consists of INPUT(S) → PROCESSES → OUTPUT(S) and, in addition, able to receive FEEDBACK, which enables the system to respond and adapt to stimuli in the form of feedback.

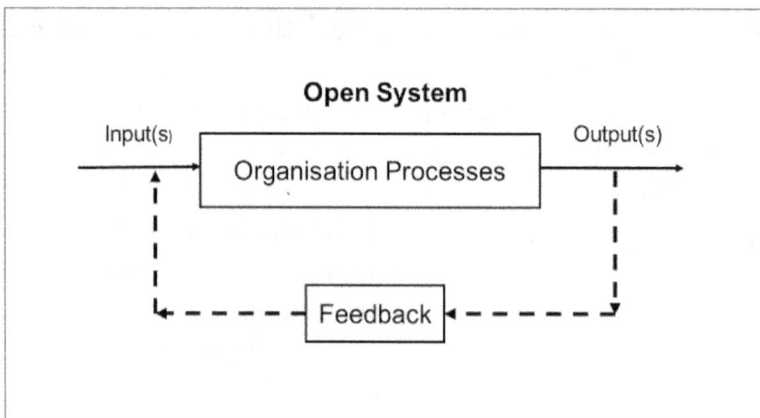

Open System

Input(s)   Output(s)

Organisation Processes

Feedback

Figure 2.2:   Open system
Source: CIL[27]

---

[26]   Centre for Innovative Leadership (CIL). 1993. *Manual for executive education: Systems Thinking for Sustainable Leadership and Transformation (STSLT).* http://www.cil.net Date of access: 13 February 2017.

[27]   Centre for Innovative Leadership (CIL). 1993.

Forrester[28] explains systems of information feedback control as "fundamental to all life and human endeavour, from the slow pace of biological evolution to the launching of the latest space satellite ... Everything we do as individuals, as an industry [as a city government] or as a society is done in the context of an information feedback system."

3.4 Systems dynamics

The presence of "feedback loops" is what makes a system dynamic and capable of behaving in different ways. A feedback loop is the basic building block for describing and modelling complex, dynamic, open systems. In the conventions of the SD modelling terminology, feedback loops reflect the causal relationships between selected variables. The quantum of a variable is known as a "stock"[29] and the strength between two variables is known as the "flow" between variables. Feedback loops together with stocks and flows are the basis of Forrester's[30] [31] SD modelling. SD models are logic-rich models based on causal loop diagrams. The basis of SD modelling is causal logic between variables. The relative rate of change between one variable and another that are linked in a causal loop relationship constitutes a differential calculus, that is, a mathematical relationship.

Stella and *iThink* software developed by Richmond and others (see Table 2.2) simplifies the mathematical calculations within a model described by a causal loop diagram of a complex dynamic system. By adjusting selected parameters in the model and then iterating the model into the future, the modeller can demonstrate the resulting pattern of behaviour over time of specific variables. Forrester was interested in using SD modelling to uncover counter-intuitive outcomes and patterns of behaviour over time for specific variables within a complex system. Logical causal links and loops differentiate this modelling methodology from most other modelling that uses data as their basis. SD models are particularly useful when developing plausible storylines for scenarios beyond a ten-year time horizon where is becomes difficult to demonstrate plausibility in the 10–25 year time frame in different scenarios.

SD modelling was first used to model urban dynamics and later expanded to encompass industrial dynamics.[32] [33] In 1972, SD emerged on a global scale as a suitable instrument for modelling the sustainable

---

[28] Forrester, J.W. 1961. *Industrial dynamics*. Cambridge, MA: MIT Press, p. 15.

[29] Meadows, D. 2008. *Thinking in systems*. White River Junction, VT: Chelsea Green.

[30] Forrester, 1961.

[31] Forrester, J.W. 1969. *Urban dynamics*. Cambridge, MA: MIT Press.

[32] Forrester, 1961.

[33] Forrester, 1969.

use of resources to study global limits to growth. Work in this regard was published in the report of the Club of Rome, known as *Limits to growth*.[34] The robustness of Forrester's SD modelling was demonstrated when a 30-year retrospective review of the 1972 Club of Rome Report,[35] completed in 2002, revealed similar results. This review found that all the major parameters in the 1972 model were on track with current unfolding data sets such as population, pollution, agriculture, resource availability and price, socio-political and capital. The model has thus been proven to be a highly suitable instrument for strategy and policy formulation on a 20–25 year planning time horizon. Forrester's inventions and work gathered a cadre of protégés and experts at the Massachusetts Institute of Technology (MIT) in the so-called Systems Dynamics group, part of the Sloan School of Management at MIT (see Table 2.2).

Table 2.2: First generation systems dynamics expertise

Systems dynamics expert	Contribution
John Sterman	*Business dynamics: Systems thinking and modelling for a complex world* (2000)
Peter Senge	*The fifth discipline* (1990), *Fifth discipline field book* (1994) and *Dance of change* (1999)
Donella Meadows	*Limits to growth*, Club of Rome Report (1972, 1992, 2004), *Thinking in systems* (2008)
Dennis Meadows	*Limits to growth* (1972)
Phyllis Fox and Alexander Pugh	DYNAMO the early industry standard for SD Modelling (1986)
Barry Richmond	Stella and iThink SD (2012)
John Morecroft	Strategic Modelling and Business Dynamics (2015)
Michael Goodman	Study Notes in Systems Dynamics (1983)
David Kreutzer	Executive Education in Systems Thinking and Systems Dynamics (1992)
Ed Roberts	First commercially successful Personal Computer (1975)

Source: Author's own research

---

[34]   Meadows, D.H., Meadows, D.L., Randers, J. & Behrens III, W.W. 1972. *Limits to growth*. London: Pan Books.

[35]   Meadows, D.H., Randers, J. & Meadows, D.L. 2004. *A synopsis – Limits to growth: The 30 year update*. Post Mills, VT: Chelsea Green.

The protégés in the above table have applied Forrester's SD methodology to a wide variety of applications in industry and government in the USA. In South Africa, SD has also been applied as part of a scenario-based strategic planning process together with capacity building in systems thinking and scenario thinking within the state-owned enterprise, Eskom.[36] First generation SD scholars and practitioners provide context to Forrester's SD legacy and a resource for capacity building in organisations and city governments. Modelling and tracking urban dynamics using SD models may also prove to be a useful method for anticipating discontinuities in the contextual environment of city government organisations in South Africa.

Based on the principles of SD, Meadows[37] conceptualises so-called leverage points as "where a small shift in one thing can produce big changes in everything else". Effective organisational structure and development practices may be dependent upon identifying leverage points as the basis for organisational interventions and adjustments. Identifying leverage points to enable resilience in organisations may also be useful for gauging the effectiveness of resilience strategies.

It is generally accepted that the level of turbulence and complexity in organisations in general and city governments in particular is accelerating. In addition, the World Economic Forum's Schwab[38] alerts us to 23 deep disruptive shifts contained in what he calls the "Fourth Industrial Revolution". This revolution consists of numerous converging technologies, which together may be disruptive, and will probably place greater demands on executive leadership and executive management in city governments. These disruptive dynamics raise the need to create more resilient organisations. Organisations that have been sufficiently responsive in the past will probably not be adequately responsive in future conditions. Specific parts of organisations may need to be adapted to deal effectively with these new resilience challenges. Collectively, these organisational subsystem changes will improve resilience in the whole organisation.

---

[36] Centre for Innovative Leadership (CIL). 2009. Scenario-based strategy report and capacity building in Eskom. (Unpublished).

[37] Meadows, 2008.

[38] Schwab, K. 2016a. *Navigating the Fourth Industrial Revolution.* http://www.biznews.com/ wef/davos-2016/2016/01/20/klaus-schwab-navigating-the-fourth-industrial-revolution/ Date of access: 23 August 2017.

4 ORGANISATIONAL SUBSYSTEMS

The organisational subsystems reflected in Figure 2.3 generally reflect the scholarly work of Kast and Rosenzweig[39] on contingency views of organisations and management. This perspective provides a useful systemic framework for the analysis of organisational subsystems, where an organisation is viewed as an open system. The essence of organisational subsystems as open systems is the presence of multiple feedback loops. These feedback loops enable responsiveness to inputs and feedback from the environment and result in dynamic behaviour to accommodate and adapt to the organisational context. Equilibrium or homeostasis along a specific growth pathway may also be maintained via these sets of feedback loops (see Figure 2.3).

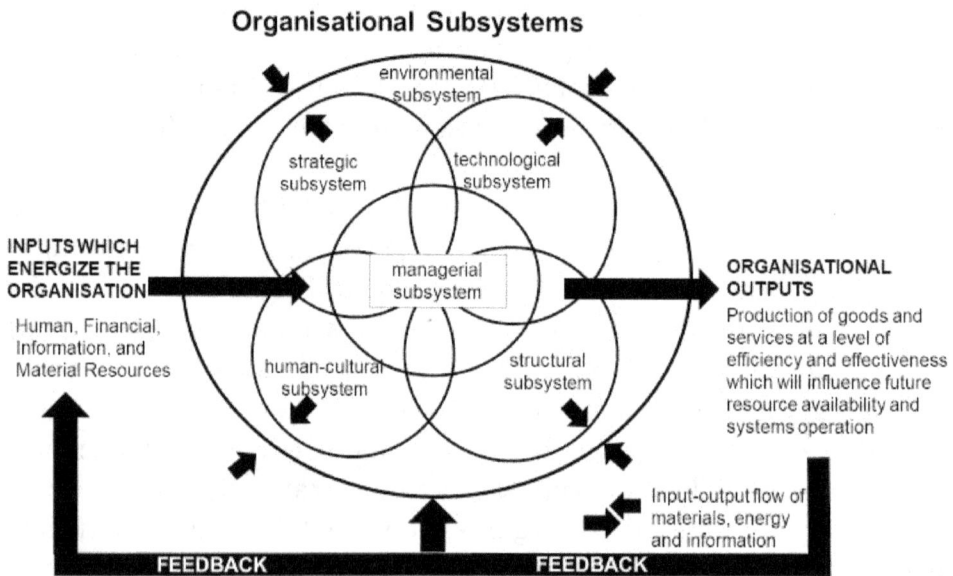

Organisational Subsystems

environmental subsystem

strategic subsystem

technological subsystem

managerial subsystem

human-cultural subsystem

structural subsystem

INPUTS WHICH ENERGIZE THE ORGANISATION

Human, Financial, Information, and Material Resources

ORGANISATIONAL OUTPUTS

Production of goods and services at a level of efficiency and effectiveness which will influence future resource availability and systems operation

Input-output flow of materials, energy and information

FEEDBACK   FEEDBACK

Figure 2.3: Organisation as an open system – A set of interdependent subsystems

Source: Adapted from Kast and Rosenzweig.[40]

According to Kast and Rosenzweig,[41] organisational subsystems consist of a managerial subsystem, technological subsystem, strategic subsystem, human-cultural subsystem and structural subsystem. All of these subsystems may be seen in the context of an environmental supra-system. In the context of an environmental supra-system, the whole organisation

---

[39]   Kast, F.E. & Rosenzweig, J.E. 1973. *Contingency views of organisations and management.* Chicago, IL: Science Research Associates

[40]   Kast & Rosenzweig, 1973.

[41]   Kast & Rosenzweig, 1973.

receives inputs in the form of human, financial, information and material resources. These are processed through its organisational subsystems to produce organisational outputs in the form of goods and services at a level of efficiency and effectiveness that influences future resource availability and systems operation efficiencies. A feedback loop from the outputs to the organisation subsystem as well as to the inputs provides the whole organisation with its capacity to anticipate, adapt and recover.

This subsystem perspective is congruent with the work of Argyris,[42] who developed theories of organisational learning. His *single-loop* and *double-loop* learning provide a model for reflective learning. Deeper, double-loop learning may result in what Whybrow[43] calls "re-tuning" the human mind. Whybrow argues that humans need to retune their minds, at scale, to survive. He continues by stressing that human thinking requires a paradigm shift – from a paradigm of economic growth to one emphasising limited growth, lower consumption and widespread recycling of resources. He goes on to argue that unless this takes place at scale, the existence of the human species may be threatened with extinction.

Morgan[44] also points towards a contingency theory for organisations adapting to environments and their fit with environments. He makes the following assertions:

- "Organisations are open systems that need careful management to satisfy and balance internal needs and to adapt to the environmental circumstances;
- There is no one best way of organising. The appropriate form depends on the kind of tasks or environment with which one is dealing;
- Management must be concerned, above all else, with achieving alignment and good fit. [In terms of fit with current and future environments as well as fit between subsystems as defined]; and
- Different approaches to management of the people in an organisation as it may be necessary to perform different tasks within the same organisation".[45]

---

[42] Argyris, C. 1992. *On organisation learning*. Cambridge, MA: Blackwell.

[43] Whybrow, P.C. 2015. *The well-tuned brain: Neuroscience and the life well-lived*. London: Norton.

[44] Morgan, G. 1997. *Images of organisations*. London: Sage, p. 44.

[45] Morgan, 1997, p. 44.

Morgan[46] proposes a contingency theory for providing organisational health, resilience and development by posing the following questions:

- "How can an organisation systemically achieve a good 'fit' with its environment?
- How can it adapt to changing environmental circumstances?
- How can it ensure that internal relations are balanced and appropriate?"

It is generally accepted that these questions have become the basis for the development of the corpus of knowledge of Organisational Development (OD) as the professional support field for management of change and transformation, and which may also be suitably competent to play a role among human resources practitioners in building organisational resilience. Examining organisations as biological entities, Morgan[47] focuses on organisations as human activity systems. The Tavistock Institute[48] termed the integration between social aspects of organisations and their technical aspects of work "social-technical systems". This approach recognises the interdependency between the technical structure and the social aspects of organisations. Organisational structures reflect an important component of social-technical systems and are therefore described below in full, to provide a comprehensive context for the evolution of paradigms over time.

5   THE EVOLUTION OF PARADIGMATIC DEVELOPMENTS IN ORGANISATIONAL THOUGHT

Over time, insight into the dynamic interaction between an organisation and its environment has grown and has led to more contemporary praxis regarding organisational design, strategies and activities. The evolution of organisational thought can be categorised into specific eras. These eras are the archetypical, classical, neoclassical and more contemporary time periods. These eras are briefly explored below.

6   ARCHETYPAL ORGANISATIONS

The *Concise Oxford Dictionary*[49] defines archetype as an "original model; prototype; typical specimen; primordial mental image inherited by all; recurrent symbol or motif". This definition serves as a rationale for drawing attention to the San Bushmen communities as example of the first simple but effective organisation for ensuring resilience. The San, who live in the western Kalahari, exist in harsh conditions which constantly test their

---

[46]   Morgan, 1997, p. 56.

[47]   Morgan, 1997, p. 34.

[48]   The Tavistock Institute. 2017. www.tavinstitute.org/ Date of access: 10 August 2017.

[49]   *Concise Oxford Dictionary* (COD). 1982. 7th ed. Oxford: Oxford University Press.

resilience and sustainability as an archetypal village community. The simple but effective social structures (*kgotla*) of the San community provide insights on this sustainability and resilience. These insights and learning may be useful for enhancing contemporary conceptions of organisational resilience.

Weisbord[50] argues that for change to be managed effectively and successfully, the whole organisational system must be represented and engaged in the change management process. Inclusive archetypal structures such as the communal conversation and decision making in a San *kgotla* may be useful for raising the probability of successful adaptive change and sustainable living. The survival of the San provides evidence of management and organisational recovery from shocks which have tested their resilience. Lewis-Williams[51] describes the images on rocks in Southern Africa as "enabling us to marvel at great achievements of the past and so form a more balanced view of western civilisation"[52] and attributes the lower status among ethnologists of rock images left by [the 'first people' in SoA] San 10 200 years Before Present (BP) to 3 990 years BP to the fact that "the low esteem the Bushmen were held in by early missionaries, researchers and explorers resulted in little attention being paid to their culture and social organisation"[53]. He goes on to explain that as our understanding of these rock images grew, an understanding of the vital part they played in the San culture and spiritual life also developed. The study of the San (Xam or "first people") language provides further insights on their belief system, social life, tradition, culture and rituals.

A closer look at San communities that have sustained themselves in these harsh desert conditions may offer learning about the archetypal organisational structures that enable their resilience. The San culture may be considered an archetypal organisation from which we can learn about the structures that enable a resilience strategy.

Kuper[54] documented some of the structural and paradigmatic elements of the San social structure. The elements have been specifically selected to enable cooperation and resilience in challenging desert conditions. At the centre of a San community is the *kgotla*. Kuper describes this structure as "an inclusive, conversation-driven forum where the San community sets

---

[50] Weisbord, M.R. 1992. *Discovering common ground*. San Francisco, CA: Berrett-Koehler.

[51] *In* Dowson, T.A. 1992. *Rock engravings of Southern Africa*. Johannesburg: Witwatersrand University Press, p. X.

[52] Dowson, 1992, p. 2.

[53] Dowson, 1992, p. X.

[54] Kuper, A. 1970. *Kalahari village politics: An African democracy*. London: Cambridge University Press.

goals, allocates accountabilities and monitors progress towards achievement of such goals".[55] This structure determines their direction as an organised community. Kuper[56] describes the proportions of the day-to-day business contained in the *kgotla* structure as follows: "About a fifth of the issues recorded are legal ... a third deal with the major public utilities, the school, education and the borehole, or ... other aspects of domestic administration, exercise of authority, and demands of various kinds from citizens."[57] He goes on to say that both domestic and external political issues are also managed through the *kgotla* conversation.

This early manifestation of an organisational structure that enables the building of alignment in the San village setting provides confirmation of what is seen as an early archetypal organisational structure. In the context of the San it constitutes the structure through which goal setting and review can take place, which ensures a greater certainty regarding achieving the goals agreed by the *kgotla* participants. In their research, Locke and Latham[58] confirmed the value of a structured goal setting and review process for raising productivity.

The structural components of the *kgotla* process described by Kuper,[59] in the context of the San, reinforce its aims to be inclusive, conversation-driven, supported by trust and developed over time through regular engagement in *kgotla* conversations. *Kgotla* members prefer sharing responsibilities with relatives or kinship groups to ensure the successful execution of *kgotla* decisions. This preference points towards trust as a part of the successful implementation of plans. In the case of the San, *kgotla* engagement with relatives and kinship groups forms the basis of trust and ensures the successful cooperation required to move the community forward to achieve the goals set by the *kgotla*.

A San village can be regarded as an open system where the presence of feedback in the form of the volatile environmental dynamics, such as climatic conditions and the fluctuating availability of food, compels the community's resilience response. This brief description of a so-called Palaeolithic organisation, in existence from 10 000 years BP, provides a starting point for describing the evolution of modern organisations as open systems.

By applying the principles of the *kgotla* to contemporary organisational

---

[55] Kuper, 1970, p. 98.

[56] Kuper, 1970, p. 100.

[57] Kuper, 1970, p. 100.

[58] Locke, C.A. & Latham, G.P. 1984. *Goal-setting: A motivational technique that works!* Englewood Cliffs, NJ: Prentice Hall, p. 15.

[59] Kuper, 1970.

resilience thinking, Van der Merwe[60] points out that this inclusive, conversation-enabled forum was used as part of the successful turnaround of Eskom in the 1980s. In the Eskom context, the *kgotla* structure was referred to as "The Top Thirty". All change initiatives were first mooted in this structure, and only after understanding, support and ownership were established were these change initiatives diffused into the organisation via its members. Similarly, the San *kgotla* was a forum for inclusive goal setting and reporting on progress, eliminating bottlenecks and unintended consequences.

7 CLASSICAL THEORIES OF ORGANISATION

Classical theories of organisation provide a typology which has been taken into common usage. The titles below use analogies such as machines and other functional descriptors to provide a useful typology.

7.1 The machine bureaucracy

Early conceptions of organisation have been labelled "machine-based" bureaucracies, since the management structure was characterised by a high degree of formalisation and specialisation. In a machine bureaucracy, decisions are made at the top level and mechanically carried out at the lower levels.

Mintzberg[61] describes the basic structure of the machine bureaucracy as "a clear configuration of the design parameters including highly specialised, routine tasks, formalised procedures, a proliferation of rules and regulations, formalised communication, relatively centralised power for decision making, and an elaborate administrative structure with a sharp distinction between line and staff functions".

7.2 Divisionalised form of organisation

Mintzberg[62] points out that the "divisionalised form" of organisations relied on market forces for the grouping of units. The dispersal of operating functions based on markets minimised the interdependence between divisions, so that each could operate as a quasi-autonomous entity, free of the need to coordinate with the others. The span of control at the apex of the divisionalised form would be rather wide. This often led to a crisis of coordination and control between and within divisions. So-called "silo

---

[60] Van der Merwe, L. 1991. Systems approach to change management: The Eskom experience. *In* Osler, C. ed. 1991. *Making their future: South African organisations on the move.* Institute for Futures Research: University of Stellenbosch Press, pp. 63–76.

[61] Mintzberg, H. 1979. *The structuring of organisations.* Englewood Cliffs, NJ: Prentice Hall, p. 314.

[62] Mintzberg, 1979, p. 381.

thinking" as the manifestation of fragmentation between divisions resulted in managerial "tunnel vision" and the absence of systems thinking. The creation of a strategy and leadership engagement forum[63] may offset this fragmentation and engage representatives of the organisation as a whole in anticipation, adaptation and recovery processes in the service of building greater resilience.

7.3   The adhocracy

According to Mintzberg,[64] the adhocracy "consists of a highly organic structure with little formalisation of behaviour, horizontal job specialisation based on formal training, a tendency to group the specialists in functional units, but deploy them in small market-based project teams to do their work". Thus, to innovate means to break away from this established pattern. In contrast, an innovative organisation cannot rely on any form of standardisation. An adhocracy must be flexible, self-renewing and organic.

The paradigmatic evolution of organisational thinking can be discerned from shifts away from mechanistic to more organic structures. Mintzberg's research[65] shows that the machine bureaucracy and the divisionalised form of organisation are inclined to be slow in responding to external forces. This is mainly due to their centralised systems and tall hierarchical structures. In contrast, resilience is dependent on organisational responsiveness which facilitates the ability to recover rapidly from shocks, adapt and then recover and develop beyond the pre-shock state. Identifying high leverage areas for gauging resilience for city government can, in the Mintzberg typology, best be drawn from organisational paradigms as machine bureaucracies and divisionalised structures. These types of organisation most closely reflect large parts of current national, provincial and city government organisations. Developing robust city government organisations for the future may need greater responsiveness to community needs and general external dynamics.

Morgan's[66] typology of organisations builds on Mintzberg's typology and includes organisations as machines, organisations as organisms, organisations as brains that learn and self-organise, organisations as cultures, organisations as political systems, organisations as psychic prisons, and organisations as flux and transformation. Brief descriptions of each are reflected on the following pages:

---

[63]   Centre for Innovative Leadership (CIL). 1992. Developing a Strategy, Leadership and Engagement (SLE) Forum. (Unpublished).

[64]   Mintzberg, 1979, p. 432.

[65]   Mintzberg, 1979.

[66]   Morgan, 1997.

7.4 Organisations as machines

Organisations are designed and operated as if they were machines, called bureaucracies. Morgan[67] describes these organisations as "machine-like" and guided by "mechanical thinking". Morgan[68] goes on to state that "this instrumentality is evident in the practices of the earliest formal organisations such as those that built the great empires, churches and armies ... If we examine the changes in organisation accompanying the industrial revolution, an increasing trend toward the bureaucratisation and routinisation of life generally is evident".

7.5 Organisations as organisms

In this perspective, organisations are regarded as "living systems" that exist in a wider environment on which they depend for the satisfaction of various needs.[69] Organisations function as open systems and need to constantly adapt to changing conditions for their health and further development.

7.6 Organisations as brains that learn and self-organise

Morgan[70] describes these organisations as consisting of "brains as information processing systems conceived as a control system similar to a computer or telephone switchboard". It has the ability to discern patterns from various sets of data and functions like a neural network that translates information into thoughts, ideas and actions.

7.7 Organisations as a result of social culture

Morgan[71] asserts that an organisation can be regarded as a "cultural phenomenon that varies according to a society's stage of development". Morgan states that although different theorists argue about the reasons for organisational transformation, most agree that societal culture plays a major role.

This perspective on organisations is relevant for building resilient metros in the South African context as they are embedded in the broader South African culture. The emerging national culture post-1994 may have an impact on the culture within metros and through this an impact on city government resilience. Greater disruptions that result from the converging

---

67   Morgan, 1997, p. 14.

68   Morgan, 1997, p. 15.

69   Morgan, 1997, p. 34.

70   Morgan, 1997, p. 74.

71   Morgan, 1997, p. 118.

dynamics in the Fourth Industrial Revolution mentioned by Schwab[72] seem to be predetermined and may, among other dynamics, result in rapidly changing the nature of work itself. This, in turn, may result in unemployment and increasing inequality due to the loss of jobs. Shifting needs within society may further influence the design of organisations. Organisations may, for example, need to adopt more responsible behaviour towards the homeless and the unemployed and become part of social investment in sustainable community development by governments. The revolution, which Schwab[73] describes as a converging set of 23 disruptive technology-enabled dynamics, may also require different competencies in city government (see to Chapter 4).

7.8   Organisations as political systems

Organisations as political systems can be positioned on a continuum of how power is exercised, for instance, between autocracy and democracy. In this regard, Morgan[74] states that political power generally acts as a leverage point in enabling resilience and state responsiveness. Morgan[75] pinpoints the following typical leverage points of power that influence organisational design and function:

- "formal authority;
- control of scarce resources;
- use of organisational structure, rules and regulations;
- control of decision processes;
- control of knowledge and information;
- control of boundaries;
- ability to cope with uncertainty;
- control of technology;
- interpersonal alliances, networks, and control of the informal organisation;
- control of counter-organisations, for example, trade unions;
- symbolism and management of meaning;
- gender and management of gender relations; and
- structural factors that define the stage of action."

---

[72]   Schwab, 2016a.
[73]   Schwab, 2016a.
[74]   Morgan, 1997, p. 171.
[75]   Morgan, 1997, p. 172.

The sources of power provide organisational executives with a variety of means for enhancing their interests and resolving or perpetuating organisational conflict.[76] Bureaucrats in government may, at different times, use these sources of power to achieve their goals.

7.9   Organisations as psychic prisons

Morgan[77] states that the communication theorist, Marshall McLuhan, noted that "the last thing a fish is likely to discover is the water it is swimming in. The water is so fundamental to the fish's way of life that it is not seen or questioned". The organisational world has many such examples, where its members become trapped in a certain way of thinking and doing.

In applying this principle to South Africa, it is evident that it resonates in the hegemony of the ruling African National Congress (ANC). The long struggle for inclusion, freedom and transformation since the founding of the ANC in 1912 has embedded specific assumptions in the ANC culture. A deep commitment, often described as a "religion", has become entrenched amongst its cadres. The Institute of Race Relations (IRR)[78] further refers to complicated challenges facing local government. Post-1994 liberation expectations have probably trapped political representatives and senior officials in municipalities into thinking that they are entitled to the benefits which flow from the struggle. Factionalism in the ruling party may also be indicative of narrow interests in the sense that supporters are caught in the "psychic prison" Morgan describes.

7.10 Neoclassical theories of organisation

As thinking on organisations and the influence of the environment on their structures and functioning evolved, new insight emerged. Neoclassical thinking can be regarded as an amorphous group of theories and approaches built on classical thought. Some of the most common characteristics of neoclassical thinking are briefly outlined below.

7.11 Organisations as a state of flux

Morgan[79] describes theoretical physicist David Bohm's perspective as "understanding the universe as a flowing and unbroken whole. He views process, flux, and change as fundamental, arguing that the state of the

---

[76]   Morgan, 1997, p. 171.

[77]   Morgan, 1997, p. 217.

[78]   Institute of Race Relations (IRR). 2014. *The 80/20 Report: Local government in 80 indicators after 20 years of democracy.* Johannesburg: IRR, p. 29.

[79]   Morgan, 1997, p. 251.

universe at any point in time reflects a more basic reality". Morgan adds that Bohm calls this reality "the implicate (or enfolded) order" and distinguishes it from the "explicate (or unfolded) order" in the world. This underlying structure provides order to what seems chaotic and unpredictable. Morgan notes that this understanding supports the so-called "four logics of change". The first logic draws on the theory of autopoiesis first described by Maturana and Varela[80], who refer to a system capable of reproducing and maintaining itself along different, alternative causal pathways due to internal interconnectedness. The second logic draws on chaos and complexity theory, explaining how ordered patterns of activity (fractals) can emerge from spontaneous self-organisation. The third logic draws on related cybernetic ideas suggesting that change is enfolded in strains and tensions found in circular relations, while the fourth logic suggests that change is a product of tensions (dilemmas) between opposites.

Bohm's study of the nature of thought shows how dialogue, a conversation where the meaning flows through the participants, enables sharing of thoughts, thus enabling learning. Dialogue points towards conversation quality and engagement and its relationship to "team learning as one of five disciplines for building a learning organisation"[81] Bohm describes dialogue where the meaning in a conversation among a team or a group of people flows through the participants in the conversation. Bohm engages the words *dia* (through) and *logos* (meaning), implying a flow of meaning in a conversation. In the context of conversation quality and engagement by executive leadership and executive management, dialogue represents a high level to which conversation quality may rise. Bohm posits that such conversations are transformative to the learning within teams as well as within the members of these teams.[82]

It is thought that dialogue was common in pre-industrial cultures such as the Native American Indian tribes and probably also the San in Southern Africa. Dialogue may have taken place in the context of the San archetypal *kgotla* structure. Systems thinking and conversation quality seem to be competencies that humans once possessed, but through the passage of time have been unlearnt. Both Senge[83] and Van der Heijden[84] posit that systems thinking, strategic conversation quality and engagement are foundational to other capabilities that enable learning and, through

---

[80]   Maturana, H.R. & Varela, F.J. 1998.

[81]   Senge, P.M., Kleiner, A., Roberts, C., Ross, R.B. & Smith, B. 1994. *The fifth discipline fieldbook*. London: Nicholas Brealey, P. 351.

[82]   Senge et al., 1994, p.356.

[83]   Senge et al., 1994.

[84]   Van der Heijden, K. 1996. *Scenarios: The art of strategic conversation*. London: Wiley.

this, organisational resilience.

Gleick[85] extends Morgan's argument of looking to the underlying structure as a way of sense-making. His seminal work on chaos is considered the birth of new science. Gleick[86] points to the underlying structure within chaotic systems by identifying the occurrence of fractals in what appear to be chaotic systems. Gleick[87] describes fractals as "[t]he Mandelbrot set and the most complex object in mathematics". Fractals, first identified and described by Mandelbrot, point towards an underlying, repetitive structure which reflects order within what appear to be chaotic systems such as clouds, coastlines, flowers and mountains. This raises the question as to whether there are repeating structures and processes [fractals] within organisations that may create order from the seeming chaos of organisations in flux and transformation. Answers to this question can be regarded as the "fifth logic" of organisational change. Identifying such structures may point towards priorities within a resilience diagnostic instrument as these structures may identify high leverage areas through which to create order from chaos. Based on the literature review, potential organisational fractal structures and processes that may ensure order include:

- goal setting and review processes;
- conversation quality and engagement (dialogue);
- a shared vision of the future for the organisation; and
- the agreed purpose for the organisation.

These processes may together be essential for building alignment, described as the potential *to act as one* for an organisation.

7.12 Laloux – paradigmatic evolution and typologies of organisations

Laloux[88] provides an evolutionary perspective on paradigmatic organisational typologies with which he emphasises and describes plausible future organisational forms. He describes an evolution from tribal chiefdoms to static command-and-control army and machine models to family and then towards dynamic self-managed organisations instead of static hierarchical pyramid organisations. These self-managing organisations are regarded

---

[85] Gleick, J. 1988. *Chaos: Making a new science.* New York, NY: Penguin Books.

[86] Gleick, 1988.

[87] Gleick, 1988, p. 221.

[88] Laloux, F. 2015. The future of management is teal. *Strategy and Business.* https://www. strategy-business.com/article/00344?gko=10921 Date of access: 17 June 2017.

as "living entities" oriented towards realising their potential. The Laloux[89] paradigmatic typology consists of "the wolf pack paradigm", "army paradigm", "machine paradigm", "family paradigm", and "living organism paradigm". Laloux[90] provides a brief description of the paradigms, reflected below, along an evolutionary trajectory of these types of organisation:

- *Wolf pack paradigm.* In this type of organisation there is a constant exercise of power by a chief to keep foot soldiers inline within a highly reactive, short-term focus. This type of organisation thrives in chaotic environments. Examples of this include some political parties, street gangs and cults.
- *Army paradigm.* An army organisation is bound together by highly formal rules within a hierarchical pyramid. Leadership is exercised through top-down command-and-control. An assumption is that the future is a repetition of the past. Examples of this include the Catholic Church, the military and most government organisations.
- *Machine paradigm.* The goal of this type of organisation is to beat the competition, achieve profit and maximise growth. A key process is management by objectives, command-and-control. Examples of this include multinational companies, investment banks and parts of metro governments.
- *Family paradigm.* The focus is on culture and empowerment to boost employee motivation. Stakeholders replace shareholders. Examples of this include businesses known for idealistic practices.
- *Living organism paradigm.* In this type of organisation, self-management replaces the hierarchical pyramid. Organisations are seen as living entities, oriented to realising their potential and signalling a higher consciousness which guides the leaders and founders. Examples include pioneering organisations and some not-for-profit organisations.

The Laloux paradigmatic typology is useful for placing organisations, including city government organisations, on an evolutionary scale and on a continuum with the potential to identify "old" paradigms as well as future paradigms.

Aspects of city government administrations can typically be located in the "army" as well as the "machine" paradigms above, with key processes such as management by objectives. This positioning provides a basis

---

[89] Laloux, F. 2014a. *Reinventing organisations: Summary.* http://www.reinventing organizations.com/uploads/2/1/9/8/21988088/140305_laloux_reinventing_organizations. pdf Date of access: 11 August 2017, p.9–12.

[90] Laloux, 2015.

for a diagnostic instrument which enables articulating aspirational and future-oriented indicators within the proposed diagnostic factors and items. Emerging organisational types, as described by Laloux,[91] will also be examined as a platform for organisations to be resilient in emergent, disruptive future conditions.

7.13 De Geus's living organisation

While De Geus's interest and scholarly contribution focused on the life span and sustaining qualities of the commercial corporation, he found that the principles he identified were equally applicable "to other types of institutions such as churches, armies and universities".[92] De Geus[93] identified four factors that characterised the "living organisation", namely:

- "sensitivity to the environment represents an organisation's ability to learn and adapt;
- cohesion and identity are aspects of an organisation's innate ability to build a community and a persona for itself;
- tolerance and its corollary decentralisation are both symptoms of an organisation's awareness of ecology: its ability to build constructive relationships with other entities, within and outside itself; and
- conservative financing is another critical element which influences the ability of an organisation to govern its growth and evolution effectively."

The idea that organisations can "learn" was stimulated by De Geus[94] with his seminal publication *Planning as learning*, which was influenced by the original work of Michael.[95] De Geus coined the term "learning organisation" which was popularised in the Peter Senge et al. Fieldbook series.[96] [97] According to De Geus, learning organisations "mimic life". Subsequently, De Geus's ideas influenced the development of the Global Living Asset Management Performance (LAMP) index as an instrument for life-mimicking organisations.[98] The component metrics of LAMP were

[91]   Laloux, 2015.

[92]   De Geus, A. 1997. *The living company*. Boston, MA: Harvard Business School Press, p. 3.

[93]   De Geus, 1997, p. 9.

[94]   De Geus, A. 1988. Planning as learning. *Harvard Business Review,* March–April: 2–6.

[95]   Michael, D.N. 1973. *Learning to plan – planning to learn*. San Francisco, CA: Jossey-Bass.

[96]   Senge et al., 1994

[97]   Senge, P.M., Kleiner, A., Ross, R.B., Roth, G. & Smith, B. 1999. *The dance of change: The challenges to sustaining momentum in learning organisations*. New York, NY: Doubleday Currency.

[98]   Bragdon, J.H. 2016. *Companies that mimic life: Leaders of emerging corporate renaissance*. London: Greenleaf Publishing.

strongly influenced by the four factors identified by De Geus.[99] De Geus's ideas serve as the basis of an emergent paradigm among neoclassical theories of organisations.

7.14 Organisations that mimic life

According to Bragdon,[100] "in the early 1990s authors began to advance the idea of economies as ecosystems and organisations as living entities within those systems". Bragdon[101] developed the global Living Asset Management Performance (LAMP) index to identify organisations with properties that were similar to life as he saw it. In 1995, he established a so-called "learning lab" to study these organisations and compare their performance to other more traditional or conventional organisations. Bragdon's LAMP index identifies organisations as living ecosystems in which their primary assets are also living. He later expanded his index to 60 organisations and studied "best of breed" performance among a representative group. The LAMP organisations consistently outperformed comparison organisations. Bragdon[102] describes the critical lifelike qualities of the organisations, including the following:

- "decentralised, self-organising networked structures, whose component parts serve the health of the whole (such as the human nervous system and the cognition architecture of our brains);
- regenerative life strategies that increase opportunities for survival, reproduction, and improving cultural DNA;
- frugal instincts that seek to optimize use of resources;
- openness to feedback that enables adaptive learning;
- symbiotic behaviours that link individual well-being to the health of the larger system in which they exist (biosphere, society); and
- the consciousness of capabilities, interdependences, and limits."[103]

While Bragdon's contribution took place within a commercial enterprise, the above principles and lifelike qualities may also be useful for gauging city government resilience in future government organisations.

---

[99]   De Geus, 1997.

[100]   Bragdon, 2016, p. 4

[101]   Bragdon, 2016.

[102]   Bragdon, 2016.

[103]   Bragdon, 2016, p. 8

7.15 Senge's learning organisations

Learning organisations were initially termed "metanoic organisations" by Kiefer.[104] The word *metanoia* was borrowed from biblical language and teachings to signal a fundamental shift of mind in relation to perspectives on how organisations functioned. "A revolutionary shift of orientation ... where people are learning to collectively create the results they want, consistent with their individual life's purposes."[105] He goes on to describe a metanoic organisation as "one that has undergone a fundamental shift in orientation from individual and collective belief that people must cope with life ... are helpless and powerless to the conviction that they are empowered to create their future and shape their destiny".

Organisational responsiveness and resilience, framed as learning, are informed by the work of Peter Senge,[106] where the term metanoic organisation, coined by Kiefer,[107] was changed to "learning organisations". These organisations are described as learning systems enabled by "five disciplines" or cross-cutting competencies among executive leadership. These so-called disciplines are:

- "building a shared vision;
- personal [self-] mastery;
- systems thinking;
- mental models; and
- team learning".[108]

By describing strategic planning as a learning process, a relationship is identified between an organisation capable of learning and its competitive advantage.[109] In the context of city government, the ability to anticipate, adapt and recover from discontinuities in the environment can also be seen as a learning process. The responsiveness during this process may determine the level of resilience of city government.

7.16 Requisite organisation

The "requisite organisation" is described as "a total system based upon a holistic perspective of organisations".[110] Jaques's systemic perspectives

---

[104] Kiefer, C. 1986. Leadership in metanoic organisation (*In* Adams, J.D. *Ed. Transforming leadership. From vision to results*). Alexandria, VA: Miles River Press, p. 185.

[105] Kiefer, 1986, p. 186.

[106] Senge, 1994 .

[107] Kiefer, 1986.

[108] Senge et al., 1994, p. v-vii.

[109] De Geus, 1988.

[110] Jaques, E. 2013. *Requisite organisation: A total system for effective managerial organisation and management leadership for the 21st century*. Orlando, FL: Cason Hall.

are also part of research on structures in organisations that are directly connected to organisational responsiveness and resilience. One of his seminal scientific contributions to a total systems approach is what he calls "the requisite organisation".[111] His finding, which he calls *requisite* is, among others, that there are optimally seven requisite hierarchical levels in any organisation, matched with a specific time focus for planning and decision making.[112] This requisite number of seven levels in a hierarchy may have a direct bearing on the responsiveness of an organisation. Where there are more than seven levels, he argues that the time delays for the transmission of decisions from the top of the hierarchy to the lower levels are longer than they need to be. These time delays inhibit the capability to react quickly to anticipate and avoid discontinuities in the external environment. Similarly, he argues that when the hierarchy is too shallow, or has fewer than the requisite seven levels, the time focus into the future from the top level is not far enough in advance to anticipate and adapt to discontinuities in time. His analysis and research has uncovered a relationship between the organisational stratum and the time it takes for a decision in a specific stratum to be shown as correct or not. He refers to this as "the time span of discretion." Jaques[113] posits "a specific time focus, and level of complexity, for decision making for each stratum, rising to 20–25 years for the highest, on the seventh stratum". This principle may be the basis for numerous human resources subsystems such as job evaluation, felt-fair pay systems on a unified pay scale, performance management systems and career planning. How these subsystems influence organisational resilience, is described in Chapter 3.

8   NATIONAL CULTURE AND ORGANISATIONAL CULTURE DIMENSIONS

Lawrence and Lorsch's[114] contingency theory underlines the important interdependence between the national culture as context and organisational culture, specifically the impact that the national culture has on human behaviour in organisations. There is a general acceptance among scholars such as Drucker and Porter that culture plays an important role in strategy execution. The intention to build resilience within an organisation is seen here as a resilience strategy. As a result of the diversity of a population, the level of intercultural competence may influence the effectiveness of a

---

[111]   Jaques, 2013.

[112]   Jaques, 2013, p. 104

[113]   Jaques, 2013, p. 105.

[114]   Lawrence, P. & Lorsch, J.W. 1967. Differentiation and integration in complex organisation. *Administration Science Quarterly*, 1(12):1–30.

resilience strategy.

Other scholars on culture, such as Trompenaars and Hampden-Turner,[115] use dilemmas and their resolution for describing culture. Their work has been applied in South Africa to describe the diversity of cultures encountered in the country. Trompenaars and Hampden-Turner have developed "dilemma mapping" as a rigorous, systemic perspective on culture and its formation. The diverse population spectrum in South Africa will probably require capacity in intercultural competence as, in the context of this research, it becomes important for enabling organisational resilience. In addition, Edmondson and Reynolds[116] in this regard state that the importance of intercultural competence cannot be overemphasised and posit that to build a resilient smart city requires future-oriented experts with their own values, skills, time frames and business models. This may lead to what Edmondson and Reynolds[117] call "a palpable cultural clash". Building resilient smart cities will require what Edmondson and Reynolds refer to as "big teaming", that is, working across functions and divisions within such city organisations.

Schein[118] defines culture as "the deeper level of basic assumptions and beliefs that are shared by members of an organisation, that operate unconsciously, and that define in a basic taken for granted fashion an organisation's view of itself and its environment". These assumptions and beliefs are learnt responses to a group's problems of survival in its external environment and its problems of internal integration. They come to be taken for granted because they solve problems repeatedly and reliably. This deeper level of assumptions is to be distinguished from artefacts and values that are the "surface levels" of culture. Culture, in this sense, is a learnt product of group experience and is, therefore, to be found only where there is a definable group with a significant history.[119] The levels of culture and their interaction are reflected in Table 2.3.

---

[115] Trompenaars, F. & Hampden-Turner, C. 1998. *Riding the waves of culture.* 2nd ed. London: Nicholas Brealey.

[116] Edmondson, A. & Reynolds, S.S. 2016. Smart cities? It takes more than a village. https://www.linkedin.com/pulse/smart-cities-takes-more-than-village-amy-c- Date of access: 20 January 2017.

[117] Edmondson & Reynolds, 2016, p. 4.

[118] Schein, E.H. 1989. *Organisational culture and leadership.* San Francisco, CA: Jossey-Bass, p. 5.

[119] Schein, 1989, p. 5–6.

Table 2.3:   Level of culture and their interaction

Level of culture	Interaction
Surface artefacts and creations Technology Art Visible and audible behaviour patterns	Visible but often not decipherable
Values Testable in the physical environment Testable only by social consensus	Greater level of awareness
Basic assumptions Relationship to the environment Nature of reality, time and space Nature of human nature Nature of human activity Nature of human relationships	Taken for granted Invisible Pre-conscious
Deeper levels Myths, folk lore, leadership heroes and villains	Unconscious

Source: Schein.[120]

Whether or not a given organisation such as the city government has a single culture in addition to various subcultures can be answered by finding stable groups within the total organisation. There may be several cultures operating within the larger social unit called the organisation, for instance, a managerial culture, various occupationally-based cultures in functional units, group cultures based on geographical proximity and worker cultures based on shared hierarchical experiences. The concept of culture is rooted more in theories of group dynamics and group growth than in anthropological theories of how large cultures evolve. The word "culture" can be applied to any size of the social unit that has had the opportunity to learn and stabilise its view of itself and the environment around it, shaping its basic assumptions. At the broadest level we have "civilisations" and refer to Western or Eastern cultures. On the next level down in terms of population size, we have "countries" or nations with sufficient commonality that we may speak of identity such as Chinese, American or Indian culture. The next level down may be cities which have sufficient commonalities such as Shanghai, Singapore, Cape Town or Mumbai. Within countries and cities, we have various "ethnic groups" to which we attribute different cultures. Even more specific is a culture at the level of "occupation, profession or occupational

---

[120]   Schein, 1989, p. 13.

community".[121] Culture has also been defined as "mental programming".[122] Hofstede[123] adds that every person carries with them patterns of thinking, feelings and potential action, which were learned throughout their lifetime". He defines culture as "mental software" and adds that "culture is the collective programming of the mind which distinguishes the members of one group or category of people from another.[124]

Figure 2.4 below provides a model for a culture which posits that culture consists of basic assumptions which are implicit.

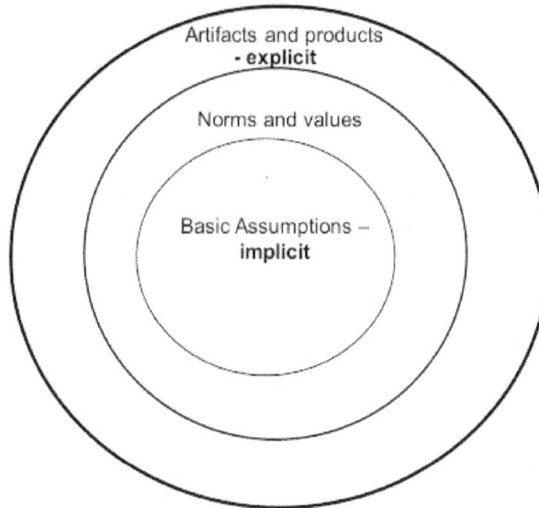

Figure 2.4:   A model of culture
Source: Trompenaars and Hampden-Turner.[125]

Trompenaars and Hampden-Turner[126] define culture "as the way in which a group of people solves problems and reconciles dilemmas". Dilemma mapping, as described in their writing, provides a scholarly rigorous and practical framework for dealing with culture. Their cultural analysis of South Africa (Table 2.4) also provides further local relevance and value for their work.[127]

The key question when observing explicit artefacts and products of culture is to enquire: How does what we observe of specific behaviour

---

[121] Schein, 1989, pp. 7, 8.

[122] Hofstede, G. 1991. *Cultures and organisations: Software of the mind.* New York, NY: McGraw Hill, pp. 4,5.

[123] Hofstede, 1991.

[124] Hofstede, 1991.

[125] Trompenaars & Hampden-Turner, 1998, p. 212.

[126] Trompenaars & Hampden-Turner, 1998, p. 6.

[127] Trompenaars & Hampden-Turner, 1998, p. 212-220.

make sense to the people in that culture? Shared norms and values, as well as implicit basic assumptions, can exert a powerful influence on the behaviour of people in a specific culture.

Khoza[128] extends the definition of culture in the context of what he refers to as "oral governance" agreements [social contracts], and he asks how leadership can better use these invisible agreements to protect the commons. The "commons" he refers to has to do with the ownership of crops cultivated by small farmers and the respect for those crops by township squatters living next to these farmlands. Culture in the form of a social contract between squatters and subsistence farmers enables their cooperation and respect, or the "oral governance" Khoza describes. These tacit agreements are strictly adhered to by stakeholders and participants as a social contract. Investing in developing these kinds of agreements in the city government/community interface can also be useful for building the responsiveness that could enhance city government resilience.

8.1 Seven dimensions of culture

Trompenaars and Hampden-Turner[129] go on to posit that "it is convenient to sort the problems solved by a group into three headings; namely, those that are from dealings with other people, those that come from [attitudes to] the passage of time and those which relate to [attitudes to] the environment".

8.2 The dilemmas that groups of people face

Trompenaars and Hampden-Turner[130] provide a frame of reference and scholarly rigour by expressing their seven cultural dimensions as *dilemmas* as follows:

- "Universalism versus particularism: Universalism describes what is good and right and always applies between people and particularism describes a particular or specific way in which we relate to others.
- Individualism versus communitarianism: Do people regard themselves primarily as individuals or primarily as part of a group?
- Neutral versus emotional: Should the nature of interactions be objective and detached or is expressing emotions acceptable?
- Specific versus diffuse: The relationship is specific to a contract, psychological or legal, versus the whole person emerges and is engaged in the relationship.

---

128 Khoza, R.J. 2012. *Attuned leadership: African humanism as compass.* Johannesburg: Penguin Books.

129 Trompenaars & Hampden-Turner, 1998, p. 8.

130 Trompenaars & Hampden-Turner, 1998, p. 10.

- Achievement versus ascription: You are judged on what is accomplished and achievements on record. Ascription means the status is attributed to you by birth, kinship, gender, age, connections and education.
- Attitudes to time: The past may be more important than the present or the future. On the other hand, the present or the future may be most important. They may be interlocking or separate from each other. Time may be seen as a line that passes one and cannot be recovered or time is drawn from one pool and more is available. Time may also be considered synchronic or sequential.
- Attitudes to the environment: Externally directed cultures see their environment as more powerful while internally directed cultures see themselves as able to shape their environment."

In the context of the so-called "rainbow nation" and the need to work effectively across the diverse cultures in South Africa, these dimensions or dilemmas may provide a valid portal to more effective communication and tolerance for different cultures. This may enhance empathy, trust and responsiveness and, through this, enhance organisational resilience. Two examples of reconciling dimensions of dilemmas in South Africa, namely, individualism versus communitarianism and internal control versus external control follow on the next page. Reconciliation of dilemmas demonstrates how their resolution takes place by embracing one dimension through the other dimension (see Figures 2.5 and 2.6).

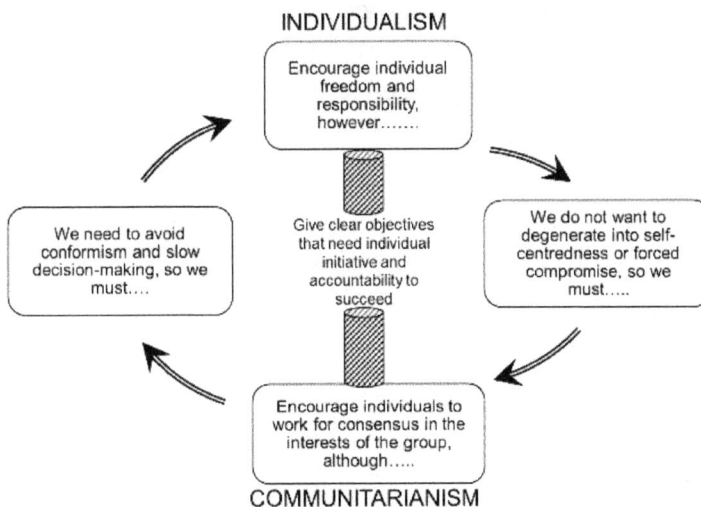

Figure 2.5: Reconciling individualism and communitarianism
Source: Trompenaars and Hampden-Turner.[131]

---
[131] Trompenaars & Hampden-Turner, 1998, p. 58.

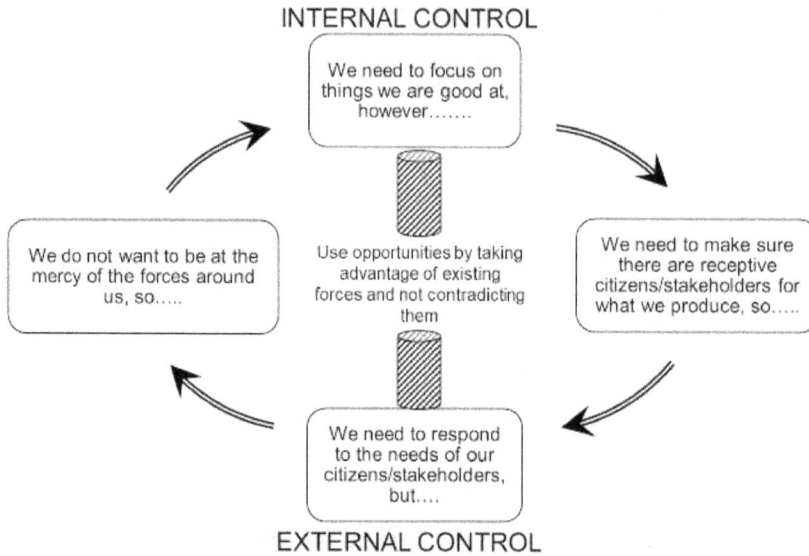

INTERNAL CONTROL

We need to focus on
things we are good at,
however.......

We do not want to be at the
mercy of the forces around
us, so.....

Use opportunities by taking
advantage of existing
forces and not contradicting
them

We need to make sure
there are receptive
citizens/stakeholders for
what we produce, so.....

We need to respond
to the needs of our
citizens/stakeholders,
but....

EXTERNAL CONTROL

Figure 2.6:   Reconciling internal control and external control
Source: Trompenaars and Hampden-Turner.[132]

8.3   Dilemma mapping in a South African sample

Trompenaars and Hampden-Turner's[133] profile for South Africa is based
on a sample of 230 participants from an urban setting in Gauteng. The
map of the South African population using the Trompenaars/Hampden-
Turner dilemma mapping approach was structured by the respondents'
language of origin. The results of the survey (see Table 2.4) confirm that
South Africa may be seen as a "microcosm of the world".[134] This competence
may be useful in enabling teamwork and responsiveness, which may in
turn enhance organisational resilience.

---

[132]   Trompenaars & Hampden-Turner, 1998, p. 153.

[133]   Trompenaars & Hampden-Turner, 1998, pp. 212-220.

[134]   Trompenaars & Hampden-Turner, 1998, p. 213.

Table 2.4: Dilemma mapping in the SA and intercultural competence

Language group	Universalism: particularism	Individualism: community	Neutrality: affectivity	Specificity: diffuseness	Achievement: ascription	Inner-outer directedness
Afrikaans	89	58	70	70	61	72
English	92	72	57	72	65	67
isiXhosa	38	73	36	84	58	61
isiZulu	78	51	65	75	58	60
North Sesotho	71	68	53	51	41	60
Setswana	40	52	61	78	63	65
South Sesotho	70	42	54	70	58	48
Xitsonga	71	22	45	58	55	49

Source: Trompenaars and Hampden-Turner.[135]

South Africa is described by Trompenaars and Hampden-Turner[136] as "one of the most pluralistic societies in the world". The authors explored the transition to democracy in the post-1994 South Africa, pointing out that –

> "… happily, things have changed in South Africa, and a man (Nelson Mandela) has been brought to power who has the creativity, courage and grandeur to reconcile cultural opposites. He is an extraordinary example of African humility. Whether his example and vision will be enough to heal decades of injustice remains to be seen. Some people rise above oppressions; most do not. South Africa's future remains in the balance."

The process of transition from the apartheid system to constitutional democracy, post-1994, can be seen in and of itself as an exercise in national resilience. Accordingly, this national transition may offer learning in terms of resilience in general. Based on the demography of a specific metro, these data may be useful in analysing culture(s) and provide a platform for intercultural competence which may enable teamwork within metro divisions/departments and across city-wide teaming processes within metros. Developing intercultural competence across the South African language groups encountered in organisations may enhance responsiveness and thereby increase organisational resilience.

---

[135] Trompenaars & Hampden-Turner, 1998, p. 213.
[136] Trompenaars & Hampden-Turner, 1998, p. 213.

The responsiveness or resilience of a metro may be facilitated or hindered by the culture of that organisation, engaging the challenge to enable resilience. Developing a resilient culture, for instance, may be dependent on the shared experience of the executive leadership and executive management and employees; in general, that is essential to leading the resilience strategy. Cultural competence and specifically intercultural competence may be important in the context of the diversity that can be found in South African municipalities and metros.

9 SYNOPSIS OF CORE ORGANISATIONAL DIMENSIONS APPLICABLE TO ORGANISATIONAL RESILIENCE IN THE CONTEXT OF CITY GOVERNMENT

The purpose of this section is to pinpoint the core organisational dimensions extracted from the literature survey in this chapter. These [theoretical] dimensions are significant in placing organisational dimensions in the context of city government resilience at the centre and then to consider these dimensions as vital for the purposes of designing a diagnostic instrument. This synopsis of core organisational dimensions serves as the first leg of data triangulation for the purposes of this study.

Lawrence and Lorsch's[137] contingency theory indicates the existence of an interactive relationship between the internal organisational structure and the level of uncertainty in the external environment. The greater the extent of uncertainties in the external environment, the less formal the internal structure of an organisation becomes and vice versa.

Smuts[138] offers a holistic perspective on organisations, and Von Bertalanffy's[139] GST represents a paradigm shift from looking at parts to looking at whole systems, across all sciences including organisational development, organisational responsiveness and organisational resilience. As stated earlier, systems may be seen either as being closed systems, without feedback loops, or as open systems, with feedback loops. The presence of feedback loops enables dynamic, adaptive, resilient behaviour. Feedback loops, control theory and causal relationships between key variables in a system enabled Forrester to develop SD as a modelling technology. SD was first used by Forrester to study urban dynamics. Urban administrations are regarded as complex interconnected systems.[140]

Defining leverage points[141] provides a guide to the high leverage places

---

[137] Lawrence & Lorsch, 1967.
[138] Smuts, 1925.
[139] Von Bertalanffy, 1968.
[140] Forrester, 1969.
[141] Meadows, 1999.

to intervene in a system in order to shift the entire system. This may also be useful for enabling resilience within city government as a system. In organisational systems, subsystems play an important part in providing structure to the overall organisational structure.

Emphasising the human characteristics of organisations, the San provide learning about resilience through their archetypal organisation. Archetypal organisational structure provides examples of how the San, or the so-called "first humans", ensured their resilience in harsh climatic conditions and offers practical ways to achieve inclusive, adaptive behaviour emphasising goal setting and peer review processes within a forum which demonstrates the ability to execute plans as agreed among the *kgotla* members.

Classical theories include Mintzberg[142] and Morgan,[143] who provide insights into hierarchical, bureaucratic structures suitable for predictable, stable environments. They both pinpoint rigid so-called machine models and bureaucracies as a commonly encountered organisational structure. Typically, national, provincial and city governments can be located within this because of the relative certainty of elected representatives flowing from a democratic constitutional system of governance in a modern government. However, in a time of factional division and the emergence of competition for political interests, we may also experience a decline in the importance of constitutional covenants. This may lead to an organisation, in this case the ANC tripartite alliance, being perceived as a psychic prison, preventing the arrest of a declining electoral support base in the face of the most recent local government electoral shift.

Neoclassical theories from Morgan and others provide insight along an evolutionary trajectory where organisations are described in people-centric terms as organisms, brains, culture creating and political systems, as well as psychic prisons. Included under neoclassical theories are "organisations that learn". Morgan offers a contingency theory for organisations adapting to their environment, which pinpoints the fit between the organisation and its environment as well as the fit between the internal subsystems. He views organisations as human activity systems, at the centre of which are the people that populate them.

Neoclassical theories include Laloux's typology of organisations from the wolf pack paradigm through army, machine and family paradigms to a living organism paradigm at the endpoint of an evolutionary track. Laloux[144]

---

[142] Mintzberg, 1979.

[143] Morgan, G. 1998. *Images of organisations*. The Executive Edition. London: Sage.

[144] Laloux, 2015.

provides an evolution-based typology which clarifies the re-emergence of a previous stage of evolutionary development, demonstrated by the constant use of power by a so-called chief to keep foot soldiers in line within a short-term reactionary focus, as well as an army-like organisation through top-down command structures.

Self-organisation in the form of disciplines of the so-called learning organisations popularised by Senge[145] [146] pinpoints the process of learning as the central adaptive property and basis for competitiveness of the so-called learning organisation. Jaques's[147] so-called requisite organisation provides a total systems perspective which posits a 20- to 25 year planning time horizon for decision makers at the seventh (highest) stratum. He also posits decision-complexity as the rationale for determining the relative value and level of jobs within his seven strata.

Bragdon's LAMP index singles out so-called "living organisations that mimic life" and demonstrates their relatively high performance levels in terms of LAMP properties. Bragdon[148] and his perspective on organisations as ecosystems identified the so-called LAMP index which describes critical lifelike qualities in organisations as the basis for exceptional performance compared to "best of breed" organisations. Bragdon's organisation that mimics life posits a higher consciousness leadership as the differentiator among the neoclassical theories.

Morgan[149] provides insight into organisations as flux and transformation in terms of four logics of change. He points towards Bohm's study of the nature of thought and conversation. He defines quality conversation as so-called dialogue and explores the transformative impact of dialogue on the thinking of participants. Mandelbrot describes fractals as underlying repetitive structures that provide order within chaotic systems. The Mandelbrot and Bohm insights enable the identification of candidate fractals within organisations in flux, which are seen as chaotic systems. Fractals may be goal setting and review processes, conversation quality and engagement, as well as building shared vision and organisational purpose.

The attributes of people-centric processes and organisations may determine how to leverage human responsiveness and therefore organisational resilience. Enablers of learning among individuals and

---

[145]   Senge et al., 1994

[146]   Senge et al., 1999

[147]   Jaques, 2013.

[148]   Bragdon, 2016.

[149]   Morgan, 1997, p. 251.

organisations, such as double-loop learning to shift assumptions in the minds of decision makers,[150] are identified together with theories of motivation from Maslow[151] and Herzberg.[152]

Culture is defined, described and positioned as playing a significant role in organisational dynamics. The resolution of dilemmas is marked by Trompenaars and Hampden-Turner[153] as the foundation of culture formation. Dilemmas are framed as a systems-based tool for resolving choices which seem irreconcilable using binary logic. Many decisions faced by executive leadership and executive management present in the form of dilemmas. Dilemma mapping, as described by Trompenaars and Hampden-Turner,[154] provides a practical, process perspective on how culture may be formed and how to effectively resolve dilemmas in general. The seven-dimension culture descriptions[155] entail the various cultures encountered among South Africans. In addition, organisations may have within them different sub-cultures. These descriptions may provide a basis for developing intercultural competence in South Africa. This competence may enable working across cultural diversity and through this, support greater resilience. The organisational culture may support or hinder responsiveness in organisations and, accordingly, support or hinder resilience. Whybrow[156] argues that global survival depends on retuning the human mind at scale to a more sustainable, resilient way of living in order to survive as a species.

10 CONCLUSION

The purpose of this chapter is to uncover the theoretical foundations of organisational structure, design and dynamics. This analysis included the fundamentals of organisational design and development that are directly interconnected with responsiveness and, in general, organisational resilience. It also explored the origins of organisations and described the subsystems within organisations.

It was established that the process of developing a resilience strategy in a complex, chaotic human activity system such as a city government organisation might require adopting a holistic, multidisciplinary, systemic

---

[150] Argyris, 1992.

[151] Maslow, A. 1954. *Motivation and personality*. New York, NY: Harper.

[152] Herzberg, F. 1987. One more time: How do you motivate employees? *Harvard Business Review,* Sept–Oct:109–120.

[153] Trompenaars & Hampden-Turner, 1998.

[154] Trompenaars & Hampden-Turner, 1998.

[155] Trompenaars & Hampden-Turner, 1998, p. 213.

[156] Whybrow, 2015.

perspective. This may in turn require uncovering interdependencies between key variables, as well identifying leverage points within the whole. Leverage points can pinpoint optimum places to intervene to raise responsiveness within a whole organisation and through this improve its resilience. A truthful, quality conversation about the current reality for specific leverage points may constitute in and of themselves feedback loops, which enable double-loop learning and the adjustment of assumptions and, accordingly, lead to greater resilience in an organisation.

The next chapter will explore models, principles and schools of thinking for organisational resilience.

CHAPTER 3

ORGANISATIONAL RESILIENCE: MODELS, PRINCIPLES AND SCHOOLS OF THINKING

---

1   INTRODUCTION

The previous chapter analysed the paradigmatic development, schools of thinking, theoretical principles, theories and models of organisations that may be significant for organisational resilience. The chapter thus laid a theoretical foundation for the broader context of organisational structure, design and functioning within a dynamic environment. This chapter aims to focus in more detail on the underpinnings of organisational resilience.

Organisational resilience thinking is generally accommodated within an emerging field of resilience models and schools of thinking which span individual, community, organisational, national and international or global resilience. Organisational resilience as a concept is often used without an explicit explanation of what is meant. It is often vague in its interpretation and hard to define. Nevertheless "resilience may be defined as the quality or fact of being able to recover quickly or easily from, or resist being affected by, misfortune, shock, illness, robustness, adaptability".[1] Braes and Brooks[2] go on to point out "that resilience will be an imperative for the 21st century as the occurrence of unforeseen, low probability high impact events increases". It may be time to assess and examine the emergent paradigms, conceptual models, theoretical principles and schools of thinking. These aspects, once clarified and understood, may be placed into a practical framework for gauging organisational resilience in the city government context.

2   ORGANISATIONAL RESILIENCE – CONTEXTUAL AND CONCEPTUAL CLARIFICATION

Traditionally, resilience has been viewed as those qualities that enable an individual, a community, a region, an organisation and a city to cope with, adapt to and recover from a disaster event. "Organisational resilience remains theoretical and methods for achieving improved resilience at

---

[1]   Braes, B. & Brooks, D. 2010. Organisational resilience: A propositional study to understand and identify essential concepts. Paper delivered at the Australia Security and Intelligence Conference organised by Edith Cowan University, p.16.

[2]   Braes & Brooks, 2010, p. 17.

both operational and strategic levels still challenge both academics and practitioners".[3] Braes and Brooks point out that what may be deduced from the resilience literature is that the emerging field is dominated by specialists in sub-domains. Resilience has become a widely used term resulting in catch-all terminology which attempts to encapsulate a complex multidimensional and multifunctional concept under a single banner. "Resilience capacity within organisations is embodied in the organisational routines and processes by which an organisation continually prepares itself to act decisively and move forward, and establishes a culture of diversity and adjustable integration that empowers it to overcome the potentially incapacitating consequences of a disruptive shock".[4]

2.1 Contextual frame of reference

Masten[5] argues that the first generation of resilience research has ended, and the second generation is beginning, witnessed by the criticisms of the construct of resilience and increasing demands for theory and process-oriented research. Scholarly perspectives on resilience include clinical perspectives focusing on individual resilience, community resilience, resilience in social-ecological systems, sustainable rural livelihoods, economic resilience of regions, disaster risk management, organisational resilience and planned cities.

Defining the concept of resilience from a range of disciplinary perspectives may clarify a definition in order to provide context and inform research policy and practice within this focus on city resilience. Resilience is defined, among other things, in discipline-specific dictionaries as the rate at which a system regains structure and function following stress or perturbation,[6] the personal quality of a person exposed to high-risk factors that often lead to delinquent behaviour but they resist[7] and a measure of a body's resistance to deformation.[8]

In the context of the individual, Windle[9] defines resilience as "the

---

[3]   Braes & Brooks, 2010, p. 16.

[4]   Braes & Brooks, 2010, p. 17.

[5]   Masten, A.S. 1999. The promise and perils of resilience research as a guide to preventive interventions (*In* Glantz, M.D. & Johnson, J.L. ed. *Resilience and development: Positive life adaptation.* New York, NY: Kluwer Academic/Plenum, pp. 251–257).

[6]   *Oxford Dictionary of Environment and Conservation.* 2007. Oxford: Oxford University Press. https://www.oxfordreference.com/ Date of access: 14 October 2017.

[7]   *Oxford Dictionary of Law Enforcement.* 2007. Oxford: Oxford University Press https://www.oxfordreference.com/ Date of access: 14 October 2017.

[8]   *Oxford Dictionary of Sports Science and Medicine.* 2009. Oxford: Oxford University Press. https://www.oxfordreference.com/ Date of access: 14 October 2017.

[9]   Windle, G. 2017. *What is resilience? A review and concept analysis.* Reviews in Clinical Gerontology. Cambridge: Cambridge University Press, p. 1.

process of effectively negotiating, adapting to, or managing significant sources of stress or trauma", pointing out that "assets and resources within the individual, their life and environment facilitate this capacity for adaptation and 'bouncing back' in the face of adversity". Windle[10] also points out that "there seems to be an increase in the research on individual resilience. Over the last two decades this has happened due to a move away from a deficit model of illness and psychopathology towards understanding healthy development despite risk, based on strengths rather than on weaknesses".

As resilience research has developed, the focus of study has moved away from factors that may be associated with resilience towards understanding the mechanisms that underpin "a dynamic *process* encompassing positive adaptation within significant adversity".[11] This emerging emphasis on the process may be useful for identifying mechanisms which offer high leverage areas for gauging resilience and also for positioning best practice for using a diagnostic instrument within a method for diagnosis and intervention to build resilience.

3   CONCEPTUAL MODELS

An organisation may be conceptualised as a community with a common purpose or a human activity system. Community resilience may emerge from four primary sets of adaptive capacities, namely, "economic development, social capital, information and communication and community competence that together provide a strategy for disaster readiness."[12] From the perspective of resilience as an interdependent set of adaptive nodal capacities, community resilience may emerge from a set of *networked* adaptive capacities. The four nodes within this networked perspective of community resilience may be interdependent with dynamics in the community for enabling responsiveness and, accordingly, the resilience of a whole community.

Specific network nodes and interdependencies may be:
- "Economic Development interdependent with: fairness of risk and vulnerability to hazards, level of diversity of economic resources, and equity of resource distribution;
- Information and Communication interdependent with: narratives,

---

10   Windle, 2017, p. 1.

11   Windle, 2017, p. 5.

12   Norris, F.H., Stevens, S.P., Pfefferbaum, B., Wyche, K.F. & Pfefferbaum, R.L. 2008. Community resilience as metaphor, theory, set of capacities and strategy for disaster readiness. *American Journal for Community Psychology,* 41:127–150. Springer Science + Business Media LLC, p. 127.

responsible media, skills and infrastructure, and trusted sources of information;

- Community Competence interdependent with: community action, critical reflection and problem solving, flexibility and creativity, collective efficacy and sense of empowerment, and political partnerships;
- Social Capital interdependent with: received (enacted) social support, perceived (expected) social support, social embeddedness (informal ties), organisational linkages and cooperation, citizen participation leadership and roles (formal ties), sense of community, and attachment to place".[13]

Norris *et al.*[14] point out that there is a primary interdependency between the four nodes, as well as the interdependencies between nodes and subordinate dynamics, which together form a resilience ecology and provide a strategic framework for disaster readiness in a community.

Since Holling's[15] seminal paper on resilience as the stability of ecological systems, the conceptualisation of resilience has developed into a perspective that comprises considering the attributes that govern a system's dynamics. Three related attributes of social-ecological systems (SES) determine their future trajectories, namely, resilience, adaptability and transformability. Resilience is defined within the SES context as the capacity of a system to absorb disturbances and reorganise while undergoing a change in order to still retain essentially the same function, structure, identity and feedback. The implications of this interpretation of SES dynamics for sustainability science include changing the focus from seeking optimal states to resilience analysis, adaptive resource management and adaptive governance. Shocks, uncertainty and local and global changes may be inherent in the dynamics of SES. In a remote rural Solomon Islands community, the SES resilience analysis may be described as:

- "people and livelihoods influenced by specific dynamics: human capability, assets and income poverty, diversification and income dependence, living conditions and competition;
- institutions and governance influenced by specific dynamics: collective action abilities, organisational and institutional capacities, governance performance and rights, access to markets and financial services, legal framework fisheries and development policies;

---

[13] Norris et al., 2008, p. 136.

[14] Norris et al., 2008.

[15] Holling, C.S. 1973. Resilience and stability of ecological systems. *Annual Review of Ecological Systems*, 4:1–23.

- natural systems influenced by specific dynamics: fishing practices, stock status and trends, biodiversity and aquatic ecosystem conditions;
- external drivers influenced by specific dynamics: conflicts with other sectors and users, land-use and population pressures, infrastructure development, macroeconomic uncertainty and climate change and environmental uncertainty".[16]

Regional definitions of resilience may be applied to explain the long-term development of urban and regional economies by adopting an evolutionary perspective. From its Latin root, *resilire,* meaning to leap back or to rebound, the idea of resilience refers to the ability of an entity or system to recover form and position elastically following a disturbance or disruption of some kind. Regional resilience may be defined "as the ability of a region to anticipate, prepare for, respond to, and recover from a disturbance".[17] A contradiction between the evolution of a region and its level of resilience may be that the more resilient the region the less that region may evolve economically. So-called "ecological resilience"[18] focuses on whether disturbances and shocks cause a system to enter another regime of behaviour. This enables linking resilience to the idea of adaptability and is thus much richer in an evolutionary sense.

> "At least four conceptual frameworks for constructing an evolutionary account of regional economic resilience can be distinguished: generalised Darwinism which emphasises variety, novelty and selection; path dependence theory which focuses on historical continuity, lock-in and new path creation; complexity theory which highlights self-organisation, bifurcations and adaptive growth; and panarchy which explicitly links resilience and adaptive cycles."[19]

---

[16] Schwartz, A-M., Bene, C., Bennett, G., Bozo, D., Hilly, Z., Paul, C., Posala, R., Sibili, S. & Andrew, N. 2011. Vulnerability and resilience of remote rural communities to shocks and global change: Empirical analysis from Solomon Islands. *Global Environmental Change,* 2:1128–1140, p. 1130.

[17] Foster, K.A. 2007. *A case study approach to understanding regional resilience* (Working paper 2007-08). Berkeley, CA: Institute of Urban and Regional Development, University of California, p. 14.

[18] Holling, 1973.

[19] Simmie, J. & Martin, R. 2009. The economic resilience of regions: Towards an evolutionary approach. *Cambridge Journal of Regions, Economy and Society,* 1–17 doi:10.1095/cjres029 p. 5.

Furthermore:

> "A distinction can be made between reactive and proactive resilience of society. A society relying on reactive resilience approaches the future by strengthening the status quo. In contrast, one that develops proactive resilience accepts the inevitability of change and tries to create a system that is capable, of adapting to new conditions ... a third type of resilience is characterised by openness and adaptation ... its key feature is a readiness to adopt new basic operating assumptions and institutional structures."[20]

While resilience may be seen as a desirable property of natural or social systems, the term has been used in different ways. The definition of resilience is best used to define specific *systems attributes* from the point of view of reactive resilience, namely:

- "the amount of disturbance a system can absorb and still remain within the same state or domain of attraction;
- the degree to which the system is capable of self-organisation".[21]

Gibson and Tarrant[22] present numerous conceptual models to clarify organisational resilience in terms of the range of interdependent factors that need to be considered in the management of resilience and to build a "resilience strategy".[23]

These conceptual models illustrate that effective resilience management may be built upon a range of different strategies that enhance both the so-called "hard" and "soft" organisational capabilities. Gibson and Tarrant[24] point out that –

> "... over the last decade, volatility in our natural, economic and social systems appears to be increasing at rates faster than many organisations can cope with. While such fast-moving events (and patterns) overwhelm many organisations, a proportion demonstrates an ability to either manage or bounce back from the adverse effects of

---

20 Klein, R.J.T., Nicholls, R.J. & Thomalla, F. 2004. *Resilience to natural hazards: How useful is the concept?* (EVA Working Paper No 9). Potsdam, Germany: Potsdam Institute for Climate Impact Research, p. 10.

21 Klein et al., 2004, p. 16.

22 Gibson, C.A. & Tarrant, M. 2010. A "conceptual models" approach to organisational resilience. *Australian Journal of Emergency Management*, 25(2):10–15.

23 Gibson & Tarrant, 2010, p. 11.

24 Gibson & Tarrant, 2010, p. 7.

system volatility. They go on to describe the so-called principles model of resilience derived from common themes which have emerged from comparisons of resilience in different disciplines".

Six key principles may provide a simple guiding foundation for conceptualising organisational resilience. They are:

- "resilience is an outcome ... it is a trait that can be observed following and in response to a substantial change in circumstances;
- resilience is not a static trait ... resilience is dynamic, it will increase or decrease as the context changes;
- resilience is not a single trait ... resilience arises from a complex interplay of many factors;
- resilience is multidimensional ... there is currently no single model that describes resilience ... the better models each describe aspects of resilience from complementary viewpoints;
- resilience exists over a range of conditions ... as an organisation focuses on and invests in resilience it should see an increasing maturity over time in its resilience capabilities from the low end reactive to a high-end adaptive level of maturity;
- resilience is founded upon good risk management ... developing resilience may be founded upon the sound assessment, treatment, monitoring and communicating about risk".[25]

Gibson and Tarrant[26] conclude with an integrated model – the so-called resilience triangle model (see Figure 3.1) – of which *capability* forms an integral part. Note that, in the resilience triangle model, the loss of *capabilities,* represented on any one side of the triangle, may result in the collapse of resilience and the integrity of the whole model. Gibson and Tarrant[27] furthermore point out that "the resilience triangle model also emphasises the fluid nature of each of the three areas of capability. This fluidity arises from organisational processes that continually review, assess and adapt capabilities on each side of the triangle to ensure that they are:

- *"fit for purpose* – their design parameters meet the job that needs to be done – requires monitoring of capability and volatility;

[25] Gibson & Tarrant, 2010, p. 7.
[26] Gibson & Tarrant, 2010, p. 10.
[27] Gibson & Tarrant, 2010.

- retain sufficient *capacity* to ensure that required organisational objectives will be achieved – this often requires that the design of the capability has some level of redundancy;
- have *tenacity* in that the capabilities continue to perform even in the face of severe disruptive consequence – requires that the design of these capabilities is either resistant or stress tolerant;
- exhibit *flexibility* to go beyond original design parameters in response to changing circumstances".[28]

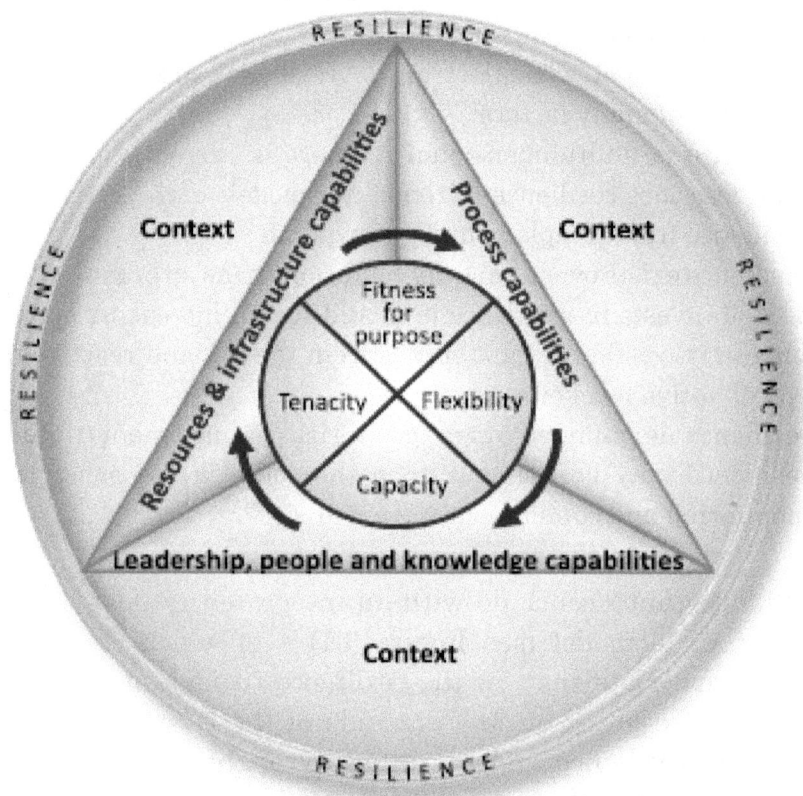

Figure 3.1: The resilience triangle model
Source: Gibson and Tarrant[29]

Gibson and Tarrant, in Figure 3.1 above, pinpoint the critical role of three areas of capability namely leadership, people and knowledge capabilities, resources and infrastructure capabilities, and process capabilities. They posit that "[a]ny loss of effectiveness of these capabilities collectively or singly will potentially degrade resilience".[30]

---

28   Gibson & Tarrant, 2010, p. 10.

29   Gibson & Tarrant, 2010, p. 10.

30   Gibson & Tarrant, 2010, p. 10.

Gibson and Tarrant[31] describe *"resilience strategies* [my emphasis] consisting of four types of strategies namely; resistance, reliability, redundancy and flexibility" (see Figure 3.2).

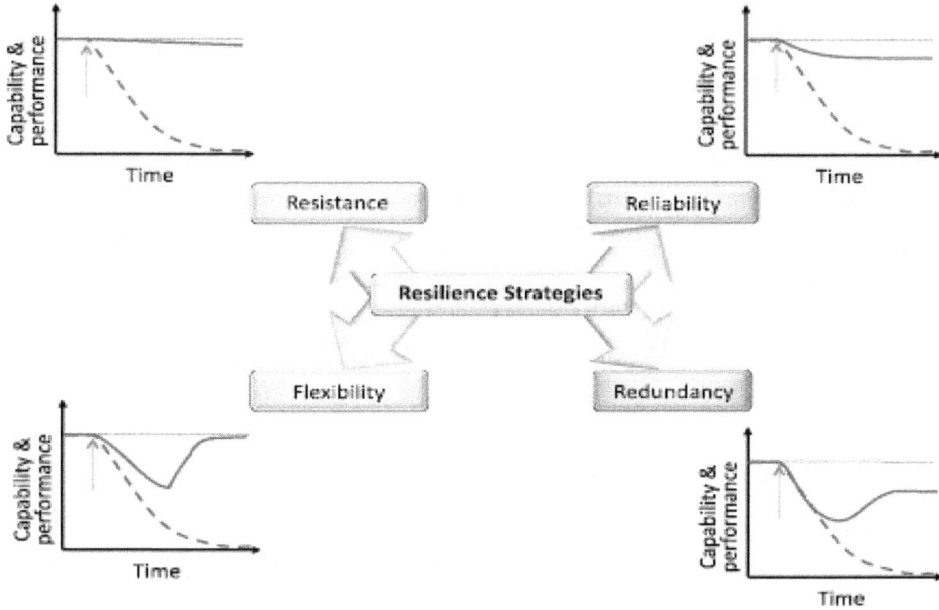

Figure 3.2:   Resilience strategies model
Source: Gibson and Tarrant.[32]

> "Each of the four types of strategies would be expected to influence the performance of organisational capability [and affect resilience] in a different manner [see Figure 3.2]. In the absence of any *resilience strategies*, organisational capability and performance [red dotted line, Figure 3.2] would be expected to show a sudden and catastrophic collapse soon after a disruptive event commenced [red arrow, Figure 3.2]. However, the presence of one or more resilience strategies would be expected to moderate this deterioration in capability and performance [blue line, Figure 3.2] depending upon the nature of the strategies in relation to the nature of the event".[33]

For example, generally, we would expect to see the following:

"Resistance strategies [own emphasis] are aimed at improving robustness and hardening the organisation to withstand the immediate effects that

---

31   Gibson & Tarrant, 2010, p. 11.

32   Gibson & Tarrant, 2010, p. 11.

33   Gibson & Tarrant, 2010, p. 11.

volatility may impose. There is usually no agility or adaptation with such approaches, resistance tries to match the organisation's strength against the event's power. Examples of resistance strategies include: land-use planning and construction standards in bushfire or flood-prone areas; use of firewalls against cyberattacks. Also, many organisational emergency response strategies can be regarded as resistance strategies."[34]

"Reliability strategies aim to ensure that key functions, resources, information and infrastructure continue to be available, accessible and fit for purpose following an event. Outputs of reliability strategies would include arrangements such as business continuity plans, multiple supplier contracts, multimode systems … Redundancy strategies provide for one or more alternatives to day to day operational approaches. Such strategies are usually designed to manage foreseeable volatility and can be fragile in circumstances where their design parameters are exceeded. Flexibility strategies enable the organisation to adapt to extreme circumstances and sudden shocks that often exceed the design parameters for the other strategies. Examples of such strategies include: training and exercising for extreme events, practising decision making in a vacuum, creating an environment for emergent leadership to flourish in, enhancing cultural aspects such as trust, loyalty and unified purpose."[35]

Responses by leadership may determine the resilience pathway as a shock affects an organisation. Leadership may consequently face choices which shape unfolding responses and determine levels of resilience.

4   LEADERSHIP RESPONSE PERSPECTIVES

Denyer[36] points out that "thought leadership" on organisational resilience has developed over the last 40 years in several different fields. Denyer[37] identifies four distinct phases with four contrasting perspectives:

- "preventative control: organisational resilience is achieved using risk management, physical barriers, redundancy (spare capacity), systems back-ups and standardised procedures, which protect the organisation from threats and allow it to bounce back from disruptions to restore a stable state;

---

[34] Gibson & Tarrant, 2010, p. 11.

[35] Gibson & Tarrant, 2010, p. 11.

[36] Denyer, D. 2017. *Organisational resilience: A summary of academic evidence, business insights, and new thinking*. BSI America and Cranfield School of Management. https://www.bsigroup.com/en-US/Our-services/.../organizational-resilience-research/ Date of access: 22 September 2017.

[37] Denyer, 2017, p. 10.

- mindful action: organisational resilience is produced by people, who notice and react to threats and respond effectively to unfamiliar or challenging situations. It soon became recognised that organisational resilience was not only about learning to bounce back but also about the ability to leap forward, to grow and prosper;
- performance optimisation: organisational resilience is formed by continually improving, refining and extending existing competencies, enhancing ways of working and exploiting current technologies to serve present customers and markets; and
- adaptive innovation: organisational resiliencies created by creating inventing and exploring unknown markets and new technologies."

The scholarly discourse on organisational resilience has been generally split between behaviours that are defensive (stopping bad things happening) and those that are progressive (making good things happen), behaviours that are consistent and those that are flexible. These four viewpoints form an integral part of a framework which is termed the "Organisational Resilience Tension Quadrant".[38] This Organisational Resilience Tension Quadrant is illustrated in Figure 3.3.

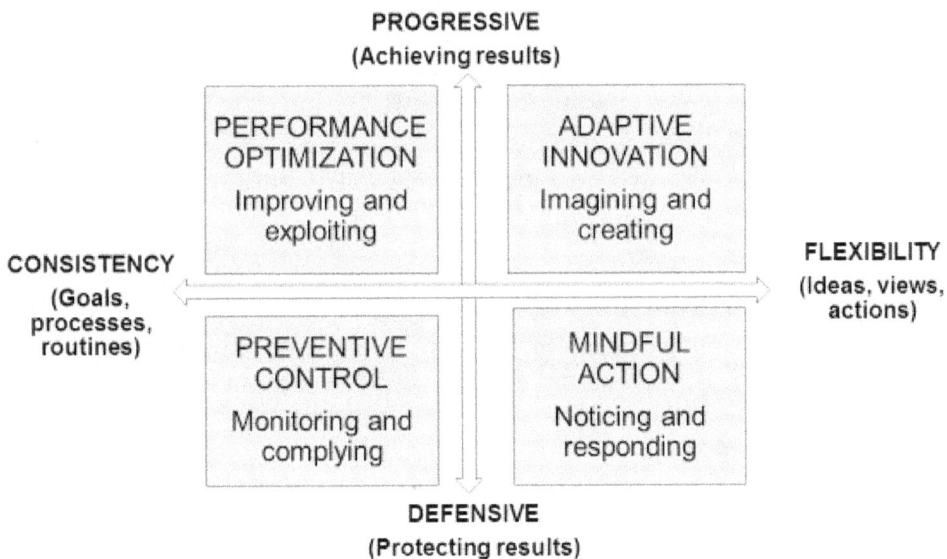

PROGRESSIVE
(Achieving results)

| PERFORMANCE OPTIMIZATION — Improving and exploiting | ADAPTIVE INNOVATION — Imagining and creating |

CONSISTENCY (Goals, processes, routines)   FLEXIBILITY (Ideas, views, actions)

| PREVENTIVE CONTROL — Monitoring and complying | MINDFUL ACTION — Noticing and responding |

DEFENSIVE
(Protecting results)

Figure 3.3:   Organisational resilience tension quadrant
Source: Denyer.[39]

---

38   Denyer, 2017, p. 9.
39   Denyer, 2017, p. 10.

Denyer[40] advocates that senior managers and executive leadership must hold and manage the tensions (dilemmas) between the four approaches effectively if organisations are to be truly resilient – this requires "paradoxical thinking".[41] Paradoxical thinking may be juxtaposed with binary thinking where a choice is made between two opposite ends of a continuum. The dilemmas he describes are defensive versus progressive. These he posits are the drivers of resilience, consistency and flexibility and may achieve resilience. Holding these tensions may create conflicts and inconsistencies that motivate a search for new possibilities and may inspire emergence, learning, discovery and creativity. "The term 'ambidextrous' suggests organisations that are able to shift structures to initiate and, in turn, execute innovation."[42] The so-called organisational resilience tension quadrant posited by Denyer may be elaborated on (see Figure 3.4) to illustrate the core dilemmas leadership face and how they may be resolved when dealing with shocks. The central dilemmas, Denyer posits, may be between control and action, innovation and optimisation – action through enabling self-control. Further interwoven dilemmas and their resolution may also exist, namely:

- performance optimisation and adaptive innovation, which may be resolved through optimisation innovation;
- adaptive innovation and mindful action may be resolved through innovation action;
- preventative control and mindful action may be resolved through action control; and
- preventative action and performance optimisation may be resolved through optimisation control.

The paradoxical thinking posited by Denyer represents a flexible leadership and management capable of shifting to various options as shocks to resilience unfold.

---

[40] Denyer, 2017, p. 10.

[41] Denyer, 2017, p. 10.

[42] Denyer, 2017, p. 15.

Performance Optimization

Improving and exploiting

Optimization::Innovation

Doing what we do better AND doing something new that is better

Adaptive Innovation

Imagining and creating

Control::Innovation

Internal consistency (risk avoidance) AND external adaption (risk taking)

Optimization::Control

Meeting productivity goals (ends) AND operating dependable processes (means)

Direction and coordination of work AND devolving ownership and responsibility

Innovation::Action

Exploring novel options and developing new business opportunities AND responding rapidly to shifting problems (fire fighting)

Optimization::Action

Preventative Control

Monitoring and complying

Action::Control

Following the rules AND taking ownership of emergent problems and formulating solutions

Mindful Action

Noticing and responding

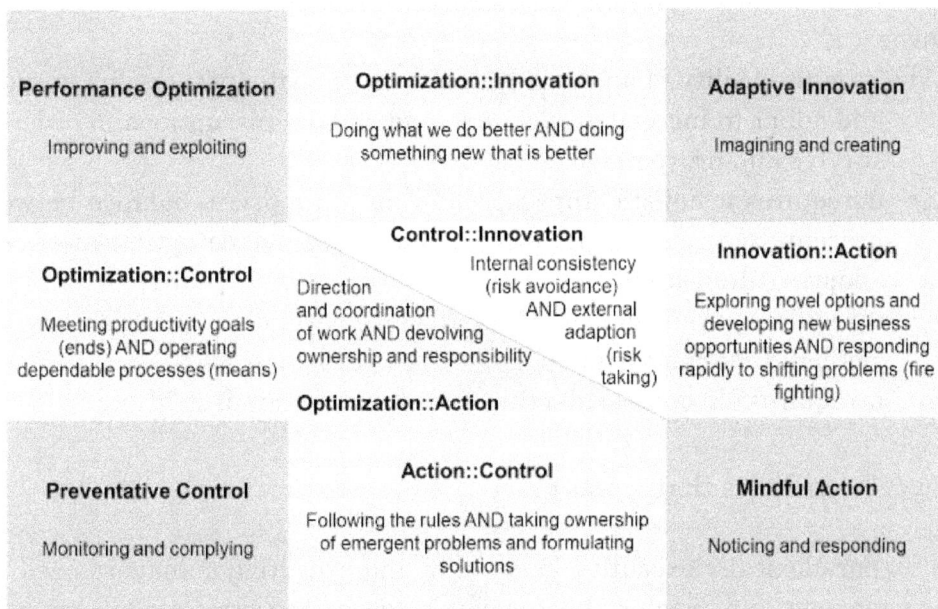

Figure 3.4: Managing the organisational resilience tensions
Source: Denyer.[43]

Denyer[44] defines organisational resilience as "the ability of an organization to anticipate, prepare for, respond and adapt to incremental change and sudden disruptions in order to survive and prosper". He adds that "it reaches beyond risk management towards a more holistic view of organisational health and success". A resilient organisation is one that not merely survives over the long term, but also flourishes. Organisational resilience can thus be regarded as a strategic imperative for an organisation to prosper in today's dynamic, interconnected world. It is not a once-off exercise but is achieved over time and for the long term. According to Denyer,[45] mastering organisational resilience requires the adoption of excellent habits and best practice to deliver organisational improvement by building competence and capability across all aspects of an organisation. This allows leadership to take measured risks with confidence, making the most of opportunities that present themselves.

---

[43]   Denyer, 2017, p. 15.

[44]   Denyer, 2017, p. 15.

[45]   Denyer, 2017, p. 15.

Denyer[46] summarises his core elements of organisational resilience as follows:

- "it is the ability of an organisation to anticipate, prepare for, respond and adapt to incremental change and sudden disruptions in order, to survive and prosper;
- it requires a holistic approach and an appropriate balance between preventative control, mindful action, performance optimisation and adaptive innovation;
- it requires paradoxical thinking to move beyond an 'either/or' towards 'both/and' outcomes; and
- it requires effective leadership and a shift in mindset."[47]

Denyer[48] concludes that –

"... paradoxically executive leadership and executive managers need to manage and master the tension between the strong supportive leadership that people want to see during times of change, and the more demanding collaborative leadership that will sustain the organisation. In leadership, as in organisational resilience, an increasingly volatile, uncertain, complex and ambiguous world calls for an appropriate balance between defence and progression, consistency and flexibility."

5   FEEDBACK LOOPS AND RESILIENCE

According to Meadows,[49] resilience arises from a "rich structure of many feedback loops that can work in different ways to restore a system even after a large perturbation. Resilience is provided by several such loops, operating through different mechanisms, at different time scales, and with in-built redundancy; one kicking in if another one fails". Meadows argues that feedback loops are essential for complex restorative and self-organising structures. Short term oscillations, periodic outbreaks, or long cycles of succession, climax and collapse may be the normal condition that resilience structures aim to stabilise. However, as far as longer-term changing paradigms are concerned, Meadows[50] warns that this perspective requires "a new way of seeing".

Organisational leadership needs to comprehend the role of *a process*

---

[46]   Denyer, 2017, p. 15.

[47]   Denyer, 2017, p. 9.

[48]   Denyer, 2017, p. 25.

[49]   Meadows, D. 2008. *Thinking in systems*. White River Junction, VT: Chelsea Green, p. 76.

[50]   Meadows, D. 2008, p. 163.

of enabling double-loop organisational learning processes supported by quality strategic conversation and engagement, which facilitates double-loop learning.

6 RESILIENCE INDICATORS

In 2011, the universities of Canterbury and Auckland in New Zealand launched the Resilient Organisations Research Programme, a cooperative research programme to investigate organisational resilience. This came about mainly as a result of the Christchurch earthquakes at that time which resulted in 185 fatalities. The research posed the following question: "What is it that makes some organisations able to not only survive, but also to thrive in the face of adversity?"[51] The result of this research was a set of resilience indicators, which is reflected in Figure 3.5.

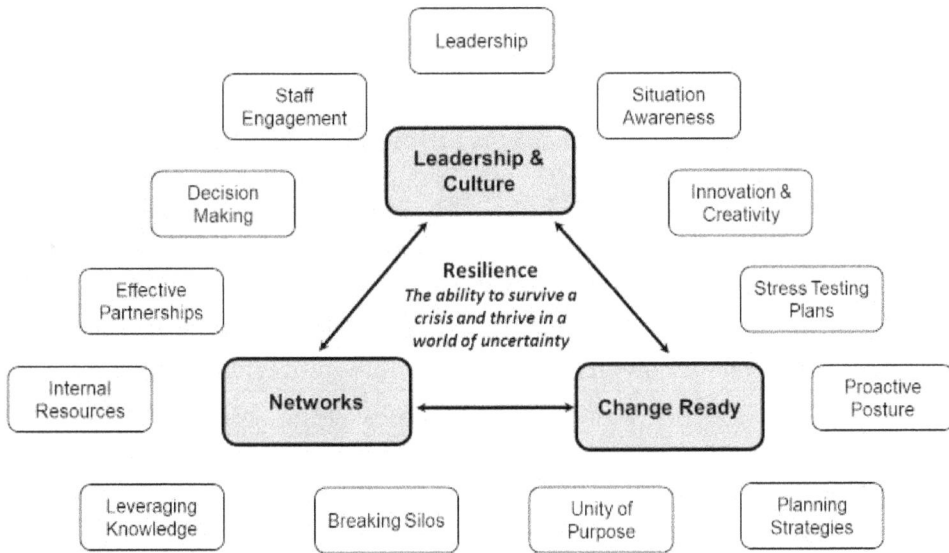

Leadership

Staff Engagement

Situation Awareness

Decision Making

Leadership & Culture

Innovation & Creativity

Effective Partnerships

Resilience
The ability to survive a crisis and thrive in a world of uncertainty

Stress Testing Plans

Internal Resources

Networks

Change Ready

Proactive Posture

Leveraging Knowledge

Breaking Silos

Unity of Purpose

Planning Strategies

Figure 3.5: Resilience indicators
Source: Universities of Canterbury/Auckland[52]

The universities of Canterbury/Auckland[53] identified 13 indicators that may be used to assess the resilience of an organisation. These indicators are described in the next section and situated within three resilience clusters namely, "Leadership and Culture, Networks and Change-ready". These clusters and their associated indicators add significant value in gauging or measuring the level of organisational resilience. As such they are essential

---

[51] Universities of Canterbury/Auckland. 2017. *Resilient Organisations Research Programme.* http://www.resorg.nz/What-is-resilience Date of access: 1 August 2017.

[52] Universities of Canterbury/Auckland, 2017, p. 3.

[53] Universities of Canterbury/Auckland, 2017, p. 4.

for building a diagnostic instrument for organisational resilience [with specific reference to city government].

6.1 Leadership and Culture cluster

Under the Leadership and Culture cluster, the following indicators were identified:

- "Leadership: Strong crisis leadership in providing good management and decision making during times of crisis, as well as continuous evaluation of strategies and work programs against organisational goals;
- Staff Engagement: The engagement and involvement of staff who understand the link between their own work, the organisation's resilience, and its long-term success. Staff are empowered and use their skills to solve problems;
- Situation Awareness: Staff are encouraged to be vigilant about the organisation, its performance and potential problems. Staff are rewarded for sharing good and bad news about the organisation including early warning signals and these are quickly reported to organisational leaders;
- Decision Making: Staff have the appropriate authority to make decisions related to their work, and authority is clearly delegated to enable a crisis response. Highly skilled staff are involved in, or able to make, decisions where their specific knowledge adds significant value, or where their involvement will aid implementation; and
- Innovation and Creativity: Staff is encouraged and rewarded for using their knowledge in novel ways to solve new and existing problems, and for utilising innovative and creative approaches to developing solutions."[54]

6.2 Networks cluster

The universities of Canterbury/Auckland[55] pinpointed the following indicators under Network cluster:

- "Effective Partnerships: An understanding of the relationships and resources the organisation might need to access from other organisations during a crisis, and planning and management to ensure this access;
- Leveraging Knowledge: Critical information is stored in numerous formats and locations, and staff have access to expert opinions when needed. Roles are shared, and staff are trained so that someone will always be able to fill key roles;

---

[54] Universities of Canterbury/Auckland, 2017, p. 5.
[55] Universities of Canterbury/Auckland, 2017, p. 6.

- Breaking Silos: Minimisation of divisive social, cultural and behavioural barriers, which are most often manifested as communication barriers creating disjointed, disconnected and detrimental ways of working;
- Internal Resources: The management and mobilisation of the organisation's resources to ensure its ability to operate during business as usual, as well as being able to provide the extra capacity required during a crisis."

6.3 Change-ready cluster

The following indicators are attached to the change-ready cluster:
- "Unity of purpose: Awareness of what the organisation's priorities would be following a crisis, clearly defined at the organisation level, as well as an understanding of the organisation's minimum operating requirements;
- Proactive posture: A strategic and behavioural readiness to respond to early warning signals of change in the organisation's internal and external environment before they escalate into crisis;
- Planning strategies: The development and evaluation of plans and strategies to manage vulnerabilities concerning the business environment and its stakeholders;
- Stress-Testing Plans: The participation of staff in simulations or *scenarios* designed to practice response arrangements and validate plans."[56]

This research[57] documented the following findings:

"Each organisation may be struck by a combination of events or circumstances that has the potential to bring that organisation to its knees. It is not just about getting through crises; a truly resilient organisation has two other important capabilities namely the foresight and situation awareness to prevent potential crises emerging, and an ability to turn crises into a source of strategic opportunity. Resilience is a strategic capability. Organisations sit within a larger system. While our research focuses on the resilience of organisations (businesses, government agencies, and institutions), an organisation sits within an ecological-like system and resilience is required at all levels of this system."[58]

---

[56] Universities of Canterbury/Auckland, 2017, p. 6.
[57] Universities of Canterbury/Auckland, 2017, p. 8.
[58] Universities of Canterbury/Auckland, 2017, p. 8.

A systemic, holistic perspective used for deriving the resilience indicators, as illustrated in Figure 3.5 above, sets a standard by which other organisations may gauge their own situation. The cluster and indicators derived from the New Zealand study form a comprehensive, interdependent perspective for organisational resilience.

The purpose of the proposed diagnostic instrument for organisational resilience, as the main outcome of this study, is to identify the most important feedback loops that ensure organisational resilience in South Africa. South Africa can be seen as a proxy for emerging economies. In the proposed diagnostic instrument, documented in Chapter 7, the feedback loops, clusters and associated indicators are aimed at provoking a productive conversation and developing a resilience strategy. A central premise is that learning is optimised when this process takes place within strategic organisational conversations that enable double-loop learning. Conversation quality and engagement[59] enable double-loop learning and, typically, the shifting of assumptions within the minds of executive leadership and executive managers that engage with the diagnostic instrument.

7   RESILIENCE STRATEGIES: SCHOOLS OF THOUGHT

As stated earlier, since 2011, scholarly work on resilience has been stimulated by the events commonly referred to as "9/11". Schools of thought regarding broad-scale resilience have thus not yet fully matured and can be regarded as emergent. It is, however, important to extract foundational parameters and theoretical principles from the field of strategic management in terms of which resilience strategies can be located and subsumed to serve as a starting point for a robust exposition of resilience strategies.

The well-established field of strategic management has similarities to the emergent field of resilience strategy. Theorist and practitioner in scenario-based strategy, Van der Heijden,[60] made a significant contribution by outlining the paradigmatic developments and theoretical principles which are relevant for resilience strategy. Van der Heijden[61] posits that there are at least three schools of thought that have arisen to interpret the way executive managers and executive leadership think. These can be labelled as rationalist, evolutionary and processual. Owing to the significance of these and other schools of thought for organisational

---

[59]   Van der Merwe, L., Chermack, T.J., Kulikowich, J. & Yang, B. 2007. Strategic conversation quality and engagement: Assessment of a new measure. *International Journal of Training and Development.* 11(3):214–221

[60]   Van der Heijden, K. 1996. *Scenarios: The art of strategic conversation.* London: Wiley.

[61]   Van der Heijden, 1996, pp. 23–25.

resilience and the design of a diagnostic instrument, each school of thought is briefly outlined below.

7.1 Rationalist school

In describing the various schools of thought in strategy making, Van der Heijden[62] asserts that the rationalist school "codifies thought and action separately". The underlying assumption of this school is that there is "one best solution", and the task of the resilience strategist (e.g. organisational executive leadership and executive management) is to search for this solution or to get as close to it as possible. Van der Heijden[63] lists the assumptions underlying the rationalist school as

- "predictability, no interference from outside;
- clear intentions;
- implementation follows formulation;
- full understanding throughout the organisation; and
- reasonable people will do reasonable things".

Elements of the rationalist school can also be found in risk assessment approaches to resilience as codified in the King lV Rules of Good Governance.[64] Through a process of analysis, the risk profile of an organisation is determined, from which a risk management strategy may be formulated.

7.2 Evolutionary school

The evolutionary school generally regards an organisation as an "organism" that gradually evolves.[65] The evolutionary school came about as a result of the realisation among researchers and scientists that decision making is not simply a rational process.[66] For example, Charles Lindblom (1959) cited in Van der Heijden[67] studied managers in organisations in the 1950s and observed that they were not "goal-seeking" but "ills-avoiding". In other words, decision makers are not merely searching for a rational solution to a problem but are also trying to avoid "pain, harm or constraint".[68]

[62]   Van der Heijden, 1996, pp. 23–25.

[63]   Van der Heijden, 1996, pp. 23–25.

[64]   King IV Report. 2016. *Report on corporate governance for South Africa.* Johannesburg: Institute of Directors (IOD).

[65]   Morgan, G. 1998. *Images of organisations.* The Executive Edition. London: Sage.

[66]   Van der Heijden, 1996, p. 133.

[67]   Van der Heijden, 1996, p. 133.

[68]   Van der Heijden, 1996, p. 135.

Mintzberg[69] coined the term "emergent strategy", which describes the evolutionary nature of strategy formulation. Mintzberg[70] goes on to describe strategy as "a plan ... a direction, a guide or course of action into the future, a path to get from here to there". Furthermore, a strategy can be regarded as a consistent pattern observable over time. Mintzberg[71] thus argues that organisations develop plans for the future, mainly the result of a pattern of decisions taken in the past. An emergent strategy thus gradually evolves from previous organisational strategies. In this regard, Mintzberg[72] differentiates between "intended" strategy and "realised" strategies. Intended strategies that are fully realised are labelled "deliberate" strategies. Those that are not realised, according to Mintzberg,[73] are referred to as "unrealised" strategies. An "emergent" strategy is regarded as a realised pattern of strategic decisions that are not expressly intended but realised.[74]

7.3 Processual school

The processual school continues to regard organisations as "living organisms", as described by Morgan.[75] Processual scholars concur with the ideas of the evolutionists that organisational situations are generally too complex to analyse in their entirety. Solutions to resilience challenges, therefore, emerge as a result of continuous learning.[76] Organisational adjustment resulting from continuous learning forms the basis of the processual school. An effective resilience strategy requires feedback that elicits and provokes a conversation about specific high leverage areas that may foster organisational resilience.

7.4 Social justice, evolutionary school

In addition to the three schools of thought identified by Van der Heijden,[77] Laloux[78] posits an evolutionary paradigm along a "social justice trajectory". This social justice school of thought is premised on foundational questions concerning the "inner rightness" of decisions. It is evolutionary since

---

[69] Mintzberg, H. 1994. *The rise and fall of strategic planning*. New York, NY: Prentice Hall, pp. 24–27.

[70] Mintzberg, 1994, p. 23.

[71] Mintzberg, 1994.

[72] Mintzberg, 1994, pp. 23–25.

[73] Mintzberg, 1994, p. 24.

[74] Mintzberg, 1994, pp. 23–25.

[75] Morgan, G. 1997. *Images of organisations*. London: Sage.

[76] Van der Heijden, 1996, p. 36.

[77] Van der Heijden, 1996.

[78] Laloux, 2014a, p. 43.

some scholars such as Bragdon[79] argue that there is an "evolution of consciousness" shifting from an outward focus to internal yardsticks of decision making. Bragdon[80] extends the arguments put forward by Laloux and describes a so-called "emerging corporate renaissance" that informs both organisational and individual decisions. Bragdon[81] argues that this "renaissance" is mainly the result of a shift away from collaborative behaviour and living in harmony with the natural world to individual actions. As humankind accumulated more knowledge and technology grew, individuals began to think of themselves as separate from and above nature. However, Bragdon[82] continues to underline the fact that environmental challenges increasingly reverse this renaissance. Issues such as rapid population growth, limited natural resources and life-altering climate change have led to a "rebirth of interest in returning to older ways of living in harmony with each other and with nature".[83] Organisations need to learn and adapt to these realities to become more resilient.

In the context of South African organisations, it may be argued that rapid urbanisation trends have removed people of African origin from a rural way of life which, in general, is in harmony with nature. This constrains the ability of people to adjust to urban life. Furthermore, elements of the social justice, evolutionary school of thought are also evident in the philosophy of Ubuntu.[84] Ubuntu philosophies were introduced into government during the Mbeki presidency with structures such as Cabinet *kgotlas* for decision making.

7.5 Self-organising system school

The fifth school of thought regarding organisational resilience strategies is the so-called "self-organising systems" school.[85] This school generally extends beyond the need to learn into the realm of self-organisation as a paradigm for strategic planning and execution. Organisations that learn and self-organise have been popularised by Senge of MIT in his work on "learning organisations". As stated earlier, Senge identified five "disciplines" which enable learning and adjustments in organisations.

---

[79] Bragdon, J.H. 2016. *Companies that mimic life: Leaders of emerging corporate renaissance.* London: Greenleaf Publishing.

[80] Bragdon, 2016, p. 198.

[81] Bragdon, 2016.

[82] Bragdon, 2016, p. 199.

[83] Bragdon, 2016, p. 199.

[84] Khoza, R.J. 2012. *Attuned leadership: African humanism as compass.* Johannesburg: Penguin Books.

[85] Senge, P.M., Kleiner, A., Roberts, C., Ross, R.B. & Smith, B. 1994. *The fifth discipline fieldbook.* London: Nicholas Brealey.

Organisational learning is posited by Senge as the foundational or ultimate basis for competitive advantage. In his work *Learning to plan and planning to learn,* Michael[86] was the first scholar to pinpoint the importance of an organisational learning process in the context of organisational strategic planning. This insight was later elaborated on by De Geus.[87] De Geus's perspective is that the process of strategic planning is a learning endeavour.

Morgan[88] summarises and provides further scholarly support for the centrality of learning for enabling resilience. His assertions generally support the AAR (Anticipation, Adaptation and Recovery) framework as described above. Morgan[89] states that learning organisations should develop capabilities and capacities to do the following:

- "scan and anticipate change in the wider environment to detect significant variations;
- develop an ability to question, challenge and change operating norms and assumptions; and allow for an emergent strategic direction and platform for organisations to adapt".

Morgan[90] underscores the notion that these capacities and capabilities will enable organisations to become "skilled in the art of double-loop learning, to avoid getting trapped in single-loop learning processes, especially those created by traditional management control systems and the defensive routines of organisational members". In the same vein, Meadows[91] states that organisations require the ability to adjust their structures and designs based on changing conditions. Just like living systems, organisations should have "self-organisation" properties. Meadows[92] continues by adding that new discoveries suggest that "just a few simple organising principles can lead to wildly diverse self-organising structures". Generally, organisational hierarchies give systems stability and resilience. Accordingly, a comprehensive set of feedback loops creates homeostasis in a system, providing the feedback it needs to spring back into the position it occupied prior to the perturbation or shock.

A diagnostic instrument for organisational resilience should contain multiple feedback loops. When followed by planned action in high leverage

---

[86]   Michael, D.N. 1973. *Learning to plan and planning to learn.* San Francisco, CA: Jossey-Bass.

[87]   De Geus, A. 1988. Planning as learning. *Harvard Business Review,* March–April: 2–6.

[88]   Morgan, 1997.

[89]   Morgan, 1997, p. 90.

[90]   Morgan, 1997, p. 90.

[91]   Meadows, 2008, p. 79.

[92]   Meadows, 2008, p. 80.

intervention areas, it will probably result in the restoration of a prior position and structure. Eliciting this strategic resilience response is the focus of this research.

7.6 Antifragile school

The sixth and final school of thought regarding organisational resilience strategies is defined by Taleb[93] as "antifragile". Antifragility goes beyond resilience and robustness. A resilient organisation tends to resist shocks and generally to remain the same, while an antifragile organisation improves its structures and functioning as a result of environmental shocks. It may thus be a property in terms of which the organisation or system "gains from disorder."[94] This property is the foundation for everything that has changed with time, such as evolution, culture, ideas, revolutions, political systems, technological innovation, cultural and economic success, corporate survival, and the rise of cities. Antifragile properties exist when disorder enables an improvement in the organisation concerned. Taleb[95] thus raises the possibility that antifragile organisations are not harmed by the adverse events and structural disruptions that create disorder but are rather strengthened by them.

The advent of technology convergence which is part of the so-called "Fourth Industrial Revolution"[96] may demonstrate Taleb's theory of antifragility. The emergence of sustainable development, green growth and smart cities may be the result of an antifragile response to converging disruptive technologies such as big data, the internet of things (IoT), the disruption of transportation and the disruption of energy. Initially, these perturbations may be disruptive. However, these disruptors may enable adaptation and recovery as well as enabling the process of sustainable development, green growth and smart cities.[97]

8   CYBERNETICS AND DOUBLE-LOOP LEARNING FOR ORGANISATIONAL RESILIENCE

Morgan[98] utilises the principles of cybernetics to analyse information exchange in organisations. The term "cybernetics" originated from the Greek word *kubernetes,* which means "steersmanship" and provides

---

[93]   Taleb, N.N. 2012. *Antifragile*. New York, NY: Random House, p. 17.

[94]   Taleb, 2012, p. 17.

[95]   Taleb, 2012, p. 18.

[96]   Schwab, K. 2016a. *Navigating the Fourth Industrial Revolution.* http://www.biznews.com/wef/davos-2016/2016/01/20/klaus-schwab-navigating-the-fourth-industrial-revolution/ Date of access: 23 August 2017.

[97]   Taleb, 2012, p. 20.

[98]   Morgan, 1997, p. 83.

useful perspectives on the way information flows in organisations. Such information exchanges guide self-regulating organisational behaviours that foster the maintenance of "steady states" (i.e. resilience).[99] Morgan asserts that "cybernetics lead to theories of communication and organisational learning". These theories stress at least the following four key principles for organisations as systems:

- "systems must have the capacity to sense, monitor, and scan significant aspects of their environment;
- systems must be able to relate information to the operating norms that guide system behaviour;
- systems must be able to detect significant deviation from these norms; and
- systems must be able to initiate corrective action where discrepancies are detected".[100]

In addition to these key principles, Morgan[101] adds that organisations need to allow an appropriate strategic direction and pattern of organisation to emerge. This strategic direction should guide the evolutionary redesign of organisations and allow them to "become skilled in the art of double-loop learning to avoid getting trapped in single-loop learning processes, especially those created by traditional management control systems and the defensive routines of organisational members".[102]

These four principles, together with the ideas of emergent strategy and double-loop learning, generally reinforce the value of a systemic, cybernetic approach to analysing organisational resilience. They also further support the validity of the appropriateness of the AAR framework for gauging organisational resilience.

Both the processual and self-organising schools of thought highlighted above suggest that the process of organisational learning in general and double-loop learning specifically play a significant role in enabling resilience. In this context, Argyris[103] describes organisational learning for improved resilience simply as "detecting error". By this Argyris means detecting any deviations from organisational strategic intent, standards or plans. The Kolb experiential learning cycle (see Figure 3.6) describes how such deviation detection may take place and how decisions may be

---

[99] Morgan, 1997, p. 83.

[100] Morgan, 1997, p. 83.

[101] Morgan, 1997, p. 83.

[102] Morgan, 1997, p. 83.

[103] Argyris, C. 1992. *On organisation learning*. Cambridge, MA: Blackwell, p. 73.

embedded in a learning process. Double-loop learning (see Figures 3.7 and 3.8) describes how assumptions in the minds of decision makers may be influenced and adjusted to facilitate greater resilience.

9 EXPERIENTIAL LEARNING THEORY

Building on earlier work by John Dewey and Kurt Levin, American educational theorist David A. Kolb posits that "learning is the process whereby knowledge is created through the transformation of experience."[104] At both a team and an individual executive leadership level, experiential learning provides an important method for building capability through capacity building. The theory of learning can be applied in a formal classroom setting as well as during on-the-job-learning (experiential). This theory of learning also guides, for example, continuous organisational improvement processes by empowering supervisors and teams to manage the quality and overall performance of organisational systems and processes, including the performance of employees. Leadership development is also guided by experiential learning in the sense that leaders may gain certain competencies in organisational performance review processes. The Kolb theory presents a cyclical model of learning consisting of four stages, numbered from 1 to 4 in Figure 3.6.

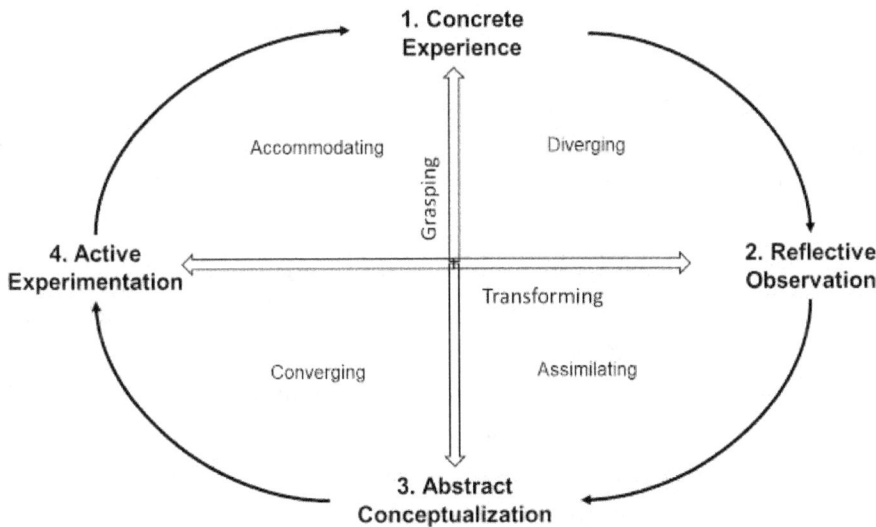

Figure 3.6: The Kolb cycle of experiential learning
Source: Kolb and Kolb.[105]

---

[104] Kolb, A. & Kolb, D.A. 2008. Experiential learning theory: A dynamic holistic approach to management learning, education and development. (*In* Armstrong, S.J. and Fukami, C.V. *Ed, The Sage handbook of management, learning and educational development*). Thousand Oaks, CA: Sage, p. 38.

[105] Kolb & Kolb, 2008, pp. 42–68.

The Kolb cycle of experiential learning may be entered at any stage but must then follow each subsequent stage in the sequence. The four stages, according to Kolb,[106] are –

1) Concrete experience (or 'Do'): This stage represents the process where learners actively engage in learning by means of actual experiences, including practical activity sessions or fieldwork.

2) Reflective observation (or 'Observe'): The second stage entails learners' reflections on their experiences gained in Stage 1.

3) Abstract conceptualization (or 'Think'): The third stage represents learners' attempts to design a theoretical model of what they observed.

4) Active experimentation (or 'Plan'): The fourth and final stage is where the learners are planning to apply the theoretical model to a new experience.

In addition to these four stages, Kolb[107] identified "four learning styles" which may be deployed during each stage. These learning styles highlight conditions under which specific learners may learn more efficiently. These styles are –

- "assimilators, who may learn better when presented with sound logical theories to consider;
- convergers, who may learn better when provided with practical applications of concepts and theories;
- accommodators, who may learn better when provided with hands-on experiences; and
- divergers, who may learn better when allowed to observe and collect a wide range of information".[108]

These learning styles are useful for enabling capacity-building processes by matching the design of learning processes with dominant learning styles of organisational members.

As stated earlier, developing an organisational resilience strategy can be regarded as a learning process. It is thus crucial to optimise the learning process itself. This includes best practice learning processes when using the diagnostic instrument as a feedback loop and a platform for reflection and adjusting assumptions among executive leadership and

---

[106] Kolb & Kolb, 2008, pp. 42–68.

[107] Kolb, D.A. 1984. *Experiential Learning: Experience as the source of learning and development*. Prentice Hall, p. 40.

[108] Kolb, D.A. 1984, p. 40

executive managers. It also includes mitigating and avoiding what may be called "learning disabilities".[109]

9.1 Single-loop learning and double-loop learning

Figures 3.7 and 3.8 differentiate between and merge single-loop and double-loop learning. As stated above, it is essential to optimise organisational learning as an instrument to facilitate organisational resilience.

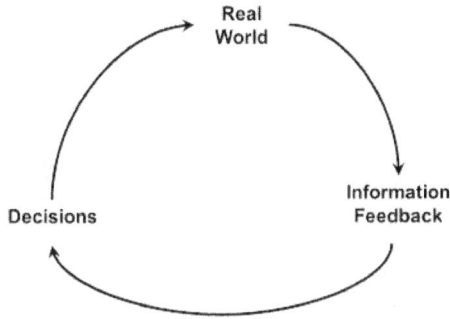

Figure 3.7: Single-loop learning
Source: Sterman[110] after Argyris.[111]

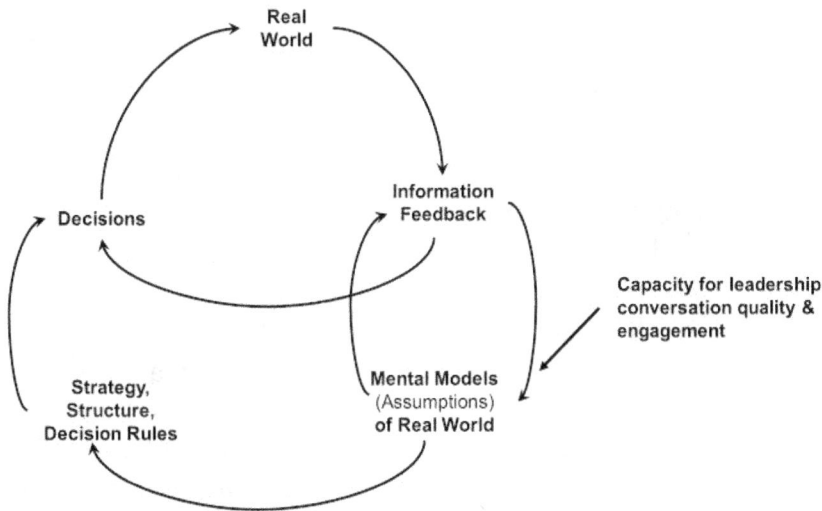

Figure 3.8: Single-loop learning and double-loop learning
Source: Based on Sterman[112] and Argyris.[113]

---

[109] Sterman, J. 2000. *Business dynamics: Systems thinking and modelling for a complex world.* Boston, MA: McGraw Hill Higher Education, p. 16.

[110] Sterman, 2000, p. 16.

[111] Argyris, C. 1982. *Reasoning, learning and action individual and organisational.* San Francisco, CA: Jossey-Bass.

[112] Sterman, 2000, p. 16.

[113] Argyris, 1992.

Argyris[114] describes single-loop learning as rational decisions based on information feedback obtained from real-world situations. When there is congruence between existing assumptions of decision makers and incoming information, new realities and facts are assimilated as learning.

Argyris[115] describes double-loop learning as a mode of learning which accommodates influences on "loosely held assumptions". In other words, decision makers allow incoming feedback to influence their existing assumptions. This open mindset enables the shifting of assumptions. In the context of organisational strategies, Wack[116] applies the principles of double-loop learning as "influencing the microcosm in the minds of decision makers about the macrocosm, the future contextual world around an organisation".

In Figure 3.9, Sterman[117] illustrates how a feedback loop (A) reflects single-loop learning, including commonly encountered learning disabilities such as "selective perception, missing feedback, time delays, bias, distortion, error and ambiguity". This may result in "implementation failure, game playing and narrow interests, inconsistency in terms of performance goals". In feedback loop (B), Sterman[118] illustrates the interactivity between "Information Feedback" and "Mental Models (Assumptions)". This interactivity indicates learning disabilities which in turn influence "Strategy, Structure and Decision Rules". This, in turn, feeds into "Decisions".

Sterman identifies typical disabilities that limit the efficiency of learning in single-loop (A) and double-loop (B) learning. These learning disabilities may be mitigated or exacerbated by the "capacity for leadership and quality conversation and engagement" (see Figures 3.7 and 3.8 above).

As far as the enhancement of conversation quality and engagement is concerned, Van der Merwe *et al.*[119] have developed a measure consisting of a checklist for "gauging conversation quality and engagement for competent leadership". They argue that a low level of conversation quality and engagement by leadership poses a capacity limit on double-loop learning and vice versa.

---

[114] Argyris, C. 1992. *On organisation learning.* Cambridge, MA: Blackwell
[115] Argyris, 1992.
[116] Wack, 1985a
[117] Sterman, 2000, p. 16.
[118] Sterman, 2000, p. 16.
[119] Van der Merwe et al., 2007, pp. 214–221.

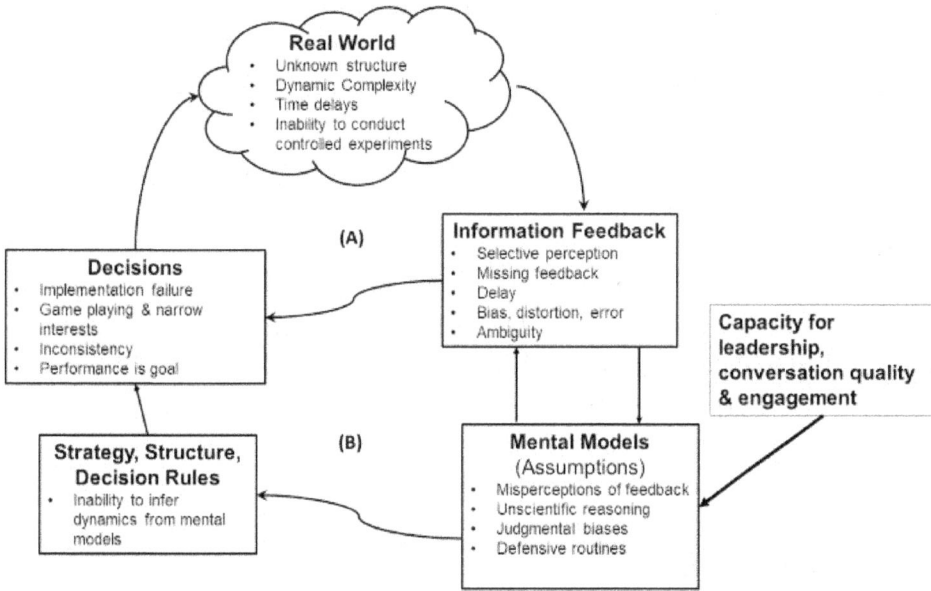

Figure 3.9: Double-loop learning: learning disabilities and enhancements
Source: Sterman.[120]

In the context of organisational strategic planning, Van der Heijden[121] argues that Argyris's learning loop model illustrates –

"... the inter-woveness of thinking and action. If action is based on planning based on a mental model [assumption], then institutional action must be based on a shared mental model. Only through a process of conversation can elements of observation and thought be structured and embedded in the accepted and shared organisational theories in use".

It follows from Van der Heijden's argument that strategic conversation is essential for sharing organisational mental models. These models are also known as "team learning" and "alignment".[122] Conversely, a limited capacity for conversation quality and engagement among organisational decision makers may limit the level of learning, which Sterman identifies as a "learning disability" (Figure 3.9), thus underlining the gravity and

---

[120] Sterman, 2000, p. 16.

[121] Van der Heijden, 1996, p. 41.

[122] Senge, P.M., Kleiner, A., Ross, R.B., Roth, G. & Smith, B. 1999. *The dance of change: The challenges to sustaining momentum in learning organisations.* New York, NY: Doubleday Currency.

consequences of this limiting ability. Furthermore, Van der Merwe *et al.*[123] posit that the attributes of strategic conversation, which enable among other things double-loop learning, can be gauged and propose what they call a "new measure". They go on to argue that both single-loop and double-loop learning may be included in an instrument to gauge the quality of strategic conversation and organisational engagement for competent leadership. Their measure for the quality of strategic conversation and engagement includes reflection on the conversation at transactional levels (i.e. Level I) and meta-levels (i.e. Level II). At a meta-level, item indicators are utilised to assess conversation processes.

Organisational disabilities and strategic conversations, as an instrument to facilitate double-loop learning, represent high leverage areas for enabling an organisational resilience strategy. As such, they serve as critical variables in the design of a diagnostic instrument for organisational resilience.

Morgan[124] identifies other areas in organisations where challenging operating norms and assumptions support continuous improvement and innovation. Such continuous improvement and innovation may be achieved by engaging double-loop learning. Morgan draws attention especially to the process of total quality management (TQM) also known as *Kaizen*, which transformed the Japanese industry in the industrial development era (post-1945). Double-loop learning is embedded in TQM, which enables structured innovation through worker engagement mechanisms such as Quality Control Circles (QCCs). Morgan[125] points out that "double-loop learning as a way to challenge assumptions, is established at strategy level". The result of this is a substantial improvement in productivity and quality through structured innovation and a lower cost of production.

10 QUALITY IMPROVEMENT AS CONTINUOUS LEARNING AND STRUCTURED INNOVATION

Morgan[126] integrates double-loop learning with TQM and pinpoints so-called "powers" associated with it to foster continuous organisational improvement. These powers are mainly vested in the fact that it encourages double-loop learning. Organisational members are asked to uncover the underlying causes of recurring problems in organisational processes. They are also encouraged to analyse existing work practices in a search for more effective, efficient and innovative ones. Employees are furthermore

---

[123] Van der Merwe et al., 2007.

[124] Morgan, 1997, p. 93.

[125] Morgan, 1997, p. 93.

[126] Morgan, 1997, p. 94.

encouraged to develop open mindsets and organisational values that stimulate learning and change. As Morgan[127] puts it: "challenging the operating norms and assumptions in this way, the approach creates information, insights and capabilities through which a system can evolve to new levels of development." As such, quality improvement fosters continuous learning and structured innovation in organisations.

In the case of South Africa, the application of the principles of TQM may be regarded as one of the key success factors in Eskom's turnaround strategy in the 1980s[128]. In the aftermath of the so-called "Koeberg incident" in 2006, where a bolt accidentally entered the generator turbine casing, causing damage amounting to approximately R623-million, the executive manager in charge of Koeberg Nuclear Power Station maintenance mentioned that "the accident ... would never have occurred if Quality Control Circles (QCCs) had been active at Koeberg".[129] He also pointed out that QCCs, as an engagement instrument, generally enable workers to raise their motivation, productivity and at the same time, by means of structured innovation and problem solving, improve the quality of their work.[130]

11 RE-TUNING THE HUMAN MIND AT SCALE

Whybrow[131] posits that the human mind is generally not tuned to deal effectively with large-scale challenges. Typical large-scale challenges include imminent climate volatility, change and the entrenched wasteful, anti-resilient behaviour that people display. Whybrow[132] designed a neurobiological model to "re-tune the human mind" from existing assumptions and behaviour that are not sustainable to assumptions that ensure behaviour that is globally sustainable, and thus greater global resilience.

The United Nations International Strategy for Disaster Reduction (UNISDR)[133] Disaster Risk Reduction Strategy 2016–2021 can be regarded as a global attempt to "re-tune" the minds of the global population. This strategy was designed in response to rising levels of disaster effects

---

[127] Morgan, 1997, p. 94.

[128] Van der Merwe, 1991

[129] Mbonyana, D. 2006. ESKOM Koeberg Nuclear Power Station Accident, Quality Control Circles [personal interview] Eskom Head Office Megawatt Park, Johannesburg.

[130] Mbonyana, 2006.

[131] Whybrow, P.C. 2015. *The well-tuned brain: Neuroscience and the life well-lived.* London: Norton.

[132] Whybrow, 2015.

[133] United Nations International Strategy for Disaster Reduction (UNISDR). 2016. Strategic Framework 2016-2021. Geneva: UNISDR.

globally. It is built on the premise that disaster risk mitigation and reduction are essential to enable sustainable development in general and city resilience specifically. In this regard, the Sendai Framework of the UNISDR[134] contains a so-called "priorities for action" list:

"Priority 1: Understanding disaster risk;
Priority 2: Strengthening disaster risk governance to manage disaster risk;
Priority 3: Investing in disaster risk reduction for resilience; and
Priority 4: Enhancing disaster preparedness for effective response, and to, 'build back better', in recovery, rehabilitation and reconstruction".[135]

The diagnostic instrument that is to be the main outcome of this study will have to incorporate rational, single-loop learning modes as well as double-loop organisational learning. An important component of the instrument is its scale of application. It should, for example, guide mitigating actions for global disaster risks, as well as foster organisational (i.e. city government) resilience. As such, the Sendai priorities for action list adds significant value to retune the minds of decision makers at scale.

12 REQUISITE ORGANISATION

According to Jaques,[136] the "Requisite Organisation" comprises design and development that can release human creativity and imagination. Jaques's[137] foundational research includes the following:
- "living organisms;
- human nature and social power;
- organisational structure; and
- managerial leadership processes."[138]

Jaques's[139] unit of analysis when studying organisations is the behaviour of executive leadership and executive management. His perspective on organisations and specifically on the so-called requisite organisational stratum enables organisational responsiveness which is directly inter-dependent with organisational resilience. In this regard, he examines plan-

---

[134] United Nations International Strategy for Disaster Reduction (UNISDR). 2015. Sendai Framework for Disaster Risk Reduction 2015-2030. Geneva: UNISDR.

[135] United Nations International Strategy for Disaster Reduction (UNISDR), 2015.

[136] Jaques, E. 2013. *Requisite organisation: A total system for effective managerial organisation and management leadership for the 21st century.* Orlando, FL: Cason Hall.

[137] Jaques, 2013.

[138] Jaques, 2013 .

[139] Jaques, 2013, p. 6.

ning time horizons, decision making and execution of decisions in organisations.

Based on the key findings of his research concerning the nature of human capability and the reasons why managers make certain decisions, Jaques[140] concludes that the existence of a managerial hierarchy (referred to as "accountable managerial hierarchies") in organisational structures may be a "reflection of discontinuous steps in the nature of human capability". Jaques thus emphasises the interdependence between an effective managerial organisation and managerial leadership. Based on this interdependence, he has formulated what he calls a "Total System for Effective Managerial Organisation and Management Leadership". By means of this system, Jaques[141] assesses the conditions that release potential in organisations through being "requisite".

In the context of the responsiveness of organisational structures to changing conditions, Jaques's requisite organisational perspectives may have implications for:

- "the requisite number of hierarchical strata in any organisational structure;
- the time focus for these levels in terms of anticipating discontinuities, planning focus and time horizons for policy and decision making;
- the relative decision-complexity in the tasks and positions within each stratum;
- strata and sub-divisions within them when tasks are based on decision-complexity may form the basis for determining the relative value of positions in a job evaluation process which uses a single criterium for evaluation;
- equitable remuneration across the strata based upon a unified pay scale which is *felt to be fair* [my emphasis] by incumbents, across the organisational hierarchy;
- containing and preventing drift between job content, titles, performance and compensation; and
- trust as an important foundation for the requisite organisation".[142]

Jaques's requisite organisation provides insight and an alternate perspective on the short-term time frames that generally characterise strategic planning and policy practice at executive leadership and executive

[140] Jaques, 2013, p. 7.

[141] Jaques, 2013, p. 72.

[142] Jaques, 2013, p. 75.

manager levels in organisations which may reflect the "short-termism" Van der Heijden[143] refers to.

12.1 Stratified organisational theory and planning focus

One of the key findings of Jaques's[144] research is the existence of a managerial hierarchy as a reflection in organisational life.

This finding may be seen to:

- "explain the continuous existence of managerial hierarchy in all post-tribal societies for the past 2000 years and suggests that it is likely to be around for the next 3000 years; and
- provide a foundation for achieving a method for and laying the basis for effective managerial leadership".[145]

Jaques's[146] perspective emphasises the systemic interdependence between, among other things, effective managerial organisation and managerial leadership. Based on this interdependence and his research into other dynamics in organisations, he has formulated what he calls "A Total System for Effective Managerial Organisation and Management Leadership". He refers to the conditions that release potential in the organisations, and through this, the organisations' whole potential as the "Requisite Organisation".[147] He points out that there is a widespread underestimation of the impact of an organisation (and structure in the broad sense) on how we go about our organisational activities and the effectiveness of managerial leadership. His research is based on, inter alia, private enterprise, public service and military organisations and their components. He posits in this regard "a universal structure and *an organisational hierarchy of a requisite seven strata*" [my emphasis].[148] Requisite strata form the basis of gauging the relative value of jobs and through this provide a basis for equitable pay within a unified pay system.[149] (See also "Pay Links" in Table 4.14.) Central to Jaques's stratified theory may be what he calls the *time span of discretion*.[150] The time span of discretion may be taken to be the time it

---

143 Van der Heijden, 1996, p. 93.

144 Jaques, 2013.

145 Jaques, 2013, p. 7.

146 Jaques, 2013.

147 Jaques, 2013.

148 Jaques, 2013, p. 72.

149 Van der Merwe, L. 1991. Systems approach to change management: The Eskom experience. (*In* Osler, C. *ed.* 1991. *Making their future: South African organisations on the move.* Institute for Futures Research: University of Stellenbosch Press, pp. 63–76).

150 Jaques, 2013, pp. 37–40.

takes for a decision on a specific stratum to be shown to be correct or not. Jaques uncovered a positive relationship between the level in a hierarchy and the time span of discretion. In other words, the higher the stratum level, the further into the future the consequences of decision making may be assessed as correct or not. In conversation with Jaques,[151] he confirmed that "the number of levels in a hierarchy within an organisation is one of the primary determinants of efficient communication within a hierarchy. Strategic responsiveness (and therefore organisational resilience) is influenced by communication within a hierarchy". He also pointed out that "the relationship between organisation stratum and time span of discretion is a constant across a large global sample of greater than 60 000 executive managers".[152] According to Jaques,[153] "planning focus in the civil service at stratum VII should be between 20- and 25 years". He outlines the time focus for planning and decision making in the civil service[154] in the USA and Great Britain in Table 3.1. This table shows Strata I to VII with the equivalent "time focus" together with the job titles at those levels. The implications of these findings in organisations are that the optimum planning time focus and decision making in general for Directors General and Deputy Directors General in the South African civil service is 20–25 and 10–12 years respectively.

Table 3.1: Planning focus and civil service stratum equivalence

Stratum	Time Focus	US Federal Civil Service	British Civil Service	South African Civil Service
VII	20–25 years	Political appointees	Permanent secretary	Director-General
VI	10–12 years	Political appointees	Deputy secretary	Deputy Director-General
V	5–7 years		Undersecretary	
IV	2–3 years		Asst. secretary	
III	1–1 .5 years		Principal	
II	3–6 months		Asst. principal	
I	1 day			

Source: Jaques.[155]

---

[151] Jaques, E. 1994. Requisite organisation. (Personal Conversation). 23 June, Boston, MIT.

[152] Jaques, 1994.

[153] Jaques, 2013, p. 136.

[154] Jaques, 2013, pp. 104, 136.

[155] Jaques, 2013, p. 136

12.2 Trust as a prerequisite for organisational resilience

Jaques[156] provides a comparative table (see Table 3.2) which itemises what he refers to as "trust inducing" and "paranoia-genic" (inducing distrust) properties in an organisation. This table is reproduced here in full as it contains a comprehensive range of aspects influencing organisational resilience. The comparison between and implications for organisations reflected in the two columns in Table 3.2 are self-explanatory. The paranoia, distrust and divisions caused by the dynamics listed in the Paranoia-genic column may have an impact on the capability of organisations to respond rapidly to discontinuities, which in turn may have an impact on their resilience.

Table 3.2: Comparison of trust inducing and paranoia-genic

Trust Inducing	Paranoia-genic (Inducing distrust)
Equitable system of distribution of pay differentials related to differentials in levels of work.	Power bargaining over pay, or phony output-related bonus "incentive" systems.
Clear definition of accountabilities and authorities in lateral working relationships.	Leaving people to sort out their lateral working relationships by means of manipulation, personal networks and power.
Managers are one stratum removed from immediate subordinates, in role and capability.	Managers more or less than one stratum removed from subordinates and "breathing down their necks" or being "pulled down into the weeds".
Managers-once-removed mentoring subordinates-once-removed on career development.	No mentoring, no career development, no real awareness of employees' potential capabilities.
Employees well informed on the context of their work, and on company vision.	Employees in the dark about what is likely to happen and why they are doing what they are doing.
Authority in line with accountability.	Accountability without equivalent authority.
Level of work in line with a person's level of potential capability.	Under-recognition and under-utilisation of capability.
Regular feedback on manager's judgement of your personal effectiveness.	Absence of feedback from manager, leaving employees in the dark about how well they are doing.
Authority as required by the work in the role.	Empowerment as a "phony gimmick".

---

[156] Jaques, 2013, p. 15.

Trust Inducing	Paranoia-genic (Inducing distrust)
Team working a matter of individuals with individual accountability and recognition working together under an accountable managerial or project team leader.	A mishmash of obscure accountability and authority in "self-managed" or in "internally accountable cross-functional teams with sponsors, coaches, and champions".
Appointments and promotions based on potential capability, commitment and knowledge.	Appointments and promotions distorted by gender, colour, ethnicity, age, religion, network, education, and so forth.

Source: Jaques.[157]

13 SHOCKLEY-ZALABAK ET AL. MODEL FOR ORGANISATIONAL TRUST

The Shockley-Zalabak *et al.*[158] Trust Model identifies five key drivers for organisational trust, namely:
- "competence;
- openness and honesty;
- concern for employees and stakeholders;
- reliability; and
- identification".[159]

In Figure 3.10, the statistical correlations between variables are indicated on the relevant connecting lines to two decimal places, 1.00 representing 100% correlation.

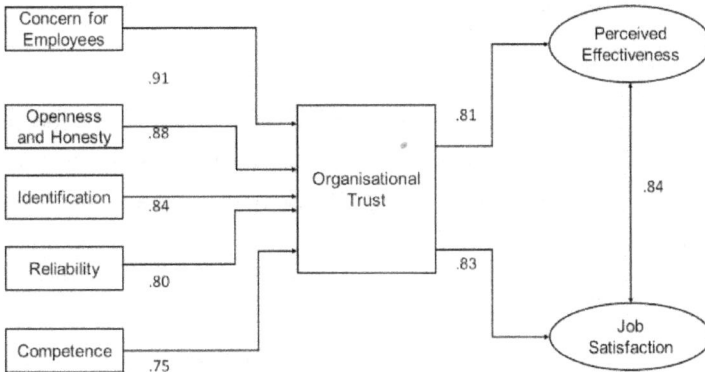

Figure 3.10: Model of organisational trust, job satisfaction and effectiveness

Source: Shockley-Zalabak *et al.*[160]

---

[157] Jaques, 2013, p. 15.

[158] Shockley-Zalabak, P.S., Morreale, S.P. & Hackman, M.Z. 2010. *Building the high-trust organisation.* San Francisco, CA: Jossey-Bass, p. 27.

[159] Shockley-Zalabak et al., 2010, p. 27.

[160] Shockley-Zalabak et al., 2010, p. 28.

The organisational trust dimensions or drivers, as described by Shockley-Zalabak et al.,[161] are briefly explained below.

13.1 Organisational trust dimensions definitions

The dimensions of the model for organisational trust in Figure 3.10 are described and defined below.

Competence

This refers to the ability of the organisation to adjust to the challenges of its environment. This competence is mainly the result of the capabilities of its leadership, strategies, systems and structures and the competencies of its employees.

Openness and honesty

This dimension refers to how organisations communicate and engage with their employees and stakeholders. Openness and honesty are promoted by confidence in the abilities of the leadership, regular and objective feedback on job performance, and commitment to the long-term strategic direction of the organisation.

Concerns for employees/stakeholders

According to Shockley-Zalabak,[162] employees need to trust the organisation. This can only be established if leaders and managers have a human resource orientation and are genuinely concerned about their well-being.

Reliability

The reliability dimension relates to organisational leadership and management consistency in keeping commitments based on promises made. They also need to inform employees about the reasons why certain things need to change.

Identification

The identification dimension refers to the sense of belonging that employees experience. They should accept the vision, mission and core values of the organisation and identify themselves with management and their colleagues.

---

[161] Shockley-Zalabak et al., 2010, pp. 20–43.

[162] Shockley-Zalabak et al., 2010, p. 24.

Trust, job satisfaction and effectiveness

Shockley-Zalabak[163] argue that the presence of the five dimensions above is also a strong predictor of the sixth dimension, namely, job satisfaction and organisational effectiveness. The findings have been found to be true for both profit and non-profit organisations.

Organisational trust can be regarded as a cross-cutting competence for gauging city government resilience. This statement is confirmed by Shockley-Zalabak *et al.*[164] and supported by other theorists such as Jaques[165] and Stephenson.[166]

14 BUILDING ORGANISATIONAL TRUST AS THE BASIS FOR ORGANISATIONAL RESILIENCE

Stephenson[167] posits that people inside organisations possess a substantial amount of knowledge, including tacit knowledge. Trust, according to Stephenson,[168] is "the utility through which this knowledge flows". In addition, Nonaka and Takeuchi[169] and Hausmann[170] refer in this regard to the significance of explicit, tacit and symbolic knowledge flows and know-how respectively in an organisation, and that this transfer of knowledge is usually achieved on the basis of reciprocal trust. A process of mentorship may provide a framework for transferring tacit knowledge, also known as know-how.

It is evident from Table 3.2 above[171] that in an organisation which generates paranoia, cooperation between individuals, departments and other parts of the organisation carries an additional cost of transacting. In addition, there may be time delays resulting from double-checking whether tasks have been executed as agreed. Political allegiances and power cross-pressures need to be tracked and may also create hesitation and further time delays in responding to change. In this regard, Shockley-Zalabak *et*

163 Shockley-Zalabak et al., 2010, pp. 20–43.

164 Shockley-Zalabak et al., 2010.

165 Jaques, 2013.

166 Stephenson, K. 2005b. Trafficking in trust: **The art and science of human knowledge networks.** (*In* Coughlin, L., Wingard, E. & Hollihan, K. *ed. Enlightened power*). San Francisco, CA: Jossey-Bass, pp. 242–264.

167 Stephenson, K. 2005a. *Quantum theory of trust.* New York, NY: Financial Times

168 Stephenson, 2005a, p. 34.

169 Nonaka, I. & Takeuchi, H. 1995. *The knowledge creating company.* Oxford: Oxford University Press, p. 224.

170 Hausmann, R. 2014. *Understanding South Africa's poor economic performance.* Johannesburg: Centre for Development and Enterprise (CDE).

171 Jaques, 2013, p. 16.

al.[172] point to the "myriad of financial regulations put in place because of breaches of trust". They go on to identify the cost of "organisational monitoring, surveillance systems, highly prescriptive contracts, rules and regulations, high supervisor to employee ratios, and a host of organisational processes which require resources both human and financial ... these decisions or processes are reflective of distrust". They also caution that "we are not going to argue that distrust is always wrong, but that it is fundamentally more expensive than trust".

In the South African context, building high-trust organisations may enable greater responsiveness and therefore improve general resilience. This may also have to do with avoiding or neutralising distrust and what Jaques[173] describes in Table 3.2 above as "paranoia-genic" attributes of organisations and the distrust and paranoia that they may generate. Gauging organisational trust may, therefore, be important as an indicator of resilience.

15 MOTIVATORS AND HYGIENE FACTORS AFFECTING JOB ATTITUDES

When executive leadership and executive management deal with the motivation of people in an organisation, there seems to be a bias towards remuneration or salary as the primary motivator. The research by Herzberg[174] may lead to a different conclusion (see Table 3.3). Remuneration may not be a true motivator but a so-called "hygiene factor". Herzberg's hygiene factors in his theory of motivation act like hygiene within a hospital, which, when absent, makes patients sick but in and of itself, does not create wellness. Therefore, when remuneration [salary] is perceived to be unfair, employees may become demotivated; however, it does not in and of itself motivate.

Herzberg's research has further implications for executive leadership and executive management and their impact on organisational responsiveness. Herzberg[175] identified factors that lead to extreme job satisfaction, so-called "true motivators". Executive leadership and executive management may need to first respond to these true motivators before addressing remuneration, which includes the following:

- "achievement;
- recognition;
- work Itself;

---

[172] Shockley-Zalabak et al., 2010, p. 10.

[173] Jaques, 2013, p. 16.

[174] Herzberg, F. 1987. One more time: How do you motivate employees? *Harvard Business Review,* Sept–Oct:109–120.

[175] Herzberg, 1987, pp. 110–112.

- responsibility;
- advancement; and
- growth".[176]

Herzberg's research suggests that true motivators which affect job satisfaction positively need to be well managed before considering hygiene factors such as adjusting remuneration as a way of raising job satisfaction and motivation levels. The higher the job satisfaction levels and motivation among people in an organisation, the more responsive they may be and therefore the more resilient that organisation may be. This research may be supported by the Eskom examples of "high leverage areas" for successful resilience and recovery described by Van der Merwe.[177]

Table 3.3: Factors which affect the attitudes and motivation of people

Factors affecting job attitudes as reported in 12 investigations	
Factors that led to extreme dissatisfaction (Hygiene Factors)	**Factors that led to extreme satisfaction (True Motivators)**
Company policy and administration	Achievement
Supervisor	Recognition
Relationship with supervisor	Work itself
	Responsibility
Working conditions	Advancement
Salary	Growth
Relationship with peers	
Personal life	
Relationship with subordinates	
Status	
Security	

Source: Herzberg.[178]

16   ENABLING FIT WITH THE FUTURE ENVIRONMENT(S) AS AN ORGANISATIONAL RESILIENCE STRATEGY

An effective resilience strategy may contain short-term components as well as medium and longer-term aspects. From a Darwinian point of view the

---

[176]   Herzberg, 1987, pp. 110–112.

[177]   Van der Merwe, 1991

[178]   Herzberg, 1987, p. 12.

purpose of a resilience strategy is to ensure that an organisation survives beyond a shock or a discontinuity in its environment. When there is a correspondence or fit between its resilience strategy and the challenge to its resilience, the organisation can conclude that its strategy is robust. During a shock there may be specific needs that in any event need to be anticipated and available in the form of essential reserves. These reserves may be in both tangible and intangible form, such as attitudes and embedded resilient responses.

16.1 Anticipating the need for essential reserves
During any shock to an organisation, there may need to be essential reserves on hand and available until initial adaptation has taken place and stability is re-established. These reserves may be, amongst others, water, food, energy, medical and sanitary supplies, and communications. An essential reserve may also be embedded emergency preparedness patterns of behaviour amongst the essential role players – essentially knowing what to do in the event of a shock. This reserve may be built up by regularly rehearsing the emergency preparedness drills until they are well known and may be automatically executed in the event of a shock. Anticipating the nature of a shock beyond the initial impact requires sense-making and appreciation of the systemic nature of the dynamic. Effectively anticipating may also require having in place methodological processes with respect to the anticipation process itself.

17 CHAOS, EMERGENCE AND COMPLEX SYSTEMS
Cronje[179] posits that when anticipating dynamics and shocks, there seems to be an impulse among executive leadership and executive management that favours prediction in order to achieve a perception or feeling of certainty. "Humans do not like uncertainty ... psychologists say the craving for certainty may be similar to a craving for oxygen or certain foods ... their response may be neurologically driven, a natural human reaction triggered by the fear that comes from not knowing."[180]

It may be said that dynamics in the environment are in a continuous state of flux because of their complex systemic interdependence. Gleick's[181] so-called "new science", referred to as "chaos", provides a frame of reference for sense-making within complex systems. Gleick[182] argues that –

---

[179] Cronje, F. 2017. A time traveller's guide to South Africa in 2030. Cape Town: Tafelberg, p. 27.

[180] Cronje, 2017, pp. 27, 28.

[181] Gleick, J. 1988. *Chaos: Making a new science.* New York, NY: Penguin Books.

[182] Gleick, 1988, p. 7.

"… traditionally, when physicists encountered complex results they looked for complex causes … The modern study of chaos began with the creeping realization, in the 60s, that simple mathematical equations could model systems every bit as violent as, for example, a waterfall. Tiny differences in input could quickly become overwhelming differences in output, a phenomenon given the name 'sensitive dependence on initial conditions'. In studying the weather for example, this is known as 'the butterfly effect'. The notion first discovered by Lorenz that a butterfly stirring the air today in Peking can transform storm systems next month in New York."[183]

This effect revealed the fine structure hidden within a disorderly stream of chaos.[184] Gleick's attractors described the concept of emergence. The idea of emergence based upon underlying structure has been supported by Bohm's implicate order, Mandelbrot's fractals, Smuts's holistic perspective and Forrester's systems dynamics.

Cronje[185] posits that a complex system displays four attributes:

- "it is made up of a great many participants or parts within the system;
- these participants interact with each other;
- participants direct what may be called feedback into the system; and
- a complex system has a fourth attribute in respect of the interaction between its participants; this is called an *emergent* characteristic".

Cronje[186] goes on to argue that "this emergent and chaotic property of complex systems makes any attempt at long-term forecasting very difficult. The solution lies in scenario-based strategic planning".[187]

According to Wack,[188] the purpose of a scenario-based strategy is "to shift assumptions and thinking in the minds of decision makers inside the organisation about what might happen in future outside the organisation".[189] Scenarios describe future conditions in the contextual environment in two, three or four internally consistent stories or narratives, supported by deep research.[190]

---

[183]   Gleick, 1988, pp. 7, 8.

[184]   Gleick, 1988, pp. 17, 29.

[185]   Cronje, 2017, p. 29.

[186]   Cronje, 2017, p. 30.

[187]   Cronje, 2017, pp. 29–31.

[188]   Wack, 1985a

[189]   Van der Merwe, L. 2008. Scenario-based strategy in practise: A framework. (*In* Chermack, T., *ed*. Advances in HRD. London: Sage, pp. 216-239), p. 219.

[190]   Van der Merwe, 2008, p. 232.

Van der Merwe[191] goes on to provide tests for the quality of scenarios:
- "relevant to decision makers using them;
- challenging existing thinking;
- plausibility based on deep research and analysis; and
- when an organisation has lived through the scenarios no important dynamic has been overlooked."

Van der Merwe[192] points out that the dynamics contained in scenarios may be drawn from the following categories: politics, economics, societal dynamics, technological, regulatory, ecological and historical. He posits that "the greatest learning accrues amongst the people who research the behaviour of specific dynamics in the environment" and goes on to add that "further deep learning takes place when using scenarios to stress-test or wind tunnel strategy and policy".[193] Stress-testing – also known as wind-tunnelling – a resilience strategy for fit or correspondence in future conditions [scenarios] for robustness, is analogous to testing an aircraft design in a wind tunnel.

18   RESILIENCE AS FIT
Figure 3.11 illustrates the principle of "fit", also referred to as correspondence, congruence or conformity with the future environment reflected in scenarios 1, 2, 3 and 4, in order for an organisation to survive and thrive. Ensuring fit is described in Figure 3.11 as "first-order fit", referring to the organisation's fit with futures (future environment scenarios 1, 2, 3 and 4) and "second-order fit" as the fit between the various "Key Strategy Enabling Processes" including specific subsystems such as "Managing Accountability and Performance" within an organisation.[194]

Key strategy enabling processes provide an indication of the cross-cutting competencies that may enable organisational learning and therefore are useful in supporting a scenario-based strategy process for anticipating the shocks and discontinuities that require a robust resilience strategy.

---

[191]   Van der Merwe, 2008, p. 232.

[192]   Van der Merwe, 2008.

[193]   Van der Merwe, 2008, p. 227.

[194]   Van der Merwe, 2008, p. 222.

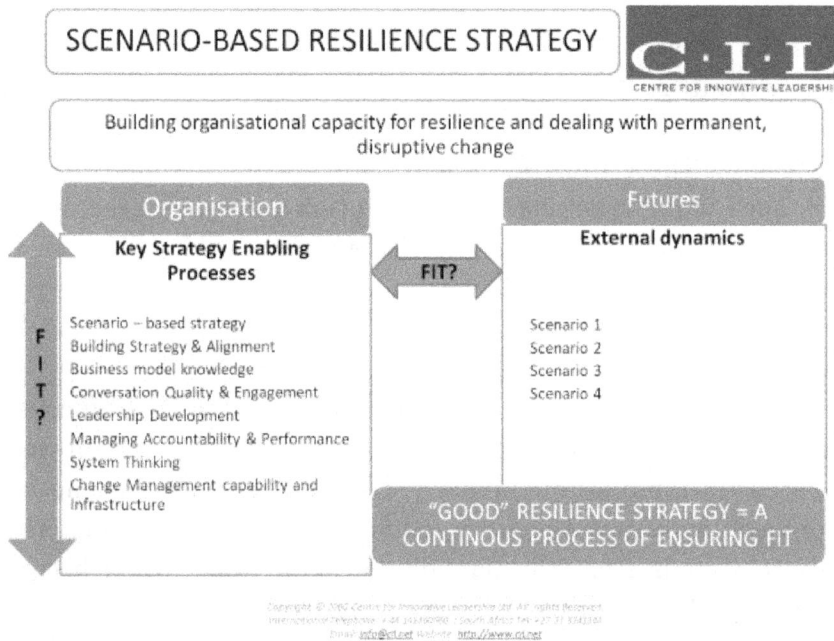

Figure 3.11: Resilience strategy as enabling fit
Source: Van der Merwe[195]

18.1 Using scenarios for stress-testing and developing robust resilience policy

Scenario-based strategy for robust policy making may be a proven way of enabling double-loop learning and dealing with an uncertain and volatile, complex future. Van der Heijden[196] points out that "the key to double-loop learning, also at an executive level, is the openness to allow incoming evidence to influence assumptions in the minds of leaders, executives and decision makers. This may shift decision making towards improved policy".[197] The foundation of a resilience strategy should be founded on anticipating discontinuities and shocks, and acting rapidly and in alignment to discontinuities and shocks.

Chermack and Van der Merwe[198] explain the basis of this:

"During this process, we may create what may be referred to as 'memory of the future' ... The trigger that seems to activate the memory of the future is contained in stress-testing or wind-tunnelling process used

---

195   Van der Merwe, 2008, p. 222.

196   Van der Merwe, 2008, p. 222.

197   Van der Heijden, 1996, p. 51.

198   Chermack, T.J. & Van der Merwe, L. 2003. The role of constructivist learning in scenario planning. *Futures,* 35:445–460, p. 449.

in testing strategies for robustness ... It is essential that during this process the 'what will we do if' question is raised while placing the resilience strategy to be tested for robustness in a specific scenario. Time paths into the future may be traced in our minds as we pose this question. These time paths may then be stored as memory and provide the capability of selective observation and rapid recognition of the unfolding dynamics in the external environment."

De Geus[199] further explains that –

"... the stored time paths serve as templates against which the incoming signals are measured. If the incoming signal fits one of the alternate time paths, the input is understood ... The message is clear ... the more memories of the future, the more open and receptive decision makers will be to signals from the outside world ... information becomes knowledge ... An organisation is not hard-wired to produce this sort of memory of the future. Management must take specific action to produce one ... this points towards using the scenario-based strategy as a means of improving an organisation's powers of perception and responsiveness ... this also explains why executive managers do not recognise external events in time to avoid crises."

An example of scenario-based strategy support for a developmental strategy and robust, resilient policy can be found in the Singapore administration. Within the scenario practitioner community, it is accepted that Singapore has successfully leveraged the value of scenario-based strategy in its development pathway from 1965 to 1990. The Singaporean administration has embedded a permanent function for scenario development and use within its government administration. The focus of the Singaporean ministry concerned is on policies that are robust in future conditions,that have high leverage for resilience and that are in the service of growing the economic wealth of Singapore. The success of the scenario-based strategy making processes is reflected in the resilience and sustained economic growth of Singapore from 1965 to 1990. "Per capita GDP in 1959 US$ 400, 1990 US$ 12,200, 1999 US$ 22,000"[200] During the leadership of Lee Kuan Yew, which may be described as servant leadership, he reminds us of a younger generation who

[199] De Geus, A. 1997. *The living company*. Boston, MA: Harvard Business School Press, pp. 36, 37.

[200] Lee, K.Y. 2000. *From Third World to First*. New York, NY: HarperCollins, p. xv.

"... took stability, growth and prosperity for granted. I wanted them to know how difficult it was for a small country of 640 sq. km with no natural resources to survive in the midst of larger, newly independent nations all pursuing nationalistic policies ... we cannot forget that public order, personal security, economic and social progress, resilience and prosperity are not the natural order of things, they depend on ceaseless effort and attention from an honest government that the people must elect."[201]

As a result of the Lee leadership between 1965 and 2000, by 2000 Singapore was positioned as globally competitive, a 35-year process. The Singapore example of scenario-based strategy informing appropriate policy is well documented.

"Singapore has been a model for all Asian countries in making the transition to a higher value service economy and ultimately to a knowledge economy. The tiny state has no natural resources to speak of save brainpower and an ability to learn ... The offshore outposts of Taiwan, Singapore and Hong Kong point to what a China, shorn of its communist legacy, can mean to the world. These are countries that have incubated a Chinese brand of capitalism ... and have succeeded famously."[202]

The Lee Kuan Yew style of leadership, together with that of Mahatma Gandhi and others, provides an example of the "personal qualities, leadership responsibilities and core values" that enable servant leadership[203] (see Figure 3.12).

19 COMPETENT, CAPABLE SERVANT LEADERSHIP

Lessons about competent servant leadership may be learnt from the leadership of Lee Kuan Yew, Oliver Tambo, Nelson Mandela, Mahatma Gandhi, Seretse Khama and Jan Smuts. We can learn from them that servant leadership may be conceptualised as the willingness, capability and capacity to take a stand for what they believe in, in the service of national interests in the present and for the future. In the case of the leadership of organisations, a stand should be taken for organisational purposes, vision or organisational interests in the widest sense. On the

---

[201] Lee, 2000, p. iii.

[202] Schwartz, P., Leyden, P. & Hyatt, J. 1999. *The long boom: A vision for the coming age of prosperity.* Reading, MA: Perseus Books, p. 128.

[203] Kleiner, A. & Roth, G. 2000. *Oil change.* Oxford: Oxford University Press, p. 108

national level, this stand and the accountability that goes with it should be informed by the supremacy of the South African Constitution.[204] The Constitution represents the shared vision for a future South Africa developed and approved by South Africans. The common denominator in the above examples of servant leadership is the leaders' ability to take a stand and the *presence* shown by their leadership, which reflects *who they are* rather than *what they do*. What they are seen to be, in terms of moral authority and their presence, is also informed by their "core value and personal qualities".[205]

Friedman[206] summarises his conceptualisation of leadership as "taking a stand". Pinpointing the focus on taking a stand "provides a systemic understanding of the essence of leadership and the position of greatest influence for leadership". He sees an organisation, or any team within it, as a chaotic human activity system which is in random motion and *needs a head*. This need can be satisfied by a person who takes a stand and holds this stand in a non-anxious manner while staying in touch with the system until that system aligns with this leadership stand. In his systemic perspective on leadership, Friedman points out that this *is all that is available* [my emphasis] to leadership.[207] Friedman reminds us that "this stand may also invite resistance and attempts at sabotage".[208] Taking a stand for what you believe may be simple but is not trivial, as there are many emotional processes and intrapersonal and interpersonal patterns of behaviour, some rooted in family systems, which may surface as a result of taking a stand. In this perspective of leadership, followership is served by the enrolment of followers through leadership. Followers are invited to enrol, literally to place their names on the shared list, for supporting the vision of what the leadership may want to create. During this process, the leader serves the followers, enabling them to enrol in building a shared vision. This process of building a "shared vision" is one of "the five disciplines for building learning organisations, together with Personal Mastery, Mental Models, Team Learning and Systems Thinking".[209] Senge goes on to emphasise that "to practise a discipline is to be a lifelong learner on a developmental path.

---

[204] South Africa. 1996. *Constitution of the Republic of South Africa, 1996.* Pretoria: Government Printer.

[205] Kleiner & Roth, 2000, p. 108.

[206] Friedman, E.H. 1985. *Generation to generation: Family process in church and synagogue.* New York, NY: Guildford Press, pp. 227–240.

[207] Friedman, E.H. 1986. Rabbi, Edwin Friedman [professional conversation]. Spiritual Counselling practise, Bethesda, MD.

[208] Friedman, 1986.

[209] Senge, 1990, p. 6

A discipline is not simply a 'subject of study'. It is a body of technique, based on some underlying theory or understanding of the world that must be studied and mastered and put into practise".[210] He describes enrolment as the leadership process where members of an organisation are enabled to choose to be part of a shared vision, and alignment as the organisation's capacity to act together. According to Senge,[211] building shared vision and alignment rests on the discipline of "Personal [Self] Mastery".

In this context, leadership is conceptualised as influence potential. Leadership, as opposed to the leader, may be seen as a distributed dynamic throughout an organisation, where everybody exercises leadership by taking a stand based on a shared vision. According to Kleiner and Roth,[212] in a generic leadership model (see Figure 3.12) "Leadership Responsibilities" include:

- "building shared vision;
- creating capacity to act;
- thinking and acting systemically;
- conversation quality and engagement to build alignment;
- sustainability and resilience;
- good governance systems and compliance;
- engaging and involving others as coach, mentor and educator; and
- building and rebuilding feedback processes".[213]

Leadership theory and practice as *presence* is arrived at through a systemic perspective based on what leadership must *be* or their "Being"[214] (see Figure 3.12). What leadership must be can be embodied in the example they set for their followers. In this model of leadership, moral authority and social capital or trust capital play an important role in developing a leader's capacity to influence followership. Mahatma Gandhi insisted that leadership should be the change they wished to create. His Satyagraha, or passive, non-violent resistance, demonstrates the powerful influence of taking a stand. For Gandhi, during his defeat of the British occupying India, leverage lay in steadfastly refusing to move from this stand or strike back, while staying in touch with the system he led until the system aligned with the stand. This approach to servant leadership requires personal qualities such as:

---

[210] Senge, 1990 p. 7.

[211] Senge, 1990 p. 6.

[212] Kleiner, A. & Roth, G. 2000. *Oil change.* Oxford: Oxford University Press, p. 108.

[213] Kleiner & Roth, 2000, p. 108.

[214] Kleiner & Roth, 2000, p. 108.

- "commitment to the truth;
- courage;
- humility;
- openness;
- compassion;
- authenticity; and
- integrity".[215]

Gandhi's servant leadership – taking a stand on a national level – was first pioneered in South Africa and later exercised in India to overthrow the British Empire in India. Because of its power, efficiency and influence, servant leadership in the form of passive, non-violent resistance has been emulated by other civil rights leaders such as Martin Luther King Jnr. and Nelson Mandela, with similar results in terms of positive influence and change.

The Proposed Leadership Model displayed in Figure 3.12 was initially developed by line management in an energy company in the USA. According to this model, "Personal Qualities (*Being*), Leadership Responsibilities (*Doing*), Core Values and Leadership Development Results" concentrates the complementary components of leadership in one interconnected space.[216]

In 1945 Japan was devastated when the USA detonated two nuclear bombs on the cities of Nagasaki and Hiroshima. This catastrophe precipitated an unconditional national surrender which ended Japan's engagement in the second world war. The adaptation and recovery by organisations, cities and the nation as a whole provide an example of collective leadership, alignment building and a resilience strategy that transformed society. This resilience strategy provides an example of embedding leadership and learning as the vehicle for continuous improvement in the quality of products and services in organisations. Japanese national leadership, under the governorship of General McArthur of the United States Army, subsequently embarked on a nationwide recovery and sustainable economic development process based on a resilient industrial strategy. The strategic priority was to deliberately create an industry culture of adopting best practice in statistical quality control management from across the world and, accordingly, raising the quality of goods and services over the next 50 years. Deming, an American statistician, was deployed to Japan to support this industrial transformation.[217] The Japanese industrial

---

[215] Kleiner & Roth, 2000, p. 108.

[216] Kleiner & Roth, 2000, p. 108.

[217] Deming, W.E. 1986. *Out of the crisis.* Cambridge, MA: MIT Press.

Personal Qualities
Commitment to the truth
Courage to take a stand
Openness
Compassion
Humility
Authenticity
Integrity

Being

Leadership Responsibilities
Building Shared Vision
Creating as well as responding to the future that is based on a clear vision which is aligned with the national and organisation's vision.
Creating the Capacity to Act
Building an environment including rewards and recognition systems, in which learning promotes both personal growth and organisational self-renewal. Setting clear direction and achieving alignment.
Thinking and Acting Systemically
Understanding complexity and interconnectedness – how the parts fit with the whole. Identifying the leverage areas in the system. Avoiding unintended consequences. Taking the long view by using a scenario-based strategy approach.
Conversation Quality and Engagement to build Alignment
Engagement in generative conversations that strengthen understanding and commitment to the larger purpose of the organisation.
Sustainability and Resilience
Lifelong learning, lowest possible cost i.t.o. carbon footprint, financial costs and time spent. Enabling early detection of error and the capacity for self-correcting.
Good Governance Systems and Compliance with them
National, organisational and community best practice governance systems and processes for encouragement and enforcement of compliance
Engaging and Involving Others as a Coach, Mentor, and Educator Demonstrating belief in the people of the organisation by giving them the freedom to create – and the accountability for producing – quality results. Creating an environment of inclusion.
Building and Rebuilding Feedback Processes

Doing

Core Values
Belief in people
Trustworthiness
Grassroots
Engagement
Excellence
Innovation
Sense of Urgency

Leadership Dev. Results
Competence-based dev.
Personal, org., national
Transformation
Results-based Performance
Individual, org capacity bldg
Continuous improvement

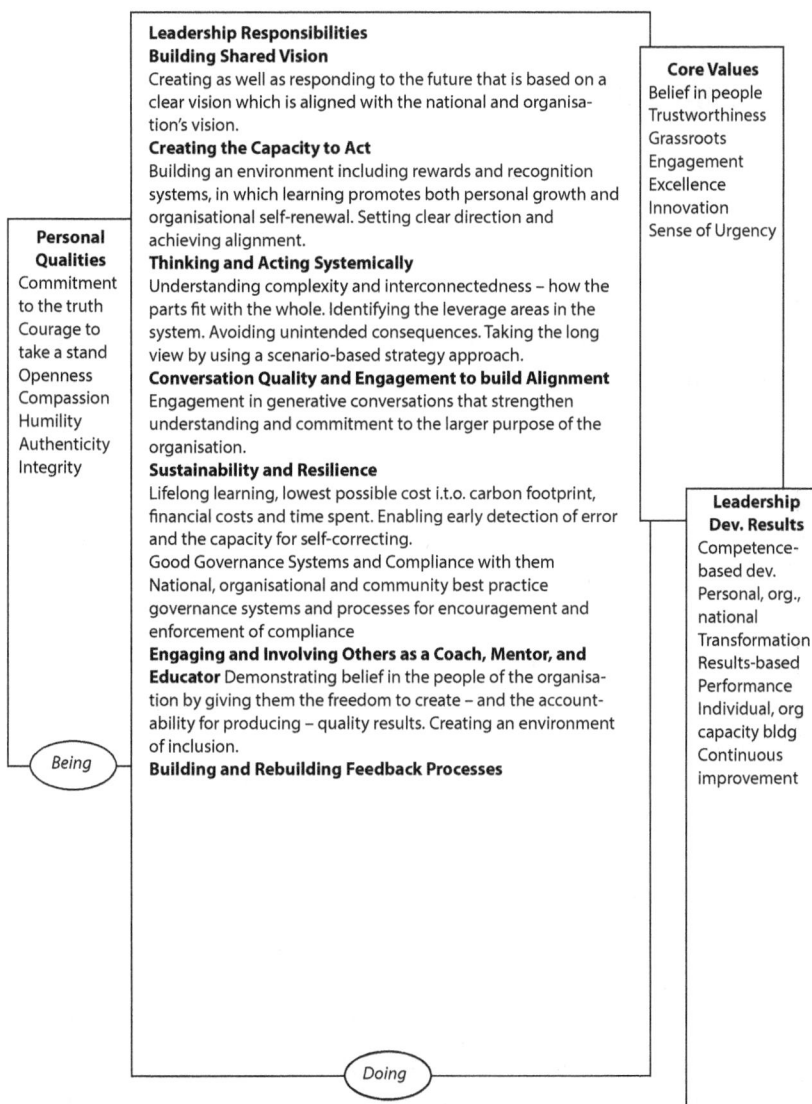

Figure 3.12: Proposed leadership model
Source: Based on Kleiner and Roth.[218]

resilience strategy and competitiveness were built on leadership which stood for eliminating wastage and continuous improvement in quality, based on a profound understanding of customer needs. Inclusive worker-driven processes, such as total quality control (TQC) and Kaizen provided a vehicle for structured innovation to better satisfy customers' needs at a lower cost. The above principles of leadership and learning have been applied in organisations and cities and at national levels.

An important part of the Japanese resilience strategy was to build

---

[218] Kleiner & Roth, 2000, p. 108.

organisational change management infrastructure to ensure that the process could be sustained over decades until the new culture was successfully embedded. Cross-functional quality councils were established in all organisations to oversee and hold the know-how for continuous quality improvement as part of successful organisational change. This infrastructure was utilised until the new way of customer-focused thinking (a new paradigm) was embedded in the culture of organisations. The Union of Japanese Scientists and Engineers (JUSE) supported the establishment of quality councils which held the knowledge for organisation-wide quality improvement. Quality was redefined as "fit for purpose". Major corporations in Japan contributed to JUSE and participated in its annual quality awards. The "Deming Prize", named in honour of Dr W. Edwards Deming for supporting the Japanese organisations in their nationwide transformation, is the apex national annual quality award. A systems approach to quality improvement and value-for-money paradigm is now firmly established within Japanese manufacturing and nationally, embodied in the quality of the products it produces. The systemic nature of the resilience strategy that transformed the Japanese industrial system is often taken for granted. This transformation took place within an economy on a small group of islands collectively the size of one of the South African provinces, with no natural resources other than its people and their willingness to lead by taking a stand and learning, as well as everybody taking personal responsibility for the success of their economic transformation in the interests of building global competitiveness.

In areas in South Africa where service delivery requires improvement, leadership by taking a stand together with learning principles for the continuous elimination of wastage and improvement of quality, as outlined above, may be applied. This may be done in the service of raising service delivery quality while at the same time reducing cost by eliminating wastage. Adopting a multifaceted approach points towards a systemic or holistic resilience strategy providing the key to success.

The Japanese example focuses on a system-wide, holistic approach to resilience strategy that is focused on organisations, recovering devastated cities and national alignment and knowledge-sharing for rebuilding. The key components of the strategy in this example illustrate a process of initial adaptation – building know-how and infrastructure for continuous improvement in quality to facilitate recovery and sustainable economic development. Since the 1945 use of nuclear weapons, nuclear materials and know-how have become more widely available, foreshadowing the inevitability of another nuclear detonation on a major metropolis, which now seems to be regarded by respected leaders as predetermined.

20 PREDETERMINED DYNAMICS IMPACTING ON CITY GOVERNMENT

Schwab[219] asserts that there are 23 deep shifts which will disrupt countries and cities globally. The deep shifts he describes (see Tables 4.15 and 4.16) will, according to Schwab, disrupt many of the key aspects of cities, such as energy use, transportation and governance. Many of these disruptions – for example, super-computing capability together with the massive free storage which enables the widely distributed sensors referred to as the IoT – may positively enable city government resilience such as the "antifragile" phenomenon described by Taleb.[220] Whybrow[221] points towards the need for re-tuning the human mind at scale among people currently living on the planet. He argues that there is an urgent need to influence assumptions and paradigms so that they will enable instead of dis-able global resilience and sustainable living. In agreement with Von Bertalanffy[222] he questions whether the human species will be able to survive if these changes in the human mind do not take place at scale.

Katz and Bradley[223] draw attention to the impending "metropolitan revolution, how cities and metros are fixing our broken national politics and fragile [and unsustainable] economy". They go on to argue that metros are more agile than nation states because they are the government front line and in direct contact with the citizenry. They argue that they are already in the process of *adaptation* [my emphasis] to discontinuities such as climate volatility and the disruptors contained in the Fourth Industrial Revolution. Metros such as Amsterdam, Singapore and others are using these predetermined disruptors as a platform for moving rapidly to sustainable development, green growth and smart cities.

Among others, the following dynamics in the current and future environment were predetermined from the literature study conducted and are therefore described in some detail below. As they seem certain to occur and may affect city government, they should be treated as predetermined dynamics that could challenge city government resilience. They include –

- living beyond the limits that planet earth may be able to support;[224]
- technology convergence by numerous deep shifts contained in the

---

[219] Schwab, K. 2016b. *The Fourth Industrial Revolution.* Geneva: World Economic Forum.

[220] Taleb, 2012

[221] Whybrow, 2015

[222] Von Bertalanffy, L. 1968. *General systems theory: Foundation development and applications.* New York, NY: George Braziller.

[223] Katz, B. & Bradley, J. 2013. *The Metropolitan revolution: How cities and metros are fixing our broken politics and fragile economy.* Washington, DC: The Brookings Institution.

[224] Meadows, D.H. 1993. *Beyond the limits.* Post Mills, VT: Chelsea Green Publishing.

Fourth Industrial Revolution described by Schwab;[225]
- cyberattack(s) on ICT [information and communication technology] infrastructure;[226]
- migration to cities;[227]
- viral attacks;
- nuclear detonations and terrorist attacks; and
- climate volatility.[228]

The above dynamics may be included in a scenario development process for the purposes of anticipation. Anticipation may also use SD modelling to anticipate the above dynamics as they are predetermined and require in-depth analysis. This analysis should extend beyond the time horizon that scenario planning may achieve, but is nevertheless necessary as a planning time horizon of 20- to 25 years for executive leadership and executive managers in a large organisation such as city government.

In 1972 the earth was viewed holistically by Meadows[229] and was modelled as one globally interconnected system. Global dynamics were modelled using Forrester's[230] SD modelling tool. This tool was used to *anticipate* discontinuities in the environment and to ask a key question: How long can the human population on the planet continue to use its resources in the current manner? The findings were published in what has become known as "the Club of Rome Report".[231] This report shows a convergence in population size and the consumption of major resources and a crisis for unsustainable living on the planet earth in the timeframe 2020 to 2030. In the 30-year synopsis and update, Meadows, Randers and Meadows[232] report that all the major dynamics in the 1972 SD model were on track as modelled. This demonstrates the robustness of SD modelling in time frames exceeding ten years. Meadows argues that the population and its consumption of resources were already "beyond the limits" of what the earth could sustain. She goes on to assert that currently 1.5 earths are

---

[225] Schwab, 2014 not in reference list please insert correct reference

[226] Center for Strategic and International Studies (CSIS). 2008. Commission on Cybersecurity for the 44th Presidency. Washington, DC: Centre for Strategic International Studies.

[227] Katz & Bradley, 2013

[228] Intergovernmental Panel on Climate Change (IPCC). 2014. Climate Change 2014. Synthesis Report. Geneva, Switzerland: IPCC

[229] Meadows, D.H., Meadows, D.L., Randers, J. & Behrens III, W.W. 1972. *Limits to growth.* London: Pan Books.

[230] Forrester, J.W. 1969. *Urban dynamics.* Cambridge, MA: MIT Press

[231] Meadows *et al.,* 1972

[232] Meadows, D.H., Randers, J. & Meadows, D.L. 2004. *A synopsis – Limits to growth: The 30 year update.* Post Mills, VT: Chelsea Green.

required to sustainably support the population already born and living on the planet. Meadows argues that the earth's population is now beyond the limits.[233] In the African context, the large number of young people below the age of 24 forms part of the challenging demographic.

The Sustainable Development Goals (SGDs), the Paris Agreement 2015 and the Sendai Framework for disaster risk reduction 2015–2030 were integrated with the UNISDR Strategy Framework 2016–2021.[234] These UNISDR initiatives could provide both goal setting and review processes in striving for global sustainability and city resilience.

The so-called predetermined dynamics above may have an impact on a resilience strategy. Capability and developing the cross-cutting enabling competencies that support the development of capability may be the functional starting point for effectively building a resilience strategy.

21 RATIONALE FOR EXTENDING THE AAR FRAMEWORK

The purpose of developing a diagnostic instrument is to provide macro- and micro-feedback loops which enable learning and high leverage action to raise organisational resilience. Executive leaders and executive managers in organisations using the instrument should have an inclusive, holistic perspective for gauging the resilience of their organisations to ensure that key dynamics are not overlooked against the broad spectrum of plausible futures. Designing a framework for gauging resilience should factor in Mouton's[235] warning that "obtaining valid constructs in social research is difficult". Accordingly, the Marcos and Macauley[236] AAR framework provids a useful starting point. Extending into interconnected dynamics that may plausibly challenge resilience in the foreseeable future may increase the value of the instrument. The need for sustainable development, the advantages of circular economics and green growth, and the possibility of leveraging technology convergence to build smart cities are closely connected and may be predetermined dynamics. Challenges to organisational resilience may be located along a continuum, reflected by the so-called "systems thinking iceberg". The iceberg analogy separates different observed levels of dynamics in the environment that may influence resilience in "events, patterns of behaviour over time and the

---

[233] Meadows, 1993

[234] United Nations International Strategy for Disaster Reduction (UNISDR). 2016a.

[235] Mouton, J. 1996. *Understanding social research*. Pretoria: Van Schaik, p. 128.

[236] Marcos, J. & Macaulay, S. 2008. *Organisation resilience: The key to anticipation, adaptation and recovery*. Cranfield School of Management http://www.som.cranfield.ac.uk/som/ dinamic-content/cced/documents/org.pdf Date of access: 26 March 2015.

structure of systems".[237] This separation clarifies the potential duration and magnitude of the impact of the resilience challenges. Van der Merwe[238] explains that the value of using the iceberg analogy is that it reminds us powerfully that uncovering patterns and structure is difficult as they may be found below the waterline and, using the iceberg analogy, may be difficult to uncover. Events, on the other hand, are above the waterline and most often what we readily observe and react to. Enabling resilience requires sense-making of unfolding patterns and understanding systemic structure to enable high leverage interventions that ensure organisational resilience. Table 3.4 provides a taxonomy of resilience dynamics. The proposed taxonomy describes the duration and magnitude, as well as numerous past and emergent examples, for each level.

Table 3.4: Proposed taxonomy of resilience dynamics and potential impact

Category level	Duration	Magnitude	Past and emerging examples
Event level impact	Instantaneous	Localised	Terror attacks, cyberattacks
Pattern level impact	Cyclical, breaching of thresholds	Regional, sectoral	Migration to cities, droughts, climate change
Structural change or disruption	Permanent, disruptive	Global including national, regional and cities	Technology convergence, disruptions to transportation and energy

Source: Author's research

One example of an events-level shock and challenge to resilience along this continuum is the 9/11 terror attack on the New York World Trade Center. It is widely accepted among global scenario-planning practitioners that there are additional examples of potentially high impact events that may occur in future such as "a nuclear detonation on a major metropolis",[239] cyberattacks on information technology (IT) infrastructure[240] and an electromagnetic shock (EMS) that seriously damages electricity generation,

---

[237] Van der Merwe, 2008, p. 221.

[238] Van der Merwe, 2008.

[355] Buffett, W. 2002. *Nuclear attack 'virtually a certainty'* https://www.google.co.za/search?rlz=1C2NHXL_enZA697ZA697&source=hp&q=Berkshire+Hathaway+Chief+Executive%2C+Buffet+nuclear+detonation&oq=Berkshire+Hathaway+Chief+Executive%2C+Buffet+nuclear+detonation&gs_l =psy-ab.12...3825.14098.0.16754.20.20.0.0.0.0.427. 3611. 2-10j1j2.13.0....0...1.1.64.psy-ab..7.10.2553 ...33i160k1j33i21k1.G8fg_R-uYc0 Date of access: 21 June 2016.

[240] Center for Strategic and International Studies (CSIS). 2008.

152

distribution and transmission infrastructure.[241]

Examples of patterns of behaviour over time that may challenge organisational resilience and that may also reach critical thresholds include extreme climate volatility resulting in hurricanes, water- and food insecurity, a viral attack on humanity of the magnitude of the Spanish influenza of 1918, and rapid urbanisation to African and other global cities. Mills and Trott[242] posit that by 2050, 80% of all people living on the African continent will be living in cities. Brand[243] insists that the rapid global migration to cities may be "the defining characteristic of the 21st century". He goes on to make the link between the dominance of western cities such as New York, London, Paris, Berlin, Frankfurt, Stockholm and Rome and western global dominance per se. He posits that as eastern cities such as Tokyo, Singapore, Shanghai, Mumbai, Beijing and others emerge, dominance may be shifting towards the east.

There may also be structural or systemic (these two words are used interchangeably) challenges to organisational resilience such as the "technology convergence".[244] Examples of disruption at a structural level come from Seba,[245] whose analysis of technology-based disruption points out that disruption takes place "when a combination and convergence of technologies makes it possible, through innovation, for entrepreneurs to create new markets".[246] These forces may also significantly transform or destroy existing products, market categories and entire industries. He specifically identifies energy and transportation disruptions. In his conference presentation, Seba[247] also provides projections based on technology cost curves, business model innovation and product innovation. His analyses posit that by 2030–2050 and beyond:

- "all new energy will be provided by solar or wind;
- all new mass-market vehicles will be electric;
- most of these vehicles will be autonomous (self-driving) or semi-autonomous;

[241]   *Economist.* 2017. The world if 2017: Electromagnetic Shock. http://worldif.economist.com/article/13526/electromagnetic-shock Date of access: 20 September 2017.

[242]   Mills, G. & Trott, W. 2015. *Poles of prosperity or slums of despair: The future of African cities.* Johannesburg: The Brenthurst Foundation.

[243]   Brand, S. 2017a. 4 Environmental heresies. TED Talk. https://www.ted.com/talks/stewart_brand_proclais_4_environm Date of access: 4 July 2017.

[244]   Schwab, 2016a.

[245]   Seba, T. 2016. Why energy and transportation will be obsolete by 2030. Keynote presentation at the Swedbank Nordic Energy Summit in Oslo, Norway. https://www.youtube.com/watch?v=2b3ttqYDwF0 Date of access: 21 July 2017.

[246]   Seba, 2016.

[247]   Seba, 2016.

- the car market will shrink by 80%;
- gasoline will be obsolete; nuclear is already obsolete; natural gas and coal will be obsolete;
- up to 80% of highways will not be needed;
- up to 80% of parking spaces will not be needed;
- the concept of individual car ownership will be obsolete;
- the car insurance industry will be disrupted; and
- the taxi industry will be obsolete".[248]

Seba's analysis, which he calls "clean disruption",[249] makes a case for disruptions that, in terms of Taleb's antifragile theory,[250] may enable organisations to gain from the disorder that results from the disruptions Seba describes. These disruptions may, over time, enable adaptation, recovery, sustainable development, green growth and smart organisations. Anticipation processes which provide a planning focus in the 20- to 25-year range, such as scenario-based strategy and SD modelling, may be required to anticipate resilience challenges.

From systems theory we know that time delays can result in a propensity for a system to overshoot or undershoot, resulting in disruption and underlining the need for anticipating discontinuities before they occur. Time delays, such as the time it takes to retrain people whose jobs have been made redundant, pose a specific systemic challenge for organisations. For another example, structural or systemic instability in electrical energy supply versus demand is a case in point for the propensity to undershoot or overshoot. It takes approximately 15 years from designing a power station concept to building a modern 3500 megawatt, coal-fired power station and starting to transmit energy. Electricity demand closely follows economic growth. If an electricity utility is to match supply with demand, this time delay in bringing additional capacity online – on time and on quality (and safely) – requires anticipating the economic growth 15 years in advance. The propensity to overshoot or undershoot may be structurally or systemically part of this industry. So long as the business model for energy generation and distribution remains as is, with large generation plants built to distribute electricity via long-distance transmission and local, municipal distribution networks, this may be true. Subsequently, technology convergence, together with the development of renewable energy resources such as the storage photovoltaic collectors and wind energy

---

[248] Seba, 2016.

[249] Seba, 2016.

[250] Taleb, 2012

154

underway, may initially disrupt this industry, resulting in the medium- to long term in a more reliably distributed, "clean" and sustainable energy system – hence supporting Taleb's "antifragility" notion. Interdependence and the need for fit between organisations and their environment fulfils the need to anticipate and adapt to events that may affect them. Patterns of behaviour over time also require adaptation as well as adjustments in development priorities in order to recover and survive intact.

Leveraging a discontinuity to enable recovery or springing back to accelerate sustainable development can be enabled by state-of-the-art, thoughtful anticipation processes such as scenario-based strategy and SD models. Thus, sustainable development may provide an economic base and a platform from which to enable green growth and smart cities.

Climate change, terror attacks and technology convergence disruptions are treated here as predetermined forces that will most likely affect organisations and challenge their resilience in the next 20- to 25 years, in some cases resulting in antifragility and, accordingly, improving whole systems.

22 TOWARDS AN INCLUSIVE, HOLISTIC FRAMEWORK FOR ORGANISATIONAL RESILIENCE

Predetermined dynamics that may challenge organisational resilience exist along the continuum of *events* (e.g. viral, nuclear, terrorist or cyberattacks), *patterns of behaviour* (climate volatility and its consequences) and *structural* challenges such as the technology convergence consisting of a number of deep shifts contained in the Fourth Industrial Revolution described by Schwab[251] and the consequences in energy and transportation for city government resilience as pinpointed by Seba.[252]

The predetermined forces described above may have an impact on organisations along the continuum of events, patterns of behaviour and systemic structure and form a basis for extending the AAR meta-framework to include sustainable development, green growth and smart cities. Capability (C), Cross-cutting Competencies (CC), Anticipation (An), Adaptation (Ad), Recovery (R) and Sustainable Development (SDev), Green Growth (GG) and Smart Organisations (SO) and, in the case of metros, Smart Cities (SC) form a comprehensive, holistic and functional framework along the continuum of dynamics that have an impact on organisational resilience.

---

[251] Schwab, K. 2016b. *The Fourth Industrial Revolution.* Geneva: World Economic Forum
[252] Seba, 2016

Meta-framework:

A meta-framework is used here to describe the overarching structure of factors and descriptions. Items that fall within these factors are grouped together based on their relevance to a specific factor within the overall meta-framework. The factors within the meta-framework are listed below.

- Capability (C)
- Cross-cutting Competencies (CC)
- Anticipation (An)
- Adaptation (Ad)
- Recovery (R)
- Sustainable Development (SDev)
- Green Growth (GG)
- Smart Organisations (SO) and Smart Cities (SC)

The meta-framework is abbreviated as C, CC, An, Ad, R, SDev, GG, SO and SC.

Functional framework for resilience C, CC, An, Ad, R, SDev, GG and SC for gauging organisational and city government resilience

The functional framework examines the purpose of the various factors and items in the diagnostic instrument. It underlines the need to view resilience holistically and as interconnected along a continuum from events that may challenge resilience through patterns of behaviour to structural, systemic shifts that may challenge resilience. National resilience and city government organisational resilience are also seen as overlapping and interdependent.

Functional analysis of a resilient city government

The modern government consists of the rule of law, accountability and capability.[253] [254] A constitution, when treated as the supreme determinant and code of legal behaviour, provides the foundation for the rule of law. Accountability for government means compliance with the rule of law. Capability may be conceptualised as "leadership, strategy and delivery".[255] The APSC[256] points out that "[t]he Australian Public Service (APS) needs to build and sustain organisational capability to respond effectively (and at

---

[253] Fukuyama, F. 2011a. *The origins of political order: From pre-human times to the French Revolution.* New York, NY: FSG.

[254] Fukuyama, F. 2011b. *Political order and political decay: From the Industrial Revolution to the globalisation of democracy.* New York, NY: FSG.

[255] APSC 2017a

[256] APSC 2017a

pace) to contemporary needs, to build capability in advance of need when emerging needs can be reasonably anticipated, and to establish resilience to cope well with the unexpected."

According to the Australian Public Service Commission:[257]

"Organisational capability extends beyond the capability of employees. It combines people skills with the organisation's processes, systems, culture and structures to deliver business outcomes. People and systems – whether ICT, financial or workforce planning – need to be consciously aligned to corporate outcomes and priorities and lines of accountability for the performance of systems will be clear. Governance systems need to ensure that large projects are managed with a strong emphasis on effective risk management. There must also be a focus on project implementation, supported by coordinated implementation strategies, the development of project management capability, and adequate business continuity planning".

The APSC goes on to explain that "[l]eadership consists of setting direction, motivating people and developing people. Strategy consists of scenario-based strategy, outcomes-focused strategy, evidence-based choices, collaborating and building common purpose. Finally, delivery consists of goal setting and managing performance, shared commitment and sound delivery models, planning, resourcing, innovative delivery".[258]

In further extensions to the AAR starting point, Fukuyama[259] [260] pinpoints capability as one of three key aspects, namely, the rule of law, accountability and capability that enable modern government. Capability, as conceptualised by the APSC, may be developed by enabling cross-cutting competencies. Therefore, capability and cross-cutting competencies are added as prerequisites for a resilience strategy and further extend the AAR framework. The factors in the meta-framework that may influence city government resilience are subsequently described as a basis for diagnosis:

- **Capability (C):** Capability as comprised of *leadership, strategy and delivery.* [261] Capability may be summarised as the ability to formulate robust strategy and policy and to execute these on time, on budget and on quality.
- **Cross-cutting competencies (CC):** Cross-cutting competencies underpin capability and may include those competencies that support

---

[257] APSC 2017a

[258] APSC 2017a

[259] Fukuyama, 2011a

[260] Fukuyama, 2011b

[261] APSC 2017a

high leverage points across the factors that enable a resilience strategy – A, A, R, SDev, GG, and SC.

- **Anticipation (An):** Anticipating immediate short-term shocks, as well as medium- and long term shocks. Scenario-based strategy enables shifting assumptions in the minds of executive leadership, executive managers and decision makers. In addition, SD modelling can be used to understand dynamics up to and including a 20- to 25-year planning time horizon.
- **Adaptation (Ad):** Absorbing short-term shocks by ensuring that water, food and effective communications are available to coordinate adaptation activities, as well as starting the process of adapting to shocks that may persist in the medium- and long term. In addition, resolution of key leadership tensions and taking an unambiguous stand for a policy that supports recovery, sustainable development, green growth and smart cities.
- **Recovery (R):** Springing back to the position that prevailed prior to the shock. There may be established change management infrastructure such as a strategy, leadership and engagement (SLE) forum. Building shared vision and a sense of urgency led by a powerful, inclusive coalition which regularly engages in the SLE strategic conversation. The SLE delivers short-term wins for the resilience strategy as well as the institutional capability to sustain recovery and embark upon sustainable development initiatives. High organisational trust enables responsiveness, agility and resilience.
- **Sustainable Development (SDev):** Compliance with the SGDs, the Paris Agreement 2015 and the Sendai Framework for disaster risk reduction 2015–2030 as well as integration with the UNISDR Strategy Framework 2016–2021;[262] enrolment in the global city mayoral parliament resolutions; focused engagement with the National Development Plan (NDP) and municipal mandate for development; small, micro and medium enterprise (SMME) development; engaging communities, including youth, in sustainable community investment programme (SCIP) development initiatives, including service delivery; attracting and nurturing talent; and enhancing education and learning quality through teacher development support.
- **Green Growth (GG):** Beyond sustainable development, there is movement towards zero carbon emissions; industrial ecological interconnectedness towards circular economics; recycling of waste as feedstock and improved utilisation of natural resources through

---

262   United Nations International Strategy for Disaster Reduction (UNISDR). 2016a

beneficiation; continuously reducing carbon footprints and reduction of consumption patterns.

- **Smart Cities (SC):** Technology-enabled, emphasising ICT-enabled cities. Leveraging relevant deep shifts[263] applicable to cities to enable smart cities; enabled by e-governance competencies; leveraging technology convergence driven disruptions to enable antifragility properties.

There are items within each factor which form part of the meta-factors framework in the diagnostic instrument. This diagnostic process provides the basis for learning and adjusting in high leverage areas through the skilful use of the proposed diagnostic instrument and double-loop learning. It should be noted that it is beyond the scope of this research to develop an instrument for gauging city government resilience that has been calibrated statistically for reliability and validity.

23 SYNOPSIS OF ORGANISATIONAL RESILIENCE DIMENSIONS

An organisation may be viewed as an ecology of human activity. Organisations, when viewed holistically, need to be led and engaged in the service of building an organisational resilience strategy. All the important interdependent aspects of organisational behaviour that affect resilience should be considered and the highest leverage areas identified to build organisational resilience with an economy of means.

Gibson and Tarrant[264] pinpoint capability as being central to a resilience strategy and provide a range of conceptual models for such a strategy. In their triangle model in Figure 3.1 which identifies resources and infrastructure capabilities, they summarise the process capabilities and leadership, people and knowledge capability at the interface between a cycle of fitness for purpose, flexibility, capacity and tenacity and the context of the organisation. Denyer[265] points towards the management and leadership responses contained in the organisational resilience tension quadrant in Figure 3.3 and goes on to identify managerial dilemmas and responses in Figure 3.4. Meadows[266] provides a systemic definition of resilience as feedback loops. In their Resilient Organisation Research Programme, the universities of Canterbury and Auckland[267] identified three clusters in terms of which resilience can be gauged, namely, leadership and culture, networks and relationships and change-ready clusters (see Figure 3.5).

---

[263] Schwab, 2016b

[264] Gibson & Tarrant, 2010

[265] Denyer, 2017, p. 9.

[266] Meadows, 2008, p. 76.

[267] Universities of Canterbury/Auckland.2017

Schools of thought on resilience strategy are identified in terms of a rationalist paradigm, an evolutionary paradigm, a processual paradigm[268] a social justice evolution paradigm,[269] a self-organising system paradigm[270] and an antifragile paradigm.[271] Organisational resilience may be framed as a learning process. Models for learning include Kolb's[272] experiential learning. In addition, Argyris[273] describes single-loop and double-loop learning, with Sterman[274] identifying learning disabilities. Capacity limits on the effectiveness of learning may be governed by conversation quality and engagement for competent leadership.[275] TQM and Kaizen are described as double-loop learning that challenges organisational thinking and assumptions and enables quality improvement as continuous learning and structured innovation.[276] Re-tuning the human mind at scale to enable sustainable development is advocated.[277]

Stratified theory on the requisite organisation specifies seven levels of hierarchy and a planning time horizon of 20- to 25 years within a total organisational system description[278]. Scenario-based strategy enables double-loop learning.[279] Jaques[280] and Shockley-Zalabak et al.[281] identify organisational trust as an enabler of responsiveness and, through this, organisational resilience. Resilience is the first-order fit with the future contextual environment. Second-order fit may be described as the fit between strategy enabling processes and cross-cutting competencies, such as scenario-based strategy, building strategy and alignment, leadership development, conversation quality and engagement, management of accountability, performance systems thinking and change management infrastructure.[282] Competent servant leadership is described in terms of displaying presence. Servant leadership is underpinned by leadership

[268] Van der Heijden, 1996, p. 23–26.

[269] Laloux, 2014a , p. 43

[270] Senge et al., 1994.

[271] Taleb, 2012, p. 17.

[272] Kolb, 2008, p. 42–68.

[273] Argyris, 1992.

[274] Sterman, 2000, p. 16.

[275] Van der Merwe et al., 2007.

[276] Morgan, 1997, pp. 93, 94.

[277] Whybrow, 2015.

[278] Jacques, 2002b

[279] Van der Merwe, 2008.

[280] Jaques, 2013, p. 5.

[281] Shockley-Zalabak et al., 2010, p. 20–43.

[282] Van der Merwe, 2008, p. 222.

responsibilities and competencies such as building a shared vision, creating the capacity to act, thinking and acting systemically, conversation quality and engagement for building alignment, sustainability and resilience, good governance systems, engaging and involving others as a coach, mentor and educator (to build capacity), building and rebuilding feedback processes,[283] and taking a stand.[284] Capability is defined as the power to do or achieve goals,[285] and organisational resilience is conceptualised as the ability to formulate robust plans and policy and to execute such plans on time, on budget and on quality.

The Japanese resilience strategy that followed the nuclear bombing of Nagasaki and Hiroshima initiated an industrial resilience strategy which developed a process methodology total quality control (TQM) and Kaizen.[286] Continuous improvement is defined as "a system for producing economically the goods and services that satisfy customer needs".[287]

The rationale for extending the AAR framework may be located in predetermined challenges to resilience emanating from events such as, among others, terror attacks, patterns of behaviour over time such as climate volatility, and structural dynamics such as energy and transportation disruptions,[288] as well as technology convergence within the so-called Fourth Industrial Revolution.[289] An extended holistic functional analysis to gauge organisational and city government resilience includes capability which consists of leadership taking a stand, scenario-based strategy and service delivery. Capabilities are underpinned by capacity building in cross-cutting competencies which enable anticipation, adaptation, recovery, sustainable development, green growth and smart cities – abbreviated as C, CC, An, Ad, R, SDev, GG, SC.

24 CONCLUSION

The purpose of this chapter was to describe the paradigmatic developments, schools of thinking, theoretical principles, theories and models for organisational resilience. An important objective is to use the AAR meta-framework as a starting point for a functional, holistic framework within which to position a diagnostic instrument.

---

283 Kleiner and Roth, 2000, p. 108.

284 Friedman, 1985.

285 *Oxford Concise Dictionary.* 1982. 7th ed. Oxford: Oxford University Press, p. 135.

286 Imai, M. 1986. *Kaizen: The key to Japan's competitive success.* New York, NY: Random House.

287 Imai, 1986, p. xxii.

288 Seba, 2016.

289 Schwab, 2016b.

Organisational resilience may be achieved within a processual paradigm, enabled by a quality, strategic conversation between executive leadership and executive managers individually, and in the context of an SLE forum consisting of an inclusive, powerful coalition of leadership. The diagnostic instrument as a frame of reference for high leverage areas may be used to focus this conversation. Diagnosis and prioritisation may take place and actions be decided which may be executed with an economy of means, together with TQM, as a basis for structured innovation of quality. This process may also result in structured innovative and continuous improvement, and value-for-money city government.

In the external environment, there are emerging predetermined dynamics that are relatively certain to have an impact on city government resilience. For example, more people on the planet than it can support, migration to cities, climate volatility, technology convergence (4IR), disruptors in transportation and energy, and terror attacks (nuclear and cyber). These challenges to organisational resilience require that the initial AAR framework be extended to include preceding AAR factors by enabling capability through capacity building in cross-cutting competencies, consequently adapting to dynamics, recovering from challenges and then extending from this basis into sustainable development, green growth and smart cities. Smart cities may be enabled by incorporating smart technologies such as sensors offered by the IoT in city government organisations, as well as massively increased portable computing power and storage. In the face of predetermined dynamics, competencies in scenario-based strategy making, SD modelling, organisational trust building and requisite organisational principles are key enablers for ensuring city government responsiveness and, through this, resilience. Urbanisation may enable city government organisations to act as the fulcrum for sustainable development projects that enable a developmental state, learning cities and greater city government resilience. Through greater city government resilience across regions, a critical mass for enabling national resilience and national sustainable development may be built.

Servant leadership, openness to learning, trust, an enabling culture, together with goal setting and a review of progress, provide the primary platform for building capability through capacity building for anticipation, adaptation, recovery, sustainable development, green growth and smart cities.

In the next chapter, city government resilience in South Africa as a proxy for emerging economies, as the primary focus of this study, will be explored.

CHAPTER 4

MODERN GOVERNMENT IN EMERGING ECONOMIES; THE REPUBLIC OF SOUTH AFRICA AS PROXY

"Anyone who stops learning is old, whether at twenty or eighty. Anyone who keeps learning stays young. The greatest thing in life is to keep your mind young."

Henry Ford

1   INTRODUCTION

In the previous chapter, paradigmatic developments, schools of thinking, theoretical principles, theories and models for organisational resilience were analysed and applied in a functional, holistic framework within which to develop a diagnostic instrument for gauging city government resilience.

The purpose of this chapter is to apply these analyses to drafting a diagnostic instrument for city government resilience within the socio-political-economic context of cities in South Africa. This will be done by identifying key systemic structures that influence city government organisational resilience. This includes identifying high leverage areas within the extended AAR framework, together with descriptors of factors and items for the process of gauging and scoring these. Capability enabled by cross-cutting competencies has been identified as the basis for capacity building. The foundations of modern government are identified together with the mandate for local government in South Africa and ways in which local government may support the developmental state. The context of cities and local government in both South Africa and across Africa is described in terms of key external and internal dynamics. In describing the socio-political-economic context, the principles and frameworks of a scenario-based strategic approach are used for the classification of various contextual forces that may influence city government resilience. Developing and testing a resilience strategy for robustness may also be best served by adopting these principles. For example, there may be predetermined contextual forces that will have an influence on city government resilience. However, many of the contextual forces may be uncertain, and their impact on cities may best be anticipated by applying a scenario-based strategic approach.

As there may be an association between economic freedom and development, the key principles of economic development and transformation are pinpointed in terms of the principles of economic freedom. The basis for attracting FDI, as well as city government revenue management and the cost of government, are also described. Capability and capacity building in cross-cutting competencies within intact management and executive teams and individuals through personal development planning are identified, describing selected high leverage processes and aspects that may enable capability. Change is assumed to be a permanent dynamic in the contextual environment that city governments need to deal with; this can be done by means of an inclusive management process and infrastructure. This suggests that infrastructure should be built that sustains a continuous successful process of ensuring fit within an unfolding context in order to ensure that city government resilience is sustained. Developmental cities will support national developmental policies by focusing on national development planning and sustainable community investment programmes. These programmes can be engaged to address specific dynamics that have an influence on cities. Disruptive dynamics may initially challenge city government resilience and then become forces for antifragility, where city government improves as a result of this disorder. In addition, circular economics are supported, which enables so-called green growth and smart cities. An inclusive, holistic diagnostic instrument is drafted consisting of two levels of diagnostics, namely, factors as a meta-framework to enable meta-diagnosis, and items within factors which are clustered within meta-categories.

A key dynamic which currently requires constant anticipation and adaptation by cities is the unresolved dilemma of policies flowing from the "official" National Development Plan (NDP) and the so-called National Democratic Revolution (NDR). Adopting a centralist NDR ideology could lead to the central government taking upon itself responsibilities that may be inappropriate for a national government. This could result in the restriction of freedom at city government level, resulting in inefficiencies, wastage and lack of resilience. Owing to migration to urban areas, specifically cities, cities have an increasingly important part to play in national development. A lack of resilience on the part of city government because of its interdependence with national responsiveness could result in a lack of resilience nationally and vice versa.

The way in which states and cities are governed has evolved over centuries and continues to evolve as their context becomes more volatile and uncertain. Many of the interconnections and interdependencies that determine resilience are unclear. The overall trajectory and evolution of government may be moving away from a government that is dependent on the values and attitudes of leadership personalities, towards inclusively agreed principles of governance as embodied in a constitution or a municipal mandate. These visionary agreements provide a basis for the rule of law, accountability and service delivery, policy and decision making. Scholars of resilience have been stimulated by events that challenge city government resilience such as terror attacks and natural disasters. Because they are closely associated, the principles of resilience and sustainable development may be addressed simultaneously by a form of governance that is in the process of evolving away from a kinship-based patrimonial system, towards a more inclusive, holistic system, termed "modern government", which will be explored below.

2 ORIGIN AND FOUNDATIONS OF MODERN GOVERNMENT

Fukuyama describes Chinese tribal society from its origins in 5000 BCE, when there were approximately 3000 polities, to 221 BCE, when there was one polity, namely the Qin Dynasty. He goes on to state that "progress in China from tribal to state-level society took place gradually with state institutions being layered on top of kinship-based social structures".[1]

Fukuyama traces the emergence and evolution of the modern nation-state and its origin in trading city-states.[2][3] He identifies the requirements for the modern government as the rule of law, accountability and capable government. These requirements also apply to city government. According to Fukuyama,[4] political accountability in a modern government means that in an "accountable government the rulers believe that they are responsible to the people they govern and put the people's interests above their own". He goes on to state that –

"... accountability can be achieved in a number of ways. It can arise from moral education, which is the form it took place in China and countries influenced by Confucianism. Princes were educated to feel a sense of responsibility to their society and were counselled by a sophisticated bureaucracy in the art of good statecraft."[5]

---

[1] Fukuyama, F. 2011a. *The origins of political order: From pre-human times to the French Revolution.* New York, NY: FSG, pp. 98–99.

[2] Fukuyama, 2011a.

[3] Fukuyama, F. 2011b. *Political order and political decay: From the Industrial Revolution to the globalisation of democracy.* New York, NY: FSG.

[4] Fukuyama, 2011a.

[5] Fukuyama, 2011a, p. 321.

Ultimately the purpose of a government is limited to specific responsibilities which may best be discharged on behalf of – and funded by taxes on – its citizens. These responsibilities are determined by the context within which a specific government functions and may be limited by what it is capable of executing.

2.1 Limits of government – new realities

The dilemma inherent in centrally directed policy as opposed to the delegated authority to act locally contains within it the two extremes of a dilemma between, on the one hand, enforcing control from the apex or centre of an organisation or, on the other hand, enabling self-control locally or on the boundary of an organisation. In terms of resolving such dilemmas effectively, lopsided thinking may result if one extreme of this continuum is favoured to the exclusion of the other. In their contingency theory, Lawrence and Lorch[6] posit that the greater the volatility in the context the more flexible the organisational structure may have to be and, conversely, the less volatile a context, the more rigid the structure. In the context of enabling city government resilience, the current volatile context, specifically in the service delivery area, may point towards greater locally based self-control at city government level while maintaining a measure of appropriate central control at the national level to discharge the minimum obligations of a modern government. In the African context, the so-called "big man" political leadership reflects a lopsided resolution of this dilemma by control from the centre with the "big man" at the apex. Mnguni (in GGA)[7] argues that the electoral and political structures and systems of many African states give a preponderant amount of power to the leader and elected governments with large majorities, with few checks and balances. Mnguni argues that "[t]his prevalence of big man politics in Africa is not only structural but also due to a defect in character among the African leaders who think that no other person can lead their countries".[8] There are indications that both elements play a role in Africa's continued tendency towards "big man" politics. This tendency results in trying to extend the stay in power for the big man and also a tendency towards centrally directed governance.

---

6   Lawrence and Lorch 1967

7   Good Governance Africa (GGA). 2017. The presidential issue. *The Journal of Good Governance,* (42), July–September. https://gga.org/ Date of access: 10 November 2017, p. 12.

8   GGA, 2017, p. 13.

Drucker[9] argues that "[t]he essence of totalitarianism is the assertion that the collective, the party, the state, the Aryan race, the ethnic group (and their 'big man') is the absolute. The definition on which all later totalitarian regimes have been based: Lenin's own party, Mussolini's, Hitler's and Mao's".[10] Drucker goes on to argue that one of the dominant political debates has been between "the believers in a 'welfare state' in which there are democratic restraints on government and on its control of the economy and society, on the one hand, and the believers in totalitarianism either of the Marxist or the Anti-Semitic persuasion, who preached and practised absolute, unrestricted government power".[11] He goes on to state that "the political doctrines which the slogans of the welfare state or of communism reflect have ceased to have much relevance or reality, politically, socially, even economically".[12] This ideological discourse may be reflected in the economic discourse in South Africa. As a contribution to this discourse, few books in history have had a greater impact on society and economics than Adam Smith's *Wealth of Nations* (1776). Smith had little love for businessmen and even less for self-interest. Smith argued that government, by its very nature, *cannot* run the economy, not even poorly. Drucker[13] adds that "soon the argument turned from what government *can* do to what government *should* do". Hayek,[14] in his anti-government tract *The Road to Serfdom*, a discourse on the relationship between individual liberty and government authority, did not argue government incompetence, but came to the conclusion that the nature of information "makes it impossible both in theory and practice for the government to manage or even to control the economy" (in Drucker[15]). Hayek was the first scholar to raise the question of the limits of government. When Margaret Thatcher became prime minister of the United Kingdom, she started to privatise many of the state-owned enterprises. Since then privatisation has not only become the programme of conservatives like Thatcher of UK or Chirac in France, "[i]t has also become the official policy of Communist China".[16] Another form of privatisation is moving faster still: letting private contractors take over public service delivery on a competitive bid basis. In

---

9   Drucker, P.F. 1994. *The new realities: In government and politics/In economics and business/ in society and worldview.* New York, NY: Harper Business, p. 6.

10   Drucker, 1994, p. 7.

11   Drucker, 1994, p. 8.

12   Drucker, 1994, p. 9.

13   Drucker, 1994, p. 59.

14   Hayek, F.A. 1944. *Road to serfdom.* Chicago, IL: University of Chicago Press.

15   Drucker, 1994, pp. 59, 60.

16   Drucker, 1994, p. 61.

light, of this trend, there may no longer be any doubt that there are limits to what government can do and alternate methods of delivering services. According to Drucker[17] there are three reasons for this dramatic change:

- "The failure of government programmes and government operations since the second world war;
- there are limits to what taxation and spending can achieve; and
- there are limits to government's ability to raise revenue".[18]

Drucker points out that "[a] government activity can only work if it is a monopoly. It cannot function if there are other ways to do that job, that is if there is competition".[19] He argues that whatever non-governmental organisations in the broadest sense (including the so-called private sector) can do better or do just as well should be not be done by the government. In the context of the emergent South African constitutional democracy, a range of ideologies, principles and concepts are currently held by different groups in government. The consequences of these ideologies, principles and concepts are in the process of being clarified. It may, therefore, be useful to further clarify the contexts in which governments may find themselves and the principles of modern government as a guide to modern city government.

2.2 Emerging government – contextual and conceptual framework

According to Fukuyama,[20] "patrimonialism characterises many of the (post-colonial) African states". He goes on to state that these "governments are staffed by the family and friends of the ruler and run for their benefit. Modern governments, by contrast, are supposed to be staffed by officials chosen on merit and expertise and run for the benefit of the broad public interest". With the outward form of a modern state, a neo-patrimonial government sometimes has a constitution, presidents and prime ministers, as well as a legal system and pretentions of impersonality. Nevertheless, the actual operation of the government remains at the core a matter of sharing state resources with friends and family. He terms this "neo-patrimonial". According to Fukuyama[21] the characteristics of African neo-patrimonial rule are:

---

17   Drucker, 1994, p. 63.
18   Drucker, 1994, p. 63.
19   Drucker, 1994, pp. 67, 68.
20   Fukuyama, 2011b, p. 287.
21   Fukuyama, 2011b, p. 287.

- "personalism – the figure of the president or big man to whom all individuals owed loyalty (virtually all African post-colonial political systems were presidential rather than parliamentary, and all presidents were male); and
- the use of state resources to cultivate political support, which resulted in pervasive clientelism".[22]

Fukuyama[23] points out that in modern government "accountable government means that the rulers believe that they are, in terms of a constitution, responsible to the people they govern and put the people's interests above their own". Formal accountability is procedural. The government agrees to submit itself to certain mechanisms that limit its power to do as it pleases – so-called checks and balances. Ultimately, these social compacts, spelt out in constitutions, "allow citizens to replace the government entirely for malfeasance, incompetence or abuse of power".[24] The South African Constitution, which has been widely hailed as the most advanced constitution in the world, also contains in it a mandate for municipalities, defining their mandate as the vanguard of the so-called developmental state.

Fukuyama provides an overview of the emergence of the modern state. [25] [26] It can be said that city government per se and city government resilience in particular, may also rest upon the premises of modern government – namely, the rule of law, accountability and capability – and by building on these foundations an effective resilience strategy can be developed.

3   CAPABILITY IN GOVERNMENT

According to Osborne,[27] "reinventing government" has erroneously been seen as referring to reinventing federal government. The solutions to problems in government have been emerging from local state government and local government. He points out that in America many dedicated people in government are trapped in ineffective government systems that are cumbersome and provide little incentive for improving performance. He pinpoints that "doing business in an outmoded way"[28] seems to be the

---

22   Fukuyama, 2011b, p. 257.

23   Fukuyama, 2011a, p. 321.

24   Fukuyama, 2011a, p. 322.

25   Fukuyama, 2011a.

26   Fukuyama, 2011b.

27   Osborne, D. 1993. Public productivity: Fiscal pressures and productive solutions. *Management Review,* 16(4):349–356, p. 349.

28   Osborne, 1993, p. 349.

fundamental problem with government. As society is transformed by both technology and social changes, the public sector should be widening its choice of service providers in line with the wide choice offered by business. According to Osborne, the move in business "to empower employees, introduce quality circles, measure performance and focus on improving quality should also be applied in the public sector".[29] In fieldwork with Gaebler, Osborne uncovered "ten principles that underscore how public entrepreneurial government organisations structure themselves. They pinpointed the points of leverage that move them from centralisation to decentralisation, from monopolies to competition, from bureaucratic mechanisms to market mechanisms, from funding inputs to funding outcomes or results".[30] Osborne and Gaebler[31] found that entrepreneurial local governments were:

- "catalytic governments, steering by using contracts, vouchers, grants and tax incentives;
- community-owned, empowering by pushing control out of the bureaucracy into the community;
- competitive, injecting competition into service delivery;
- mission-driven governments, transforming rules-driven organisations, thus enabling managers to find the best way to accomplish that mission;
- results-driven governments, funding outcomes not inputs;
- customer-driven governments, meeting the needs of customers not the needs of the bureaucracy;
- enterprising governments focussed on earning rather than spending;
- anticipatory governments preventing problems rather than curing problems with services;
- decentralised governments moving from hierarchy to participation and teamwork;
- market-orientated governments leveraging change through the market rather than administrative systems".[32]

According to Osborne and Gaebler,[33] "the impulse to control is embedded in almost every set of rules by which government operates: the budget system, the personnel system, the procurement system and the accounting system. The rule-driven government may prevent some corruption but at a

---

[29] Osborne, 1993, p. 351.

[30] Osborne, 1993, pp. 352–356.

[31] Osborne, D. & Gaebler, T. 1992. *Reinventing government: How the entrepreneurial spirit is transforming the public sector.* Reading, MA: Addison-Wesley.

[32] Osborne & Gaebler, 1992, pp. ix, x.

[33] Osborne & Gaebler, 1992, p. 112.

price of monumental waste". The findings by Osborne and Gaebler[34] with entrepreneurial local governments point towards an inclusive, holistic approach to reinventing government. In the UK Public Service, "capability reviews" were conceived in 2005 as a way to reinvent government in the UK and were launched by the Cabinet Secretary as a way "to hold government department leaders to account for improving their departments' capability to deliver".[35] In an evaluation of the capability reviews programme, it received mixed reviews among senior civil servants in a survey of 219 directors and deputy directors. These were reported as follows, "8% responded: Very effective, 56% responded: Quite effective, 25% responded: Not very effective, 3% responded: Not at all effective and 4% responded: No changes implemented yet".[36] In 2009, the UK House of Commons Public Accounts Committee published an assessment which concluded that "the introduction of capability reviews is a significant advance in bringing transparency and comparability to how government departments are assessed". It goes on to recommend that, if capability reviews are to secure sustainable improvements, there needs to be:

- "improved metrics;
- external benchmarks against which to compare;
- a much stronger culture of individual performance linked to overall delivery metrics;
- higher confidence levels;
- strong, strategically focused senior management; and
- improved insight into service delivery partners similar to private sector organisations."[37]

A number of these recommendations are touched on and reflected by the 80/20 report by the IRR[38] in which it pinpoints the "root problems facing local government." (in South Africa) as "political appointments, lack of capacity [capability] and lack of accountability".

The Australia Public Service (APS) follows and improves on the UK Capability Reviews by focusing and defining capability. The APS

34 Osborne & Gaebler, 1992.

35 *Institute for Government UK. 2005. Capability reviews: A case study by Panchamia, N. & Thomas, P. London: Institute of Government, p. 1.*

36 Sunningdale Institute, 2007. *Take-off or tail-off? An evolution of the Capability Reviews Programme.* www.nationalschool.gov.uk Date of access: 14 October 2017, p. 19.

37 United Kingdom (UK) House of Commons. 2009. *Assessment of the Capability Review Programme: Forty-Fifth Report of Session 2008–2009.* London: The Stationery Office Limited, pp. 5, 6.

38 Institute of Race Relations (IRR). 2014. *The 80/20 Report: Local government in 80 indicators after 20 years of democracy.* Johannesburg: IRR, pp. 16, 17.

positions its capability framework at the centre of its initiative to reinvent government which may provide an organisational focus in city government and a holistic frame of reference for enabling capability through capacity building. The Australian Public Service Commission's (APSC) descriptions of capability may be useful in a diagnostic instrument for gauging city government resilience.

The APS and specifically the APSC have, as a priority, to build and sustain organisational capability in order to respond effectively (and at pace) to the contemporary needs of modern government and the dynamics in the environment, and to build capability in advance of these needs. Emerging needs can be reasonably anticipated, and resilience established to cope well with unexpected shocks.[39] The APSC points out that organisational capability extends beyond the capability of employees and combines people skills with the organisation's processes, systems, culture and structures to deliver outcomes. People and systems need to be consciously aligned to overall organisational outcomes and priorities with lines of accountability that are clear for the performance of systems. Governance systems need to ensure that large projects and contractors are managed with a strong emphasis on effective risk management. There should also be a focus on project implementation, supported by coordinated implementation strategies and the development of project management capability.

According to the APSC, "it has developed this capability framework (see Figure 4.1) as a basis for its capability assessment process". The APSC goes on to state that "[i]t is deliberately selective and focuses on the most crucial [high leverage] areas of capability and key enablers of successful performance namely leadership, strategy and delivery".[40] The APSC describes these aspects of its capability assessment framework as follows:

- "leadership: the critical juncture between government policy and strategy execution and delivery;
- strategy: the high level strategy developed by public service agencies to meet the government's policy directions; and
- delivery: the capability that agencies need to deliver on time and on budget the government's policy through high quality programs and services".[41]

---

[39] APSC, 2017b Capability Assessment. http://www.apsc.gov.au/capability-reviews

[40] APSC, 2017b Capability Assessment. http://www.apsc.gov.au/capability-reviews

[41] APSC 2017b

The APSC adds:

"... the 10 elements of the model, grouped under these three key
enablers, allow emphasis to be placed on capabilities that are of high
importance and high leverage and are often unique to the public sector,
for example, evidence-based policy development and collaboration
across sectors and with other agencies to resolve cross-cutting issues."

The APS capability model (see Figure 4.1) provides a framework and
common language for discussing and assessing organisational capability.[42]

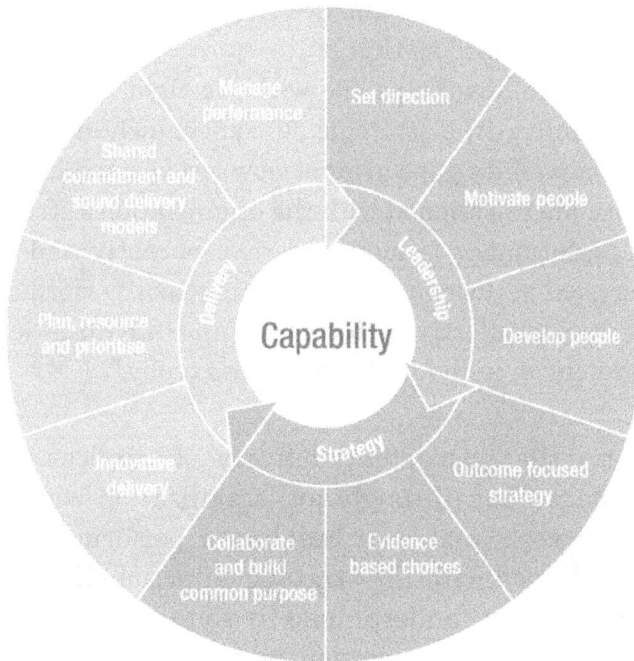

Figure 4.1: APS capability model
Source: APS Commission[43]

The APSC capability model contains three clusters which each contain
descriptors of functionalities:
  • "Leadership: Set direction, Motivate people, Development of people;
  • Strategy: Outcomes-focused strategy, Evidence-based choices,
    Collaborate and build common purpose; and
  • Delivery: Manage performance, Shared commitment and sound
    delivery models. Plan, resource and prioritise, innovative delivery".[44]

---

[42] APSC 2017b

[43] APSC 2017b

[44] APSC 2017b

According to the APSC, leadership plays a key role in transforming organisational capability in the APS. In the APS model of capability, "leadership capability emphasises setting direction, motivating people and continuously developing employees as the key characteristics".[45] One of the primary responsibilities is "setting direction". By enrolling followers in a compelling and coherent vision for the organisation, leadership demonstrates its capability to set direction, together with leading and managing change and galvanising action. The APSC adds that "addressing and overcoming resistance when it occurs, is a critical leadership capability in a rapidly changing environment".[46] To develop people, leaders need to ensure that systems such as personal development planning and processes to build capacity are in place so that –

- "the organisation has the people with the right knowledge, skills and attitudes to deliver the strategic outcomes, including identifying and addressing capability gaps evident now or expected in the future;
- staff performance is aligned with the organisation's strategic priorities and that performance is managed transparently and consistently – rewarding good performance and tackling poor performance; and
- the organisation effectively identifies and nurtures leadership and manages talent in individuals and across teams".[47]

The APSC asserts that consistent delivery of services depends upon performance management through an organisation-wide performance management framework, aimed at building a performance culture that is responsive and aligned with the strategic direction of the organisation. Performance management, underpinned by sound, well-resourced service delivery models which enable innovation, is required to build organisational capability.[48]

4 EXECUTION OF PLANS

The execution of strategy and plans, according to Bossidy *et al.*,[49] depends upon what they refer to as the missing link and the main reason why organisations and leadership fall short of their promises. According to Bossidy *et al.*,[50] to understand execution three important points must be accepted:

---

[45] APSC 2017b

[46] APSC 2017b

[47] APSC 2017 b

[48] APSC 2017b

[49] Bossidy, L., Charan, R. & Burck, C. 2002. *Execution the discipline of getting things done.* New York: Crown Business.

[50] Bossidy et al., 2002.

- "execution is a discipline and integral to strategy;
- execution is the major job of organisational leadership; and
- execution must be a core element of an organisation's culture".[51]

Bossidy *et al.*[52] assert that there needs to be a system of getting things done through questioning, analysis and follow-through. In addition, there needs to be an embedded discipline of comparing intent, strategy and policy with an honest assessment of current reality and aligning people's energy with desired policy and goals. They go on to describe the building blocks for execution by citing leadership, building capability, culture change, choosing the right people, as well as a line-of-sight connection between divisions, departments and jobs with their role in executing policy. Regular reviews of current reality provide feedback on progress against goals.

5   THE SOUTH AFRICAN CONSTITUTION AS THE FOUNDATION FOR THE RULE OF LAW

Building a shared vision within a municipality in South Africa may be built in alignment with the South African Constitution. The South African Constitution and the mandate for municipalities may be seen as the shared vision for city government in South Africa.

Following the first democratic elections in 1994, the South African Constitution was developed and approved by Parliament in 1996.[53] It reflects a widely agreed, shared national vision for a future South Africa. The South African Constitution rose like the proverbial phoenix from the ashes of apartheid and was heralded by many in the world as the most advanced constitution in existence. Section 4.2 above explains how Fukuyama[54] describes the transition from a kinship-based tribal, patrimonial form of government to modern government. Modern government is represented by the transition away from rule by a tribal chief (or the "big man") to accountability to the rule of law as embodied in and mandated by an agreed constitution. This mandate provides the basis of accountability by government to citizens, and places an obligation on all citizens to uphold the Constitution based upon the rule of law. Enabled by capability within government, as defined above, taxes collected are applied in the service of complying with the mandate contained in the Constitution. The mandate to government in the South African Constitution cascades down to pro-

---

[51]   Bossidy et al., 2002, p. 21.

[52]   Bossidy et al., 2002.

[53]   South Africa. 1996. *Constitution of the Republic of South Africa, 1996.* Pretoria: Government Printer.

[54]   Fukuyama 2011a

vincial and local government through specific mandates upon them. The mandate for municipalities governs their priorities, policies and decisions. The focus of this study is on the properties of a resilience strategy for city government and developing a diagnostic instrument to support city government in achieving this. Describing the municipal mandate within the context of the South African Constitution provides a frame of reference for city government resilience strategy.

8 The mandate for local government

The local government sphere in South Africa consists of three categories of municipalities, namely eight metropolitan, 44 districts and 205 local municipalities. These municipalities obtained their mandate from the South African Constitution (Chapter 7, Section 151). Furthermore, the White Paper on Local Government[55] resulted in legislation pertaining to the local government sphere. The priorities, policies and structures of municipalities that may facilitate or hamper city government resilience are described comprehensively below in the municipal mandate.

Section 151 –

(1) "The local sphere of government consists of municipalities, which must be established for the whole of the territory of the Republic.
(2) The executive and legislative authority are vested in its Municipal Council.
(3) A municipality has the right to govern, on its own initiative, the local government affairs of its community, subject to national and provincial legislation, as provided for in the Constitution.
(4) The national or provincial government may not compromise or impede a municipality's ability or right to exercise its powers or perform its functions".

Section 152 –

(1) "The objects of local government are:
  (a) to provide democratic and accountable government to local communities;
  (b) to ensure the provision of services to communities in a sustainable manner;
  (c) to promote social and economic development;
  (d) to promote a safe and healthy environment;

---

[55] South Africa. 1998. The White Paper on Local Government. *Government Gazette* No 30137 of 01-August 2007. Pretoria: Government Printer.

(e) to encourage the involvement of communities and community organisations in the matters of local government.

(2) A municipality must strive within its financial and administrative capacity to achieve the objects set out in subsection (1)".

Subsections (1)(b), (c) and (e) and (2) in section 152 above may have a bearing on ensuring the city government resilience contained and reflected in the municipal mandate. The primary accountability of municipalities is to the Constitution as well as the various pieces of local government legislation, including the following:

- Local Government: Municipal Structures Act of 1998
- Local Government: Municipal Systems Act of 2000
- Local Government: Municipal Finance Management Act of 2003
- Local Government: Municipal Property Rates Act of 2004
- Local Government: Municipal Systems Amendment Act of 2011

The Constitution provides municipalities with a measure of autonomy and gives them the responsibility to formulate local strategy and policy and to enact municipal legislation except for the departments of Education and Health. Municipalities have a specific responsibility to execute a developmental policy. However, this is limited by their capability and financial and administrative capacity.

6   STRUCTURE, ROLES AND RESPONSIBILITIES OF LOCAL GOVERNMENT IN SOUTH AFRICA

Local government is structured into Categories A (metro), B (local) and C (district) municipalities. The overall objective and constitutional mandate of these municipalities is to focus on growing local economies and providing infrastructure and services to those living under their jurisdiction.[56] Municipalities classified as metropolitan municipalities (aka metros) must have more than 500 000 voters within their city boundary. Metropolitan councils may decentralise powers and functions, with the proviso that all original legislative and executive powers remain vested in the metropolitan council. A metropolitan council is run by a council, with the number of councillors varying depending on the municipality. Half of the councillors are elected through a proportional representation ballot, and the other half are elected as ward councillors by the residents in each ward.

The main sources of operating revenue for municipalities are relatively

---

[56]   IRR 2014 Institute of Race Relations (IRR). 2014. *The 80/20 Report: Local government in 80 indicators after 20 years of democracy.* Johannesburg: IRR.

stable over time and are reflected in Table 4.1. To highlight the potential impact of FDI on municipalities, FDI is reflected in the context of the main revenue sources below.

Table 4.1: Main revenue sources – municipal operating revenue 2012/2013

Source of revenue	Proportion percentage
Property rates	16.0
Service charges or tariffs	55.0
Interest earned – external investments	1.0
Other revenue	8.5
Transfers from government	19.5
Foreign direct investment (FDI) in metros	?

Source: National Treasury.[57]

Other possible sources of income include external loans, internal loans, government grants, donations and public contributions, public-private partnerships (PPPs) and FDI in local industries. The final line item in Table 4.1 above raises the question of if and how cities may attract FDI from other cities as well as from investors.

As at 31 December 2013, the aggregate municipal debt owed to municipalities was R93.3 billion, of which 63.2% or R59 billion was owed by households.[58] This may be offset by efficient revenue management systems which enable revenue owed to municipalities to be collected and effectively applied. Irregular expenditure further compounds the difficulties of inefficient revenue management by reducing the funds available to city government for the provision of services and may have an impact on a resilience strategy. Table 4.2 reflects irregular expenditure at local government levels. As can be seen in Table 4.2, in 2015-16 irregular expenditure increased by 51% (R5.68 bn) from the previous year. According to the Auditor General,[59] "the irregular expenditure was the highest since we started tracking the values. The number of municipalities incurring such expenditure had increased to 236. A total of 217 (92%) of these 236 municipalities had also incurred irregular expenditure in the previous year".[60]

---

57 National Treasury. 2011. *Local Government Budgets and Expenditure Review*. 10 October. Pretoria: National Treasury.

58 Institute of Race Relations (IRR). 2014, p. 10.

59 Auditor General of South Africa (AG). 2016, p. 40.

60 Auditor General of South Africa (AG). 2016, p. 40.

Table 4.2: Three-year trend in irregular expenditure by municipalities by province

Province	Rand value		
	2013–14	2014–15	2015–16 (% increase over previous year)
Eastern Cape*			R 5.66 bn (60)
Free State			
Gauteng			
KwaZulu-Natal*			R 2.36 bn (117)
Limpopo			
Mpumalanga*			R 2.28 bn (162)
North West*			R 2.25 bn (117)
Northern Cape			
Western Cape			
Total irregular expenditure	R 11.33 bn 225 municipalities	R 11.14 bn 232 municipalities	R 16.81 bn 236 municipalities

Source: AG 2016.[61]

Note: Municipalities that were the main contributors to % increases are marked (*)

In an assessment by the IRR,[62] of the overall performance of municipalities, including their financial spending, the worst- and best performing municipalities were identified using the following indicators:
- "the employment rate;
- the proportion of people aged 20 and older who have passed grade 12;
- the poverty rate;
- the number of houses which are owned but not fully paid off;
- the proportion of households that use electricity for lighting;
- the proportion of households that have access to piped water inside dwelling or yard;
- the proportion of households that have piped water within one kilometre of the household;
- the proportion of households that have their refuse removed by the local authority or private company;

---

[61] Auditor General of South Africa (AG), 2016. *Consolidated General Report on Local Government Audit Outcomes, 2015/16*. Pretoria.
[62] Institute of Race Relations (IRR), 2014.

- the proportion of households that have a flush or chemical lavatory; and
- the number of households that have no lavatory".[63]

Scores were aggregated on a ten-point scale. These indicators may be useful for modelling the city government dynamics that play a role in city government resilience.

Table 4.3: The 10 best and the 10 worst municipalities in South Africa

10 Best performing (score above 7.5)			10 Worst performing (score below 3.0)		
Municipality	Province	Score	Municipality	Province	Score
Saldanha	WC	7.88	Ntabankulu	EC	2.56
Siyancuma	NC	7.86	OR Tambo	EC	2.56
Overstrand	WC	7.66	Mbhashe	EC	2.61
Umdoni	KZN	7.65	Mbizana	EC	2.73
Drakenstein	WC	7.62	Msinga	KZN	2.73
Mossel Bay	WC	7.61	Engcobo	EC	2.88
Swartland	WC	7.61	Ezinqoleni	KZN	2.90
Stellenbosch	WC	7.55	Amathole	EC	2.91
Gamagara	NC	7.54	Emalahleni	EC	2.95
Cape Town	WC	7.53	Pt St Johns	EC	2.96

Source: IRR.[64]

According to the IRR the root problems facing local government are –
- "political appointments, which have undermined the morale of the public servants and citizens' confidence in the state;
- lack of capacity which is caused by many vacancies and inability to attract talent; and
- lack of accountability because of lack of consequences for poor performance and lapses in leadership and governance".[65]

---

[63]   Institute of Race Relations (IRR). 2014, p. 15.
[64]   Institute of Race Relations (IRR). 2014, p. 16
[65]   Institute of Race Relations (IRR). 2014, p. 16

These root problems often have their origins in the socio-political-economic context of these municipalities. For this reason, the contextual socio-political and economic dynamics impacting on city government are briefly examined in the section below.

6.1 Contextual socio-political-economic dynamics impacting on city government

The global context provides a basis for comparison at country level between Africa and other countries. Continental Africa may be segmented into regions, consisting of Francophone West Africa, Anglophone West Africa, North West Africa, East Africa and Sub-Saharan Africa. Colonial history and history per se play a significant role in determining the characteristics and development pathways of specific countries. This provides context for the cities in specific African countries.

6.2 African city dynamics in context

According to the United Nations World Urban Prospects statistics (in ISS),[66] the population trends illustrated in Table 4.4 indicate that by 2050 more than 58% of people in Africa will be living in cities.[67] Urbanisation poses a complex challenge to city government resilience as this influx of people affects various dynamics in cities such as housing, property prices, schools, crime and transportation. Dynamic complexity arises when several interconnected dynamics are triggered by a specific interconnected dynamic such as population influx into an urban area. This demonstrates the difficulty with comprehending the dynamic complexity inherent in a large inflow of people into a city. Understanding how these interrelated dynamics may play out beyond a ten-year time horizon can best be understood using SD modelling support.

Table 4.4: Migration to African cities

	2016	2020	2030	2040	2050
Total African population m/bn	468 m	563 m	701 m	1.1 bn	1.4 bn
% Urban population	40	42	48	53	58

Source: United Nations World Urban Prospects.[68]

---

[66] Institute for Security Studies (ISS). 2016. *Africa's future is urban.* https://issafrica.org/events/africas-future-is-urban Date of access: 27 April 2017.

[67] Institute for Security Studies (ISS), 2016.

[68] Institute for Security Studies (ISS), 2016.

The Institute for Security Studies (ISS) posits that as the world's cities continue to grow in size, "[b]y 2030, six of the world's 41 megacities (of more than 10 m inhabitants) will be in Africa".[69] Cairo, Lagos and Kinshasa, which currently have populations greater than 10 million inhabitants, will each contain more than 20 million people. Johannesburg, Luanda and Dar es Salaam will each contain more than 10 million people. The ISS adds that cities have the potential to be key drivers of their countries' economic performance and may provide a connection between Africa and the global economy. By 2035, approximately 30 million people could be living in Lagos, turning Nigeria's commercial hub into the largest megacity on the African continent (see Table 4.5).

According to Brand,[70] urbanisation and the development of informal settlements adjacent to African cities are probably indicators of the structure of future cities in Africa. These settlements reflect informal cash economies in which all inhabitants are working, engaging and trading their way *out of poverty*. Van der Merwe[71] supports this argument by Brand by identifying the informal traders within the formal city limits as a social and economic transformation at work.[72] However, this spontaneous community development may not be sufficient to offset the overall trend towards income disparity and poverty in African cities.

7   URBANISATION AND DEVELOPMENT

According to the ISS, Africa could develop rapidly, but slow economic structural transformation, poverty, inequality and violence will probably hold back growth in Africa. The rapid pace of urban population growth in African urban settings (see Table 4.5) is outpacing social, economic and institutional development. The ISS concludes that "[u]rbanisation is more likely to compound Africa's challenges and resilience than encourage sustainable development".[73]

---

[69]   Institute for Security Studies (ISS), 2016.

[70]   Brand, S. 2017b. What squatter cities can teach us/TED Talk/TED.com. https://www.ted.com/talks/stewart_brand_on_squatter_cities Date of access: 8 August 2017.

[71]   Van der Merwe, L. 2016b. *Failing our future: Why SA needs to develop competent teachers at scale.* http://www.biznews.com/thought-leaders/2016/08/12/eating-our-children-why-sa-needs-to-develop-competent-teachers-at-scale/ Date of access: 13 August 2016.

[72]   Van der Merwe, 2016b

[73]   Institute for Security Studies (ISS), 2016.

Table 4.5: Expected population size of Africa's current and emerging megacities (million people), 2014–2050

City	2014	2030	2035	2040	2045	2050
Cairo	18.4	24.5	26.1	27.7	29.2	30.8
Lagos	12.6	24.2	29.3	34.7	40.2	45.4
Kinshasa	11.1	20.0	23.8	27.8	32.1	36.4
Johannesburg	9.2	11.6	12.3	13.0	13.4	13.8
Dar es Salaam	4.8	10.8	13.2	16.0	19.1	22.4
Luanda	5.3	10.4	12.8	15.5	18.4	21.4
Abidjan	4.9	7.8	9.0	10.2	11.6	12.8
Nairobi	3.9	7.1	8.6	10.2	11.9	13.7
Kano	3.6	6.2	7.5	8.8	10.3	11.6
Ouagadougou	2.4	5.9	7.2	8.8	10.6	12.5
Addis Ababa	3.2	5.9	7.3	8.9	10.7	12.6
Bamako	2.5	5.2	6.4	7.8	9.3	10.8
Dakar	3.5	6.0	7.0	8.0	9.1	10.2
Ibadan	3.1	5.5	6.6	7.9	9.1	10.3

Source: ISS.[74]

According to the ISS, there is a link between urbanisation and economic development. However, in Africa this link may be weaker than elsewhere in the world such as China. In other words, urbanisation may, in Africa, not be synonymous with economic development. "Urban population growth has been outpacing economic development, partly because of the lack of productive employment creation".[75] The ISS goes on to point out that the single most important driver of urban growth in Africa is natural urban population growth or the predominance of births over deaths in urban areas. This nett growth rate accounts for around 60% of urban population growth, while rural-urban migration accounts for about 30%. People living in rural areas in Africa move to cities because of better service provision as well as changing, volatile weather patterns, land pressures, natural disasters and conflict.[76] The ISS adds that "[i]ncidences of violence, whether politically or criminally motivated, are common in Africa's cities and towns, and, like

---

[74] Institute for Security Studies (ISS), 2016.
[75] Institute for Security Studies (ISS), 2016.
[76] Institute for Security Studies (ISS), 2016.

poverty, violence seems to be urbanising".[77] The ISS's arguments support the IRR 2014 report, which cites that riots and protests are on the rise. The ISS warns that "unplanned, overcrowded settlements populated with marginalised youth can be hotbeds for violence".[78] The dynamics identified by the ISS and the IRR reports may have the nett result of creating a *lack of resilience* in cities. In the context of developing resilience, the ISS report indicates the need to focus on the role of cities in accelerating and sustaining economic development by enabling sustainability through job creation and institutional capability and capacity building.

7.1 Sustainability and development

Fabricius[79] supports many of the propositions put forward by the ISS in his scenarios for Africa to 2030. He makes salient points that have parallels in South Africa, which have a bearing on city government resilience. Fabricius[80] posits that "Africa will miss most of its Sustainable Development Goals (SDGs) but might just reach its 'escape velocity' enabling it to break out of its extreme poverty orbit by 2045 or 2050". He posits that "Africa would need sustained growth of at least 7% year on year to make a significant dent in poverty".[81]

The United Nations Economic Commission for Africa (ECA)[82] "urges Africa to build credible institutions to boost industrialization". The ECA goes on to say "[t]ransforming Africa's industrial landscape has failed partly because of weak institutional structures and poor policy design throughout its post-independence history".[83] These propositions underline the importance of the meta-factor "sustainable development (Sdev)" and its association with and role in gauging city government resilience.

Harvey,[84] on the other hand, posits that "the most exciting dimension may be Africa's ability to address negative externalities such as hidden environmental and social costs". With this, he points towards an antifragile

[77]   Institute for Security Studies (ISS), 2016.

[78]   Institute for Security Studies (ISS), 2016.

[79]   Fabricius, P. 2017. *Peering into a murky crystal ball: Where will Africa be in 2030?* https://issafrica.org/iss-today/peering-into-a-murky-crystal-ball-where-will-africa-be-in-2030?ct= (FFD_February_2017) Date of access: 21 March 2017.

[80]   Fabricius, 2017.

[81]   Fabricius, 2017.

[82]   Economic Commission for Africa (ECA). 2014. *Dynamic industrial policy in Africa.* http://www.uneca.org/eca/ Date of access: 4 June 2017.

[83]   Economic Commission for Africa (ECA), 2014.

[84]   Harvey, R. 2012. *The Fourth Industrial Revolution: Potential and risks for Africa.* https://theconversation.com/the-fourth-industrial-revolution-potential-and-risks-for-africa-75313?utm_medium=email&utm Date of access: 31 March 2017.

property inherent in Africa which may provide a cushion against catastrophic disruptions. Harvey[85] goes on to explain that a country's growth trajectory usually follows the hypothesised *Environmental Kuznets Curve*, where income growth in pre-industrial economies is accompanied by environmental degradation and pollution. Post-industrial economies, such as service economies reduce environmental degradation while maintaining income growth. New technologies and technology convergence make it possible to transition to a technology-enabled service economy and leapfrog over the environmental degradation phase posited by the *Environmental Kuznets Curve*. Africa and African cities may be beneficiaries of this transition. Harvey[86] further describes the post-industrial economy phase of the Kuznets Curve as the transition to a "circular economy", which decouples production from natural resource constraints. The premise of a circular economy is that nothing that is made in a circular economy becomes waste as waste becomes feedstock for the next process in a value chain. In this regard, the IoT enables the tracking of material and energy flows to create efficiencies along product value chains. Perhaps most importantly for African countries, renewable energy offers the possibility of devolved, deep and broad access to solar-generated electricity. However, Harvey[87] warns that premature de-industrialisation to a technology-enabled, information economy will result in a decline in the demand for jobs for unskilled people in transition to higher-skilled jobs. Cities, as the primary sites for development and job creation, could take on an important role in identifying and investing in reskilling labour in advance of the demand for the new jobs. Harvey[88] advocates "rapidly improving access to electricity as the foundation for future growth and to build clear strategies that engage the benefits of a fourth Industrial revolution. If not, they risk being left behind".[89] He implies that African governments (and city governments) should be proactive in adopting new and more sustainable technologies as it pays in the long run to craft inclusive institutions that promote widespread innovation. The purpose of developing an instrument to gauge city government resilience is to engage and accelerate the positive prospects in city governments discussed above through feedback on their current resilience strategy reality. Developing a city government resilience strategy may be seen in the context of disruptors as being a result not only of technology convergence but also of other dynamics in their context that

---

[85] Harvey, 2012.

[86] Harvey, 2012.

[87] Harvey, 2012.

[88] Harvey, 2012.

[89] Harvey, 2012.

may influence city government resilience positively. With this continental perspective as a vantage point, the next section focuses specifically on the socio-political and economic dynamics affecting city government in South Africa.

8 DYNAMICS AFFECTING CITY GOVERNMENT

One of the key principles of scenario-based strategy, which may be applied to developing a robust resilience strategy, lies in stress-testing a resilience strategy for robustness across all the scenarios. This can be done by confronting the resilience strategy with all plausible scenarios for external forces that may have an impact on a city government resilience strategy. The implication of this approach is that all the plausible forces at work that may have an impact on a city government resilience strategy need to be identified as context. Anticipating futures that may plausibly influence city government resilience may be used as an important meta-factor in the diagnostic instrument.

The dynamics identified in section 4.7.5 are cited as examples of plausible dynamics which may be reflected in scenarios for anticipating challenges in a future context in general and to a resilience strategy specifically. Anticipation, abbreviated as (An), as a key meta-component of a resilience strategy diagnostic instrument contains a wide, inclusive range of different dynamics. The relevance to executive leaders and executive managers in city government and, accordingly, encouraging the use of scenarios may depend on "the key concerns and uncertainties on the minds of the decision makers".[90] The quality and value of scenarios to the executive leaders and executive managers in a specific city may depend on their "relevance" to decision makers, how the scenarios "challenge" and widen their thinking, and using deep systemic research to increase "their plausibility".[91] Van der Merwe adds another quality criterion from Wack,[92] who encouraged inclusivity so that once the future had unfolded and been lived through no important dynamics were overlooked. The examples listed have been identified to draw attention to specific dynamics that may challenge city government resilience in the context of city government in South Africa. Their selection may vary from city to city based on current concerns.

Forces and dynamics that may have an impact on city government resilience in South Africa can be divided into two broad categories: those forces *outside* the cities that may have an impact on cities and their governments which may be the focus of scenarios, and those dynamics

---

90   Van der Merwe, 2008, p. 228.
91   Van der Merwe, 2008, p. 231.
92   Wack, 1985a

within city government and cities which may be the focus of organisational capability review dimensions which has been included in the diagnostic instrument. The forces in the external environment or context of cities may be identified under the headings of political, economics, societal, regulations, technology, ecological and historical, and may be sorted into two broad categories:

- "external forces that are certain to impact upon cities, so-called 'predetermined' dynamics; and
- external forces that are uncertain and may have a high impact upon cities, so-called 'key uncertainties'".[93]

Because there may be little or no data about future dynamics that could have an impact on city government resilience, being inclusive may avoid omitting important dynamics.

8.1 External dynamics in the future environment

External dynamics which can affect cities in the future are identified below. They may be in play currently or may in the future have an impact on cities. Within external dynamics, there are dynamics which are certain aka predetermined dynamics, those that are uncertain aka key uncertainties, as well as those that are uncertain with a low probability yet with a very high impact if they occur aka black swans. These dynamics are explored in more detail below.

8.2 Predetermined dynamics

- Cyberattacks, natural disasters, and economic or social upheaval;[94]
- Widespread unrealistic expectations in South Africa;[95]
- Rapid urbanisation;[96]
- Climate volatility resulting in prolonged, extreme weather conditions;[97]
- Water insecurity in terms of quality and quantity;[98]

---

[93] Van der Merwe, 2008, p. 225.

[94] Rockefeller Foundation. 2017. *100 Resilient Cities Network*. https://www.rockefellerfoundation.org/our-work/initiatives/100-resilient-cities/ Date of access: 15 November 2017.

[95] Cronje, F. 2014. *A time traveller's guide to South Africa to our next ten years*. Cape Town: Tafelberg, pp. 7–10.

[96] ISS, 2016.

[97] Bohatch, T. 2017. What's causing Cape Town's water crisis? *Groundup*: https://www.groundup.org.za/article/whats-causing-cape-towns-water-crisis Date of access: 15 November 2017.

[98] Bohatch, 2017

- An increase in service delivery protests;[99]
- Large young populations[100] (see also Table 4.6);
- Technological convergence and acceleration during the so-called World Economic Forum's (WEF) Fourth Industrial Revolution;[101]
- Transformation of work, job redundancy, job losses and need for retraining;[102]
- E-governance competence requirements for technology-impacted services;[103]
- Peer-to-peer financial transactions safely and securely enabled by blockchain/Bitcoin, so-called open ledger technology and cryptocurrencies;[104]
- Energy disruption by solar and wind technologies;[105]
- Transportation disruption by electric and autonomous vehicles;[106]
- Need for compliance with the United Nations office for Disaster and Risk Reduction (UNISDR) including the Sendai framework and SDGs.[107]

Specific predetermined dynamics have been highlighted and described, thus providing the context within which a city government resilience strategy may be developed. The significance and size of the youth population – approximately 26.5 million, or 49% of the total South African population of 54 million – justifies special attention when considering a city government resilience strategy. The fact that this dynamic is predetermined may further require that greater importance be attached to the large youth population when developing a city government resilience strategy.

---

[99]   Institute of Race Relations (IRR), 2014.

[100] StatsSA. 2014. Statistics South Africa http://www.statssa.gov.za/?m=2014&gclid= EAIaIQobChMI2tWHooCj7QIVCU4YCh39xwPiEAAYASAAEgLiWfD_BwE   Date   of Access: 23 June 2017.

[101] Schwab, K. 2016a. *Navigating the Fourth Industrial Revolution.* http://www.biznews.com/ wef/davos-2016/2016/01/20/klaus-schwab-navigating-the-fourth-industrial-revolution/ Date of access: 23 August 2017.

[102] Schwab, 2016a

[103] Van der Waldt, G. 2016a. Towards an e-governance competency framework for public service managers: The South African experiment. *African Journal of Public Affairs,* 9(4):114–129.

[104] Schwab, 2016a

[105] Seba, T. 2016. Why energy and transportation will be obsolete by 2030. Keynote presentation at the Swedbank Nordic Energy Summit in Oslo, Norway. https://www.youtube.com/ watch?v=2b3ttqYDwF0 Date of access: 21 July 2017.

[106] Seba, 2016

[107] United Nations International Strategy for Disaster Reduction (UNISDR). 2016a. Strategic Framework 2016-2021. Geneva: UNISDR.

Table 4.6: RSA youth demographics 0–24 years old

	Age 0–4	Age 5–9	Age 10–14	Age 15–19	Age 20–24	TOTAL
Black	4 936 601	4 541 523	4 303 892	4 357 984	4 417 106	22 557 106
Coloured	420 171	428 867	444 983	451 117	427 547	2 172 685
Asian	99 256	96 953	93 863	101 609	109 668	501 347
White	263 301	269 367	280 988	306 851	312 797	1 433 304
Total	5 729 329	5 336 710	4 944 347	5 231 566	5 267 118	26 509 070
	Ratios for youth 0–24 of 26 million			Ratios for entire population of 54 million		
Black	84.6%			80.0%		
Coloured	8.2%			9.0%		
Asian	1.8%			2.5%		
White	5.4%			8.5%		
Total	100%			100%		

Source: StatsSA. [108]

StatsSA continues to provide its statistics by racial grouping. While a racial reflection of population statistics is not desirable in terms of the South African Constitution, it enables insight into the relative size of the youth component as well as the decline in the percentage of certain racial groups in terms of the total population. Demographics such as those reflected in Table 4.6 provide insight into the predetermined dynamics as defined,[109] where all of these young people will achieve working and voting age at a specific time in the future. The values and attitudes held by this population demographic and shaped by the context in which they grew up, will probably determine their future behaviour as a group. The leading edge of this group is probably among the so-called #Feesmustfall protesters and Fanon ideologues demonstrating at South African universities. Considering the disruptive forces at work in the approaching Fourth Industrial Revolution, which may render many traditional jobs redundant, there will be a need for the retraining of current workers at scale to equip job seekers for the new world of work, post-revolution. As education falls outside the municipal mandate, city government is required to work in collaboration with the national government in this area. There may also be an opportunity to leapfrog into the new world of work, provided that educational institutions in cities anticipate this new world and develop appropriate competencies in advance of the loss of jobs that will result from the so-called revolution. A competency framework for e-governance has been compiled by Van der

---

[108] Stats SA. 2014.

[109] Van der Merwe, 2008, p. 225.

Waldt[110] and is used to assess the competencies required for e-governance among current city government job incumbents. This competency framework has the potential to uncover priorities for vocational training to prepare for a post Fourth Industrial Revolution future. An initial list of key uncertainties, high impact and poorly understood dynamics, drawn from various scenario-based strategy processes, is reflected below and provides insight into this category of external dynamic that may influence a city government resilience strategy.

8.3   Key uncertainties

The following key uncertainties can be highlighted:

- technology convergence: 23 deep, converging shifts which are part of the so-called Fourth Industrial Revolution;[111]
- rising economic and societal inequality;
- increasing interventions by the national and provincial government;
- societal expectations and demands since 1994 asynchronous with current realities; and
- university protests against the rising cost of higher education.

Further risks are documented based on the findings in the Institute of Risk Management South Africa (IRMSA) Report and reflected in Table 4.7. This identifies important risks in South Africa which are ranked by "Likelihood" and "Consequence".[112]

These dynamics and their ranking provide an indication from the IRMSA perspective for policy priorities with which to offset these risks. Conspicuous by its absence or subsumed in other items, such as "Unemployment" above, is the predetermined risk of 26.5 million young people under the age of 24 years making up the so-called "youth bulge" in the South African population demographic (see Table 4.6). However, being inclusive when describing the context may avoid omissions and unpleasant surprises. While the IRMSA identifies these risks as national risks in South Africa, they may also have an impact on city government resilience. Besides "key uncertainties" there may be another category of forces in the context of cities that might challenge their resilience.

---

[110]   Van der Waldt, 2016a.

[111]   World Economic Forum (WEF). 2015. Survey Report – Deep Shift: Technology tipping points and societal impact. https://search.yahoo.com/search?p=wef%20survey%20report%20 deep%20shiftselect&fr=yset_chr_cnewtab&type=newtab Date of access: 9 February 2017.

[112]   Institute for Risk Management South Africa (IRMSA). 2015. *South Africa Risks Report.* Johannesburg: IRMSA, pp. 8, 9.

Table 4.7:IRMSA report – South Africa risks 2015 rank order

By likelihood	By consequence
Corruption	Corruption
Unemployment	Governance failure
Infrastructure failure	Unemployment
Political and social instability	Infrastructure and networks
Organised crime	Critical Infrastructure
Cyberattacks	Fiscal crisis
Financial mechanisms failure	Financial mechanisms failure
Income disparity	Economic and resource nationalisation
Urbanisation	Cyberattacks
Data fraud	Income disparity

Source: IRMSA.[113]

8.4 Low probability/high impact dynamics (potential black swans)

So-called "black swans"[114] represent the impact of unanticipated events, analogous to the unexpected appearance of a black swan outside of the general awareness of executive leaders and executive managers. A number of dynamics which are outside of the awareness have been identified in this section. In the event of one or more of these dynamics coming to pass, they will most probably be labelled as so-called black swans to register their unexpected occurrence. To be precise, Taleb[115] argues that black swans are unknowable. However, were a low probability/high impact dynamic to materialise, such a dynamic could have an impact on a city government resilience strategy. For instance, Berkshire Hathaway Chief Executive, Warren Buffet, stated at his company's 2002 AGM that in his view "a nuclear detonation, on a major metropolis, was now a virtual certainty".[116] Buffett is widely acknowledged by the investment community for his ability to anticipate the future. His view, in this case, may be based on the increasing availability of weapons-grade fissionable material used in

---

[113]   Institute for Risk Management South Africa (IRMSA). 2015, pp. 8, 9.

[114]   Taleb, N.N. 2007. *The black swan*. London: Penguin.

[115]   Taleb, 2007.

[116]   Buffett, W. 2002. *Nuclear attack 'virtually a certainty'* https://www.google.co.za/search ?rlz=1C2NHXL_enZA697ZA697&source=hp&q=Berkshire+Hathaway+Chief+Executive %2C+Buffet+nuclear+detonation&oq=Berkshire+Hathaway+Chief+Executive%2C+ Buffet+nuclear+detonation&gs_l=psy-ab.12...3825.14098.0.16754.20.20.0.0.0.0.427.3611.2-10j1j2.13.0....0...1.1.64.psy-ab..7.10.2 553...33i160k1j33i21k1.G8fg_R-uYc0 Date of access: 21 June 2016.

nuclear power programmes. Many of these nuclear power programmes are being developed in unstable parts of the world such as Iran, North Korea and Pakistan. It may, therefore, be useful and in the interests of developing a robust resilience strategy to consider this possibility. Considering such a possibility and asking what we would do in the event of this dynamic may already create resilience because, by considering it plausible, awareness is raised in decision makers.

Another example of a black swan is what has become widely accepted among futurists, namely a viral attack on humans similar to the 1918 so-called Spanish flu epidemic. While this dynamic is seen as predetermined, the timing of such a pandemic may be unknown and unknowable. Hence, a resilience strategy should take into account the possibility of such a pandemic. The Spanish flu epidemic is estimated to have caused the loss of 20- to 50 million lives worldwide.[117] Since the above passage was written, the Covid-19 virus has spread across the entire globe with devastating impact on health and the economy as a result of the lockdown strategy implemented by most countries. Singapore and a handful of other government organisations probably anticipated this dynamic as it has a scenario-planning function embedded in its government organisation. With a planning time horizon of 20- to 25 years, planners should anticipate that there will be another episode where a pathogenic virus impacts on society during this timeframe. It remains unclear if the structures such as wet markets etc. that were the cause of Covid-19 have been dismantled. If not, planners should anticipate another viral attack and prepare a resilience strategy for it in advance.

Systems Dynamics (SD) practitioners are aware that a systemic phenomenon such as climate change may reach thresholds after which the dynamic accelerates or declines rapidly and unexpectedly. Thresholds being breached are reflected in the prolonged, unseasonal droughts in the Cape which threaten water security and expose poor city government resilience strategies. According to Bohatch,[118] "we shouldn't see the current water crisis in the Cape as a temporary phenomenon that will resolve in a year or two. It's a long-term problem". This conclusion may have implications for other cities in the Southern African region. Reaching a threshold is also reflected in the exponential increase in the number of cyclones in the United States of America.

Another example of a plausible black swan is an electromagnetic shock (EMS). An electron ejection by the sun causes an EMS, and an

---

[117] Influenza pandemic. 2017. *Flu pandemic: Facts & summary*. www.history.com/topics/1918-flu-pandemic *Date of access: 28 August 2017*.

[118] Bohatch, 2017.

EMS could inflict permanent damage on a country's electrical generation, transmission and distribution system which would also affect cities. Storm Analysis Consultants in Duluth, Minnesota,[119] maintain that an "Electromagnetic shock (EMS) may be caused by a coronal mass ejection from the sun as occurred on 13 March 1989, which had a startling impact on Canada. Within 92 seconds, the resulting geomagnetic storm took down Quebec's electricity grid for nine hours". They posit that "it could have been worse, had it hit the United States of America, the resulting geomagnetic storm would have destroyed a quarter of high voltage transformers". They add that "a prolonged interruption of electricity supply may be life-threatening, removing up to 90% of the population as a result of the prolonged absence of electricity". According to Storm Analysis Consultants in Duluth, Minnesota "future geomagnetic storms are inevitable". They go on to point out that "[a] nuclear blast 40 km above the earth, over the USA, for instance, could also generate an EMS".[120]

If city government resilience is to be robust, there is a need for cities to anticipate and prepare for these eventualities in their resilience strategies. The Rockefeller Foundation posits that there are generic dynamics, which they have labelled "acute internal stresses", that have become "the new normal" for cities across the globe. These include:
- "poverty;
- endemic crime and violence; and
- failing infrastructure that weakens cities over time".[121]

In the South African city context, the internal dynamics listed below are visible almost daily in the media and can have an impact upon city government resilience.

8.5 Internal city government and city dynamics
The following internal dynamics and general dynamics around cities are applicable:
- factional divisions, dysfunctional competition for jobs and conflict;
- patronage politics;
- trust deficit and paranoia;
- erosion of public accounting quality;
- erosion of accountability to the South African Constitution and the rule of law;

---

[119] *Economist.* 2017. The world if 2017: Electromagnetic Shock. http://worldif.economist.com/article/13526/electromagnetic-shock Date of access: 20 September 2017.

[120] *Economist,* 2017.

[121] Rockefeller Foundation, 2017.

- accelerating irregular expenditure and corruption;
- erosion of capability within government institutions and state-owned entities;
- uneven capability at national government, provincial government and city government levels to execute plans on time, on budget and on quality;
- lack of capability resulting in unreliable service delivery;
- deteriorating personal safety and security;
- decline in health and life expectancy caused by, among other things, increasing HIV/AIDS infection levels; and
- policy ambiguity between the NDP and NDR flowing from "unresolved dilemmas" (see section 4.8.6).

Source: Author's research

Trompenaars and Hampden-Turner[122] posit that many policy choices present in the form of dilemmas, as seemingly apposing choices in tension with each other. When left unresolved they create ambiguity and uncertainty. The uncertainty resulting from policy ambiguity in and of itself creates a lack of resilience at all levels of government. Such ambiguity may inhibit clear signalling of priorities and government policy which in turn creates hesitation and an inability to act decisively in the event of a challenge to resilience.

8.6 Unresolved dilemmas, policy ambiguity and uncertainty

The following unresolved dilemmas, policy ambiguity and uncertainties are critical to monitor:
- supremacy of the Constitution versus primary loyalty to a faction and its narrow interests;
- narrow African nationalism versus global internationalism and national competitiveness;
- the National Democratic Revolution (NDR) versus National Development Planning (NDP);
- leveraging a national crisis to transform society by edict as part of the crisis response;
- social transformation via statute and regulation versus leveraging economic freedom, effective developmental economic policies and sustainable community investment programmes (SCIP) for sustainable social transformation; and

---

[122] Trompenaars, F. & Hampden-Turner, C. 1998. *Riding the waves of culture.* 2nd ed. London: Nicholas Brealey.

- learner-centred quality education for embedding critical thinking skills as a prerequisite for economic development and democracy versus teacher and institution directed education by rote learning.

Source: Author's research

Dilemmas, as defined by Trompenaars and Hampden-Turner,[123] express culture as a systemic structure where the "horns of a dilemma" are in tension with each other. The productive resolution of dilemmas determines and shapes culture.[124]

According to Lawrence and Lorsch,[125] contingency relationships exist between the degree of uncertainty and stability in the environment and the internal structure of an organisation. This contingency relationship points to the likelihood of city government organisations embodying elements of the national culture, as they are influenced by aspects of this culture. Trompenaars and Hampden-Turner[126] define culture thus: "Culture is the way in which a group of people solve problems and reconcile dilemmas." The unresolved dilemmas listed above, besides creating unambiguity and uncertainty, may over time harden into national cultural dynamics and enter the culture of city government organisations. The context for local government may also be determined by the level of interventions from the central government. The events and patterns over time with interventions by the national government in municipalities provide an indication of the underlying structure of interventions. The official reasons for interventions as well as the underlying intentions underpinning them provide a further level of complexity to internal dynamics within municipalities.

8.7 Interventions by the province and the national government in municipalities

In terms of section 139 of the South African Constitution[127] and the constitutional support for provincial and national government interventions in local government, there seems to be a rising trend in interventions in the affairs of municipalities. That this is justified may be deduced from the level of irregular spending reflected in Table 4.2 above: "Irregular expenditure

---

[123] Trompenaars & Hampden-Turner, 1998.

[124] Trompenaars & Hampden-Turner, 1998, p. 6.

[125] Lawrence, P. & Lorsch, J.W. 1967. Differentiation and integration in complex organisation. *Administration Science Quarterly,* 1(12):1–30.

[126] Trompenaars & Hampden-Turner, 1998, p. 6.

[127] South Africa, 1996.

by municipalities by province". Van der Waldt and Greffrath[128] assert that "these trends can be seen against the broader context of state dysfunction". They assert that "poor service delivery and lapses of governance may not be exclusively at play in interventionism. Political factors may also serve as more covert reasons to intervene to influence the balance of power in a given province, municipality or within the party itself".[129] Van der Waldt[130] cautions that "government interventionism is multifaceted and multidimensional, political, economic and social". He goes on to cite common failures that have triggered section 139 interventions. The most common failures include:

- "governance failures, political infighting, a conflict between senior management and councillors, and human resource management issues;
- financial failures, specifically inadequate revenue collection, ineffective financial systems, fraud, misuse of municipal assets and funds; and
- service delivery failure, for example, breaches of sections 152 and 153 of the South African Constitution which outline the service delivery obligations of municipalities."[131]

According to Van der Waldt and Greffrath,[132] in the context of local and district municipalities, metros are seen by government in terms of the government classification system for municipalities in distress as "Class 4: Low vulnerability". In terms of failure to honour their municipal mandate, maintaining best practice service delivery requires that capacity building takes place constantly to enable their capability. This may also be true for enabling city government resilience. The low vulnerability status of metros provides a platform for further improving their resilience. Greater resilience amongst metros will, in aggregate, probably raise the resilience of South Africa as a whole. As a result of migration to cities, metros take on a more economic and politically important role in development in general and the developmental state specifically. The dilemma between a centrally directed model (NDR) and a distributed market-friendly model (NDP), regarding the preferred economic development model, creates ambiguous signalling for policymakers and investors. It may, therefore, be useful to clarify the basis of economic policy which supplements democratic principles. In a democracy, individual choice lies at the heart of the

---

[128] Van der Waldt, G. & Greffrath, W. 2016. Towards a typology of government interventions in municipalities. *African Journal of Public Affairs,* 9(2):152–165.

[129] Van der Waldt & Greffrath, 2016.

[130] Van der Waldt, 2016a.

[131] Van der Waldt, 2016a, p. 121.

[132] Van der Waldt & Greffrath, 2016, p. 157.

election process that underpins democratically elected representatives. The principle of individual, informed choice may thus be an essential part of the political dynamics in a constitutional democracy. There may also be an economic equivalent which posits that an economy and economic development may best be driven through distributed self-control versus an ideology of centrally controlled policy and governance. The role of government thus becomes providing the context for self-control and freedom to act. According to The Heritage Foundation, economic freedom as defined, may yield better economic results in terms of development and societal transformation.

9 ECONOMIC FREEDOM OF CHOICE AS THE FOUNDATION FOR DEVELOPMENT AND TRANSFORMATION

Milton Friedman, in alignment with the arguments put forward by Drucker[133] above, argues that government has three primary functions:

- "provide military defence of the nation;
- enforce contracts between individuals; and
- it should protect citizens from crimes against themselves or their property".[134]

In the context of the size of government, Friedman[135] argues that when governments, with the best of intentions, try to rearrange the economy, legislate morality, or help special interests, the cost comes in inefficiency, corruption by middlemen, lack of motivation and loss of freedom. Friedman, supported by Drucker,[136] insists that "government should be a referee, not an active player".[137] According to Friedman,[138] freedom to choose probably lies at the heart of economic freedom, market-friendly policy, the free enterprise system itself, wealth creation and job creation. He argues that greater efficiencies may be derived from freedom of choice. He points out that "[t]he free enterprise system is not only about profits but also about losses. Sustained losses and bankruptcy is the free enterprise way of getting rid of management that makes bad or wasteful strategic decisions".[139] He asserts that it is inappropriate for the government

---

[133] Drucker, 1994

[134] Friedman, M. 2017. *Milton Friedman quotes.* https://www.goodreads.com/author/quotes/5001.Milton_Friedman Date of access: 30 August 2017.

[135] Friedman, 2017.

[136] Drucker, 1994.

[137] Friedman, 2017.

[138] Friedman, 2017.

[139] Friedman, 2017.

to engage in activities which the free enterprise system may be able to deliver. "When the government engages in free enterprise activities and makes bad strategic decisions or wastes resources, the same management will most likely approach the treasury to ask for taxpayers' money to keep them in business."[140] He argues that the result is usually to perpetuate poor leadership, wastage and bad strategic decisions. He concludes that "[t]his also often creates a co-dependence between government institutions and the citizens' taxes masquerading as investment and business which actually only enrich a few politically connected people".[141]

9.1 The Heritage Foundation and economic freedom ranking in 2015

Institutes and think tanks in the United States of America such as the Fraser Institute and the Cato Institute provide reliable information on economic freedom and its associations that are in alignment with the findings of The Heritage Foundation (THF).

Table 4.8 describes The Heritage Foundation's perspective on economic freedom. The association between these criteria and gross domestic product (GDP) per capita in Figure 4.2 demonstrates that there is a positive association between The Heritage Foundation ranking criteria for economic freedom and GDP per capita. The Heritage Foundation economic freedom index country ranking is based on the criteria reflected in Table 4.8. Descriptions of each criterion are provided in the table.

Table 4.8:The Heritage Foundation 2015 economic freedom

THF Index criteria
1. **Rule of Law** which includes property rights and freedom from corruption
2. **Government size** which includes fiscal freedom and government spending
3. **Regulatory Efficiency** which includes business freedom, labour freedom and monetary freedom
4. **Open Markets** which includes trade freedom, investment freedom and financial freedom

Source: The Heritage Foundation[142]

The association. reflected in Figure 4.2, between economic freedom of countries, as defined above, and successful economic development creating wealth, reflected as GDP per capita, or purchasing power parity (PPP$), is

---

[140] Friedman, 2017.

[141] Friedman, 2017.

[142] Heritage Foundation. 2015. *Index of Economic Freedom*. www.heritage.org
Date of access: 4 April 2017.

becoming widely accepted by evidence-based leadership and policymakers across the world. Singapore, South Korea and Australia are cited as leading examples of free economies and effective sustainable economic development and wealth creation.

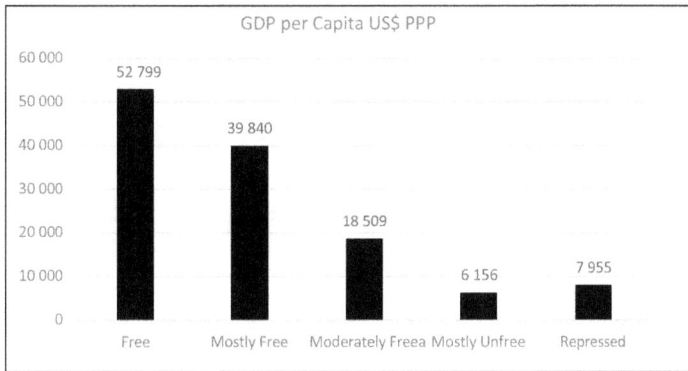

Figure 4.2: GDP & economic freedom
Source: The Heritage Foundation[143]

Closely held assumptions may blind observers because "political slogans outlive political reality. The slogans of the welfare state century will similarly be with us for a long time, yet the political doctrines which the slogans of the welfare state or of communism reflect have ceased to have much relevance or reality, politically, socially, even economically".[144] Drucker points out that "policies that may turn out to be counterproductive to development may be put forward by policymakers by virtue of good intentions and not based upon hard evidence".[145] Evidence of an association between economic freedom and wealth creation can be seen and conclusions reached from inspection of the data reflected in Figure 4.2 above. It may be concluded from these data that the "more free" the economic system, the greater the wealth that is created. It is probably also true that when free enterprise is conducted in a sustainable and socially responsible manner, it reduces inequality. In this context, a socially responsible government may provide a safety net through appropriate legislation. However, there is a balance to be struck between supporting citizens' needs for a safety net and creating a co-dependency with government handouts, where citizens cease to take responsibility for themselves.

Friedman[146] draws our attention to a contradiction by explaining that "a major source of objection to a free economy is that it gives people what

---

[143] Heritage Foundation. 2015.

[144] Drucker, 1994.

[145] Drucker, 1994.

[146] Friedman, M. 1980. *Free to choose*. Chicago, IL: Harcourt.

they want, and not what a particular group thinks they ought to want. Underlying most arguments against the free market is a lack of belief in freedom itself". He adds that "national leadership may not deliberately set out to destroy its own economy. It usually happens incrementally, the result of policies which are counterproductive, informed by outdated ideology, economic illiteracy, narrow factional interests and short-sightedness".[147] Over time, different policies in countries result in these countries separating economically from each other based upon levels of economic freedom as defined by THF. A selection of countries is reflected in Table 4.9 to highlight economies that may be relevant to Southern Africa and current policymakers in South Africa.

9.2   Country rankings evidence for developmental policy – a selection

The relative numerical ranking in Table 4.9 reflects a country's relative economic freedom according to The Heritage Foundation index. Learning from these patterns and understanding the links between the various components of the index and its underlying structure may be a fruitful approach to macroeconomic policy in South Africa, as well as for city government sustainable development policy. This would also be preferable to waiting to see the outcomes and unintended consequences after 20- to 25 years of good policy intentions. For example, when Zimbabwe, Cuba, North Korea and Venezuela are held up by politicians as a basis for policy, it is self-evident from their relative ranking in The Heritage Foundation Economic Freedom index that such policies may turn out to reduce rather than promote development, wealth creation and jobs. Further comparisons of evidence-based patterns between South Africa and other companion countries are useful from an economic developmental policy point of view. The other BRICS countries, namely Brazil, Russia, India and China, are, according to The Heritage Foundation, index all less free than South Africa. Learning from these countries as a basis for economic development policy may thus have unintended consequences, such as a lack of resilience and counterproductive outcomes.

---

[147]   Friedman, 1980, p. 17.

Table 4.9: Global ranking: a selection of the 186 countries ranked by the freedom index score

Free	Mostly free	Moderately free	Mostly unfree	Repressed
1. Hong Kong	6. Canada	36. Botswana	91. Swaziland	155. Lesotho
2. Singapore	9. Ireland	72. South Africa	92. Uganda	158. Angola
3. New Zealand	10. Mauritius		93. Namibia	166. CAR
4. Australia	12. USA		100. Zambia	168. DRC
5. Switzerland	13. UK		109. Tanzania	175. Zimbabwe
	14. Taiwan		118. Brazil	177. Cuba
	16. Germany		120. Nigeria	178. North Korea
	17. Netherlands		126. Malawi	179. Venezuela
	23. Sweden		128. India	
	29. South Korea		139. China	
	31. Malaysia		143. Russia	

Source: Index of Economic Freedom – The Heritage Foundation[148]

The selected countries reflected in Table 4.9 show their relative ranking according to economic freedom criteria. It may be concluded from the evidence in Tables 4.8 and 4.9, together with Figure 4.2, that economic freedom can be associated with sustainable development (SDev) and thus enables city and national government resilience. Decision makers formulating policy for both city government and national government will probably learn more from Hong Kong, Singapore, New Zealand and Australia, which are ranked as "Free", as well as Mauritius ranked as "Mostly Free" (see Table 4.9). In the Sub-Saharan region, Mauritius leads the way on economic freedom followed by Botswana, which is ranked "Moderately Free". Significantly, the Mauritius government which is a "Mostly Free" country in the Southern African (SoA) region (see Table 4.9) is in the process of encouraging greater use of their port facilities by acquiring the entire Singapore harbour container clearing system to speed up the traffic through their own harbours. Singapore is effectively able to clear a container in 12 minutes as opposed to weeks in other harbours. Sustainable economic development at city government level, shaped by a policy that enables economic freedom as defined by The Heritage Foundation, will probably raise the level of development, reduce inequality and improve city government resilience.

Key lessons may be drawn for a city resilience strategy and policy from the evidence in Figure 4.2, which demonstrates the association between economic freedom as defined in Table 4.8 and GDP per capita. Emulating strategy and policy from the countries with the highest levels

---

[148] The Heritage Foundation, 2015.

of economic freedom and GDP per capita may provide appropriate evidence and guidance for an effective resilience strategy.

Property rights have a long and conflicted history in most countries which were occupied by the colonial empires of England, Germany, France and Holland. Moreover, property rights are a key component of economic freedom as defined by The Heritage Foundation index. A description of the origins of property rights is therefore justified to enable a deeper understanding as the basis for policy at national level as well as at city government levels. This issue is analysed in the next section.

9.3   Origins of property rights

The protection of property rights is one of the criteria for economic freedom defined in Table 4.8 above and stated as "Rule of Law which includes property rights and freedom from corruption".[149] Property rights and the restoration of property are often positioned in the media by politicians as the top priority for alleviating poverty and inequality. The demand and priority, among many competing social needs, for the restoration of property rights and the distribution of property as the basis for economic development may thus be more closely interrogated. It seems that the sentiments among a sample of the population indicate that there are other "serious unresolved problems" that may outrank "property distribution". In a field survey relying on a representative sample of 2291 people across all the racial groups in South Africa, one of the survey questions under the heading, "Most serious unresolved problems" that the RSA faces post-1994, was put to respondents in a face-to-face interview. Respondents ranked "Distribution of Property" tenth in a ranked list of ten items and "Unemployment" as the top of the list of issues, therefore first.[150]

Emphasis on the distribution of property, some argue "without compensation", is probably used in the service of short-term populist vote-harvesting rather than as evidence-based policy for the purposes of sustainable developmental needs among the population, as the IRR survey results demonstrate. This contradiction between perceptions and evidence provides an example of judging a policy by intention, in preference to basing policy on the evidence of proven results. Lack of adequate protection of property rights may also deter FDI and result in a decline in economic wealth resulting from a lack of investment. Appropriate policy in the service of the protection of property rights may require greater clarity regarding the origin of these rights. "Property rights had their origin in ownership of land. According to THF they now include all property including equity

---

[149]   The Heritage Foundation, 2015.

[150]   IRR, 2017a pg. 3.

ownership in markets, companies and intellectual property. Property rights in the sense of rights to own land are a relatively recent introduction to society".[151] Malchik explains that –

"... the point [of property ownership] was for an individual or family to gain the means for an independent life, not grow rich from land ownership. The Magna Carta, agreed in 1215 by England's King John at the insistence of his barons, protected those nobles from losing their lands at the whim of whatever sovereign they were serving."

The Magna Carta is a charter of rights agreed to by King John of England at Runnymede, near Windsor, on 15 June 1215. It may be widely cited as the foundation of modern democracy. In pre-democratic tribal Africa, and in parts of South Africa today, land ownership remains at risk at the whim of the local tribal chief.

Having argued in favour of economic freedom as policy at both national and city government level, evidence may be found within the official economic development policy embodied in the NDP[152] for national macroeconomic policy and city government policy respectively. The NDP provides a focus on key dynamics such as –

- "building an economy that will create more jobs;
- building capabilities;
- improving infrastructure;
- building environmental sustainability and resilience;
- improving quality of education;
- health care for all;
- safer communities; and
- fighting corruption".[153]

The unresolved policy dilemma between complying with the market-friendly NDP or centrally directed NDR may create confusion among policymakers and investors. It also violates what Deming, the father of the Japanese industrial revolution, identifies as "[t]he crippling disease: lack of constancy of purpose and an emphasis on the short term".[154] The fact that China has derived most of its recent growth from market-based

[151] Malchik, A. 2017. *Who owns the earth? Aeon essays.* https://aeon.co/essays/is-it-time-to-upend-the-idea-that-land-is-private-property Date of access: 14 January 2017.

[152] National Planning Commission (NPC). 2012. *National Development Plan 2030: Our future – make it work.* Pretoria: Department of the Presidency.

[153] National Planning Commission (NPC). 2012, pp. 23–63.

[154] Deming, W.E. 1986. *Out of the crisis.* Cambridge, MA: MIT Press, p. 98.

policies seems to have been lost on the adherents to the NDR. "China's pre-communist trajectory of a rural, family, and community-oriented economy, combined with overseas networks, created an indigenous tradition of flexible labour and networked capitalism that others now emulate. The Maoist promotion of education and health was as important as any privatisation initiatives to develop a globally competitive labour force".[155] Attractiveness to investors forms the basis for placing capital at the disposal of industries within national and local government jurisdictions. Consequently, government policy and capability may encourage or discourage such investments.

9.4 Foreign direct investment and city government attractiveness

According to the International Monetary Fund (IMF), it is widely accepted for emerging economies and for cities that an important part of enabling economic development is their attractiveness for foreign direct investment (FDI). FDI has become an important source of private external finance for economic development. It represents an investment in production facilities and may have great significance for developing economies because FDI can add to investible resources and capital formation. FDI is also a means of transferring production technology, know-how, skills, innovative capacity, and organisational and managerial practices to local situations. FDI often also provides access to international marketing networks. "Since the early 1980s, world FDI flows are now attributable to almost 54 000 transnational corporations. They have grown rapidly – faster than either world trade or world output. During 1980–1997, global FDI outflows increased at an average rate of about 13 per cent a year".[156]

The IMF describes policy framework and trends in developing countries and the determinants of FDI in terms of "Host country (and city) determinants, Type of FDI classified by motive of firms and principal economic determinants in host countries (and cities)".[157]

9.5 Type of foreign direct investment – host country and city determinants

Development in cites may be dependent on FDI flows. It may therefore be helpful for appropriate policy formulators to understand motives and priorities of investors.

---

[155] Sheppard, E. 2010. Adam Smith in Beijing: Lineages of twenty-first century by Giovanni Arrighi. *Clark University,* 86(1):99–101. www.economicgeography.org Date of access: 29 August 2017.

[156] International Monetary Fund (IMF). 1999. Foreign direct investment in developing countries. *Finance and Development,* 36(1):114–140

[157] IMF, 1999.

9.6 Policy framework for foreign direct investment

Motives for FDI described by the IMF[158] may inform policy that enhances attractiveness to investors. According to the IMF, these motives typically are the following:

- "economic, political, and social stability;
- rules regarding entry and operations;
- standards of treatment of foreign affiliates;
- policies on functioning and structure of markets (especially competition and policies governing mergers and acquisitions);
- international agreements on FDI;
- privatization policy;
- trade policy (tariffs and non-tariff barriers) and coherence of FDI and trade policies; and
- tax policy".[159]

9.7 Business facilitation

The IMF[160] points out that this motive for FDI describes business aspects that enhance and facilitate attractiveness for investors. This includes the following:

- "investment promotion (including image-building and investment-generating activities and investment-facilitation services);
- investment incentives;
- costs (related to corruption and administrative inefficiency); and
- social amenities (for example, schools, quality of life)".[161]

9.8 Type of foreign direct investment classified by motive of firms and principal economic determinants in host countries

The IMF[162] points out that this motive for FDI describes how business and other economic determinants enhance attractiveness for investors in terms of the potential magnitude of return on investment (ROI).

9.9 Market-seeking FDI

- "market size and per capita income;
- market growth;

---

[158] IMF, 1999.

[159] IMF, 1999.

[160] IMF, 1999.

[161] IMF, 1999.

[162] IMF, 1999.

- access to regional and global markets; and
- country-specific consumer preferences".[163]

9.10 Resource/asset-seeking FDI

This motive for FDI describes the resources that may be available that enhance attractiveness for investors in terms of locally available factors of production and existing assets that may form the basis of ROI.

9.11 Structure of markets

The structure of markets and availability of the factors of production enable investors to operate efficiently, thereby maximising ROI. Key components of the structure of markets are –
- "raw materials;
- low-cost skilled labour;
- skilled labour; and
- technological, innovative, and other created assets (for example, brand names), including as embodied in individuals, firms and clusters".[164]

9.12 Efficiency-seeking FDI

This motive for FDI describes the ease of doing business in terms of physical movement of goods and potential ROI which enhances attractiveness for investors, for example physical infrastructure (ports, roads, power, telecommunications). These efficiencies include the following:
- "cost of resources and assets listed above, adjusted for labour productivity;
- other input costs, such as transport and communication costs to/from and within the host economy and other intermediate products; and
- membership of a regional integration agreement conducive to the establishment of regional corporate networks".[165]

To establish a priority among attractors for FDI, consulting firm Kearney[166] surveyed investors to establish a rank order for factors which most influenced their investment decisions in a foreign market. Table 4.10 reflects the results of this survey. While the Kearney surveys are aimed at a country level, many of the attractors may be made available by city

---

[163]   IMF, 1999.

[164]   IMF, 1999.

[165]   IMF, 1999.

[166]   Kearney, A.T. 2017. *2017 AT Kearney Foreign Direct Investment Confidence Index: Glass half full.* https://www.atkearney.com/documents/10192/12116059/2017+FDI+Confidence+Index+-+Glass+Half+Full.pdf/5dced533-c150-4984-acc9-da561b4d96b4 Date of access: 12 August 2017.

government through strategy, policy and municipal legislation. City-to-city networked relationships may provide a gateway for industrialists from one city to invest in another city. Cities attracting investment may already have built or possess many of the properties that may attract investors, as listed below.

Table 4.10: Attractors for foreign direct investment (FDI)

Rank number	Description
1	General security environment
2	Efficiency of legal and regulatory processes
3	Tax rates and ease of tax payment
4	Technological and innovation capabilities
5	Transparency of government regulation and lack of corruption
6	Domestic market size
7	Domestic economic performance
8	Ease of moving capital into and out of the country
9	Strength of investor and property rights
10	Government incentives for investors
11	Government participation in trade agreements
12	Cost of labour
13	Availability of financial capital in domestic market
14	Availability of land or real estate
15	Talent and skill level of labour pool
16	Research and development capabilities
17	Availability of raw materials and other inputs
18	Quality of transportation infrastructure
19	Quality of telecommunications infrastructure
20	Quality of electricity infrastructure

Source: Kearney[167]

The above attractors may be embedded in city government policy making, where such policy is within the municipal constitutional mandate for city government. Attracting greater FDI may enable sustainable economic development and city government resilience. Among the highest-ranked

---

[167] Kearney, 2017, p. 10.

priorities for attracting FDI in Table 4.10 above are criteria that are directly interdependent with and within the ambit of national government policy. Among some of the highly ranked factors that investors may consider are:
- "technological and innovation capabilities;
- lack of corruption;
- government incentives for investors;
- availability of land or real estate;
- talent and skill level of labour pool;
- research and development capabilities;
- quality of transportation infrastructure; and
- quality of telecommunications infrastructure".[168]

City government may also influence and determine the policy that influences the factors that influence investors specifically cost of city government. Cost of government as perceived by potential investors may constitute an important attractor for foreign direct investment in a specific city. These costs typically include:
- "cost of labour;
- general security environment;
- regulatory transparency;
- the efficiency of legal and regulatory processes; and
- tax rates and ease of tax payments".[169]

Costs of government may also be determined by shifting social and political dynamics as well as expectations of what governments must do.

10 COST OF GOVERNMENT

Drucker[170] pinpoints new realities which may bring pressures to bear on the government to perform. He posits that these pressures may emanate from small highly organised minorities, single-cause or single-interest in their focus and totally political in the form of new mass movements. He argues that to try and satisfy them through charisma may result in mis-leadership and mis-performance. The "new realities" he describes "will make totally different demands on political leadership".[171] Drucker points out that "[f]or almost two centuries we hotly discussed what the government *should* do. We almost never discussed what government *can*

---

[168] Kearney, 2017, p. 10.

[169] Kearney, 2017, p. 10.

[170] Drucker, 1994.

[171] Drucker, 1994, p. 56.

do".[172] Drucker adds that it has become widely accepted, and evidence now demonstrates, that "there are limits to what government can do". He points out that "there are three reasons for this change". Drucker describes these reasons in the following manner:

- "the failure of government programmes and government operations since the second world war;
- there are limits to what taxation and spending can achieve; and
- there are limits to government's ability to raise revenue".[173]

The unrealistic expectations that accompany assumptions about what government should do will, in the face of the above realities, inevitably result in disappointment and frustration for governments and citizens. This may, in turn, lead to protests and antisocial behaviour in society.

10.1 The role of expectations and pressure on government cost

In the context of rising expectations of government from citizens at both national and city levels in South Africa, Cronje[174] points out that "[o]ur critics ask why if we are correct in suggesting that living standards have improved so quickly, is there so much violent protest action and antisocial behaviour in our society". He goes on to argue that "as life improves in any society, people begin to expect continued improvement in their living standards and what city government should do". Where the economy becomes unable to secure such improvements, a dramatic political reaction is likely to be triggered by exactly what we see in South Africa today".[175] Pressure from rising expectations of government may result in greater demands and at the same time demands for lowering the cost of government. This dynamic may reflect the "new realities" Drucker describes above in the local context. Drucker argues that because we know there are limits to government's ability to raise revenue, city government may need to return to a more focused and back-to-basics, business-like approach for discharging its mandate. City government may need to prioritise carefully and engage with its citizens regarding its strategies and policies. Cronje[176] warns that "expectations may be outpacing realities currently on a national level". This phenomenon is true for any process of transformation and must be taken into account for the change to succeed.

---

[172] Drucker, 1994, p. 59.

[173] Drucker, 1994, pp. 61, 62.

[174] Cronje, F. 2017. *A time traveller's guide to South Africa in 2030.* Cape Town: Tafelberg, p. 51.

[175] Cronje, 2017, p. 51.

[176] Cronje, 2017, p. 51.

Osborne and Hutchinson[177] advise that a back-to-basics approach for municipalities emphasises getting back to the fundamentals of sound value-for-money government. This approach may also enhance sustainability and ensure resilience through the capacity to formulate robust plans and capably execute such plans. Osborne and Hutchinson[178] provide certain basic frameworks and principles for a back-to-basics approach for government in general, which may also be applicable to city government. Osborne and Hutchinson offer a perspective on cost-cutting and austerity from New York in the USA and the effects on other government institutions following the New York example. They point out that:

> "Bloomberg, the mayor of New York, announced a layoff of 3,400 city employees and the closure of eight firehouses. The following day the city Department of Education cut 3,200 jobs. America's largest city faced a budget shortfall of $3.3 billion, despite an 18.5 percent increase in the city property tax and elimination of 14,000 city jobs since Mayor Bloomberg took office."[179]

Starting from the perspective of resource availability in preference to expectations that may be unrealistic, and only then deciding what ought to be done by government, could enable city government to apply downward pressure on the costs of government.

The principles put forward by Osborne and Hutchinson can also be of value to municipalities in South Africa. Specifically, their financial emphasis may add value as this is one of the key vulnerabilities, resulting from the large-scale wastage in municipal government as a result of the irregular spending described above (see Table 4.2). The Osborne and Hutchinson approach include goal setting and review as a key process for improving productivity and quality of services in city government. Evidence from Locke and Latham[180] supports this emphasis. Osborne and Hutchinson provide tactics for "smarter government" and an approach for providing better results for citizens, as reflected in Tables 4.11 and 4.12, respectively. Tactics for smarter government include many of the modern management approaches used in successful business ventures. So-called problems are analysed before setting the price that the government may

---

[177] Osborne, D. & Hutchinson, P. 2004. *The price of government: Getting the results we need in an age of permanent fiscal crisis.* New York, NY: Basic Books.

[178] Osborne & Hutchinson, 2004.

[179] Osborne & Hutchinson, 2004, p. 2.

[180] Locke, C.A. & Latham, G.P. 1984. *Goal-setting: A motivational technique that works!* Englewood Cliffs, NJ: Prentice Hall.

have to fund. This is, therefore, an inclusive process where priorities are chosen and realistic goals are set. Purchasing priorities set on a competitive basis ensure that such services are provided at optimal costs.

Table 4.11: Smarter government

No.	Tactic	Analysis
1	Getting a grip on the problem	Is it short- or long term? Is it driven by revenue or expenses or both?
2	Setting the price of government	Determining how much the citizens are willing and able to pay
3	Setting and communicating the priorities of government	Deciding which results citizens value most
4	Setting the price of each priority	Deciding how much the government will spend to produce each of these outcomes
5	Purchasing the priorities	Deciding how best to produce the desired results at the price citizens are willing (and able) to pay

Source: Adapted from Osborne and Hutchinson[181]

Osborne and Hutchinson argue that the best results may be obtained as a result of regular reviews to eliminate projects that are no longer needed. They also advocate deciding what *not to do* as a means of focusing on strategic areas for services. In addition, they advocate the elimination of patronage among employees by focusing on competence for building capability. They argue that approaching the provision of means in terms of services should be evidence-based and the results delivered to citizens should be assessed from their point of view.

Table 4.12: Better results for citizens – approaches for providing the means

Number	Approaches
1.	Strategic reviews: Divesting to invest. Shutting down projects that have become entrenched and are no longer needed
2.	Consolidation around strategic focus areas. Deciding what *not to do*
3.	Rightsizing: Elimination of patronage focusing on competence for building capability
4.	Buying services competitively
5.	Rewarding performance, not good intentions
6.	Smarter customer service: Putting customers in the driver's seat

---

[181] Osborne & Hutchinson, 2004, p. 13.

7.	Don't buy mistrust – eliminate it
8.	Using flexibility to get accountability. Enabling the person closest to management information to take responsibility and be accountable
9.	Making administrative systems allies not enemies
10.	Smarter work processes: Use tools from industry to create efficiencies and continuous improvement of quality, productivity and value

Source: Adapted from Osborne and Hutchinson[182]

Leveraging the recommendations shown in Tables 4.11 and 4.12 above may require leadership that takes a stand, and at the same time is accountable and capable of formulating appropriate policies and plans. Such plans for delivery of services need to be executed on time, on budget and on quality. Rebuilding confidence in citizens following a lapse may be easier at the city and town levels because of the proximity of citizens to their representative on the governing body.

10.2 Service delivery (water, sanitation, health, housing and nutrition)

The IRR[183] describes the current violent protests as "service delivery protests". It goes on to point out that "these protests are taking place against the background of widespread public violence". A count by the IRR shows that 45 people have died in these protests over the past decade, most of them at the hands of the police. These figures exclude the fatalities at Marikana. According to a recent statement by the police, 1 882, violent protests occurred between April 2012 and March 2013. "Grievances include lack of water, or housing, or sanitation, or electricity. In some cases, promises made had not been met, while in others delivery has been interrupted".[184] Barber, Rodrigues and Artis[185] describe their service delivery framework, which they call "deliverology", under the following headings:

- "develop a foundation for delivery;
- understanding the delivery challenges;
- plan for delivery; and
- drive delivery and create an irreversible delivery culture".[186]

---

[182] Osborne & Hutchinson, 2004, pp. 13–17.
[183] Institute of Race Relations (IRR), 2014.
[184] Institute of Race Relations (IRR), 2014, p. 24.
[185] Barber, M., Rodrigues, N. & Artis, E. 2016. *Deliverology in practice*. London: Sage.
[186] Barber et al., 2016, p. 6.

Categories of what Barber et al. posit as foundations for "deliverology" stand out, as they provide an actionable frame of reference for city government. These categories are:
- "building a delivery unit;
- understanding the current reality, and from that base;
- developing a plan to reform the current delivery strategy, while at the same time;
- improving the quality of execution; [see Figure 4.3] and
- *establishing routines* [my emphasis] to drive and monitor performance ensures that there is adequate pressure to perform".[187]

According to Barber et al.,[188] "[b]uilding capacity *all the time* [my emphasis] constantly raises capability". They assert that this is a constant investment in capability through capacity building as capacities underpin capability. During the Japanese industrial revolution, capacity building was done on the job. They point out in Figure 4.3 "Map of delivery" that successful delivery requires "boldness of reforms and quality execution" to achieve improved outcomes and a transformation to a delivery culture.

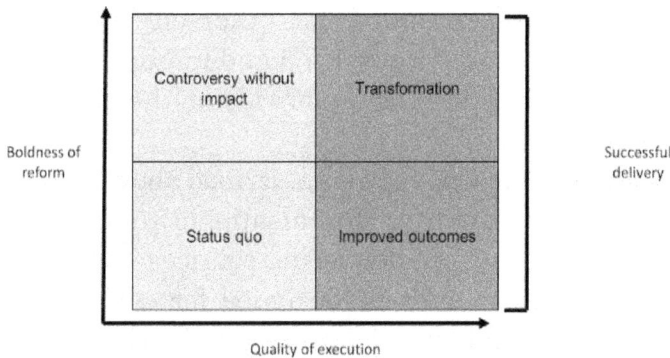

Figure 4.3: Map of delivery
Source: Barber[189]

Barber et al.[190] advocate benchmarking as a scientific method for goal setting and review. They describe five types of benchmarking (see Table 4.13), which may also be useful as the basis for a review of performance and basis for continuous improvement processes.

---

187   Barber et al., 2016, p. 6.
188   Barber et al., 2016, p. 7.
189   Barber, M. 2015. *How to run a government so that citizens benefit and taxpayers don't go crazy.* London: Penguin Random House, p. 6.
190   Barber et al., 2016, p. 13.

Table 4.13: Benchmarking

Type of benchmarking	Example of questions to be asked
against history	What levels of performance have we achieved in the past?
against the world	What levels of performance are achieved in systems like this elsewhere in the world?
against other similar systems	How do we compare to other systems like ours (e.g. among Australian provinces or German *länder*)?
within the system	What levels of performance are achieved by the best performing units in the system (e.g. a hospital, a school, a police force)?
against organisations that are altogether different but have some similar relevant functions	What can we learn from them about how they do that?

Source: Barber[191]

It may be appreciated that calibrating to benchmarks set by other governments' levels of performance locks the city government into using benchmarking as followers. When a city government wishes to lead by *setting the standard or benchmark* for other city governments, it will require continuous structured innovation and improvement systems, such as may be found in TQM and Kaizen, for raising the quality and value for money of services.

Goal setting and review have been described above as high leverage for raising productivity and quality. Organisational routines, where specific steps in a structured process of delivering services – what Barber et al.[192] refer to as "deliverology" – may be designed for embedding goal setting and reviewing progress and quality improvement. These may be used over time by the city government to create and embed an irreversible delivery culture.

11 ATTRACTING AND NURTURING TALENT

Attracting FDI capital is important to growing an economy. However, attracting and nurturing human capital in the form of talent is just as important and requires a deliberate strategy to succeed. According to Lee Kuan Yew, the priority for and importance of nurturing and attracting talent to Singapore was the basis of its success. Lee[193] posits that "[t]alent is a country's [and a city's] most precious asset. For a small country

---

[191] Barber, 2015, p. 14.

[192] Barber et al., 2016.

[193] Lee K.Y., 2000. *From Third World to First*. New York, NY: HarperCollins.

with two million people in 1965 it was the defining factor". Singapore may also be viewed from the perspective of being a successful city-state. Yew[194] describes the Chinese workforce in Singapore as descendants of agricultural labourers and many of the better-educated citizens had emigrated to access better career opportunities in countries such as Canada, New Zealand and Australia. In 1980, Lee formulated a specific recruitment strategy that included structures for placement and social integration. Further dimensions of Lee's strategy for attracting talent that may be relevant to city government were the following:

- "meeting promising students at their universities to try and interest them in jobs in Singapore;
- for the exceptionally bright, Singapore tried to 'green harvest' by offering jobs before graduation, on the basis of performance before final examinations;
- scholarships in the hope that some would remain because of better job opportunities in the city government;
- change our outmoded, bureaucratic immigration policy; and
- elimination of fear of competition both at professional and lower levels; there was a resistance to an inflow of talent".[195]

A significant component of Lee's relentless focus on the development of Singapore may be clearly observed in his focus on attracting talent with the competence required to support the growth strategy. Retaining and nurturing talent that was attracted through meaningful jobs that leveraged the "true motivators" identified by Herzberg above, involved motivating incumbents by providing

- "a sense of achievement;
- recognition through regular performance feedback;
- the work itself;
- real responsibilities;
- advancement;
- personal growth; and
- other true motivators".[196]

Attracting and nurturing talent formed a foundation for the growth and ultimate success of Singapore in becoming a capable state that remains

---

[194] Lee K. Y., 2000.

[195] Lee K.Y.,, 2000, pp. 135–144.

[196] Herzberg, F. 1987. One more time: How do you motivate employees? *Harvard Business Review,* Sept-Oct:109–120, p. 112.

internationally competitive and resilient. Yew[197] provides a benchmark for building capability by developing competence that supports strategy. Van der Merwe[198] identifies "Key Strategy Enabling Processes" based on cross-cutting capabilities and competencies. Examples of these include the following:

- "leadership development;
- strategy engagement forum;
- scenario-based strategy;
- building strategy and alignment;
- business model development;
- performance management;
- systems thinking;
- change management; and
- an enabling organisational culture".[199]

These areas of competence are, amongst others, candidates for developing cross-cutting competence for a city government resilience strategy.

12 CAPABILITY CAPACITY BUILDING IN CROSS-CUTTING COMPETENCE AREAS (KEY STRATEGY ENABLING PROCESSES)

Prioritising the development of the capacity to support building capability for a city resilience strategy comprises integrating the formal part of a performance management system (PMS) with a personal development planning process (PDPs). These PDPs may be formulated for intact executive teams and for individual executive leaders and executive managers. As with the PMS, the responsibility for learning should reside with the learner. This requires personal development goal setting as part of the PMS. Developing capacity in a learner-directed mode commences with a self-diagnosis of needs based on a truthful assessment of competencies. In 2000 United Nations Development Programme (UNDP), as part of their Southern African capacity building initiative, commissioned the development of a competency profile for "strategic leadership". CIL developed this profile for the purposes of self-assessment among the UNDP development professionals in the various UNDP missions in Botswana, Lesotho, South Africa, Namibia and Mozambique. The competency profile consisted of competencies and behaviour descriptions across competencies

---

[197] Yew, 2000.

[198] Van der Merwe, 2008, p. 222.

[199] Van der Merwe, 2008, p. 222.

identified by the UNDP executive leadership. Competence descriptor categories included: "Knowledge (what must be known by the incumbent), Skills (what the incumbent must be able to do), and Attitudes (the way the incumbent should go about doing their tasks)."[200] Once self-assessment was completed and numerical scores according to "None, Basic, Competent and Advanced" allocated, priorities could be set for individuals based on scores. Learning resources could then be identified and brought to the learner or group of learners; this could be done on the job and be delivered digitally.

12.1 Team and individual capacity building

In alignment with the perspective of holism and the *primacy of the whole* principle, capacity building should take place within teams first, as the primary site, and then with individuals in the executive team. PDPs may be included as part of a performance contract in a formal performance management system (PMS), where the team and the individual are held accountable for their development. PDPs enable goal setting and regular reviews to assess progress. Role clarification and contracting for performance (see Figure 4.4), goal setting and accountability may incur the responsibility for developing appropriate competence within the team and within the individual. When executing a resilience strategy, there are numerous cross-cutting competence areas that determine the capability to execute a city government resilience strategy. In the face of a resilience challenge, this execution may be identified as the bridge between formulating a resilience strategy and city government resilience itself.

12.2 Public service training and education

Capacity development takes on a certain significance in city government as the first investment in building capability. To date, the ANC government staffing policy has comprised so-called cadre deployment, where loyalty to the ANC tripartite alliance in preference to competence to do the job has been the main criterion for most executive and managerial appointments. As reported above by the IRR,[201] this policy has resulted in the absence of capability and capacity to perform the basic functions of modern government. It therefore follows that competence areas that are useful for ensuring city government resilience may be extensive and should be focused on supporting the development of capability as well as city government strategic priorities such as sustainable economic development

---

[200] Centre for Innovative Leadership (CIL). 2000. United Nations Development Programme (UNDP) Southern Africa Capacity-building initiative (SACI) CIL Competency Profile (Unpublished), pp. 2, 3.

[201] IRR, 2014.

through a focus on the NDP. For city government support the focus of policy should be on building a developmental state.

The White Paper on Public Service Training and Education (PSTE) of July 1997 outlines, in detail, the framework for a new system of PSTE. The school of government established in the National School of Governance (NSG) aims to "contribute to establishing a capable professional and responsive public sector that is committed to and has institutionalised the values of a developmental state. A public sector that delivers services that are able to address the challenges of poverty and inequality".[202] The NSG goes on to say that –

> "… the NSG is responsible for learning and development programmes in a uniform public sector with the objective of developing a professional, responsive and capable public sector, driven by the imperative of a developmental state. Culture and ethos of service will be imbued throughout the public sector, meeting the expectations of stakeholders and communities, and based on policy commitments of government."[203]

The legislative mandate for the NSG is derived from section 4 of the Public Service Act.[204] The NSG describes its mandate as follows on their website:

> "There shall be a training institution listed as a national department (in Schedule 1).
>
> 1) The management and administration of such institution shall be under the control of the Minister.
>
> 2) Such institution:
>
> • Shall provide such training or cause such training to be provided or conduct such examinations or tests or cause such examinations or tests to be conducted as the head of the institute may with the approval of the Minister decide or as may be prescribed as a qualification for the appointment or transfer of persons in or to the public service;
>
> • May issue diplomas or certificates or cause diplomas or certificates to be issued to persons who have passed such examinations".[205]

---

202   National School of Governance (NSG). 2017. www.Thensg.gov.za Date of access: 3 March 2017.

203   National School of Governance (NSG), 2017.

204   South Africa. 1994. *Public Service Act 1994*. Pretoria: Government Printer.

205   National School of Governance (NSG). 2017.

On examination of the curricula offered by the NSG it was found that none of the competencies that may be required by e-governance, cross-cutting competence listings and building a resilience strategy for city government was being offered. Capability and capacity building has been positioned as the first priority that should be considered in the proposed diagnostic instrument for gauging city government resilience.

The competence areas reflected below have been identified for the purposes of the diagnostic instrument. However, providing reliable and validly calibrated behavioural descriptions for each level of each competence is beyond the scope of this research. Nevertheless, details of specific competence areas have been provided based on relative importance and where novelty, subtleties and complexity could result in misunderstandings in acquiring such competencies. As part of the diagnostic instrument, simple descriptions have been developed which should be perceived as relevant, clear and applicable by users of the instrument.

12.3 South Africa Constitutional knowledge and metropolitan, municipal mandate

As stated earlier the supremacy of the South African Constitution and specifically the mandate for municipalities should be well known by leadership in the widest sense as a shared vision and should be reflected in policy to which public servants are held accountable. This requires that city executive leaders and executive managers have an intimate, practical knowledge of the South African Constitution and their municipal mandate as well as certain amendments. Anecdotal reports indicate that in the face of cadre deployment and the ANC historical hegemony to date, it is likely that this capacity may need to be more widely built. As an enabling process, goal setting and review, including the development of capacities using a PDP process, can be viewed as the first priority of capacity building.

13 GOAL SETTING AND REVIEW – PERFORMANCE MANAGEMENT SYSTEMS

Managing accountability and performance is most effective when embedded in the context of an organisation-wide goal setting and review process. According to Locke and Latham,[206] goal setting motivates and raises productivity and they noted an average gain of 20% in performance over numerous tasks. They go on to reference Likert,[207] who argues that "group goal setting fosters a higher degree of cooperation and communication than

---

[206] Locke, C.A. & Latham, G.P. 1984. *Goal-setting: A motivational technique that works!* Englewood Cliffs, NJ: Prentice Hall.

[207] 'Likert, R. 1967. *The human organisation.* New York, NY: McGraw Hill.

individual goal setting and is preferable. When tasks to be accomplished are highly interdependent, group goals are indeed appropriate". [208] In addition, the transparency of group goal setting mobilises social pressures from peers to perform to the goals set in an inclusive manner.

While much has been written about managing performance per se, implementation of a PMS as a free-standing process in organisations such as metros may result in disappointment and, consequently, the urgency of introducing a PMS system may be short-lived. When not part of a regular routine or fully embedded in creating a performance culture, it will probably not raise performance. Van der Waldt[209] points in this regard to "a clear link between improving service delivery and performance improvement". Continuous improvement of productivity and quality may require a medium term of five years to a long term of 25 years for establishing organisational routines that result in changing assumptions and, over time, changing paradigms and embedding an organisational culture. The foundation for the "deliverology practice" advocated by Barber et al.[210] can be created by establishing organisational routines which enable a shift to a "demanding delivery culture" becoming embedded in a city government organisation. A PMS may need to be seen to fit within the context of broader organisation goal setting and alignment with organisation-wide strategic priorities. In this context, an organisation-wide PMS within a team and for individuals may be seen as part of the strategic conversation referred to by Van der Heijden.[211]

Strategy making and alignment should take place within an established routine of skilful strategic goal setting and review conversations, also referred to as strategic conversation, which take place within an intact team as well as one-on-one. Regular (weekly) and quarterly review of goals identified, culminating in an annual performance assessment, represents an embedded process of goal setting and review. Ideally, this assessment is integrated with recognition and rewards that comprise the "true motivators" mentioned above.[212] Measurement of performance using scorecards has been shown to be useful, although it is generally agreed that measures on their own will not increase performance, raise productivity and quality or improve service delivery. It is widely accepted that effective leadership is important in the achievement of agreed goals.

---

[208] Locke & Latham, 1984, p. 15.

[209] Van der Waldt, G. 2004. *Managing performance in the public sector: Concepts, considerations and challenges.* Landsdowne: Juta, p. 4.

[210] Barber et al., 2016, p. 151.

[211] Van der Heijden, K. 1996. *Scenarios: The art of strategic conversation.* London: Wiley.

[212] Herzberg, 1987, p. 112.

Leadership as taking a stand is based on systemic principles for leadership advocated by Friedman.[213] For Friedman, taking a stand on what leadership believes in and holding that stand until the system aligns with the leadership stand constitutes the essence of a systemic perspective on leadership.[214] In the context of a PMS, this principle of taking a stand may be applied to specific agreed and contracted tasks, as well as productivity and quality goals. This systemic leadership principle may also ensure capability in city government and help to establish continuous improvement and innovation and raising service delivery standards. Figures 4.4 and 4.5 illustrate these principles. Capability and capacity building should be used in a complementary way. In Figure 4.4, goal setting takes place through agreement on desired results and purpose, and at the same time within the context of an honest and truthful view of the current reality. Goal setting for the whole organisation, and for teams and individuals, is done by taking cognisance of the strategic leverage areas of the whole organisation and each cluster. The goal setting cluster can also be used for specific aspects of city government such as a resilience strategy itself, building capability or raising levels of service delivery and so on. Describing the virtuous cycle in Figure 4.4: "goal setting" leads to "accountability" through role clarification, contracting and action planning. Accountability leads, through quality conversation, to leadership and engagement and then to "performance review". This, in turn, reinforces "goal setting" to complete a virtuous cycle. The result of a virtuous cycle may be the continuous improvement of the "level of productivity and quality" over time, as illustrated in Figure 4.5.

---

[213] Friedman, E.H. 1985. *Generation to generation: Family process in church and synagogue.* New York, NY: Guildford Press.

[214] Friedman, 1985.

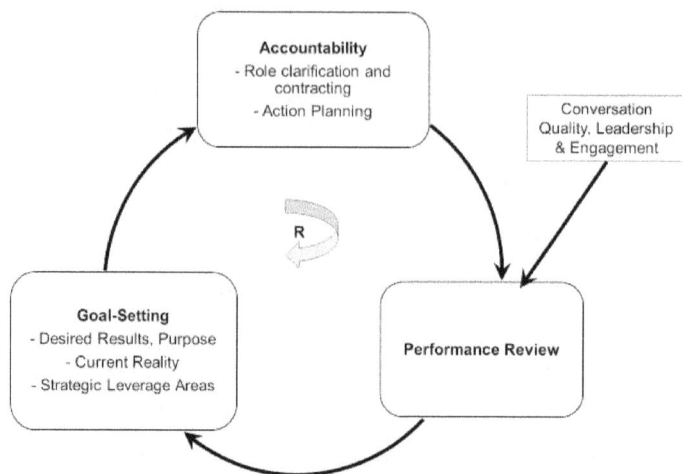

Figure 4.4: Goal setting, accountability and performance review
Source: CIL[215]

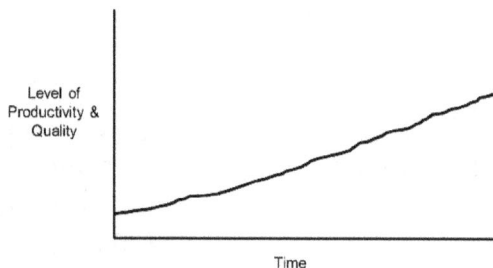

Figure 4.5: Goal setting, accountability and continuous improvement of productivity and quality
Source: CIL[216]

Goal setting may be integrated vertically within an organisation via Likert "linking pins", as illustrated in Figure 4.6. Performance reviews can take place in teams as well as on a one-on-one basis between leadership, that is, the linking pin, and the individuals in the team. Regular, routine reviews weekly, quarterly and formally once a year, enabled by quality conversation, leadership and engagement skills, will promote organisational responsiveness and continuous improvement using the linking pin concept in a PMS. The result may be the development of organisational alignment so that the organisation may respond as one. In addition, there will be the accountable execution of agreed goals on time, on budget and on quality.

---

[215] Centre for Innovative Leadership (CIL). 1998. Manuals for managing accountability and performance installation. Shell Europe Oil Products (SEOP). (Unpublished).

[216] CIL, 1998

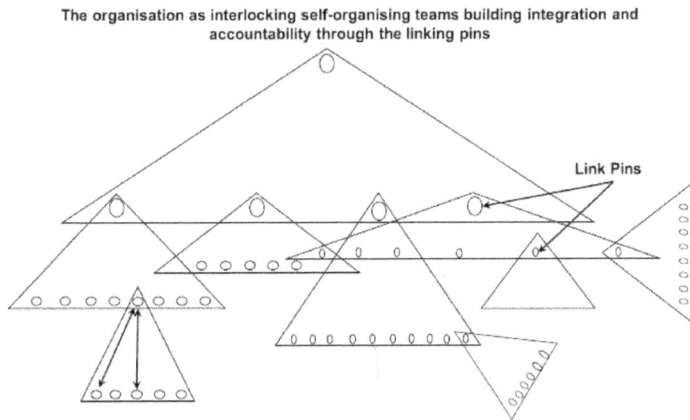

The organisation as interlocking self-organising teams building integration and accountability through the linking pins

Link Pins

Figure 4.6: Vertical integration through Likert linking pins
Source: Likert[217]

Figure 4.6 illustrates the role of Likert's linking pins, namely to ensure vertical integration. The role of linking pins is also to ensure alignment and responsiveness from the whole organisation to shocks from the external environment. In the service delivery process, the quality assurance of services can also take place by means of linking pins. Goal setting and review processes can use the linking pins to ensure that the chain of accountability and responsibility is secured through a system of interlinking performance agreements.

Successful organisational change management
Ensuring city government resilience in the sense of adapting rapidly to and recovering from resilience challenges can be seen as the capability to manage change effectively. Kotter[218] warns that "two out of three attempts to manage change in organisations fail and do not produce the intended change". Kotter identifies several reasons for successful change, which are the converse of the "eight problems" described by Endres[219] below. Kotter's reasons for ensuring success are as follows:
- "establishing a sense of urgency;
- forming a powerful guiding coalition;
- creating a shared vision;
- communicating the vision;

---

[217] Likert, 1967.

[218] Kotter, J. 1995. Leading change: Why transformation efforts fail. *Harvard Business Review*, (March-April):59–67.

[219] Endres, J. 2005. *Change management in cities: An international comparison*. Norderstadt: Books on Demand GmbH.

- empowering others to act on the vision;
- planning for and creating short-term wins;
- consolidating improvement and producing still more change; and
- institutionalising new approaches".[220]

The eight problems that are contra to reasons for ensuring success are the following:
- "allowing too much complacency;
- failing to create a sufficiently powerful guiding coalition;
- underestimating the power of a vision;
- under-communicating the vision by a factor of 10 or 100;
- permitting obstacles to block the new vision;
- failing to create short term wins;
- declaring victory too soon; and
- neglecting to anchor changes firmly in the organisational culture".[221]

The above imperatives for successful management of change and the contra problems they address may provide the basis for identifying high leverage items and descriptors in the proposed diagnostic instrument. Building and ensuring the effective management of city government resilience challenges should take place at the same time as effectively managing the day-to-day dynamics and complexity of city government and its administration. This conflict of priorities presents a key dilemma for managing change successfully. Resolving this dilemma successfully can play a key role in the Adaptation (Ad) and Recovery (R) phases of the expanded AAR diagnostic framework. Failure to resolve this dilemma productively may be identified as one of the common threads that tie together Kotter's eight reasons for why many change efforts fail. The implication of this is that in two out of three cases, failure to adapt and recover will be an important limiting dynamic in a city government resilience strategy. Successful management of change may, therefore, be an important differentiator for this diagnostic instrument. The establishment of a strategy and engagement forum which engages a representative group of executive leaders and executive management from across the organisation is supported by Weisbord,[222] when he advocates the engagement of the whole organisation in any change process. The participants in the forum should link to the entire organisation via Likert linking pins. This structure may

---

[220] Kotter, 1995.

[221] Endres, 2005, p. 40.

[222] Weisbord, M.R. 1992. *Discovering common ground.* San Francisco, CA: Berrett-Koehler.

enable communication with and the engagement of the whole organisation.

Trompenaars and Hampden-Turner's[223] dilemma mapping may be used to map and demonstrate the effective resolution of this dilemma by creating the strategy, leadership and engagement (SLE) forum described in the figure below. In the dilemma map illustrated in Figure 4.7, lopsided thinking is represented in D1 and D2, where *either* city government resilience strategy *or* city government administration are engaged in a lopsided manner on their own. Reconciling this dilemma: The SLE forum may engage the city resilience strategy through management in terms of goal setting and capacity building among SLE members (see Figure 4.7). The SLE forum enables adaptation and recovery as a continuous change management process and avoids the pitfalls Kotter warns against and which are the causes of failure of change management processes.

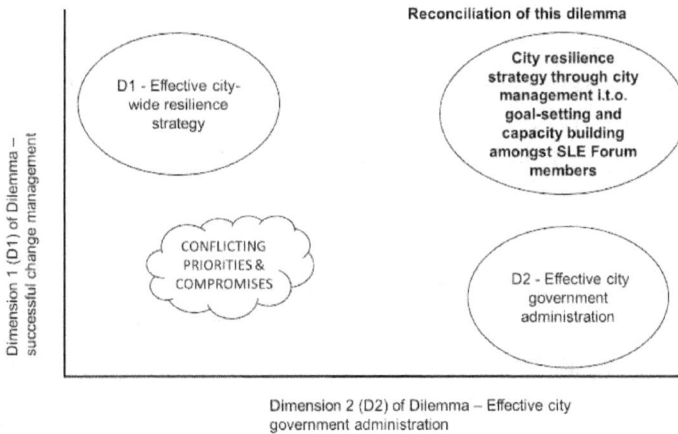

Figure 4.7: Resolving the key dilemma for enabling successful change management

Source: Van der Merwe.[224]

Change management is often treated, mistakenly, as a project with a finite beginning and end. This may also be a mistaken assumption for building a resilient city government. As the frequency of disruptions increases and challenges city government resilience, there may be a case for using the SLE forum as the infrastructure for managing change on a continuous basis. The SLE forum may also be useful for developing and exercising

---

[223] Trompenaars & Hampden-Turner, 1998.

[224] Van der Merwe, L. 1991. Systems approach to change management: The Eskom experience. (*In* Osler, C. *ed.* 1991. *Making their future: South African organisations on the move.* Institute for Futures Research: University of Stellenbosch Press, pp. 63–76), p. 66.

capability, which is defined by the APSC[225] as "Leadership, Strategy and Delivery". City administration needs to execute its mandate efficiently and cost-effectively and, at the same time, it needs to build a resilient city government strategy in order to engage its capability to respond resiliently in adapting to and recovering from shocks. Capability in terms of leadership, strategy and service delivery may have been built in advance of resilience challenges experienced by city government through capacity building. The positioning of capability and capacity building has been designed to stimulate a conversation regarding these two aspects at the outset of gauging resilience as they are the basis and foundation of the remaining six factors.

Regarding appropriate membership of the SLE, the Executive Mayor and the Mayoral Executive Committee (MECs) in city government, as defined in the South African Constitution, satisfies the guidelines for good governance. However, the membership of this group is probably not inclusive enough to take the entire city government organisation, along with the changes required to build and execute a city government resilience strategy. In addition to the MEC leadership, membership of the SLE forum could include the leadership of functional silos reporting to the MEC. Informal leadership and constructive heretics, as identified by Kleiner,[226] from the middle ranks of city government, may also form part of the SLE forum. Kleiner refers to heretics as people who, in the context of city government, are loyal to the organisation and who, at the same time, hold a contrarian view of the city government priorities, policy and how city government should be managed and led.[227] Heretics often provide innovative insights into complex organisational dynamics. These heretics, or informal leadership, may also be gatekeepers who manage the flow of information and signalling from executive levels to the middle and lower strata of organisations. It is, therefore, an advantage to include them in the SLE. Accordingly, forum membership should be structured inclusively so that the entire city government organisation is represented, thus eliminating what may be called "silo thinking" and communication gaps between divisions.

---

[225] APSC, 2017a

[226] Kleiner, A. 1996. *The age of heretics.* New York, NY: Doubleday.

[227] Kleiner, 1996.

14 BUILDING ORGANISATIONAL INFRASTRUCTURE FOR SUCCESSFUL CHANGE MANAGEMENT

Weisbord,[228] in his description of his "Future Search" change management methodology, advocates "[g]etting the whole system in the room". He suggests that the change leadership should include the whole organisation in a strategic conversation about change. According to Weisbord,[229] this should be done to enable ownership and the successful execution of change. This may be achieved in a structural intervention by building infrastructure for the strategic conversation that is inclusive and cross-functional. This type of forum has already been referred to as the SLE forum (see Figure 4.7). The SLE forum includes executive leadership and executive management and other representatives who, together, are capable of taking the whole organisation along, as well as forming a critical mass and a powerful guiding coalition of leading change successfully. Building this infrastructure may be essential for a successful city government resilience strategy. In this forum, shared leadership may assist in sustaining a resilience strategy focus over time until the strategy is embedded in the culture and the paradigms of the city government organisation. This kind of forum may be found in the JUSE in Japan, as well as organisational quality councils in Japanese TQC and Kaizen strategies in large industrial organisations.

In the early 1980s, Eskom was technically bankrupt as a result of the accelerated building of new power stations to match the demand forecast for electricity which in turn is based on an economic forecast. The high leverage areas described by Van der Merwe[230] that were engaged are identified in Table 4.14. The Eskom turnaround engagement forum called the "The Top 30" in Eskom played an important role in the successful turnaround. In the 1990s, the Open University (OU) used a similar forum to engage the leadership of the OU in scenario development and change management. The purpose, design and functionality of the SLE forum have been described in-depth.[231] CIL[232] reminds us that the purpose of this forum is to build infrastructure for ownership, shared leadership and the alignment of strategic priorities across the organisation to manage change sustainably and successfully. An important aspect of the SLE forum process is the conversation quality and engagement in strategic conversation.

---

[228] Weisbord, 1992, p. 47.

[229] Weisbord, 1992

[230] Van der Merwe, 1991, p. 69.

[231] Centre for Innovative Leadership (CIL). 1992. Developing a Strategy, Leadership and Engagement (SLE) Forum. (Unpublished).

[232] CIL, 1992.

A conversation which enables double-loop learning assists executive leadership and executive management to change the assumptions they hold and to then change their decisions and actions that follow. Typical results from the SLE forum listed by CIL[233] are the following:

- "maintaining momentum;
- broadening ownership;
- building critical mass for change;
- preliminary conversations about change initiatives;
- management of resistance;
- elimination of silo thinking;
- activating linking pins to build vertical integration;
- raising the level of accountability and performance; and
- capability and capacity building".[234]

The successful Eskom recovery and resilience organisational development experience in the 1980s identified a number of high leverage interventions and areas for building resilience, which enabled successful recovery and turnaround. High leverage areas are reflected in Table 4.14. The cluster headings and items listed below are self-explanatory. Cluster headings for high leverage areas are the following:

- "leadership and alignment;
- training and development [capacity building];
- participation [inclusion];
- recognition and rewards [in alignment with the items above];
- recruitment, promotion and succession [based on merit and peer assessment]; and
- communication [regular inclusive, evidence-based communication from leadership to all internal and external stakeholders]".[235]

As an indicator of the success of this recovery process it may be noted that on completion of this 1989 resilience strategy process, the international ratings agencies granted Eskom in the 1990s an AAA+ credit rating status – a better credit rating than the South African government at the time. An ad hoc and high leverage intervention not reflected in this table was initiated by the late Dr James Nkosi and his colleague Andrew Mariti. They proposed that they take the members of the executive team, one at a time, into a township and spend an evening in one of the popular shebeens.

---

[233] CIL, 1992.

[234] CIL, 1992.

[235] Van der Merwe, 1991, p. 69.

Less than 5% of people in South Africa who are white had ever visited a township. Sadly this statistic is still valid. A shebeen or speakeasy as they are sometimes called is usually patronised by its local community in a particular neighbourhood. The host would often be a household with an entrepreneurial matriarch providing a livelihood for her family by offering this community service. It was an unusual experience for members of the executive team. The combination of uncertainty and personal contact sharing beer quarts over a friendly conversation with random regulars played a pivotal role in broadening the perspective and assumptions of the executive team. Thirty years later, the memory of these visits remained vivid and, in retrospect, provided a watershed in learning and personal adaptation to participants.

Table 4.14: High leverage areas for organisation recovery and resilience (Eskom circa 1985-89)

High leverage areas for organisation recovery and resilience
Leadership and alignment • Vision and strategies ["Top 30" aka Strategy, Leadership and Engagement (SLE) Forum] • Evaluate [strategic and business] plans • Individual results • Performance review (conversation quality and engagement) • Pay Links [to job evaluation and on job results delivered]
Training and development (competency-based capacity building) • Management [executive management, mid-management] • Supervisors • Trainers/facilitators • Human resources [staffers]
Participation (inclusion) • Problem-solving teams [cross-functional at mid-management levels] • Quality Circles [Part of TQC, Kaizen and TQM] • Productivity measurement and improvement [REALST modelling]
Recognition and rewards [alignment with items above]
Recruitment, promotion and succession [Based on merit & peer assessment]
Communication [regular, inclusive, evidence-based communication from leadership to all internal and external stakeholders]

Source: Van der Merwe[236]

The Eskom case study as a state-owned enterprise (SOE) falls within government; its successful resilience strategy may provide valuable learning for successful organisation change for city government. Disruptions

---

[236] Van der Merwe, 1991, p. 69.

in energy and transportation with taxi-hailing systems, autonomous vehicles and solar photovoltaic (PV) are already having an impact on jobs and industries. These disruptions are the forerunners of a number of technology and business model-driven disruptors which, according to Schwab[237] of the World Economic Forum, constitute a revolution equal in magnitude to previous industrial revolutions.

15 THE FOURTH INDUSTRIAL REVOLUTION AND TECHNOLOGY-DRIVEN DEEP SHIFTS

Schwab[238] posits that disruptions and changes will be the result of what he has termed the "Fourth Industrial Revolution". This revolution has been preceded by three previous revolutions, each with a specific focus (see Table 4.15). These revolutions have transformed organisations, industries and countries. Jobs have disappeared, and new jobs have been created. The so-called Fourth Industrial Revolution may have a similar effect. As it is currently seen by many as predetermined and unpredictable, this revolution may have an impact upon city government resilience and require specific strategies to minimise damage from disruptions.

Table 4.15: The Fourth Industrial Revolution and city government resilience

Industrial revolution	Year	Information
First	1784	Steam, water, mechanical production equipment
Second	1870	Division of labour, electricity, mass production
Third	1969	Electronics, IT, automated production, robotics
Fourth	?	Cyber-physical systems, and 20 deep shifts (destruction of all jobs that can be automated, Internet of Things (IoT), enabling smart cities, direct engagement of and feedback from citizens, education enabled by massive open online courses (MOOCs) and auto-didactism via smart phones)

Source: Schwab[239]

Schwab[240] warns that the fourth revolution is distinct from the previous revolutions because of its "high velocity, wide scope, structural disruptions and systems impact".[241] He goes on to say that "the speed of current

---

[237] Schwab, K. 2016b. *The Fourth Industrial Revolution*. Geneva: World Economic Forum.

[238] Schwab, 2016b

[239]   Schwab, 2016a, p. 6

[240] Schwab, 2016a.

[241]   Schwab, 2016a, p. 3.

technology-driven breakthroughs has no historical precedent when compared to previous industrial revolutions".[242] According to Schwab, the fourth revolution is evolving and approaching at an exponential rather than a linear pace. Moreover, Schwab tells us that it will disrupt almost every industry in every country, and the breadth and depth of these changes herald the transformation of entire systems of production, management, government sectors and governance. The predetermined nature, as well as the potential magnitude of their impending impact, the so-called "20 deep shifts" mentioned by Schwab,[243] are reflected in Table 4.16.

A global sample of 800 executives was surveyed by the WEF Global Agenda Council to identify their perceptions of the convergence of various technologies. The resultant 20 deep shifts were identified. Respondents were also requested to indicate and describe the tipping point (TP) for a specific deep shift and whether the TP will have been reached by 2025. The percentage of participants in the survey that indicated that the TP will have been reached by 2025 is indicated. The potential social impact is described in the fourth column. The deep shifts that may be relevant to city government resilience have been identified with an asterisk (*).

Table 4.16: The Fourth Industrial Revolution – 20 Deep Shifts

Deep Shifts	The Tipping Point (TP)	By 2025 what % said TP reached	Social Impact
Shift 1: Implantable technologies	First implantable cell phone	82	Pacemakers and cochlear implants are only the beginning of this shift. Smart tattoos for IDs
*Shift 2: Our digital presence	80% of people with a digital presence on the internet	80	Present on more than one of these; Facebook, Twitter, Linked In, Tumblr blog, Instagram etc. develop virtual relationships globally
Shift 3: Vision as the new interface	10% of reading glasses connected to the internet	86	Eyes and vision access to the internet. Eye-tracking becomes "intelligent" navigation, instruction
*Shift 4: Wearable internet	10% of people wearing clothes connected to the internet	91	Wristwatches e-connected, chips embedded in clothes, self-managed healthcare

---

[242] Schwab, 2016a, p. 9.

[243] Schwab, 2016b, pp. 120–172

Deep Shifts	The Tipping Point (TP)	By 2025 what % said TP reached	Social Impact
*Shift 5: Ubiquitous computing	90% of population with regular connection to the internet	79	Today 40% of the world's population is connected to the internet. Will become a basic right
*Shift 6: A supercomputer in your pocket	90% of the population using smart phones	90	Many of the current smartphones contain more computing power than what were formerly known as supercomputers. Global smartphone subscribers estimated at 3.5 bn by 2019 which is 50% smartphone penetration
*Shift 7: Storage for all	90% of people have unlimited and free (advert-supported) storage	91	Commoditising of storage capacity. Prices have dropped exponentially by factor ten every five years
*Shift 8: The internet of things (IoT)	1 trillion sensors connected to the internet	89	Continuously increasing computing power and falling hardware prices in line with Moore's Law
*Shift 9: The connected home	Over 50% of internet traffic delivered to homes for appliances and devices (not for entertainment or communications)	70	Control of lights, shades, ventilation, air conditioning, audio and video, security systems, and home appliances. Additional support by connecting robots for all kinds of services such as vacuum cleaning etc.
*Shift 10: Smart cities	The first city with more than 50 000 inhabitants and no traffic lights	64	Many cities will connect services utilities and roads to the internet ... manage energy, material flows, logistics and traffic ... Singapore and Barcelona are already implementing intelligent parking solutions, smart trash collection and intelligent lighting. Smart cities are continuously extending their sensor technology and working on their data platforms, which will be the core for connecting the different technology projects and adding future services based on data analytics and predictive modelling

Deep Shifts	The Tipping Point (TP)	By 2025 what % said TP reached	Social Impact
*Shift 11: Driverless cars	Driverless cars equalling 10% of all cars on US roads	79	Trials of driverless cars are already being run by Audi in Singapore and by Google and others. Greater efficiency and safety. Reduce congestion. Disrupting existing models for car ownership, public transport and logistics
*Shift 12: Artificial intelligence and decision making	The first artificial intelligence (AI) machine on a corporate board of directors	45	AI can learn from previous situations to provide input and automate complex decision processes, easier and faster with concrete solutions based on data and past experiences
*Shift 13: AI and white-collar jobs	30% of corporate audits performed by AI have occurred	75	AI is good at matching patterns and automating processes, which enable it to replace a range of functions performed today by people
*Shift 14: Robotics and services	The first robotic pharmacist in the US	86	Robotics is beginning to influence many jobs from manufacturing to agriculture and services. Currently there are 1.1 million working robots in the world. Machines already account for 80% of the work in manufacturing a car
*Shift 15: Bitcoin and the blockchain	10% of global domestic product (GDP) stored on blockchain technology	58	Bitcoin and blockchain currencies are based on the idea of a distributed trust mechanism called the "blockchain", as a way of keeping track of trusted transactions. Currently the worth of Bitcoin in the blockchain is around US$ 20 billion or about 0.025 of global worth of US$ 80 trillion. The open ledger approach enables peer-to-peer financial transactions, disintermediating financial institutions that currently provide this service

Deep Shifts	The Tipping Point (TP)	By 2025 what % said TP reached	Social Impact
*Shift 16: The sharing economy	Globally more trips/ journeys via car sharing than in private cars	67	Technology-enabled ability to share the use of physical assets in terms of goods and services, such as vehicles, space, accommodation and provide these at increased efficiency not available before. This benefit of increased efficiency and utilisation passed on to end-user. Early examples are Amazon, Airbnb and Uber
*Shift 17: Governments and the blockchain	Tax collected for the first time by a government via a blockchain	73	Both opportunities and challenges for countries (and metros). Loss of control over monetary policy creates new opportunities for taxing mechanisms built into the blockchain itself
*Shift 18: 3D printing and manufacturing	The first 3D car printed in production	84	3D printing has the potential for creating very complex products without complex equipment. It is already being used to make wind turbines and toys
*Shift 19: 3D printing for consumer products	5% of consumer products printed in 3D	81	Anyone with a 3D printer can print typical consumer products on demand
Shift 20: Designer beings	The first human genome that was directly and deliberately edited is born		First entire human genome was created in 2003 at a cost of US$ 2.7 bn. By 2009 the cost of one genome was US$100 k and this has fallen to US$1000 for sequencing one human genome
Shift 20: Neuro-technologies	The first human with a fully artificial memory implanted in the brain		The Human Brain Project funded by the European Commission and former President Obama's Brain Research through Advancing Innovative Neuro-technologies (BRAIN)

Source: Schwab[244]

[244] Schwab, 2016b, pp. 120–172.

The convergence of numerous technologies is bringing down costs and making technology available to many more users. Component technologies such as computing capacity, memory size and cost, data storage, battery storage and the miniaturisation of components has enabled drones and the proliferation of sensors, which may result in the disruption and transformation of many of the taken for granted components of daily life and industry today. In the biological and social spheres, genetic engineering is genetically modifying plant and animal species. In addition, social media and the internet are disrupting the way we assimilate information and learn. These technologies have also enabled the development of aggregated applications such as smartphones. Open ledger technology may create secure peer-to-peer money transfers, thus bypassing the banking sector, and cryptocurrencies are set to replace Reserve Bank guaranteed currencies. Disruptive business models for transportation and energy may soon be a reality, including electric vehicles and solar- and wind-generated energy. In addition, disruptive business models are disrupting transportation with taxi-hailing software and accommodation rentals. This technology convergence may also enable so-called green growth and smart cities.

Many of the above-mentioned technologies have the potential to affect city government, thus disrupting and enabling city government resilience strategies. Capability, as defined by the APSC, and capacity building in specific cities may determine a unique pathway to the future of individual cities. The overall effect of the application of many of these converging technologies is the so-called Fourth Industrial Revolution (4IR).

According to Schwab,[245] "[t]he possibilities of billions of people connected by mobile devices, with unprecedented processing power, storage capacity and access to knowledge, are unlimited."[246] He posits that there are four major areas that the Fourth Industrial Revolution will impact on, namely:

- "customer expectations;
- product (and service) enhancement;
- collaborative innovation; and
- organisational forms".[247]

Schwab argues that "these disruptors may impact upon countries and cities. Amongst a range of disruptions, these disruptors may create redundancy of many competencies and jobs as machines take over these

---

[245] Schwab, K. 2016a. *Navigating the Fourth Industrial Revolution.* http://www.biznews.com/wef/davos-2016/2016/01/20/klaus-schwab-navigating-the-fourth-industrial-revolution/ Date of access: 23 August 2017.

[246] Schwab, 2016a.

[247] Schwab, 2016a.

functions".[248] Resisting disruptions may be futile as they represent systemic changes at a structural level that can lower costs and improve convenience and efficiencies permanently. The more resistance, the more relentlessly the disruption will proceed on its pathway through rapid adoption among users because of the benefits being offered. The choices for city government seem to be adapt or be left behind. On the other hand, these technologies have the potential to enable so-called smart cities. For example, autonomous, electric vehicles – once they are in common use – may reduce the number of cars, with estimates ranging between a 60- and 80% reduction.[249] This reduction will have a positive effect on air pollution, the use of highways and roads in general. City parking currently taken up by commuter vehicles may also be reduced by approximately the same percentage and will be free to be used for other purposes. Seba goes on to warn that as a result of technological advances from large investments in developing energy storage, solar photovoltaic cells and wind turbines will provide almost all future energy by 2050.[250]

Tapscott[251] posits that Bitcoin, which is based on the underlying structure of blockchain, and the so-called open ledger, can protect rights, identity and peer-to-peer financial transactions through a chain of immutable records. Peer-to-peer financial transactions may create a strong economy, end the cost of transferring remittances and reduce or eliminate the role of intermediaries such as banks. Blockchain, Tapscott tells us, "will also enable citizens to own and monetise their data, protect the privacy and ensure compensation for the creation of value and intellectual property".[252] This will probably change the way in which municipalities render and settle accounts and transact financially. The intermediary role of banks may become obsolete because of the lower transaction costs. Open ledger and blockchain promise to be as influential in the financial transaction arena as the internet was in transforming communication in society.

Scholars have yet to publish substantially on this emerging technology. From the 2017 Davos meeting, and reports in the media on blockchain, "the protagonists of blockchain tell me it is now similar to where the internet was in 1996. It is on a trajectory to become another disruptive

---

[248] Schwab, 2016b, p. 35.

[249] Seba, T. 2014. Clean disruption of energy and transportation. https://www.youtube.com/watch?v=2b3ttqYDwF0 Date of access: 9 September 2017.

[250] Seba, 2014

[251] Tapscott, H.D. 2016. *Blockchain revolution: How the technology behind Bitcoin is changing money, business and the world.* New York, NY: Penguin Random House.

[252] Tapscott, 2016.

technology that may rival the impact of the internet in its transformative properties".[253] Blockchain and cryptocurrencies such as Bitcoin and Etherium that are based on blockchain may offer early adopters in city government an advantage that can enhance resilience and lower the cost of transacting financially between it, its citizens and with foreign direct investors. In addition, many of these disruptive technologies discussed above may enhance the capabilities of city government once engaged.

16 DISRUPTORS ENABLE ANTIFRAGILITY

Early anticipation and adaptation by city governments of the disruptors reflected in the 20 deep shifts Schwab describe in Table 4.16 may result in what Taleb[254] describes as antifragile properties, where city governments with effective resilience strategies gain from the disorder these disruptors create. Cities may adapt and recover through an antifragile response to disruptors and transform to improved sustainable development and evolve to green growth and smart cities.

For city government to be robust against the impact of this revolution, executive leadership and executive management should stress-test strategy, policy and plans in well-researched scenarios which include the range of effects these disruptors may have on city government. Anticipating and exploiting specific effects on city government and their citizens may enable efficient adaptation through appropriate policy and early recovery.

16.1 Retraining for new jobs – alignment and upgrading of education

City government may need to retrain people whose jobs have disappeared as a result of disruptions. Anticipating effectively in this regard means correctly identifying which competencies will be disrupted and disappear and which new competencies may be needed. Personnel planning, as well as city government resilience strategy and policy, may require the use of a scenario-based strategic approach to achieve fit with these future conditions.[255] Moreover, new competencies will be required in city government and among citizens to deal with this revolution and its disruptive impact on jobs. High quality city schools which provide appropriate education that anticipates and adapts to disruptors in the Fourth Industrial Revolution may become an important resource for

---

[253] Hogg, A. 2017. *Davos Diary Day 4: Trump's sole attendee, frostbite & Blockchain killed the* ...https://www.biznews.com/wef/davos-2017/2017/01/20/davos-diary-blockchain Date of access: 20 January 2017.

[254] Taleb, 2012.

[255] Van der Merwe, 2008, p. 222.

creating city government resilience in the face of these disruptions.

Schwab posits that "in future talent more than capital, will represent the critical factor of production. This will give rise to the job market increasingly being segregated into 'low-skill/low-pay' and 'high-skill/high-pay' segments which in turn will lead to social tensions".[256] City governments may need to attract top talent from the best schools and fast track this talent into key positions such as service delivery, policy formulation and strategy making areas. High leverage, cost-effective areas for rapidly raising the quality of learning in schools may be best achieved by focusing on the quality of teaching in schools.[257] Van der Merwe describes how, amongst other things, Singapore cost-effectively achieved high quality learning by prioritising learner-focused, quality teaching where teachers stimulated learning among their students and enabled critical thinking skills. Van der Merwe posits that the most accomplished teachers from high quality schools may be used as academic support resources and for mentoring teachers in other city schools. Identifying master teachers who wish to mentor other teachers could raise the average quality of learning at all schools in a city. Van der Merwe[258] compares this to the way government and educators mistakenly follow the latest educational fashion or fad that promises to raise the quality of schools and education easily and transform outdated approaches to teacher-centred learning in many schools. City government may choose to invest in leveraging the improvement of the quality of education in other city schools in general by raising the quality of teaching of appropriate competencies across all schools in the city. Table 4.17 separates high leverage interventions for raising the quality of teaching in schools from low leverage interventions.

Technology may also have an effect on governance at the national level and specifically city governance. A competency-based approach could enable a learner-directed, low threshold to entry for learners and thus build capacity rapidly and efficiently to enable city government capability.

---

[256] Schwab, 2016a.

[257] Van der Merwe, 2016b.

[258] Van der Merwe, 2016b.

Table 4.17: Raising and developing the quality of teaching in all city schools

High Leverage
Feedback to pupils Meta-cognitive strategies. (Helping pupils to think about their own learning more explicitly) Peer mentoring among teachers Collaborative group learning
Low Leverage
Reducing class size to <20 Individual instruction Mentoring of pupils Teaching assistance Improving school buildings Streaming by ability

Source: Van der Merwe[259]

16.2 The Van der Waldt e-governance competency framework

Van der Waldt[260] encourages the government to build capacity for e-governance in advance of the advent of the Fourth Industrial Revolution to enable its application in the cities of the future. New and different competencies may be required for government administrators, for good governance. New jobs will be created by the revolution and thus enable the transformation that follows. Van der Waldt[261] has developed a "Comprehensive e-governance competency framework" (see Table 4.18) for senior civil service managers. These competencies are required for the transformation of cities to enable the adoption of e-governance. Van der Waldt argues that these competencies should be developed *in advance* of the impact of disruptions, thereby leveraging e-governance and resulting in good electronically enabled governance.

Van der Waldt argues that good governance is a prerequisite for performance. He takes good governance to mean, "the process of decision making and the process by which decisions are implemented [or not implemented]".[262]

---

[259] Van der Merwe, 2016b

[260] Van der Waldt, 2016a.

[261] Van der Waldt, 2016a.

[262] Van der Waldt, G. 2004. *Managing performance in the public sector: Concepts, considerations and challenges.* Landsdowne: Juta, p. 4.

According to Van der Waldt,[263] there are eight major characteristics of good governance:

- "participation;
- rule of law;
- transparency;
- responsiveness;
- consensus orientated;
- equity and inclusiveness;
- effectiveness and efficiency; and
- accountability".[264]

Van der Waldt goes on to integrate good governance with its effect on improving service delivery and its linkage to public service performance.

According to Schwab,[265] the positive effect of the Fourth Industrial Revolution and, specifically, e-enablement "will be a greater engagement of citizens with government, voicing their opinions, coordinating their efforts and even circumventing the supervision role of public authorities". Van der Waldt[266] has identified a number of key e-governance competencies that are required to perform efficiently in both government and city government. He posits that the utilisation of information and communication technology (ICT) in government may be experiencing exponential growth globally. Several key ICT areas, including electronic (e-) government bluetooth-connected devices, broadband wireless (Wi-Fi), IoT, cloud computing, and big data may be increasingly becoming intertwined with the way society is governed. In addition, at the local sphere of government, the emergence of smart cities may give rise to the creation of so-called networked local governance associated with ICT applications for basic service delivery. These trends are congruent with the reinvention of the public service by the so-called New Public Management. Networked governance paradigms may lead to the blurring of lines between the private and public sectors. This blurring supports the argument for engaging competitive bidding for the delivery of specific services. As e-governance enables greater interactivity, it may gradually revolutionise the way government interacts with its citizenry. Van der Waldt posits that there seems to be a "general" consensus that "civil service managers, as custodians and administrative leaders of e-governance endeavours, generally lack the necessary compe-

---

[263] Van der Waldt, 2004.
[264] Van der Waldt, 2004, p. 10.
[265] Schwab, 2016a
[266] Van der Waldt, 2016b

tence to adequately cope with these new realities and to adequately adjust functional operations for e-governance endeavours".[267]

To remedy the perceived general lack of competence amongst civil service managers, Van der Waldt developed a comprehensive e-governance competency framework for civil service managers which may enable capacity building amongst senior civil service management. While Van der Waldt's research focuses on the public service at the national level, it may also be applied to city government metros. Prioritising and funding capacity building using the Van der Waldt competency framework would probably enable metros to leapfrog over redundant jobs by means of capacity building, thus entering this new era of e-governance, green growth and smart cities with a minimum of disruption.

The Van der Waldt competency framework enables self-assessment as well as a formal assessment. The framework reflects a progression of competency levels, namely, Basic/emerging, Intermediate, Advanced and Expert/specialist. The framework describes competency type in terms of cognitive ability and e-governance (technical and managerial).

Table 4.18: Towards a comprehensive e-governance competency framework for senior civil service managers

Competency level	Competency type	
	Cognitive	E-governance (technical and managerial)
Basic/emerging	Creativity and entrepreneurship Adaptability Communication Innovation and continuous learning Teamwork Personal integrity Leadership	Basic ICT skills for office work Basic understanding of e-governance transformation and reforms such as change management, organisational development, general IT literacy, and the utilisation of appropriate hardware and software
Intermediate	Knowledge management Ability to shape the future (vision) Service delivery innovation Problem solving and analysis Client orientation and customer focus	Identify, design and execute e-governance projects Manage related knowledge and competencies required to execute ICT projects

[267] Van der Waldt, 2016a, p. 115.

Competency level	Competency type	
	Cognitive	E-governance (technical and managerial)
Advanced	Policy advice Strategic orientation Adapted leadership	Direct e-governance programmes and applications Direct e-governance strategic orientation in government Contract management Management stakeholders and external relations Manage the ICT resources to implement a department's e-government strategy in accordance with its overall strategy and government policy
Expert/ specialist	Systems thinking Systems dynamics Complexity theory Global vision and perspectives	Management of networks (e.g. PPPs) Specialist skills in the areas of technology and management such as programme management, IT security, and IT audits Manage organisational changes resulting from e-government programmes

Source: Van der Waldt[268]

A PDP approach may be engaged whereby teams and individual members of executive leadership and executive management take collective and personal responsibility for their capacity building. This process should commence with self-assessment, first within management teams and then through individual self-assessment within that team. Competencies that might already be present within the team may be identified and leveraged throughout the whole team. For instance, individuals with sufficient competency could become the designated capacity builders for other members of the team. As building capability through capacity development is fundamental to modern government and a city government resilience strategy, this is an example of using resources that may be currently resident in specific parts of an organisation to build capacity – so-called "bootstrapping" – which will enable the process of capacity building to start as soon as possible. Individuals may use the competency framework for defining new jobs and roles together with competencies that go with them.

---

[268] Van der Waldt, 2016a

A PMS process may also be applied as it includes the self-assessment of competencies resulting in a PDP which may form part of a performance contract for development. In addition, appropriate learning resources may be identified for areas where capacity needs to be developed individually or within an intact work team. Progress should be reviewed regularly as part of routine performance review processes. Rapidly building the competency that enables greater resilience in advance of the substantial discontinuity that Schwab warns against may also be supported by Van der Waldt's competence framework.

A competency-based approach may also be used for developing competency areas that have been identified as part of cross-cutting competencies in the diagnostic for enabling city government resilience. As city government is the face of government because of its proximity to citizens, it is well placed to enable development in specific communities in the city as well as in the whole city.

16.3 Developmental city government
The South African Constitution provides a vision for the whole of South African society and provides sufficient latitude for municipalities to play a significant role in building a developmental state within municipalities, including cities. The White Paper on Local Government provides guidelines on the characteristics of a developmental local government.

16.4 The White Paper on Local government
In Section B of the White Paper on Local Government, the roles of developmental local government are listed as follows:

Characteristics of developmental local government;
- "Maximising social development and economic development;
- Integrating and coordinating;
- Democratising development, empowerment and redistribution; and
- Leading and learning."

Developmental outcomes of local government;
- "Provision of household infrastructure;
- Creating of liveable, integrated cities, towns and rural areas; and
- Local economic development."

Tools and approaches for the development of local government;
- "Integrated development planning, budgeting and performance monitoring;
- Performance management; and
- Working together with local citizens and partners".[269]

In summary, this section of the White Paper puts forward a vision for a developmental local government that engages local communities in working together to find sustainable ways to meet their needs and improve the quality of life in communities. A focus on developmental outcomes is encouraged, such as "the provision of household infrastructure and services; the creation of liveable, integrated cities, towns and rural areas; and the promotion of local economic development and community empowerment and redistribution".[270] Three approaches are provided which may assist municipalities in their developmental role, namely:
- "integrated development planning and budgeting;
- performance management; and
- working together with local citizens and partners".[271]

16.5 National development plan

Developmental city government is bounded by the South African Constitution, the White Paper on Local Government and the NDP. The National Planning Commission (NPC) was appointed in 2010 to draft a vision and develop a national development plan. In 2011, the Planning Commission's Diagnostic Report was released, setting out South Africa's achievements and shortcomings since 1994. Failure to implement policies and an absence of broad partnerships were cited as the main reasons for slow progress. The NPC set out nine primary challenges:
- "too few people work;
- the quality of school education for black people is poor;
- infrastructure is poorly located, inadequate and under-maintained;
- spatial divides limit inclusive development;
- the economy is unsustainably resource intensive;
- the public health system cannot meet demand or sustain quality;
- public services are uneven and often of poor quality;
- corruption levels are high; and
- South Africa remains a divided society".[272]

---

[269] South Africa, 1998

[270] South Africa, 1998.

[271] South Africa, 1998.

[272] National Planning Commission (NPC), 2012, P. 25.

Four thematic areas were identified following the diagnosis: rural economy, social protection, regional and world affairs, and community safety.[273] The Commission also asserts that "[t]he plan draws extensively on the notion of capabilities. Key capabilities that emerge from the development literature include:

- "political freedoms and human rights;
- social opportunities arising from education, health care, public transport and other public services;
- social security and safety nets;
- an open society, transparency, disclosures and a culture of accountability; and
- economic facilities, work, consumption, exchange investment and production".[274]

In addition, the NPC asserts that "[m]aking the plan work will require a complex interplay of actors and actions, and progress in any one area is almost always dependent on progress in another. The plan will provide a common focus for action across all sectors and sections of South African society".[275] The NPC points out that "South Africa has an urbanising youthful population. This presents an opportunity to boost economic growth, increase employment and reduce poverty. The Commission, recognising that young people bear the brunt of unemployment, adopted a 'youth lens' in preparing its proposals".[276] The Commission goes on to summarise the report in brief and to identify and list critical actions that need to be taken as follows:

- "a social compact to reduce poverty and inequality and raise employment investment;
- a strategy to address poverty and its impacts by broadening access to employment, strengthening the social wage, improving public transport and raising rural incomes;
- steps by the state to professionalise the public service, strengthen accountability, improve coordination and prosecute corruption;
- boost private investments in labour-intensive areas, competitiveness and exports, with adjustments to lower the risk of hiring younger workers;

---

[273] National Planning Commission (NPC), 2012, P. 25.
[274] National Planning Commission (NPC), 2012, P. 26.
[275] National Planning Commission (NPC), 2012, P. 27.
[276] National Planning Commission (NPC), 2012, P. 30.

- an education accountability chain with lines of responsibility from the state to the classroom;
- phasing in of national health insurance, with a focus on upgrading public health facilities, producing more health professionals and reducing the relative cost of private health care;
- public infrastructure investment at 10 per cent of gross domestic product (GDP), financed through tariffs, public-private partnerships, taxes and loans and focussed on transport, energy and water;
- interventions to ensure environmental sustainability and resilience from future shocks;
- new spatial norms and standards – densifying cities, improving transport, locating jobs where people live, upgrading informal settlements and fixing housing market gaps; and
- reduce crime by strengthening criminal justice and improving community environments".[277]

The above critical actions have been extracted from Chapters 3 to 15 of the report where objectives and actions have been described in detail. The municipal mandate contained in the Constitution provides for municipalities to play their role in achieving the objectives set out by the NPC in the NDP. The diagnostic instrument for gauging city government resilience may directly address many of the developmental aspects as described in the NDP. While the NDP describes the developmental state from a macro national perspective, cities may focus on their micro component of the NDP within their municipal mandate. Investment in sustainable community programmes could provide a focus for local community development in cities. Aspects of city government capability such as service delivery may be supplemented with delivery by external service providers such as through joint ventures, PPPs and an alternate development approach such as a rights-based sustainable development investment programme.

17   SUSTAINABLE COMMUNITY INVESTMENT PROGRAMME

According to Geerts,[278] the sustainable community investment programme (SCIP) developed by Reynolds and successfully tested in Zimbabwe fits into an alternative development approach which the NPC has identified as people-centred development, where people take responsibility for their

---

[277]   National Planning Commission (NPC), 2012, p. 34.

[278]   Geerts, S. 2014. A conceptualization and analysis of the community investment programme with reference to South Africa case studies: Towards a new model. University of South Africa (PhD Thesis).

own development. "The facilitating organisation, in this case, the South African government [and city government], should play a supporting role".[279] Facilitating the SCIP has been included as one of the competencies required by municipalities in South Africa to fulfil their role as a developmental city government. The essence of this community-focused programme is described by Geerts[280] diagrammatically in Figure 4.8.

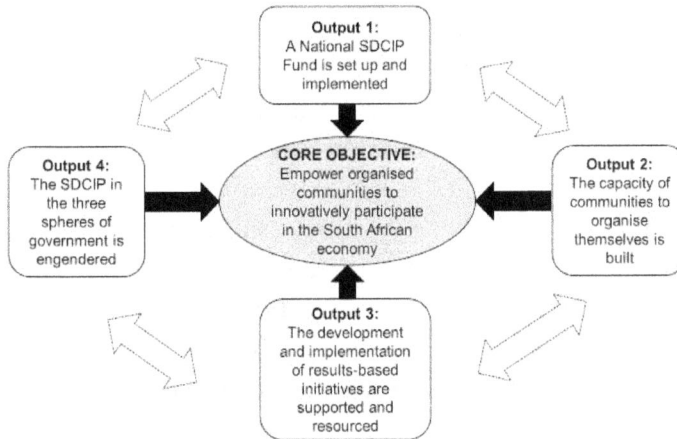

Figure 4.8: Outputs of the implementation of SCIP by the South African Government

Source: Geerts[281] Based on Reynolds[282]

The SCIP is also referred to as the Sustainable Development Community Investment Programme (SDCIP) by the South African government. This programme, as defined, builds institutional structures for community investment by government and ownership by specific communities. The core objective is to empower a community to organise itself to undertake economic development in the service of social transformation.

The SCIP, the precursor to the SDCIP, was developed by Reynolds.[283] The SCIP enables the government to invest in employment creation and livelihoods among community members. The community individually and collectively takes responsibility using the SCIP model for building community resilience through sustainable business development. The core notion of the SCIP development approach is that it empowers communities to take responsibility for their own economic welfare. This approach is

---

279 Geerts, 2014, p. 46.

280 Geerts, 2014.

281 Geerts, 2014, p. 94.

282 Reynolds, N. 2007. A trusteeship for Zimbabwe: Citizens as Mai actors. *EPS Quarterly*, 20(2):1–2.

283 Reynolds, 2007.

more sustainable and is therefore preferred to other transfers from the government such as social grants which, without capacity building, create a co-dependency between government and beneficiaries.

The SCIP may be typically described as a *rights-based initiative* [my emphasis] that is identified and launched by the community itself using "rights programmes" which focus on specific dynamics in the community such as, for example, youth employment rights, child education rights and health rights. This is done within a clearly bounded community focus to enable locally responsible ownership, management and contributions. The initial investment to seed the community-based development initiative may be made by one of the various national or local spheres of government. Alternatively, sources of seed capital may be made available through FDI from other cities both locally and abroad or from socially responsible industrialists as part of their corporate social investments (corporate social responsibility [CSR]). Resources already present within communities may also be leveraged to support SCIP development. Geerts[284] outlines diagrammatically the various governance structures that may be set up to enable national government support, community ownership, fund flows, sharing of returns and benefits and the prevention of wastage and corruption. This infrastructure may be built at both the national level and local city levels. A community coupon system or other currencies may be introduced within defined boundaries to enable the internal circulation of money through payment for products and services within the system (see Figure 4.9).

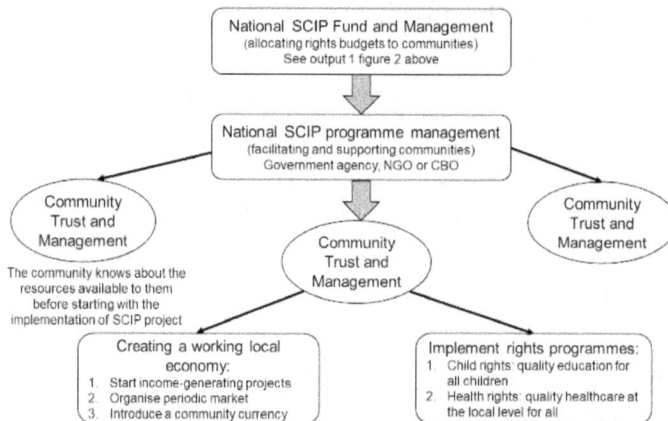

Figure 4.9: Schematic view of SCIP as envisaged by Reynolds
Source: Geerts[285]

---

[284] Geerts, 2014.

[285] Geerts, 2014, p. 96.

Critical components for the SCIP may be summarised as –

- seed funding from government and other resources, transparency;
- institutional structures as vehicles for engaging specific communities;
- community capacity-building; and
- a rights-based foundation through which to engage the community, including children's education rights, quality health care rights, youth rights to employment and others to be determined.

Economic principles for a successful SCIP include –

- defining the economic boundary around a specific community;
- containing the circulation of money and resources within this boundary;
- substituting products that are acquired from outside the SCIP system with locally manufactured products and services or going without;
- keeping money and resources circulating within the SCIP system is the primary goal. Once money circulates more than four times within this community its local micro-economy starts to grow; and
- creating a virtuous microeconomic cycle of economic growth which results in community wealth creation, self-respect and dignity from job creation.

The SCIP could be a vehicle for delivering the community services that municipalities may be incapable of delivering, such as sanitation, water, waste management and fuel provision, thus supplementing local government service delivery. The informal or invisible economy described by Van der Merwe[286] may also be engaged, formalised for social transformation within communities and by communities using SCIP governance structures. Kibbutzim in Israel are similar in structure to the SCIP developmental initiative developed by Reynolds. Initially, the Kibbutzim were government-sponsored, but now many are privatised. According to the Jewish Virtual Library[287] –

"The kibbutz [Hebrew word for communal settlement] started as a unique rural community; a society dedicated to mutual aid and social justice; a socio-economic system based on the principle of joint ownership of property, equality and cooperation of production,

---

[286] Van der Merwe, 2016a

[287] Jewish Virtual Library (JVL). 2017. *The Kibbutz and Moshav: History and overview.* http://www.jewishvirtuallibrary.org/history-and-overview-of-the-kibbutz-movement Date of access: 4 May 2017.

consumption and education. The fulfilment of the idea "'from each according to his ability, to each according to his needs'".[288]

Joint ventures and public-private partnerships may also be a way of enabling development by supplementing government capability to deliver services at national and city government levels.

18 JOINT VENTURES AND PUBLIC-PRIVATE PARTNERSHIPS

Joint ventures (JV) may be another structure through which to enable development in cities, as defined in the White Paper on Local Government. The "Debswana JV" between DeBeers and the Botswana government was initiated in 1969 and provided an example of successful public-private JV. Once the availability of diamonds became public knowledge in Botswana, the Botswana government formed the 50:50 public-private partnership or JV, called Debswana, between the government and De Beers. The purpose of the Debswana JV is to engage De Beers' mining expertise to exploit the diamond resources to the benefit of both De Beers and the Botswana nation. The Debswana JV provides an example of how city governments may create a platform for sustainable FDI in cities and through this propel the developmental state at city government level. JVs may be a way of expanding capability for quality service delivery and value-for-money government. The public-private partnership created to construct and operate the Gautrain is another example of a successful city-based JV. The structure of the Gautrain Management Agency and Bombardier and its success could be the basis of learning and ensuring the success of other public-private JV partnerships.

19 THE INFORMAL ECONOMY

Van der Merwe[289] describes what he refers to as the "invisible economy", consisting of spontaneous entrepreneurial ventures which currently provide livelihoods to those initiating them. He goes on to say that this invisible economy has become a substantial component of the national economy and its ability to resiliently adapt to economic shocks. Van der Merwe[290] points out that according to Alcock,[291] a substantial part, approximately 15% of the national economy in GDP terms is now taken up by the invisible economy, comprising roadside and township food service

---

[288] JVL, 2017.

[289] Van der Merwe, 2016a

[290] Van der Merwe, 2016a

[291] Alcock, G.G. 2016. *Kasinomics: African informal economies and the people who inhabit them.* Johannesburg: TMP.

providers, grocery shops (spazas), tabletop vendors, stokvels, taxis, and traditional medicine (muti) vendors. Van der Merwe emphasises that this is an example of wealth creation through informal, practical developmental economics, through small businesses at work. These entrepreneurs are using economic freedom as a basis for spontaneous entrepreneurship and small business development. Cities could formalise this sector and support a developmental economy at the city level as a contribution to the developmental state.

20 GREEN GROWTH

Climate volatility is increasing, and as this realisation increases multilateral governance bodies such as the United Nations (UN) and others are encouraging countries and cities to reduce carbon emissions by reducing and recycling waste. There are a number of waste streams that could be reduced or provide feedstock to downstream production processes. This perspective which reflects a sustainable industrial ecology as an interconnected system, is represented by the factor "Green Growth" in the diagnostic instrument.

20.1 Recycling of waste streams

Certain waste categories in cities require specific treatment to reduce their impact on the environment and should be recycled when possible. Table 4.19 reflects and ranks the waste streams in the European economy based on aggregated tonnage.

Table 4.19: Waste treatment by waste category in EU28, 2012

Category of Waste	Million Tonnes
Total	2 309.00
Mixed ordinary waste	1 720.40
Recyclable waste	233.60
Metal	86.30
Animal and vegetable waste	84.30
Wood	52.90
Paper and cardboard	38.80
Chemical and medical waste	30.00
Glass	15.50
Plastic	12.70
Common sludges	12.60

Category of Waste	Million Tonnes
Equipment	10.20
Discarded vehicles	4.80
Rubber	2.40
Textile	2.40
Batteries and accumulators	1.60
Waste containing PCB	0.04

NOTE: PCB (polychlorinated biphenyls) are a class of man-made chemicals which are released from landfills containing transformers, capacitors etc.

Source: European Parliamentary Research Service[292]

While recycling waste may be in its infancy in South Africa, there seems to be no upper limit to what is possible. With the political will from the city government, the benchmarks set by European countries like Sweden and the UK may be achievable when enabled by the political will and capability to set such goals. In its 8 December 2016 edition, *The Independent*[293] reported that "[l]ess than 1 per cent of Swedish household waste was sent to land-fill last year or any year since 2011. The UK has made strides in the proportion of waste recycled under an EU target of 50 per cent by 2020". In 2012, the South African Department of Environmental Affairs set a precedent in the area of recycling rubber waste. In terms of legislation reflected in the *Government Gazette* No 35927, it placed a levy on the prices of new tyres which funds the collection and recycling of 150 000 tonnes of used tyres per annum. The relatively small levy tipped the balance towards establishing institutional capability by forming a government partnership with REDISA and making the recycling of waste rubber financially sustainable. This initiative may be a useful new business model for other waste streams. This example also demonstrates the potential for PPPs to enhance municipal capability for delivering recycling services. Technology convergence may also contribute to the more efficient management of waste streams through the increase in capability to track materials along the entire value chain. Technology-enabled cities may also benefit from technology convergence by applying the applicable shifts to integrated and more efficient management and coordination of city infrastructure and services.

---

[292]   EPRS European Parliamentary Research Service
[293]   *Independent*. 2016. 8 December 2016. Edition. https://www.independent.co.uk/environment/sweden-s-recycling-is-so-revolutionary-the-country-has-run-out-of-rubbish-a7462976.html Date of access: 21 March 2017.

21 SMART CITIES

Enabling competencies for so-called smart cities entails the use of both hard technologies in terms of networks and computational power and soft competencies such as fostering behaviour in citizens that allows them to live happily in new technology-enabled environments.

21.1 Smart city knowledge

Among the key enablers of the Fourth Industrial Revolution is increased capability in ICT. The WEF has developed a metric for the infrastructure that may enable this capability, referred to as the Networked Readiness Index (NRI). The Global Information Technology Report[294] documents the latest iteration of the NRI: The NRI "represents a key tool in assessing countries' preparedness to reap the benefits of emerging technologies and capitalize on the opportunities presented by a digital transformation and beyond".[295] The NRI measures and assesses the factors, policies and institutions that enable a country to fully leverage its ICT for development. "The NRI provides a global ranking at country level in the form of the NRI".[296] Using the NRI, countries are assessed over four categories of indicators:

- "the overall environment for technology use and creation (political, regulatory, business, and innovation);
- networked readiness in terms of ICT infrastructure, affordability, and skills;
- technology adoption/usage by the three groups of stakeholders (government, the private sector, and private individuals); and
- the economic and social impact of the new technologies. Whenever relevant, the Index looks at what the different actors in society, both private and public, can do to contribute to the country's networked readiness".[297]

These categories may, individually and together, contain candidate items for the diagnostic instrument and have therefore been cited comprehensively. According to the WEF,[298] "[a]n important channel by which digital technologies can contribute to increased development and prosperity is via their impact on innovation". This index ranking has been

---

[294] World Economic Forum (WEF). 2016. *The Global Information Technology Report 2016: Innovation in the digital economy.* http://www.org/gitr Date of access: 14 February 2017.

[295] WEF, 2016, p. 3.

[296] WEF, 2016, p. 4.

[297] WEF, 2016, p. 4.

[298] WEF, 2016, p. 3.

established at a national level; however, it may evolve to city level as a way of measuring the same dimension for cities. Recently IMD has developed a Smart City Index which reflects the citizens' view of their city. See IMD Smart City Index 2019 for a dedicated index with which to gauge smart cities.

The promise of the smart city is described by Edmondson and Reynolds[299] as, "state-of-the-art, innovative, energy-saving technology, sustainable food production, resilient infrastructure and smart transportation". They go on to posit that, "rapid urbanisation and concerns about environmental sustainability point to cities as the most important site of innovation".[300] Edmondson and Reynolds' observations support the notion of cities enabling antifragile properties through the innovative use of technology. E-governance may provide the capability to leverage technology in the service of innovative governance in smart cities. Competencies documented by Van der Waldt in his "Competent e-governance framework for public service managers"[301] may be used as a platform for assessing current competencies and to undertake capacity building among public service managers so that they are equipped to deal effectively with administration in smart cities. Resilient city governments may have the greatest capacity to deal effectively with the major disruptive forces at work that will transform lives in cities, nation states and globally. City governments with resilient, responsive capabilities may be the first to deal with these and other dynamics that may test city government resilience. The convergence of technologies that Schwab refers to may require rapid learning to anticipate them effectively as well as new competencies across a broad front. Factors for the diagnostic instrument have been established to gauge city government resilience across macro- or meta-dimensions. Current and emergent dynamics which may be considered predetermined and which may challenge city government resilience have been included to provide for emergent dynamics.

Fukuyama establishes the foundations of modern government in the rule of law, accountability in terms of the rule of law and capability to execute plans to provide services.[302] [303] Drucker points out that as a

---

[299]   Edmondson, A. & Reynolds, S.S. 2016. *Smart cities? It takes more than a village.* https://www.linkedin.com/pulse/smart-cities-takes-more-than-village-amy-c- Date of access: 20 January 2017.

[300]   Edmondson & Reynolds, 2016.

[301]   Van der Waldt, 2016a.

[302]   Fukuyama, F. 2011a. *The origins of political order: From pre-human times to the French Revolution.* New York, NY: FSG.

[303]   Fukuyama, F. 2011b. *Political order and political decay: From the Industrial Revolution to the globalisation of democracy.* New York, NY: FSG.

result of what he calls the new realities a shift has taken place among stakeholders in government from what government *can* do to what government *should* do. He argues that government, by its very nature, cannot run the economy – not even poorly.[304] He goes on to assert that even traditional, progressive-thinking people no longer doubt that there may be limits to what government can do, stating three reasons for this change – failure of government programmes, there are limits to what taxation and spending can achieve and there are limits to government's ability to raise revenue. He adds that whatever non-government organisations can do better or just as well should not be done by government.[305] This argument is also supported by Smith, Friedman and Hayek.

The emerging context and concepts of government described by Fukuyama[306] pinpoint patrimonialism as the dominant characteristic of most post-colonial African states, where the "big man" ensures that governments are staffed by family and friends and run for their benefit. This may be compared to modern governments where staffers are supposed to be chosen on merit and expertise, and governments run for the benefit of the broad public interest. The modern government may be characterised by a constitution, presidents and prime ministers, executive leadership and executive managers, a legal system and a professional administration. Fukuyama goes on to restate the foundations of the modern state as the rule of law, accountability and capability.[307] [308]

The Australian Public Service Commission (APSC)[309] describes capability as consisting of leadership, strategy and delivery.[310] In South Africa, the mandate for government and local government is bounded by the South African Constitution as well as the White Paper on Local Government, which may be seen as a "mini-constitution" for local government. Combined with the various acts governing local government, these provide a measure of autonomy and freedom to execute a developmental policy at local government level. The White Paper on Local Government sees the municipalities as the vanguard of the developmental state. Key external dynamics that may have an impact on local government include, inter alia, urbanisation, large numbers of young people, as well as internal dynamics such as factionalism, wastage and corruption. Predetermined dynamics

---

[304] Drucker, 1994, pp. 59, 60.

[305] Drucker, 1994, pp. 61–68.

[306] Fukuyama, 2011b, p. 287.

[307] Fukuyama 2011a.

[308] Fukuyama 2011b. Fukuyama 2011a

[309] APSC, 2017b

[310] APSC, 2017b

that may challenge city government resilience include the capacity limits to the global carrying capacity, rapid urbanisation, youth dynamics, terror attacks – both nuclear and cyber, another viral epidemic similar to the so-called Spanish flu, and climate volatility. Furthermore, unresolved dilemmas between the NDP and the NDR may create policy ambiguity and uncertainty for investments and a confusing leadership style.

For evidence-based leadership, economic freedom is defined by The Heritage Foundation as the rule of law, government (small) size, regulatory efficiency and open markets. These may be associated with wealth creation as gauged by GDP per capita measured by PPP$ and wealth. Greater economic freedom as defined by The Heritage Foundation[311] may be associated with greater GDP per capita. The main sources of revenue are currently reflected without any substantial FDI included. This raises the question of how FDI might be attracted and benefit city government in its developmental role. Attracting direct foreign investment is described by the International Monetary Fund[312] in terms of various motives for investment. A list of investor criteria reflecting investment priorities was provided by Kearney[313] in a survey of investors.

The cost of government draws attention to what the government can do. Drucker[314] points out that, increasingly, the limits and function of government may become the issue. Once expectations have been raised and pressures that emanate from these expectations manifest themselves, the realities of what governments can do may be outpaced and lag behind, risking negative social consequences.[315] Osborne and Gaebler[316] describe what they identify as entrepreneurial governments. They advocate a smarter back-to-basics approach to government.[317] The use of proven structured business approaches such as prioritisation, business planning, TQM and Kaizen as a way to innovate and continuously improve services may result in better services and value for citizens. Osborne and Gaebler[318] successfully introduced capability reviews in the UK government.

---

[311] Heritage Foundation, 2015.

[312] IMF, 1999.

[313] Kearney, 2017

[314] Drucker, 1994.

[315] Cronje, F. 2017. *A time traveller's guide to South Africa in 2030.* Cape Town: Tafelberg, p. 51.

[316] Osborne & Gaebler, 1992

[317] Osborne, D. & Hutchinson, P. 2004. *The price of government: Getting the results we need in an age of permanent fiscal crisis.* New York, NY: Basic Books, p. 13–17.

[318] Osborne & Gaebler, 1992.

The APSC[319] defines capability in its APS capability review process as reviewing leadership, strategy and service delivery clusters. They provide details within each cluster. Scenario-based strategy may be used to enable city government to anticipate dynamics that may have an impact on city government, anticipate such dynamics and learn about specific dynamics by analysing their underlying structure.

Further learning may take place when scenarios are used to wind tunnel or stress-test scenarios for robustness. Attracting and nurturing talent and investing in capacity building may be an important counter-measure for the lack of capacity pinpointed by the IRR.[320] Public service training and education may not be keeping abreast of the competencies required for e-governance, as reflected in the Van der Waldt competency framework.[321] A number of cross-cutting competencies that have been identified for developing capacity include, for instance, constitutional knowledge, goal setting and review, PMSs and processes, organisational change management infrastructure, leveraging deep technology convergence shifts, as well as specifically retraining for new jobs in general as a requirement for adapting to the convergence of technology described by the WEF in the Fourth Industrial Revolution shifts and disruptions.[322]

Kotter[323] describes why efforts to change organisations fail. Cases of successful organisational change, such as Eskom in the 1980s and the Open University, demonstrate the value of a leadership and strategy forum in which the whole organisation may be engaged in a strategic conversation. This forum can describe the building of organisational infrastructure required for successful organisational change. Disruptions from the technology convergence described by the WEF as the Fourth Industrial Revolution promise to transform governance; the four major areas that may be transformed by this convergence are customer expectations, product and service enhancement, collaborative innovation and organisational forms. The open ledger may do for financial transactions what the internet did for communications. Furthermore, technology-driven disruptions may initially challenge city government resilience and later enhance and improve city governance through a process that Taleb[324] describes as antifragility.

---

[319] APSC, 2017b

[320] IRR, 2014, pp. 16, 17.

[321] Van der Waldt, 2016a.

[322] Schwab, 2016b, pp. 120–172.

[323] Kotter, J. 1995. Leading change: Why transformation efforts fail. *Harvard Business Review*, (March-April):59–67.

[324] Taleb, N.N. 2012. *Antifragile*. New York, NY: Random House.

The national development planning for macroeconomic policy[325] proposes a market-friendly national plan for development. City government, in its role as the vanguard for the developmental state, may engage in a number of alternative community development processes. The SCIP developed by Reynolds[326] and described by Geerts[327] engages bounded communities in taking responsibility for their own development. The SCIP, together with JVs and other PPPs may enable city governments to take on a greater role in executing a developmental policy on behalf of the state. Resilience for city government may consist of adapting to shocks and recovering by engaging in sustainable development. Sustainable development may lead to the management of waste streams and recycling, resulting in a circular economy and green growth where waste provides feedstock to the next manufacturing process. Green growth and smart cities may be enabled by ICT infrastructure when measured by the WEF NRI,[328] which provides a ranking of countries in terms of their readiness to transition and leverage technology in the service of green growth and smart cities.

A draft diagnostic instrument to gauge city government resilience includes events, patterns of behaviour and structural aspects within the extended AAR continuum. This continuum includes Anticipation (A), Adaptation (A), Recovery (R), Sustainable Development (SDev), Green Growth (GG) and Smart Cities (SC). Best practice in the use of the diagnostic instrument and the learning it promotes is described, indicating the scoring protocols for scoring factors and scoring items within factors.

22 CONCLUSION

The urbanisation currently under way globally is set to be the defining dynamic of the twenty-first century. In South Africa, this flow contains a significant number of people (26 m) below the age of 24, who are moving towards cities. This may initially be a challenge for city government resilience but later become an opportunity, depending on how cities anticipate and adapt to this dynamic. Capable city governments may have built capacity in advance of shocks as a result of efficient anticipation, well-planned adaptation and sustainable recovery. An antifragility dynamic in city governments that are resilient may enable leapfrogging into a post-revolution phase, thus avoiding the intermediate carbon-inefficient

---

[325] NPC, 2012, p. 34.

[326] Reynolds, 2007.

[327] Geerts, 2014, p. 94.

[328] WEF, 2016, p. 3.

developmental phases described by Kuznets.[329] Convergent technologies may initially disrupt city governments across a broad front and then, over time, promote antifragile properties in resilient city governments. Predetermined dynamics such as migration to cities, climate volatility, terror attacks and viral attacks could create a coalition between citizen leadership and politicians with the will required to recover from these dynamics. Developing a powerful, dominant public and private coalition, in and among cities globally, may be required to respond resiliently at scale. Anticipating in terms of a 20- to 25-year planning horizon may be required in order to avoid being surprised by predetermined shocks. In addition, an appropriate policy that attracts FDI to cities may lead to deep societal and economic development and transformation on a national level. Thus, semi-autonomous, networked, developmental cities may provide a foundation for resilient developmental states.

In the next chapter the quality of strategic conversation will be described, and an instrument for measuring the quality of strategic conversation is provided. This dimension of strategy is often referred to, but seldom is a concrete instrument provided. One of the keys to effective strategy formulation and execution is the quality of strategic conversation. There is also evidence that conversation quality and organisational trust are associated.

---

[329] Kuznets, J. 2019. *Environmental Kuznets Curve*. https://www.economicshelp.org/blog/14337/environment/environmental-kuznets-curve/ Date of access 9th July 2020.

PART III

Key Competencies for Effective Practice

Contents

CHAPTER 5

AN INTRODUCTION TO CONSCIOUS STRATEGIC CONVERSATION

---

1   INTRODUCTION

Archaeological evidence suggests that the evolution of language took place approximately 100 000 BCE. Recent studies of more than 500 languages by Dr Quentin Atkinson, a biologist at the University of Auckland, indicate that all languages evolved from a single prehistoric African language. His ground-breaking research, based on analysing the variations and number of different sounds in language, was based on an analysis of what are known as phonemes. He posits that the number of phonemes decreases in direct proportion to the distance from the origin of language. From this frame of reference, he found that language originated in Africa and specifically Southern Africa (SoA), the epicentre where all modern languages originated. At approximately the same time, early humans began to migrate from the African continent, eventually spreading around the rest of the world. Atkinson found that the language spoken by the Xu (Southern Africa), for example, has 141 phonemes, while Mandarin (China) has only 32 and the Inuit (Greenland) 22. His hypothesis is that the number of phonemes decreases in proportion to the distance from the origin of language. This points to SoA as the origin of language. The highest number of phonemes are found among the Xu in SoA, the epicentre of language. The development of language and the advantage that it provides to humans coincides with the so-called "big bang" of brain development in Homo sapiens (wise man) or simply Sapiens. Symbolic language and conversation is a uniquely human trait and forms the basis of culture. It enabled humans to cooperate more effectively as well as securing a competitive advantage over other humans of that era, such as the Neanderthals who had not yet developed a sophisticated language capability. In Western Europe, Neanderthals became extinct in a relatively short time in the face of competition for resources from Sapiens. It has been estimated that the genetic difference between Sapiens and Neanderthal was less than 5%. However, this small difference resulted in the extinction of Neanderthal. Language can be seen as simply the ability to communicate, however, a symbolic language carries many other attributes such as values, attitudes, emotions and cultural messages.

A recent Centre for Innovative Leadership (CIL) study uncovered a positive association between strategic conversation quality and organisational trust[1]. It has become widely recognised among scholars that an increase in trust lowers the transaction costs between individuals in an organisation or human activity system. In a high-trust organisational environment decisions can be taken faster and better. Action planning and action can also follow more efficiently. The converse is also true and reflects the high cost of distrust often caused by inappropriate interpersonal competition and rivalry between factions competing for vested interests. Strategic conversation exists whenever members of organisations or interest groups communicate about a common organisational purpose, as well as the direction and roles in achieving these superordinate aspirations. The quality of conversation and the engagement of leaders may, therefore, influence the agility, resilience and competitive advantage of an organisation through robust strategy making and rigorous, relentless execution.

The effectiveness of scenario planning is thought by some to be based on the ability of facilitators to engage organisational members in genuine conversation.[2] [3] [4] [5] [6] Many scholars agree that effective conversation and communication between and among organisational decision makers is important.[7] [8] In this view, scenario planning is a tool for fostering the strategic conversation – an ongoing dialogue about possibilities, opportunities and change.[9] The more authentic this conversation, the more effective joint action can be. The general observation has been made that it is extremely difficult to manage a scenario-planning project via online participation. The face-to-face interaction and dialogue is thought to be the mode by which the benefit of scenario planning happens, where assumptions are influenced and widened. While there is much conceptual

[1]   Centre for Innovative Leadership (CIL). 2014. The association between organisational trust and conversation quality and engagement for competent leadership. (Unpublished).

[2]   Chermack, T.J. & Van der Merwe, L. 2003. The role of constructivist learning in scenario planning. *Futures,* 35:445–460.

[3]   Georgantzas, N.C. & Acar, W. 1995. *Scenario-driven planning: Learning to manage strategic uncertainty.* Westport, CT: Quorum.

[4]   Schwartz, P. 1991. *The art of the long view.* New York: Doubleday.

[5]   Senge, *et al.*1994

[6]   Van der Heijden, K., Bradfield, R., Burt, G., Cairns, G., & Wright, G. 2002. *The sixth sense: Accelerating organizational learning with scenarios.* New York: John Wiley.

[7]   Georgantzas and Acar, 1995.

[8]   Senge, et al., 1994

[9]   Manning, T. 2002. Strategic conversation as a tool for change. *Strategy & Leadership,* 35(5):35–38.

work that outlines how this occurs in theory, there has been no rigorous study of the phenomenon. There have been no attempts to assess the quality of strategic conversations as a valuable component of planning in organisations.

2 REVIEW OF MAJOR CONCEPTS

The purpose of this chapter is to provide a multidimensional rationale for viewing strategic organisational conversation as the key to strategy making and strategy execution. A brief description of scenario planning is once more provided, followed by a detailed literature review of the concept of strategic conversation. Little has been published in this domain as it is an emerging component of strategy making that is only now beginning to receive attention. Once concepts are established, an instrument is provided here that measures the quality of strategic conversations reliably and validly. This instrument is the product of 30 years of practise. The results of CIL research efforts is described to examine the validity and reliability of the instrument scores using a sample of 204 managers in a strategic context.[10]

2.1 Scenario Planning

The scenario-planning literature increasingly features the term "strategic conversation" as one of the key inputs as well as outputs of the scenario-planning process. Skilful strategic conversation enables shifting assumptions in the minds of decision makers. In short, because of this property scenario planning is an approach to strategy that accounts for uncertainty in ways that traditional strategic planning falls short.

Scenarios have been defined as tools for ordering one's perceptions about alternative future environments in which one's decisions might be played out. Alternatively, "a set of organised ways for us to dream effectively about our own future".[11] Scenario planning has been defined as "a process of positing several informed, plausible and imagined alternative future environments in which decisions about the future may be played out, for the purpose of changing current thinking, improving decision making, enhancing human and organisation learning and improving performance".[12]

---

[10]   Van der Merwe, L., Chermack, T.J., Kulikowich, J. & Yang, B. 2007. Strategic conversation quality and engagement: Assessment of a new measure. *International Journal of Training and Development,* 11(3):214–221.

[11]   Schwartz, 1991, p. 4.

[12]   Chermack & Lynham, 2005. pg. 4

While there are many methods for conducting scenario planning, the Centre for Innovative Leadership[13] has identified six steps, or phases, which mirror most of the methodologies available publicly today. These are:

1) identification of a strategic organisational agenda, including assumptions and concerns about strategic thinking and vision;

2) systematically examining the organisation's external environment to improve understanding of the structure of key forces driving change;

3) challenging of existing assumptions of organisational decision makers by questioning current mental models about the external environment;

4) synthesis of information about possible future events into two, three or four alternative plots or storylines about possible futures;

5) development of narratives about the storylines to make the stories relevant, compelling and plausible to decision makers; and

6) use of stories to help decision makers "re-view" (aka wind-tunnelling or stress-testing) their strategic thinking.

Scenario planning is assumed by many to be a vehicle for fostering strategic conversation. The term "strategic conversation" requires some clarification and discussion.

2.2 The strategic conversation

The strategic conversation is a phenomenon that has been described as the simple conversations and interactions that occur among organisational members in everyday formal and informal situations. While this strategic conversation includes the formal planning process and the associated meetings and retreats, it also includes the more subtle interactions that can only be classified as informal and undocumented. Van der Heijden[14] is commonly credited for coining the term in his book *Scenarios: The Art of Strategic Conversation* in which he wrote:

> "The crux of the institutional aspects of the processual paradigm is conversation. The learning loop model shows the interwovenness of thinking and action. If action is based on planning on the basis of a

---

13 Centre for Innovative Leadership (CIL). 1995. *Strategic management: Introduction to scenario thinking public workshop.* Rivonia, South Africa: The Centre for Innovative Leadership.

14 Van der Heijden, K. 1997. *Scenarios, strategies and the strategy process.* The Netherlands: Nijenrode University Press.

mental model, then institutional action must be based on a shared mental model. Only through a process of conversation can elements of observation and thought be structured and embedded in the accepted and shared organisational theories in use."[15]

Certainly, the strategic conversation is an abstract phenomenon – difficult to describe and pin down. However, there are some suggestions in the scenario-planning literature for what is required in order to achieve this strategic conversation. Van der Heijden[16] wrote that an effective strategic conversation requires 1) a common language, 2) the alignment of ideas, 3) a willingness to engage in rational argumentation, and finally, 4) it contains the evolution of ideas inside the organisation.

2.3 Common language

The requirement for a common language is logical and not complex. Stated simply, organisation members participating in any process need a common understanding of the process to be used and some way to define and sort

2.4 Alignment of ideas

The strategy literature increasingly includes reference to the notion of alignment.[17] [18] While most of the strategy literature refers to alignment among the organisation, process and individual goals, the strategic conversation aims to produce alignment among *ideas and assumptions* also known as mental models. Wack[19] stresses the importance of revealing and analysing mental models in scenario planning. In this context, the notion of idea alignment, which enables the ability to act in the same direction, can be considered as an output of building a collective mental model. Sharing assumptions, values and the basic scaffolding of a unified purpose are critical to establishing this kind of alignment.[20] Action, based on a collective mental model will automatically be aligned by this shared mental model. Alignment is defined as the ability of an organisation to act as one. This ability can be seen in the moments of extraordinary, aligned play where a world-class team in sport or the arts comes together. In these rare moments their alignment is both rational and intuitive. Do you

---

[15]   Van der Heijden, 1997, p. 41.

[16]   Van der Heijden, 1997.

[17]   Manning, 2002.

[18]   Mintzberg, H. & Lampal, J., 1998. Reflecting on the Strategy Process. *Sloan Management Review*. 40(3).

[19]   Wack,1985

[20]   Manning, 2002.

think this happens only by chance? There are principles and disciplines that enable us to recreate these moments. They are reflected in the work popularised by Peter Senge and the learning organisation. Learning faster than competitors remains an enduring competitive advantage.

2.5 Willingness to engage in rational argumentation

The scenario-planning process is one of dialogue, challenge, and willingness to critique ideas. Thus, participants must be comfortable engaging in conversation and must be open to having their ideas challenged by other participants in a skilful, conscious conversation. By definition, learning happens when people begin to see things in a new way. Without this critical piece, the strategic conversation becomes lip service and none of its implications is taken seriously as there is no learning and no novel insights.

2.6 Evolution of Shared Ideas inside the Organisation

This final requirement can be thought of as the result of the previous three requirements. This is the goal. The stage for the evolution of ideas within an organisation is set by developing a common language, working toward aligning ideas, and with a willingness to critique and be critiqued by the majority of people in an organisation. Often, scenarios are just a starting point for ideas to be sparked, which leads to a revision of the scenarios and further debate and dialogue until assumptions are either shattered or persist as plausible and become shared.

2.7 Dialogue

Van der Heijden's initial components of the strategic conversation do not include the notion of dialogue which was developed by Bohm.[21] [22] [23] Dialogue is an additional critical component that cannot be ignored in considering the quality of the strategic conversation. Bohm's[24] work on the nature of thought has suggested much about the ways in which people communicate. Given the positioning of communication in this chapter and in the larger context of scenario planning, it is useful to consider the nature of communication. Bohm's work sheds considerable light on the subject.

> The meaning of the word "dialogue" used by Bohm is somewhat different from
> what is commonly understood. The derivations of words often help to suggest
> a deeper meaning. "Dialogue" comes from the Greek words "dia" and "logos".
> Logos means "the word" or in this context, we would think of the "meaning of

---

[21] Bohm, D. 1989. *Quantum theory*. London: Dover Publications.

[22] Bohm, D. 2002. *Wholeness and the implicate order*. London: Routledge.

[23] Bohm, D. 2004. *On dialogue*. London: Routledge.

[24] Bohm, 2002.

the word". And dia means "through" – it doesn't mean "two". A dialogue can take place among a number of people, not just two. The picture or image that Bohm suggests is a stream of meaning flowing among and through participants and between members of a group. "This will make possible a flow of meaning in the whole group, out of which may emerge some new understanding."[25]

Contrast this with the word "discussion", which has the same roots as "percussion" and "concussion", which means to break things up. It emphasises the idea of analysis, where there may be many points of view, and where everybody is presenting a different one – analysing and breaking up. That obviously has value, but it is limited, and it will not get us very far beyond current points of view.[26]

Conscious conversation includes a perspective where the person engaged in conversation is self-conscious during a conversation. A meta-perspective which includes in-the-moment observation and adjustment, thus continuously improves the quality of conversation and through this raises the level of trust and learning. These requirements of strategic conversation are intended to clarify the essence of a quality strategic conversation. While becoming something of a cliché in organisations, clear definitions and descriptions do not yet exist and are not arrived at by simply reviewing the little that has been written. Various authors[27] [28] [29] have referred to the strategic conversation as a means by which to continuously improve the quality of strategy making in organisations. However, they are silent on precise descriptions of what constitutes quality in these conversations.

Dialogue that reflects a quality conversation is an important part of communicating and diffusing any idea throughout an organisation. However, there are few clear ways of measuring dialogue and communication in an organisational context. Additionally, since we are primarily concerned with the scenario-planning phenomenon, also known as scenario-based strategy, we have found that there are no useful instruments that reliably measure or gauge the quality of communication, conversation or dialogue in the context of organisational planning. Conversation, as has been mentioned above, can be seen as a distinctly human trait. An instrument which determines its quality in the context of planning will probably also determine quality in general.

---

[25] Van der Heijden, 1997, p. 6.

[26] Van der Heijden, 1997, p. 7.

[27] Chermack, T.J. 2005. Studying scenario planning: Theory, research suggestions and hypotheses. *Technological Forecasting and Social Change, 72*(1), 59–73.

[28] Van der Heijden, 1997.

[29] Van der Heijden et al., 2002.

3   DEVELOPMENT OF AN INSTRUMENT TO GAUGE STRATEGIC CONVERSATION QUALITY AND ENGAGEMENT

An instrument to gauge strategic conversation quality and engagement began with a need to understand the communication abilities of scenario-planning participants in practice. While business interventions in the world of work (WOW) certainly have an analytical and fact-driven side, they also have an intuitive, relationship-driven side. The same principles for quality conversation apply in the world of family (WOF). The resources engaged to develop this instrument have been drawn from both the WOW and the WOF domains. The basis for the instrument was established from key works in the counselling literature, the transformational change literature and the action science literature. The goal of the instrument was to measure individual skills in conversing with others and also to take some measure of the level of engagement in conversations overall. Each theoretical component is described briefly in the next section.

3.1   Theoretical background of the instrument

The foundations of the instrument include: 1) Carl Rogers' work on person-centred communication theory,[30] 2) Nunnally's work on communication in families,[31][32][33][34][35] 3) Argyris's work on balancing advocacy and inquiry,[36][37] and 4) Lewin's work on group dynamics.[38][39]

---

[30]   Rogers, C. 1961. *On Becoming a Person*. Boston, MA: Houghton Mifflin.

[31]   Miller, S.L. 1971. The effects of communication training in small groups upon self-disclosure and openness in engaged couples' systems of interaction: A field experiment. (Doctoral Dissertation, University of Minnesota, 1971). Dissertation Abstracts International, 32, 2819A–2820A. (University Microfilms No. 71–28, 263).

[32]   Miller, S.L., Nunnally, E.W., & Wackman, D.B. 1976. A communication training program for couples. Social Casework, 57, 9–18.

[33]   Miller, S., Wackman, D. & Nunnally, E.W. 1982. *Straight talk: A new way to get closer to others by saying what you really mean*. New York: Signet Publishers.

[34]   Nunnally, E.W. 1971. Effects of communication training upon interaction awareness and empathic accuracy of engaged couples: A field experiment. (Doctoral Dissertation, University of Minnesota, 1971). Dissertation Abstracts International, 32, 4736A. (University Microfilms No. 72–05, 561).

[35]   Nunnally, E.W., & Moy, C. 1989. *Communication basics for human service professionals*. New York: Sage Publications.

[36]   Argyris, C. & Schon, D.A. 1996. *Organizational learning II. Theory, method, and practice*. New York: McGraw Hill.

[37]   Bolman, L.G. & Deal, T.E. 1997. *Reframing Organizations. Artistry, choice and leadership*, San Francisco, C.A.: Jossey-Bass.

[38]   Lewin, K. 1948. *Resolving Social Conflicts. Selected papers on group dynamics*. New York: Harper and Row.

[39]   Lewin, K. 1951. *Field Theory in Social Science*. New York: Harper and Row.

Rogers' work on person-centred communication theory. Carl Rogers spent much of his career focusing on individual experience. He eventually posited conditions for relational health, namely: 1) congruence, 2) openness, 3) honesty, 4) respect, 5) unconditional positive regard, and 6) empathetic understanding. By using the term "congruence" Rogers means "a match or fit between an individual's feelings and outer display".[40] "Unconditional positive regard" was simply an attitude that Rogers consciously tried to hold toward people and found that he experienced deeper levels of trust by doing so.[41] [42] Another of Rogers' conditions, "empathetic understanding", involves deep listening from *within the other*; a willingness to explore what it is like to be another person is a skill that Rogers found brought him closer to those he was trying to help. It also changed the relationship between them.[43] These components are embodied in several of the items on the instrument, such as "I use active listening to understand another person's point of view", and "I encourage others to make choices that support engagement in the conversation".

Nunnally's work on communication in families. Nunnally has developed a large body of work (with co-authors Miller and Wackman) in the area of communication among family members and interpersonal relationships. These works[44] [45] [46] [47] [48] [49] feature the self-awareness wheel as the primary contribution that informs the instrument. The self-awareness wheel helps individuals recognise their own sensations, feelings, intentions and actions in the context of how they relate to others.[50] Items such as "I know my personal patterns of behaviour and 'hot buttons' and can intervene effectively and make choices" and "I do my best to be explicit about the assumptions underlying my opinions" reflect this work from the counselling literature.

---

[40] Rogers, C. 1957. The necessary and sufficient conditions of therapeutic personality change. *Journal of Consulting Psychology 21*(2), 95–103, p. 97.

[41] Rogers, C. 1961.

[42] Rogers, C & Skinner, B.F. 1956. Some issues concerning the control of human behavior. *Science 124*(2): 1057–1065.

[43] Rogers, 1961.

[44] Miller, 1971.

[45] Miller *et al.*, 1976.

[46]   Miller *et al.*, 1976

[47] Miller et al., 1982.

[48] Nunnally, 1971.

[49] Nunnally & Moy, 1989.

[50]   Miller et al., 1976

Argyris and Schon's work on advocacy and inquiry. Argyris and Schon[51] have argued for a balancing of advocacy and enquiry in organisations. Typical organisational conversations are lopsided in the direction of advocacy at the cost of enquiry which is where learning is enabled. This means a combination of pushing for individual aims and respecting that the individual is part of the larger whole. Best known for differentiating Model I and Model II learning loops, Argyris and Schon[52] have proposed that a shift takes place when individuals begin to consciously pay attention to their own behaviour and evaluate it as they would another person's behaviour. An emphasis on common goals and shared interests and the group efforts to achieve them contributes to the key idea of reflection on the learning process. The theoretical background of the instrument and this reflection is known as Model II learning or double-loop learning. Model II represents a meta-perspective by observing the self through a process of self-differentiation. These ideas can be seen in items such as "I define personal and organisational boundaries and review them when necessary" and "I constantly question my opinions with the intent of reaching observable data". Level II Skills in the CIL instrument reflect the meta-level, Argyris's Model II, where my capability to rise above the transactional conversation level (Level I Skills) provides additional learning.

Lewin's work on group dynamics. Lewin's famous t-groups were a breakthrough in understanding interpersonal communication, intra-personal processes and personal growth among t-group members.[53] The key contribution arose when researchers allowed a participant to be present for an analysis of her observed behaviour earlier in the day. The participant happened to be a woman and she argued directly with Lewin about his inaccurate interpretations of things she did. Conversation ensued and a new method of intergroup skills training was born. "I maintain balance between asking questions and stating my opinions" and "I paraphrase what is said to ensure deeper understanding" are examples of items that draw from both Lewin's and Argyris's research.

This brief review of the theories and suggestions regarding their influence on the initial instrument provides practitioners with insight as well as resources with which to enlarge their own perspective on conversation quality. The face validity of the CIL instrument may be evident in the items on Level I Skills and Level II Skills. The CIL questionnaire clearly reflects some of the concepts. Additional face validity may be

---

51   Argyris & Schon, 1996.

52   Argyris & Schon, 1996.

53   Lewin, K. 1951.

extended based on its use by prominent scenario planning and other practitioners. However, its use and additional applications such as in the area of performance management can add considerably to the credibility of the instrument and its overall validity and reliability in strategic contexts. The next sections described the research study which examined these characteristics. The detailed description of the research methodology and statistical analyses are beyond the scope of practitioner guidelines and have been omitted for the sake of ease of access to the conclusions of the analyses and the effective use of the instrument to raise the quality of strategic conversation.

4   CONCLUSIONS AND CONTRIBUTIONS TO SCENARIO-BASED STRATEGY PRACTICE

In short, the CIL analysis found a highly reliable set of instrument scores by measuring two key components which are labelled 1) Active leadership and engagement in conversations and 2) Awareness of individual communication patterns and tendencies – the major components of conversation quality and engagement skills in a planning context. In addition, the results have revealed that these constructs are multidimensional. These components appear to be critical for the effectiveness of internal organisational strategic conversation and this validation procedure lends some credibility to the instrument. Besides that credibility the reliability and validity has been scientifically calibrated within a substantial sample of more than 300 US managers and came out with flying colours.

This research study has confirmed the basis of reliability and validity for an instrument developed primarily in practice. In addition, it seems that strategic conversation may indeed be a component of strategic planning that should draw further attention in the future and may result in a need to adjust current planning models to include this component.[54] The CIL analysis has resulted in a practical instrument with acceptable reliability and validity scores that measures participant conversation quality and engagement skills in strategic contexts. While this instrument is eminently suitable but has not yet been used in other contexts – for instance, in performance evaluation conversations, organisation development and team-building interventions – its applicability to these situations seems reasonable. In particular, the Rogers' person-centred approach was successfully applied in a context of extreme racial diversity in South Africa in 1986. In that context the person-centred approach was seen to develop trust, cohesion and empathy among participants. In short, the

---

[54]   Chermack, T. 2005.

CIL instrument may prove a valuable measure of individual conversation quality and communication skills in a variety of contexts. CIL therefore encourages scenario-planning professionals and other practitioners to use this instrument and continue to build the credibility of its use through continued examination of the reliability and validity properties of its scores[55] (see CQE instrument in Table 5.1).

5 CONVERSATION QUALITY AND ENGAGEMENT (CQE) CHECKLIST

Please assess your conversation and engagement skills and score yourself.
Ask other colleagues to also score your skills and compare scores. This checklist can be used in work settings such as strategy making, coaching and performance management, as well as other settings such as leadership, social and even family settings. Keep practising and reflecting on skill levels and improving your CQE skills in realtime whenever conversation quality is important. Work on improving Level I Skills first, then move to Level II Skills

Note: To be used in conjunction with CIL skills development workshops and executive mentoring

FEEDBACK – IN STRATEGY AND LEADERSHIP, AND MANAGING ACCOUNTABILITY AND PERFORMANCE ROLES

Complete the assessment sheet by providing scores which indicate levels that reflect typical behaviour in conversations in team and one-on-one settings. Each score can also be accompanied by a description of a specific behaviour, if possible, in specific situations, as further support and a basis for learning. Start a self-assessment process by using the following introduction:
In assessing strategy, leadership or performance conversations I (insert an item wording) then provide scores for the items 1–20.

Table 5.1: Conversation Quality and Engagement (CQE) Checklist

	Never	Sometimes	Often	Usually	Always
LEVEL I SKILLS					
1. I use active listening to understand another person's point of view	1	2	3	4	5
2. I repeat a summary of and paraphrase what is said to ensure deeper understanding	1	2	3	4	5

---

[55] Van der Merwe et al., 2007

	Never	Sometimes	Often	Usually	Always
3. I take responsibility for myself by choosing language that indicates this	1	2	3	4	5
4. I listen to what is being said and am self-aware when judging	1	2	3	4	5
5. I maintain a balance between asking questions and stating my opinions	1	2	3	4	5
6. I do my best to be clear about the assumptions underlying my opinions	1	2	3	4	5
7. I constantly question my opinions for concrete evidence to support them	1	2	3	4	5
8. I use concrete examples to describe behaviour, sensing, feelings and impact	1	2	3	4	5
9. I stay engaged by identifying events that could assist in understanding underlying patterns of behaviour and structural aspects	1	2	3	4	5
10. I use open-ended questions to clarify the patterns and structures	1	2	3	4	5
Subtotal Level I Skills					
LEVEL II SKILLS					
11. I avoid third-party involvement (triangulation) by dealing directly with others and with the issues at hand	1	2	3	4	5
12. I confront others constructively when I disagree with their opinions	1	2	3	4	5
13. I take a stand and express the results I want while remaining engaged with the conversation at hand	1	2	3	4	5
14. I make informed choices about my personal behaviour in the conversation by balancing the purpose of the conversation with its desired results and current reality	1	2	3	4	5
15. I encourage others to remain engaged in the conversation	1	2	3	4	5
16. I define personal and organisational boundaries and review them when necessary	1	2	3	4	5

	Never	Sometimes	Often	Usually	Always
17. I know my personal patterns of behaviour and "hot buttons" and can intervene effectively and make choices	1	2	3	4	5
18. I understand the origins of my behavioural patterns and "hot buttons"	1	2	3	4	5
19. I apply conflict resolution skills as required	1	2	3	4	5
20. I use applicable coaching skills such as deep listening, empathy, respect, concreteness and genuineness as appropriate	1	2	3	4	5
Subtotal Level II Skills					
Overall Total – Levels I & II Combined					

SCORE	DESCRIPTION AND INTERPRETATION GUIDELINES
0–25	Low potential for leadership. Others feel out of touch and no effort is made to be in touch, even disrespect. Conversations easily escalate into conflict and leave feelings of frustration. General lack of trust and alignment. Low morale and commitment is common. Open, authentic conversations are difficult and seldom happen. Teams and individuals don't know what their priorities and roles are, and results are unclear.
26–50	Medium potential for leadership. Others feel that you are somewhat distant. Conversations are often unsatisfactory and people don't know where they stand. Trust is at a low level. Open and authentic conversations sometimes happen and when they do the contrast is immediately noticed. Indirect behaviour with third parties is commonplace and many areas that are undiscussable develop. Priorities are often unclear and choices are difficult to make, boundaries are also unclear and easily violated.
51–75	Average to above-average potential for leadership. Trust levels are building. Practising conversation and engagement skills in real time is accepted and encouraged. Regular feedback and coaching for the purposes of learning is commonplace. Priorities are clear and tough choices are made and adhered to. Boundaries are often the focus of conversations. Systems thinking is applied as a way of looking at the world and influencing it and this informs many choices at interpersonal and intrapersonal levels.

76–100	High potential for leadership. Priorities are clear and there is continuous improvement with little wastage. Raising of performance standards and changes in direction are both easily executed. Others experience openness and authenticity in the leadership process. Relationships are characterised by confidence, humility, courage, firmness, vulnerability and openness. Confronting in a tough yet compassionate and constructive way occurs frequently and is skilfully executed using conversation and engagement skills naturally, and sometimes intuitively. Thinking and actions are informed by a systems perspective and self-knowledge. Trust is continuously being built and the team performs at a high level and in alignment with the overall goals and with each other.

Leadership is conceptualised as *influence potential*. Leadership is executed through the capacity to take a stand and then skilfully, in a non-anxious manner, hold this stand while staying in touch with the system you lead, using conversation and engagement skills, until the followers align themselves with your stand.

Competent conversation and engagement consists of frequent face-to-face communication one-on-one as well as one-on-many, which are characterised by openness and authenticity, together with a tough-minded focus on agreed purpose and results. This enables high performance through robust, trusting relationships and a learning climate. In this approach, individuals and teams take personal responsibility and are accountable, which enables rapid self-correcting, which in turn supports the capacity for self-organising at individual, team and organisational levels.

Select one or two of the skills that you would like to improve and include them in your personal development planning. Create practice areas in different settings where you can raise your level of competence, including contracting for regular structured feedback processes with mentors.

DEVELOPING CONVERSATION QUALITY AND ENGAGEMENT SKILLS – SCORES FOR THE PURPOSES OF PERSONAL DEVELOPMENT PLANNING (PDP)

Conversation quality and engagement skills can improve the quality of your relationships both at work and in your family. These essential life skills are the foundation for strategy making, learning, leadership and building trust.

CHAPTER 6

SCENARIO-BASED STRATEGY: A FRAMEWORK FOR ANTICIPATING THE FUTURE AND APPLIED SYSTEMS THINKING

"Your assumptions are your windows on the world. Scrub them off every once in a while, or the light won't come in."

Isaac Asimov

Scenario-based strategy is a crucial process to enable organisational learning. The field of practice was developed by its pioneers in Royal/ Dutch Shell Group planning to enable informed strategic conversation and to shift assumptions in the minds of decision makers about how the external, contextual environment might unfold. This work was preceded by that of Herman Kahn, a futurist who worked for the RAND Corporation. During the 1960s, he wrote the original *Thinking About the Unthinkable*. He had noticed that decision makers had not shifted their assumptions about the likelihood of a nuclear holocaust. Deeper learning at assumption level is required to retune the human mind from a model which is based on extraction, beneficiation, use and then discard, to enable using planet Earth's finite resources sustainably.

1 SCENARIO-BASED STRATEGY: A FRAMEWORK

The primary use of successful scenario practice is to shift and enrich the assumptions in the minds of decision makers, knowing that assumptions are the basis of decisions. This chapter documents the essential elements and underlying principles of scenario-based strategy practice. Essential principles and the overall approach have been learnt directly from the first and second generation pioneers of the scenario-based strategy method. Guidelines for practitioner development represent a set of foundations and quality standards for sound scenario practice. Detailed process choices and decisions may be based on these guidelines once they have been mastered and internalised. General management and specialists such as human resources development (HRD) professionals and other professionals whose organisational contributions require a good knowledge of scenario-based strategic thinking may also benefit from this framework. Potential scenario-based strategy practitioners who wish to enter this field will find this chapter and other chapters in this book key to ensuring success as a resilience practitioner. An outline is provided below of the knowledge, skills and attitudes needed by competent practitioners. The first part of this chapter identifies a number of key phenomena which led to the birth of scenario-based strategy as a method. The second part describes some of the essential process elements, their origins and the competencies needed for process choices, facilitation and execution. The goal is to provide a set of reliable "handrails" for learner practitioners and guidelines for identifying useful further learning resources.

As a result of the increasing rate of change and complexity in our environment, strategy making is moving towards a more emergent and learning-based focus. An article in the *Harvard Business Review* (*HBR*) by Arie de Geus titled "Planning as Learning" marks a watershed between designing organisations and their internal processes from a command-and-control point of view and that of learning and responding to the emergent elements in the environment. This watershed article was preceded by an earlier contribution by the late Don Michael titled *Learning to plan and planning to learn*. Pioneer Pierre Wack said about Don Michael's contribution that Don Michael was the first to put learning at the heart of planning.

Argyris defines learning as "detecting and correcting error". In the context of organisational strategy, learning serves precisely that purpose – that of detecting an error in assumptions and decision making. The emergence of the "learning organisation" as a breakthrough in organisation design and leadership was popularised in the best-selling series of field books by Peter Senge. These field books can be directly linked to De Geus's far-sighted work in the *HBR* in 1988. This shift has opened the strategy making process to specialists in learning, rather than leaving it in the realm of analysts, economists and finance specialists.

Designing a scenario-based strategy process and facilitating such design with learning in mind fits closely with the competence of the HRD professional. Many of the methods as practised by Pierre Wack lie firmly within the current remit of the HRD discipline and organisation development (OD). HRD practitioners require an understanding of adult learning, group process and a multitude of organisation development processes which are also critical for successful scenario planning.

The general framework provided in this chapter is a practical approach that has been handed down from the first two generations of scenario-based strategy "masters". Traditionally, a novice practitioner would navigate this pathway under the tutelage and guidance of an experienced professional using a mentorship model for learning. However, masters of the scenario-based strategy method are relatively scarce, and practice varies between so-called masters. For the first time, this pathway, together with the essential principles, is documented in a publication in such a way that a novice practitioner may find his or her own way through this diverse landscape.

Strategy making and specifically scenario-based strategy can be described as a divergent process which also converges at times. When dealing with a divergent problem, there are no clear, set steps. There is no defined procedure that suits all situations, only cycles and areas of enquiry and learning. In a divergent problem, the first step influences the next steps and often determines the style, character and content of the subsequent steps in the process.

1.1 Guidelines for aspiring scenario-based strategy practitioners

Scenario planning is a subtle and highly complex process, and it would be impossible for any single chapter to cover all of the crucial aspects of the method in great detail. A structured course was developed which codified and practised many of the key processes first developed by Pierre Wack and Ted Newland at Royal/Dutch Shell.

There are, however, guidelines and broad principles that inform judgement and decisions, which enable continuous cycles of application and learning. A divergent process (in this case, scenario-based strategy) further requires an aspiring practitioner to develop a sense of judgement on how to navigate each fork in the pathway to building and using a set of scenarios with a high level of competence and expertise. This approach to planning also requires that the aspiring practitioner adopt a specific worldview that looks at the interconnections between parts rather than snapshots or fragments of particular dynamics.

This way of viewing the world is known as systems thinking. Systems thinking can be extended to systems dynamics (SD) and complexity theory. Omissions that may compromise the quality of scenario work can be avoided by drawing attention to critical phenomena and by describing a practical framework for understanding and working through the major components of a scenario-based strategy process. The practice of scenario-based strategy varies between practitioners, and this variation provides aspirant practitioners with a richer repertoire from which to develop their own approach. However, practitioners should first understand and master the general framework used by the founders before inventing alternatives that may not necessarily improve the result. Dr Peter Senge would often say to practitioners wishing to innovate prematurely, "Master Sonata-form first before attempting to alter Sonata-form."

1.2 Increasing Use of Scenarios in Strategy making

According to Napier Collyns, one of the first generation scenarists in Shell Group planning, "Scenario planning is suddenly on the leadership agenda in many of the major corporations around the world."

As the environment becomes more uncertain, and the risks to individuals and organisations grow, the need to mobilise every ounce of intelligence and creativity to deal with this volatility is greater than ever. The problem of dealing with this complexity is that it requires state-of-the-art process technologies carefully embedded in organisational strategy making and strategy execution . Scenario-based strategy is one such method. Cutting-edge practice in using this method should enable the strategy process to function like an organisational radar or early warning system that identifies emerging discontinuities and opportunities in the environment that the organisation has to face well in advance of being affected by them Wack.

The rising complexity and volatility of external dynamics in the organisational environment are driving the demand for scenario-based strategy and opening numerous opportunities for practitioners with related expertise. Specifically, this may be an opportunity for aspirant practitioners to develop their competence and thus occupy a more mainstream or strategic role in their organisations as they adopt a practice that will enable them to become part of the organisational strategic conversation.

1.3 The structure of this chapter

This chapter proceeds with two major sections. In section one, it offers some basic approaches that apply to strategy making and specifically the scenario-based strategy process. These approaches are gleaned from more than 30 years of consulting and executive education in organisational strategy throughout the world. The major topics of this subsection include:
- problems with prediction;
- systems thinking; and
- strategy as "fit".

The second section, the larger of the two sections, focuses on some essential, more specific elements for emerging scenario-planning practitioners. Elements in this section include:
- generations of scenario pioneers and uses of scenarios;
- a typical scenario development process;

- an example of systemic analysis for water;
- SD modelling;
- quality criteria for scenarios;
- using scenarios to test strategic robustness; and
- a competency profile for scenario-planning practitioners;
- practitioner guidelines for facilitating scenario projects.

2 SECTION 1: APPROACHES IN THE SCENARIO-BASED STRATEGY METHOD

Three phenomena in strategy making that form the foundations for scenario-based strategy are: 1) inherent problems with prediction, 2) increasing complexity in the external environment and the need for practical systems thinking, and 3) strategy as a continuous learning process with the purpose of achieving "fit" between the organisational intent of leadership and the dynamics in the external environment. These approaches evolved primarily in a practical environment where a practitioner had to do what worked in terms of purpose and desired results. Citations of authoritative scholars, where available, are provided in the narrative of the various aspects of scenario-based strategy, as potential learning resources. Citation of sources is the basis of this author's own practice, pinpointing what has worked best and why this forms the basis of the argument(s) in this chapter.

2.1 Problems with prediction

The most commonly used method for understanding what might unfold in future is by studying what has happened in the past and then using this as a basis for predicting the future. The central problem with this approach, however, is deeply buried in the principles of cognition. Once a prediction has been widely agreed, the way in which people then observe the future becomes limited to a narrow band of variability. Schumacher reminds us that when faced with complexity, we tend to reduce this complexity to an "either/or" dialectic in order to cope. In addition, the official blessing that these predictions receive from top leadership often prevents people from seeing emerging forces and discontinuities outside of "the official future" (see Figure 6.1). This official "blessing" by executive leadership (according to Brenard – a CEO of Shell) also changes the nature of the conversation in the organisation from revealing risk to concealing risk.

People who have worked in large command-and-control organisations have experienced this phenomenon. "The official future" cuts across all forms of learning, information sharing and decision making. The classical command-and-control organisation requires that everyone in a leadership role supports and adheres to the officially enunciated policy. Deviation from the norm is often seen as disloyalty and is sanctioned and corrected. Mavericks are usually unaffected by this requirement to conform, hence their value in stimulating alternate perspectives on the future. The corporate incantation that "mavericks make the best hamburgers" signals their vulnerability in the face of pressure to conform. In this type of organisation, the thinking is usually done at the top of the organisation while managers and supervisors are expected to act out these decisions. Learning is limited to the top and reactions to changes in the environment are slow. Hesitation and delays can sometimes be fatal to the organisation because it no longer fits with the environment in which it finds itself. One important purpose of scenario-based strategy is to address these issues.

Shell engaged Pierre Wack to contribute to the planning process in the 1970s because they had noticed that their predictions were never accurate enough, and that predictions, once accepted as official policy, altered the conversation and learning processes about external dynamics inside Shell. Shell was only interested in one prediction – the future price of oil. Planning teams noticed that once management had pronounced what the predicted price of oil was, this prediction changed the quality of the conversation about oil price dynamics and possibilities. It was not acceptable to deviate from the predicted price (aka the "official future") when compiling business plans and budgets and exploring specific strategies (see Figure 6.1). Because senior management had created an official future, there was no space to think the unthinkable, let alone discuss the unthinkable, without risking personal reputation.

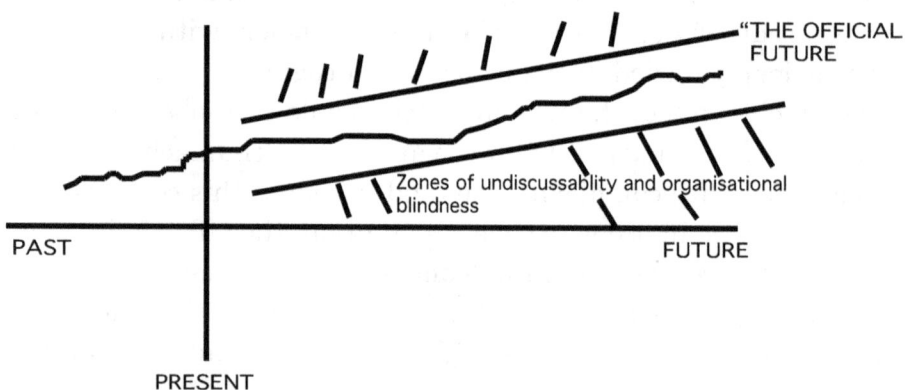

Figure 6.1:Predictions, Scenarios, and the dangers of the "Official Future"

Source: Van der Merwe, L. Scenario-based Strategy In Practice: A framework. (In Chermack, T., *ed* Advances in HRD, London: Sage, pp 216-239).

Pierre Wack's stated purpose of scenarios emphasises the shifting of assumptions in the minds of decision makers.

> "The most important purpose of the scenario building process is to shift the thinking amongst the leadership inside the organisation about what might happen, in the future, in the external environment."

This purpose statement represents one of the key guidelines for practitioners when designing scenario-planning workshops, and highlights a purpose consistent with avoiding predictions in planning. Attempting to predict which scenario is most likely is a variation on creating a false sense of certainty and should be avoided. This tendency, often encountered among novice practitioners, violates a fundamental principle of scenario-based strategy, i.e. shifting assumptions, which creates a set of equally plausible, internally consistent scenario narratives. The further implication of Wack's statement is that the scenarios must take the thinking beyond the current assumptions and the official future. Wack was confronted with the tendency for decision makers to choose an "official future", and his solution was to use the "official future" as a device to engage the decision makers to take ownership of the scenarios to learn about worlds beyond the boundaries of their assumptions. "It is useful," he wrote, "to encourage the decision makers to walk out into the official future and once there, (they may be willing) to consider other more divergent futures."

> "Our real target was the microcosm in the minds of our decision makers; unless we influenced the mental image, the picture of reality held by critical decision makers, our scenario would be like water on stone."

2.2 Increasing complexity in the external environment and practical systems thinking

Much has been written about systems thinking in recent years. The term has become overused in many organisations and organisational literature, but systemic worldview is still uncommon. For example, take the common wisdom which questions the human causes of climate volatility and its potential threat to human existence. The capability to see wholes and interconnections is critical in scenario planning. Given the wealth of resources on systems thinking, this manual provides only a brief overview; however, the importance of understanding and seeing systems cannot be overstated in scenario-based strategic planning. Note that one of the recent developments in the field of seeing interconnections and identifying underlying patterns and structures is the field of complexity theory, aka chaos.

Systems thinking is the label for a worldview that looks at interconnections and causal relationships rather than at snapshots, fragments and "independent" parts. This worldview aims to allow the individual to see that which is not immediately obvious. This perspective forms the foundation of building an organisation capable of detecting error, learning and self-correcting errors, as it pursues its goals and strategies. This is also known as a learning organisation.

Systems thinking has been described as "uncommon sense" by Davidson in a book of the same title. When faced with the complexity in the external or internal dynamics of an organisation, the systems lens enables decision makers to see beyond events and detect underlying patterns over time, as well as the forces and causal relationships – the structure – that hold these patterns in place. A systems worldview, together with tools and techniques to make structure visible, is important for building quality scenarios. An understanding of how underlying causal relationships drive specific dynamics in the external environment is difficult but essential work. Once this structural level is better understood, we may more accurately build theories of how a specific dynamic might unfold over the scenario period.

The iceberg analogy is a useful entry point into uncovering structure. It provides a practical way for enabling practitioners and decision makers to adopt and use a systems perspective and start to appreciate how different variables are interconnected (see Figure 6.2).

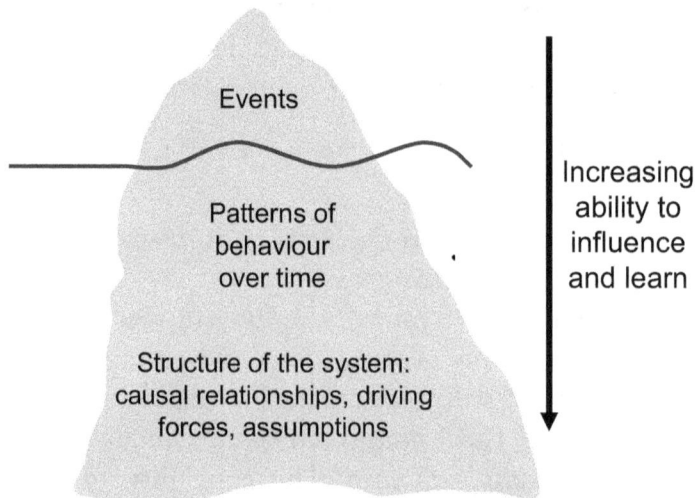

Figure 6.2: Systems Thinking using the Iceberg Analogy
Source: Source: Van der Merwe, L. Scenario-based Strategy in Practice: A framework. (In Chermack, T., *ed* Advances in HRD, London: Sage, pp 216-239).

We typically observe the world at an events level (the visible part of the iceberg). We are predisposed as humans to notice events more easily. The media, for instance, look for a *"who event"* not a *"what event"* to write about or broadcast. When we look through this lens we are trapped in a reactive mode, because we see only a small part of the dynamic and react to counter what we observe. Only when we start to look below the surface (the part of the iceberg that exists underwater and beyond obvious sight) to identify the patterns of behaviour over time can we begin to better understand the events-level information and therefore build better scenarios about how a pattern may play out in future. The key to even more substantial learning is in understanding the structural level of a dynamic, the key variables and the causal relationships between them. Using this insight and learning to develop scenarios creates a forum in which decision makers can explore the structural level of various forces having an impact on the organisation.

In order to provide a practical example of systems thinking, exploring and comparing the structure of HIV/AIDS and SARS provides a useful basis for learning. Doing so enables us to see the impact of small but important differences in their structure and the relative time delay from infection to showing visible symptoms. This helps us to respond in a better way when trying to outline how this specific dynamic might play out in future. Southern Africa, in particular, is dealing with a serious level of HIV/AIDS infection and scenarios have been used a number of times in examining the future of this dynamic in the country. Effective scenarios for the future of Southern Africa must consider the HIV/AIDS epidemic and how it may unfold.

One of the most subtle, and therefore most difficult, structural aspects of the HIV/AIDS dynamic is the lengthy time delay between infection and visible symptoms. This is also true for Covid-19. This structural property creates a tendency to misread the level and timing of impact of the pandemic. A wait-and-see position is then adopted, which results in either not doing enough or perhaps doing too much. The time delay is exacerbated by cultural taboos which deny the existence of infection and inhibit testing. The key structural or systemic insight is to appreciate the effect of time delays and then to deal with it more effectively in scenario development. A dynamic which contains a time delay tends to result in what is called overshoot or undershoot. An effective intervention should appear to be an overreaction in order to deal with a built-in time delay. An overreaction enables the intervention to overcome the backlog, which the time delay has masked. The taboos in the African culture around human sexuality stifle talk about such matters. Because of this, feedback is concealed and therefore prevents a clear understanding of potential causes. This phenomenon provides an incomplete picture of what is going on and therefore inhibits responding effectively. It is, as a result, difficult to know how to deal with this problem at an individual and a collective level.

SARS on the other hand, has a short time delay between infection and symptoms. Governments can see the impact immediately and respond more rapidly. The key structural difference is tied up in this variation in the time it takes to get feedback in these two systems. The leverage in dealing effectively with HIV/AIDS resides in providing an immediate feedback process on infection levels. This is why testing for the HIV/AIDS virus is so important. Scenarios exploring the future of Southern Africa will be very different depending on how the importance and consistency of HIV/AIDS testing is dealt with. A 14-day latency period in Covid-19 before symptoms appear in the infection cycle also places testing and contact tracing as the highest leverage for preventing exponential infections. The role of feedback in any structure cannot be overemphasised. Where systems cannot self-correct it is because feedback is either misunderstood, hidden or deliberately concealed. Many examples of this exist around us such as crime dynamics and global climate change, to mention but a few.

3   STRATEGY AS FIT

Describing strategy as a process of fit presents an ongoing learning process of detecting deviation from good fit and correcting for such deviation. This provides a useful view of how organisations succeed or fail. When an organisation fits with the future environment it will prosper, and when it does not fit it will falter and perhaps fail. Porter called this first-order fit.[1] According to De Geus[2] the average life expectancy of a Fortune 500 type company is less than 50 years. In my experience, the most important internal organisational processes that enable an organisation to fit are reflected in Figure 6.3. These are called "key strategy enabling processes" and "cross-cutting competencies" elsewhere and are the focus of capacity building. Assessing and developing capability remains the first priority for executing a resilience strategy. Internal organisational processes require what Porter called a second-order fit,[3] meaning that these internal processes have to fit with each other to provide the organisation with optimum capability and capacity to respond and create fit with changes in the environment. These processes may also be called strategy enabling or resilience enabling processes.

---

[1]   Porter, M.E. 1998

[2]   De Geus, A. 1997

[3]   Porter, M.E. 1998

ORGANISATION		FIRST ORDER FIT ⟷	FUTURES
SECOND ORDER FIT	**Key Strategy Enabling Processes** • Scenario-based strategy • Building strategy and alignment • Leadership development • Conversation quality and engagement • Management of accountability and performance • Systems thinking • Change management organisational infrastructure		**External Dynamics** • Scenario 1 • Scenario 2 • Scenario 3 • Scenario 4

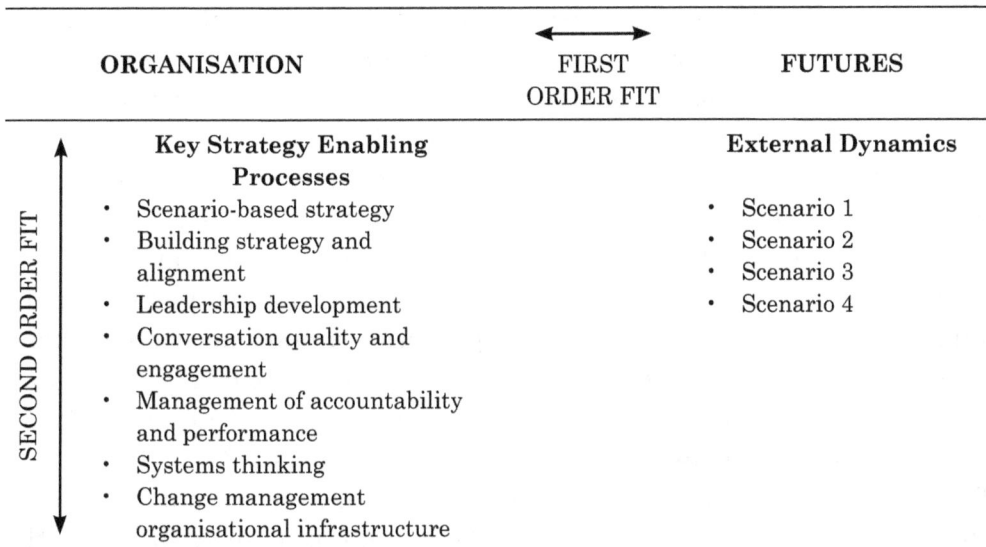

Figure 6.3: Strategy as fit
Source: based on Porter.[4]

Ensuring the internal fit of the various processes that affect strategy making and execution represents one of the key areas of design in which practitioners already have expertise. For example, leadership development is often included in HRD academic and executive curricula, as well as change management, organisational learning and organisation development. While not an exhaustive list, these are four key areas in scenario-based strategy that fall directly within the domain of HRD, and within the competence of the modern HRD practitioner. The point is that many processes critical to effective scenario-based strategy are currently within the remit of HRD and OD practitioners, provided we continue to frame strategy as a learning process. The knowledge and skills related to adult learning will probably become the foundation of organisational strategy making.

It is beyond the scope of this chapter to discuss each of the key strategy enabling processes shown in Figure 6.3 in detail. However, one process deserves mention as it is often poorly executed. The area of performance management is often the key to connecting strategy to individual jobs and job descriptions. [5] [6] [7]

Performance management is singled out not only because it is often poorly executed, but also because performance is at the heart of the

---

[4] Porter, M.E. 1998.

[5] Porter, M.E. 1998.

[6] Rummler & Brache, 1995.

[7] Rummler, 2005.

HRD contribution in any organisation. Specifically in strategy execution, performance is heavily reliant on the quality of thinking, which in turn is dependent on the quality of strategic conversation.[8] In general, the all-round capacity or competence (knowledge, skills, and attitudes) of the people in the organisation creates real strategic options. A real option is defined here as when there is a match between competencies and emergent external dynamics or stakeholder requirements. The rising complexity, the need to constantly adapt and create fit with the environment as it unfolds, requires specific strategy enabling capabilities among decision makers, managers, supervisors and staff in general. Lack of capacity places an immediate limit on the ability of an organisation, as a human activity system, to adapt in a resilient manner by executing strategy rapidly and effectively. One key organisational capability, aka alignment, is usually absent and requires constant work. Alignment is defined here as the ability to act together, act as one, and in the same direction, strategically.

Although we constantly hear the mantra of "people are our most important asset", this area of building capability to perform together is usually disconnected from the strategy making and execution process.[9] This is akin to being a captain at the helm of a ship, trying to navigate a difficult passage, with no connection from the ship's helm to the rudder! This is an area of expertise in which HRD and OD practitioners have a clear opportunity to add value to the performance of an organisation.[10] Ensuring that roles are clear and that the performance management process is designed to connect the strategy making and prioritisation process directly to jobs can best be done by HRD practitioners. When the reviewing process is done well[11] by means of skilful strategic conversation there will probably also be an increase in the productivity and quality of services.

These three phenomena, 1) problems with predictions, 2) increasing complexity and systems thinking, and 3) strategy as "fit", provide the basis for adopting scenario-based strategy as the preferred mode of strategy making. The organisational environment has grown too complex for single line forecasting tools alone. Organisational problems, and business problems specifically, are inherently complex and often require a synthesis or systems view in *addition* to an analytic view. In addition, the various organisational processes must be in alignment with each other so that the

---

[8]   Van der Merwe et al., 2008.

[9]   Rummler, 2005.

[10]   Rummler, 2005.

[11]   Rummler & Brache, 1995Cannot find in reference list

organisation may respond as a whole. This leads to the conclusion that yesterday's approaches to strategy are simply no longer adequate.

Section 2: Essential process elements, founding personalities and key competencies for scenario-based strategic practice

The second part of this chapter provides a short history of the pioneering thinkers in scenario planning and a framework for practising scenario-based strategy. Scenario-based strategy has been described as a divergent process,[12] [13] thus the framework provided is flexible and is intended to allow practitioners a degree of freedom so that they may bring their individual competencies to bear, as long as they respect underlying foundations and principles as outlined. That is, most scenario projects will include the elements described here. The depth and concentration on each element, however, will vary from process to process and expertise in this art can best be gained through continuous practise, preferably under the guidance of a competent practitioner. The remainder of this chapter, however, provides some critical components and useful practitioner tips for practising and developing scenario-based strategic competencies.

3.1 Generations of scenario pioneers – prioritising sources for learning

Traditionally, knowledge and expertise in scenario building has been passed on through an apprenticeship process. Pierre Wack[14] was of the opinion that it took at least a year in apprenticeship mode for a practitioner to learn the basics of the method. The CIL started the process of codifying and teaching scenario-based strategy in South Africa in 1992 in a four-day CIL course called "Thinking and Acting with Scenarios (TAS)". This CIL offering was conceptualised as a simulation of all the essential elements of a first generation scenario building process. The remainder of this chapter provides a snapshot of the essential elements from this four-day course.

In 2002 Shell International marked 30 years of scenario planning under the directorship of Ged Davis the then head of Group Planning at Shell International. Under his instruction, Shell International Group Planning gathered together 30 scenario practitioners whom they considered "the next generation of scenarists" from across the world. Significantly, CIL was among those invited to this celebration of the "coming of age" of the scenario method. This method has its roots deeply buried in the history of Group Planning at Royal Dutch Shell.

---

[12]   Chermack & Van der Merwe, 2003.

[13]   Schwartz, 1991.

[14]   Wack, P. 1985a

This background is provided by way of an introduction to locate the roots of the scenario-planning method and acknowledge these early pioneers who, at times, risked reputation and position so that this important method could be developed, tested and become widely available to organisations and governments.

It is accepted that the Shell scenario method is founded on the early work of writer Herman Kahn. Pierre Wack was an early protégé of Herman Kahn and took the tools the RAND Corporation developed for "thinking about the unthinkable" into a corporate organisational setting when he became the head of long-range planning at Royal/Dutch Shell.[15] Individual practitioners continued to learn, mainly from other practitioners, and often in Shell. Some of the pioneers have written about the method in a way that informs practice.[16] [17] The practice still varies widely among practitioners and any formalised or standardised best practice or comprehensive theory is still elusive.

Art Kleiner, editor in chief of the management journal *Strategy + Business* provides a useful outline of the individuals and characters who pioneered the method during the 1970s and '80s.[18] Table 6.1 provides potential practitioners with a perspective for identifying and prioritising their learning by using this table to identify further key resources. This table also enables the elimination of contributions not close to the mainstream of an emerging body of literature.

Table 6.1: Generations of Scenario Pioneers

First Generation	Second Generation	Beginning of a Third Generation
Ted Newland Pierre Wack Napier Collyns Peter Schwartz	Arie de Geus Kees van der Heijden Stewart Brand	Graham Galer Ged Davis Guy Jillings 30 International scenario practitioners – selected and acknowledged by Shell International Group Planning

The scenario-based strategy method has grown up in applied practice. Given this, the process has not yet established clear academic roots and is often rejected by business schools that still hold the economic/analytic

---

[15]   Kahn, H. & Wiener, A.J. (1967). The next thirty-three years: A framework for speculation. *Daedalus, 96*(3), 705–7.

[16]   Schwartz, 1991.

[17]   Van der Heijden, K. 1996. *Scenarios: The art of strategic conversation.* London: Wiley.

[18]   Kleiner, A. 1989

views of strategy[19] and strive to emulate the practices of the Harvard Business School. Practitioners of the method, who are also expert in organisational learning, generally agree that scenario-based strategy provides the most sophisticated and proven organisational learning process. This is only beginning to be explored and acknowledged through scholarly research.[20] [21] [22] Scenario-based strategy rightfully belongs among the processes through which the level of learning in an organisation may be enhanced. From a practitioner point of view, the theory development underway will confirm or refute relationships that have long been unsubstantiated claims by practitioners and taken for granted. This research will move practitioners of the method closer to an accurate model of best practice in scenario-based strategy. The demand for and credibility of written material on the scenario method is expected to increase as organisations continue to adopt a learning perspective in their strategy practices.[23] However, Pierre Wack's[24] and Peter Schwartz's[25] publications, which can now be considered somewhat out of date, still stand out as the standard references on the topic.

Recent theory-building efforts in the domain of scenario planning deserve mention as they synthesise current knowledge about the phenomenon.[26] [27] The intent behind these theory-building efforts is to arrive at a model that captures an effective portrayal of the phenomenon in reality. While these models will never truly reflect reality and all of its complexity, they will eventually contribute to a significant representation of the process as a whole.

3.2   Uses for scenarios – A methodology with a wide range of applications

There are several different applications for scenarios (see Table 6.2). While the general framework remains the same, the uses and applications

---

[19]   Mintzberg et al, 1998

[20]   Chermack, Lynham & Van der Merwe, 2004

[21]   Burt, G. & Van der Heijden, K. 2002. Reframing industry boundaries for structural advantage -- the role of scenario planning. In G. Ringland (Ed.), *Scenarios in Business*. New York: John Wiley, pp. 223–232.

[22]   Burt, G. & Van der Heijden, K. 2003. First steps: Towards purposeful activities in scenario thinking and future studies. *Futures 35*(10), 1011–1026.

[23]   Burt & Van der Heijden, 2002.

[24]   Wack, 1985a

[25]   Schwartz, 1991.

[26]   Chermack, T.J. 2005. Studying scenario planning: Theory, research suggestions and hypotheses. *Technological Forecasting and Social Change, 72*(1), 59–73.

[27]   Chermack, Lynham & Van der Merwe, 2006

can shift the timetable and depth, and reduce or amplify other important components of the process. For example, using scenario-based strategy to examine and maintain fit with the external environment will look different to the scenario-based strategy used to test the viability of investment in a new product line or the robustness of a city government resilience plan. These projects will use the same general steps, but each step may vary in depth and intensity.

Table 6.2: Uses of the Scenario Method

DIFFERENT USES OF THE SCENARIO METHOD	
Type/description	**Purpose**
1. *Decision scenarios*	To test decisions for robustness
2. *Normative scenarios*	To push a community towards a specific perspective
3. *Community dialogue problem solving, conflict management*	To engage a community of leaders to explore the future
4. *Policy alignment*	To enable various ministries to align policies with each other
5. *Organisation alignment and engagement*	To provide an umbrella focus for strategic conversation and alignment in the organisational support for organisation development
6. *Environmental scanning*	To enable the organisation to learn about and take a position on specific assumptions upon which strategy is based
7. *Scenario thinking*	A way of thinking embedded in all decision making or choices
8. *Leadership mentoring using scenarios*	Stimulating a personal inquiry on which to base personal strategies

Note: Examples of these different uses of scenarios are often not publicly available.

Source: This table has been compiled by the author to provide practitioners with a sense of the wide range of uses of the scenario method.

Decision scenarios. Decision scenarios are used to improve the quality of decision making by focusing on particular decisions the organisational leaders are entertaining. They are, therefore, based on deep analysis and research. Full-time planning staff provide the capability to track specific trends and driving forces and renew the scenarios every three to four years.

Normative scenarios. Normative scenarios are used to push their readers in a specific direction. The "high road, low road" scenarios used during the South African transition in 1994 helped all South Africans to look into the abyss of the "low road" scenario and start the work of building the "high road".

Community dialogue. Scenarios provide a neutral space within which a wider strategic conversation can take place. When participants enter a way of thinking where the future is assumed to be plural, they will seriously consider and talk about a wider range of futures. The danger is that these conversations lack the rigour of decision scenarios and often miss important dynamics. For example, the Mont Fleur scenarios from the early '90s were initially silent on the crime and corruption dynamics in South African society.[28]

Policy alignment. The Singapore government invests substantially in developing and continually updating a set of scenarios for its own use in formulating robust policy. It then insists on using them in all the ministries to test decisions and national policy for robustness. This has the benefit of enabling each ministry to function as autonomously as they wish in policy making, yet by testing policy in a common set of scenarios ministries across government are automatically aligned with each other.

Organisational alignment. Organisational alignment can be defined as the capability to act as one.[29] Working from a common set of planning assumptions, embedded in the minds of decision makers, automatically ensures alignment of decisions and actions across an organisation.

Environmental scanning. The focus of scenario development is always aimed at the external dynamics and how they might unfold over the next number of years. Tracking and continuously updating the scenarios and focusing on specific key driving forces (KDFs) in the scenarios keeps decision makers who use the scenarios up to date on all the important dynamics that may have an impact on their decisions.

Scenario thinking. Scenario thinking represents a perspective that uses this way of thinking for all decision making. This perspective consists of at least two important components – seeing the future as plural, and as unpredictable beyond the confidence horizon for predicting. Scenario thinking can be used to guide many things, including career decisions within the family context, decisions in small businesses and work teams, complex decisions in a multinational corporation, and decisions relevant to national and global policy.

---

[28] Kahane, A. 2002. Civic scenarios as a tool for societal change. *Strategy & Leadership, 30*(1), 32–37.

[29] McLean, 2006

Leadership coaching using scenarios. Scenario thinking provides a useful and comprehensive framework for coaching leadership. While a personal strategy is often an intensive, introspective process, scenario thinking compels leadership to reflect on dynamics in their context which may confront their plans in future.

4   A GENERAL SCENARIO DEVELOPMENT FRAMEWORK

Optimal learning during the application of the scenario method occurs in two important components of the process, namely, 1) building scenarios and 2) using the scenarios to test plans for robustness, and through this embedding scenario thinking as a way of thinking and operating in a particular organisation.[30] Strategic learning in this approach to strategy is thought to occur more intensely with involvement in developing scenarios, as well as involvement in testing strategy using the wind-tunnelling process.[31]

A typical scenario-based planning project usually unfolds over a period of six- to nine months and consists of several general phases. These general phases are included in Table 6.3 and may be labelled as follows; 1) interviews, 2) feedback, sorting and structuring of external dynamics, 3) rigorous analysis, 4) building capacity for strategic conversation, 5) constructing a scenario workbook or website, 6) sustaining strategic conversations, and 7) documenting noticeable results. Each phase is described briefly.

Table 6.3: A Scenario Development Framework – Overview of Critical Phases

Phase	Description
One-on-one meetings (interviews) (Conduct, document, analyse, feedback)	The purpose of these meetings is to ground the scenario development in the concerns of organisational leadership. Conduct 10–25 interviews, two tranches; first tranche with decision makers; second tranche includes the next generation of decision makers and informal leadership.
Feedback, sorting and structuring of external dynamics	(Optional) Initiate internal dynamics work with function head, start with feedback on the internal dynamic analysis.

---

[30]   Chermack & Van der Merwe, 2002

[31]   De Geus, 1989

Phase	Description
Rigorous analysis	Analysis and research punctuated by three to four, two-day work sessions (WI – WIV) to consolidate and integrate a set of 2-3-4 scenarios.
Building capacity for strategic conversation	Ranking space, use of tools such as systems loops and links, story maps, ladder of inference, left and/right-hand column etc. See also conversation quality checklist – see Table 5.1 in Chapter 5.
Challenging the assumptions and stretching the logic of the scenarios	Use outside contributions from people who may hold different views, also called "remarkable people" (RPs) or "thought leaders". These contributions raise the quality of thinking and logic of the scenarios, exclude blind spots and raise the credibility of the scenarios.
Scenario workbook, website or other	Develop a workbook that attends to the learning of the decision makers. Reflect both rational aspects as well as aesthetic aspects. Use a wide variety of tables and illustrations to reflect both explicit and implicit aspects of the storylines. Make them memorable using a set of vivid titles.
Embedding scenario thinking among decision makers	Integrate the use of scenarios into the planning cycle as a "wind-tunnelling" process. Develop processes that integrate the use of scenarios into the decision maker's routines.
Sustaining the strategic conversation	Assemble a Strategic Engagement Forum which may include links to the whole organisation or to talk about how the strategy is working regularly, tracking emerging dynamics in the external environment and identifying capacity limits in the organisation.
Documenting noticeable results	Survey scenario impact reflecting both quantitative and qualitative dimensions. See Scenario Impact Questionnaire (SIQ) at the end of this chapter. Administer other metrics: conversation quality, strategic thinking, trust etc.

Note: Table 6.3 above forms part of the CIL training course for scenario practitioners. During this executive education course, practitioners are assisted by this framework to develop an organisation-specific plan for a scenario development process. Table 6.3 reflects the important phases.[32]

---

[32]   CIL Ltd, 1994

One-on-one meetings (interviews). An important question is who to interview and who to include in the scenario building team. Ideally, the same people should participate in both processes. In terms of change management principles, the rule is to be inclusive. Typically, as many of the top leadership as possible are selected on a hierarchical basis. This usually results in between 10 and 25 interviews. Besides this initial group, there is a second group of people who are important to engage, namely informal leaders. They are scattered at the middle strata of the organisation. The informal leadership may not occupy senior positions, but they are often gatekeepers in the organisation networks. They regulate the information flow between the lower levels of the organisation and the top leadership and vice versa.[33] [34]

Informal leadership should be included in the interviews and involved in all the learning processes that are part of developing and using the scenarios. They usually add substantial value in terms of learning about external dynamics, but are often mistrustful of top leadership. Thus, by including informal leadership in important organisational processes, buy-in may be developed, and as a result, people in these informal leadership positions feel ownership and a stake in the organisation. Engaging informal leadership in the scenario-based strategy process opens a doorway for building trust. Informal leadership will often also shift their position from resistance to support as they learn more about how the external environment might impact on the organisation.

Conducting the one-on-one meetings/interviews to establish "the natural strategic agenda". Shell developed seven questions which are used to guide the interviewer. They are referred to by scenario practitioners as the so-called "seven questions". The interviewer is trained to write down verbatim what is said in response to these questions, without filtering. Examples of these questions are: "If I (the interviewer) were an oracle and could answer any question you had about the future, what would you ask?" Another example: "If you could write your epitaph, what would you write?" On analysis of the responses, the interviewer is looking for the key concerns and uncertainties on the minds of the decision makers. The themes and patterns identified amongst interviewees are referred to as the natural strategic agenda and form the starting point for developing relevant scenarios.[35]

Sorting, structuring and feedback of external dynamics. Contracting

---

[33] Stephenson, K. 2003 *The quantum theory of trust: power, networks and the secret life of organizations*. Prentice Hall.

[34] Kleiner, A. 2003 The man who saw the future. *Strategy and Business* – Spring 2003.

[35] De Geus, 1991 No 1991 in reference list – author to add full ref

with decision makers to feedback the results of the one-on-one meetings must be obtained *before* the interviews commence. This contracting follows standard survey feedback principles.[36] Interviews provide crucial information about the natural concerns of the decision makers as well as providing a basis for building a relationship with the organisation. Interviews, usually conducted by two practitioners working as a team, are confidential and recorded verbatim. Interview data are analysed for common themes amongst interviewees. These data are then structured to bring out the patterns and underlying causal relationships driving external dynamics. An initial list of key driving forces (KDFs) is developed with the organisation. Decision makers are engaged to sort and rank these forces by their *relative impact* on decisions and, after that, their *relative uncertainty* about how particular forces may play out over the scenario period.

Rigorous systemic analysis and building capacity for strategic conversation. A series of scenario building workshops should be individually designed to meet organisational needs and desired results for the scenario-based strategy exercise. This should typically involve a series of three to four workshops of two days each, set six to eight weeks apart, to allow deep systemic analysis between workshops as well as critical reflection time in between. A typical first generation scenario development process for a medium- to large organisation follows a number of phases over a period of months. Figure 6.4 outlines a generic framework of these phases as a guideline.

The capacity for strategic conversation should be regularly tested, starting with baseline measurements at the beginning of the process and then again regular measurements at set intervals until the process is complete. The author has developed a questionnaire for measuring the quality of strategic conversation and engagement within organisations which provides both a measure as well as a checklist to assess and develop competencies required for a productive conversation. This questionnaire has been tested for reliability and validity.[37]

Challenging the assumptions and stretching the logic of the scenarios. Pierre Wack spent time with George Gurdjieff a Russian philosopher, mystic, spiritual teacher, and composer while he was living in Paris. Gurdjieff was. Gurdjieff also wrote a book titled, "Meetings with Remarkable Men". During Wack's visits with Gurdjieff he noticed that when visitors,

---

36   French, W.L. & Bell, C.H. Jr., 1984. *Organisation development.* (3rd ed.). Prentice Hall.

37   Van der Merwe, L., Chermack, T.J., Kulikowich, J. & Yang, B. 2007. Strategic conversation quality and engagement: Assessment of a new measure. *International Journal of Training and Development,* 11(3):214–221.

passing through Paris, joined in the conversations with Gurdjieff and his associates they had a disproportionate influence on shifting thinking and assumptions. As a result of this learning Wack introduced carefully selected outside people into the scenario development process named remarkable people (RPs) to influence and stretch thinking amongst participants and decision makers. Once a first draft of the scenarios is available, one or two of these RPs are invited to examine the scenario narratives and comment on their plausibility or on any omissions they noticed, with the purpose of challenging existing assumptions. RPs are people who think differently from the French "remarkable" meaning different thinking.

Scenario workbook, website or other. A scenario workbook reflects the investment in how forces may drive future conditions and is a medium through which the scenarios may be viewed as a set. The scenarios must be memorable and labelled with evocative titles for the set. The scenario stories should travel among decision makers in the organisation as a kind of "oral history of the future". Often the benefits of scenarios are restricted to key decision makers at the apex of the organisation. The leading-edge scenarios attend to widening their use among the various layers and learning styles of the decision makers across the organisation, to middle management levels. This is done by providing a more user-friendly workbook or by enabling wider participation by placing the information from the scenario workbook on a website.

- Key components of the workbook are:
- a memorable set of names which is relevant to the organisation or industry and which captures the essential qualities or *gestalt* of specific scenarios;
- the ranking of the key driving forces used in the scenarios;
- When using the deductive method a four box matrix is used to spread the proto-scenario narratives apart;
- proto-scenarios are usually made up of eight to ten bullet points for each scenario quadrant reflecting the key themes;
- a optional systems diagram for each scenario;
- illustrations for the scenarios and the key dynamics they contain;
- a list of contributors; and
- a brief description of the methodology used.

For the *individual scenarios*, a memorable name is given to each scenario which captures the key theme of that scenario, a brief description of that theme, a summary, a story map, internally consistent details of each part of the story map, key patterns across the storyline and a systems diagram showing the dynamics at work in the storyline.

Embedding scenario thinking among decision makers. One of the critical ways to embed scenario thinking among decision makers is for them to use the scenarios to test decisions. This can best be done by structuring the strategy process so that scenario thinking must be engaged during the strategy making process; for example, using the scenarios as "wind tunnels" to stress-test a strategy or a specific decision for robustness. Building scenarios, and stress-testing for robustness is where the richest learning amongst participants takes place. [38] The process of wind-tunnelling is briefly outlined below under the heading, "Testing strategies for robustness aka wind-tunnelling".

Sustaining strategic conversation. Building infrastructure for strategic conversation is essential to sustaining this conversation.[39] The natural way to do this is to establish a strategy engagement forum that contains this conversation. Such a forum needs to be designed and well run to sustain itself beyond three or four meetings. A successful forum will focus the attention of the organisation on key dynamics and continue the process of building alignment. The main goal of this forum is effective dialogue as an "inside conversation" with the leadership, where current dynamics having an impact on the organisation and concerns are on the agenda. Specific problems and capacity limits in the organisation should also be addressed and resolved. Current decision making and control structures in the organisation should not be disturbed. Resist degenerating into formal feedback on progress. .

Documenting noticeable results. Scenario-based strategy also builds intangible assets in the organisation such as alignment, confidence and trust. It is essential to measure both tangible and intangible results where possible and to document the results that flow from the process. A standard practice is to provide documentation of specific dimensions using checklists and questionnaires where available. Typically, baselines are established at the beginning of the process and then measured annually or on a regular basis throughout the process. In addition, qualitative results can be assessed using state-of-the-art qualitative research methods.[40]

It is essential that practitioners of this method see scenario planning as a multigenerational process. First generation scenarios are useful, but only with second, third and fourth generation scenarios are deeper systemic understanding and learning developed. With repeated use, supported by research and analysis, new and innovative opportunities, as

---

[38]   Chermack & Van der Merwe, 2004

[39]   Van der Merwe et al., 2008

[40]   Denzin & Lincoln, 2000

well as hidden risks and discontinuities, can be uncovered (see Figure 6.4). Pierre Wack[41] was adamant about this point. Continued use and rigorous analysis are at the heart of organisational learning in the scenario-based strategy method.

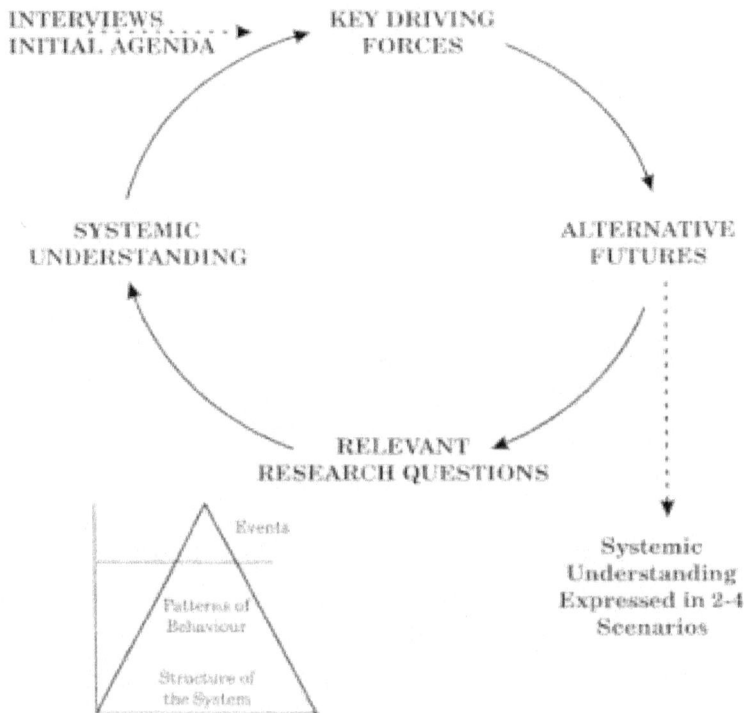

Figure 6.4: The Pierre Wack Scenario Approach: Building Multigenerational Scenarios
Source: This figure forms part of the CIL executive education in scenario building.

The cyclical or multigenerational nature of scenario development advocated by Wack encourages practitioners to build infrastructure for ongoing scenario thinking in their organisation. (See also Van der Heijden, 1996.)

5   QUALITY CRITERIA FOR SCENARIOS

Useful anchors for scenario novice scenario practitioners are the quality criteria provided in Table 6.4. Quality criteria provide a basis on which the scenario team can assess the likelihood that their work will get through to managers and provoke new perspectives. Three key quality criteria have emerged informally from the scenario literature. Walton[42] has shed light on

---

[41]   Wack, 1985a

[42]   Walton, J.S. 2007. *Scanning Beyond the Horizon: Exploring the Ontological and Epistemological Basis for Scenario Planning.* Advances in HRD

the possible roots of these criteria for scenario practitioners. These criteria state that any given scenario must be relevant, challenging and plausible in order for it to be useful and elicit buy-in from managers. These three criteria have been sequenced in a specific order to emphasise a logical structure and are usually evaluated after each generation of scenarios is completed.

Table 6.4: Quality Criteria for Scenarios

Criterion	Impact	Practitioner tip
Relevant to the concerns of the decision makers	Deepens ownership by sponsor(s) and decision makers through feedback on external dynamics and internal dynamics (optional)	Independent, in-depth interviews are done by outside practitioners. Uncover both external dynamics and internal dynamics for feedback and joint action planning
Challenging current assumptions	Expands thinking beyond current knowledge to enable changes in assumptions	Use of outside thought leaders/remarkable people (RPs) to challenge and enrich thinking and documentation
Plausible because they are based on deep systemic analysis and research, and also because they are internally consistent	Creates plausibility and credibility for storyline(s) when they can stand up to scrutiny	Deep systemic analysis and research into key dynamics to understand key variables that support them. Ensure also that the scenario narratives are internally consistent

Relevant. Notice that the first two criteria – relevant and challenging – are in tension with each other. The scenarios must be anchored in the current concerns and *at the same time* take the thinking beyond current assumptions. The relevance component of scenarios lays the foundation for ownership by decision makers. When the relevance criterion is met, decision makers recognise their specific concerns within the scenarios. These are usually presented as feedback from interviews with decision makers in the early scenario development workshops. Because decision makers see their specific concerns in the scenarios, they are more likely to take ownership of a set of scenarios that will shed light on these concerns. A set of scenarios must always be tailored to the concerns of the decision makers.

Challenging. Each scenario must provide a story that is, in some way, surprising. Given Wack's stated purpose to "shift the thinking",[43] scenarios should enable users to see things differently. If the scenarios are too challenging, decision makers may not engage or seriously entertain the content of the scenarios. If the scenarios are not challenging enough decision makers may become bored or disappointed at having invested time and energy in a set of scenarios that provides no novel insights or information.

Plausible. The plausibility of scenarios is based on deep analysis and research. Scenarios must be able to stand up to scrutiny in terms of the plausibility of the storylines. Internal consistency in individual scenario narratives reinforces their plausibility.[44] Scenarios must be realistic in that the internal assumptions and events must be plausible. When scenario-based planning is criticised for being too "soft",[45] it is because there has not been a multigenerational scenario process in place or quantitative elements are absent. Essential foundations are analysis and research to support the narrative of each scenario with both qualitative and quantitative data where possible. Deep, data-driven analysis is a cornerstone of high quality, high utility scenarios.

A typical response to a high quality set of scenarios should be: "No, that cannot happen!" However, on deeper enquiry into the underlying logic and structure, decision makers will accept that the scenarios are plausible and say, "Now that you show me the causal relationships I can see that it is a challenging and alternative view of the issue that I had not previously considered." This response is what is usually achieved when scenarios feature these important criteria. In summary, scenarios must be relevant in that they capture the elements that are of concern to the decision makers who will use them, challenging in that they stretch the internal thinking of the decision makers, and plausible in that they are well-researched and provide detail and data to support the events in the storylines. Wack insisted on a further acid test for quality scenarios and that was, having lived through the scenario period, looking back, did the scenarios miss any important dynamics? For instance, the Mont Fleur scenarios which were used to engage the incoming political leadership in South Africa prior to the 1994 elections were initially silent on the crime and corruption dynamics in post-apartheid South Africa. The result of this omission was that the government and business leadership were caught unawares by these damaging dynamics and are still struggling to deal

---

[43]   Wack, 1985a

[44]   Schwartz, 1991.

[45]   Mintzberg *et al.* 2005

with it years later. Finally, in the case of multigenerational scenario use, hindsight provides a valuable learning tool in that dynamics that may have been left out of previous generations of scenarios can be included in future iterations.

6   TESTING STRATEGIES FOR ROBUSTNESS AKA WIND-TUNNELLING

The term "wind-tunnelling" is used because of the similarity between testing a strategy in a given set of scenarios and testing the design of an aircraft in a wind tunnel. A wind tunnel varies the operating conditions to which the aircraft is subjected to expose design errors or successes. In the planning context, scenarios represent the different future conditions within which a strategy, business model, budget or other decisions must fit. Wind-tunnelling is used to test decisions for robustness and for exposing both opportunities and risks. An important additional benefit of wind-tunnelling is that the leadership engaged in wind-tunnelling are continually adjusting their assumptions as they enter the different worlds described in each scenario. As leaders check their decisions or business models in the set of scenarios, they are required to adjust their thinking based on evidence of flawed assumptions. This process is filled with critical learning opportunities in the scenario-based strategy framework and draws greatly on learning principles. Chermack and Van der Merwe provide a detailed description of the cognitive processes at work in scenario planning and wind-tunnelling.[46]

The key to intense learning in this process is when decision makers suspend disbelief and treat the scenarios as reality. This is similar to what one does in a good theatre performance when entering the worlds being described by the scenarios. This will only happen to those who are trying to use them in well-crafted scenarios that are relevant, challenging and plausible. The key question that triggers this learning is "What would I do if ...?" This question also triggers what has been called "future memory". This is stored memory of the future(s) reflected in scenarios which enable decision makers to recognise and recall discontinuities before other decision makers who have not engaged scenarios, and act earlier than them.[47]

---

[46]   Chermack & Van der Merwe, 2004.

[47]   Chermack & Van der Merwe, 2004.

Table 6.5: Testing Strategies for Robustness aka Wind-tunnelling

Testing strategies for robustness – how to "wind tunnel"	What to wind tunnel?
• The key question to ask as you enter these different worlds; "What would I do if …?" • Look for both opportunities and risks • List for each scenario – look for patterns across scenarios For the scenarios as a set: important conclusions, challenges, opportunities, questions for further analysis	Consider each of the following elements in each scenario: • strategy, • strategic priorities, • business models, • business plans, • budgets, • specific decisions, • leadership development programme, • organisational structure, • senior leadership succession, • other.

Note: Scenarios are regarded as different future operating conditions in the contextual environment of the organisation using the scenario method

Stated another way, decision makers can use scenarios to consider the important organisational elements. For example, useful questions would include: "Will the current strategy hold up in scenario 1, 2, 3, and 4? Or is the current strategy only viable in a single scenario?" The same questions may be asked about organisational structure, culture, leadership competencies, business plans, budgets and specific decisions, among other elements. Using this process allows decision makers to see where and under what conditions certain organisational elements may need to be revised in order to build "robustness".

7   COMMON MISTAKES AND TRAPS: PRACTITIONER GUIDELINES

The final section of this chapter provides a series of guidelines for practising scenario-based strategy. These guidelines include a number of common mistakes in developing scenarios, problems associated with assigning probabilities, an additional quality criterion, and the need to ensure that scenarios are used for considering important aspects of organisations.

Some common scenario development mistakes. The following are mistakes made by learner practitioners in constructing scenarios and should be avoided by novice practitioners learning the science and art of scenario development and use:

- putting all the good news in one scenario and all the bad in another;
- best case, worst case, and status quo scenarios;
- developing unrealistic, implausible scenarios;

- assuming that scenario development is the product of a brainstorming process;
- falling into the probability trap; and
- stopping when the first generation of scenarios are done.
- Not engaging the organisation in strategic conversation in purpose-made organisational infrastructure such as a forum developed for strategic conversation, and;
- Not regularly gauging the effect of the scenario work.

Good news, bad news. By putting all the good news in one scenario and the bad news in another, we start to move toward identifying preferences and influencing the users of such scenarios to consider only the good scenario. This is good practice for normative scenarios (see Table 6.2 above) but not for decision scenarios, where all the scenarios should be equally plausible.

Best case, worst case and status quo. Best case, worst case and status quo as a set usually lack deep analysis to uncover counter-intuitive, plausible turns in how the scenarios might unfold in the future. This type of analysis is more akin to sensitivity analyses than quality scenario work.

Unrealistic, implausible scenarios. Scenarios that are seen as unrealistic or implausible will not be taken seriously by decision makers. Scenarios that are the result of brainstorming lack the deep analysis required to produce a plausible basis for the storylines reflected. Bear in mind – constantly – that quality criteria for the scenarios reflected in Table 6.4 are essential if the scenarios are to be included in the decision making process.

Quality scenarios enable participants to do what actors and scriptwriters refer to as "suspending disbelief". The reader mentally and emotionally enters the story and treats it as reality. This is an essential property if scenarios are to influence and change assumptions in the minds of decision makers.

The probability temptation. Most managers and executives are trained to establish some level of certainty. There is a natural temptation for analytically trained managers to want to assign probabilities to each scenario. Once probabilities are assigned, the most probable scenario will be seen as the official future; consequently, the other scenarios will be left behind and the purpose of shifting the thinking will be lost. Often, novices inadvertently imply that a specific scenario is more probable than another because they, in turn, would like to be seen as "right" about an aspect of the future. This destroys the plausibility and value of the scenarios as a set.

It is not expected that any scenario narrative will unfold in reality as told. However, it is important that the scenarios as a portfolio of stories about the future contain the full range of variability for all key driving forces identified in the various workshops and interviews. The iterative, multigenerational scenario-based strategy process represents an important framework for contracting with an organisation considering using this method.

Moving beyond scenario development – don't stop there. Engage the organisation in a continuous strategic conversation. Because the scenario workbook is often the most tangible part of the deliverables, it is often mistakenly thought of as the product or final deliverable. It is therefore essential to contract, from the outset, for both developing the scenarios and putting them to use to test strategy and decisions for robustness. A scenario project is never really complete, but must not end with the production of the scenarios. The practitioner must ideally contract for an iterative multigenerational approach to scenario development from the outset. The scenarios are most useful if they are used for learning, which is solidified in using the scenarios to consider critical decisions of the organisation. Embedding scenarios as a process for regularly testing decisions usually entails restructuring the strategic planning cycle to include the robustness testing process as part of the cycle.

Nobody would dispute rising volatility and discontinuities in an organisation's contextual environment. Few organisations or countries were prepared for the Covid19 pandemic. Yet organisations that have built the organisational infrastructure or have the capability to deal with permanent volatility are rare. Shell continues to use the method. Singapore government has an embedded scenario planning capability in one of its ministries. The simplest scenario development process would have uncovered the cyclic nature of viral attacks on the human species. How many organisations or countries are now developing scenarios to anticipate the next viral attack or develop robust strategies to mitigate the looming climate volatility.

This chapter has provided some key reference points and practitioner "handrails" in strategy making as well as a general framework for scenario-based strategy. Quality criteria for scenarios and a competency profile for scenario-planning practitioners have also been presented. Whereas the scenario method has traditionally been taught through an apprenticeship approach, current demand for competent scenario-based strategy professionals is growing. When one considers how long it is taking to get important issues such as climate change in the minds of decision makers, it is essential that the scenario method is adopted as widely as possible, in both the public and private sectors as well as non-governmental organisations and civil society in general. One key purpose of this chapter has been to support novice scenario-planning practitioners specifically in city and town governments. As cities and towns take on greater significance in supporting their own as well as national resilience, it is essential to expand their capacity for scenario-based strategy to improve the quality of decision making and leadership.

8 THE COMPETENT SCENARIO-BASED STRATEGY PRACTITIONER

The foundation for competence in scenario-based strategy naturally exists within the HRD and OD professions.[48] [49] The required additional competencies need to be assessed and developed at an individual level using a personal development plan (PDP). While it is possible for an individual to develop personal expertise in scenario planning through experience, another efficient method remains to work under the tutelage of an accomplished scenario planning practitioner. Table 6.6 reflects a selection of key competencies that enhance the performance of an aspirant practitioner.

Table 6.6: A Competency Profile – Scenario-based Strategy Practitioner

A KNOWLEDGE:	B SKILLS:
Organisational sustainability knowledge, distinctive competence, competitive advantage Strategic planning process Business planning process Scenario practice and application Theory of the business (business modelling) Systems thinking, worldview and mapping of a structure Adult learning Conflict resolution Organisation development Group process	Process design Facilitator Conversation quality Visual representation Systemic representation Organising
C ATTITUDES: Role versatility Intellectual versatility Attention to detail Continuous improvement	

Source: Centre for Innovative Leadership Ltd (CIL)

---

[48] Cummings & Worley, 2001.

[49] Torraco, R.J. & Swanson, R.A. 1995. The strategic roles of human resource development. *Human Resource Planning,* 18(4): 3–38.

Overview of Systems Dynamics (SD) Models and an Example of Systemic Analysis of Water Security Circa 2008

In 2008 Klaus Schwab, founder of the WEF, established the Global Agenda Council on Strategic Foresight.

The global agenda council consisted of 17 futurists and policy experts. The first task given to its members was to compile two essays. We were requested to produce two essays each in topics of our choice. One essay was to describe a useful global futuring method and the second essay was to identify an impending global crisis or dynamic that was not yet on the policymaker's and decision maker's radar. I chose SD modelling as a recommended futuring technique and Water scarcity as a global dynamic not yet on decision-maker's radar. Remember that in 2008 few countries or cities were yet concerned about water supply and demand. These two essays are reflected below verbatim. Note: Figures and Tables are not in numerical sequence.

Systems thinking and systemic analysis are essential complements of scenario thinking and scenario development. Developing useful scenarios requires unravelling the complexity ahead and tracing out plausible storylines into the future on a 20- to 25 year planning time horizon. In the first essay, systems dynamics (SD) has been included as the recommended method for developing plausible narratives beyond the ten-year planning time horizon.

The second essay demonstrates how the iceberg analogy – *events, patterns of behaviour and systemic structure* – may be used as a departure point to analyse a specific key driving force (KDF), in this case water security, in preparation of developing scenario narratives for which water security is one of the KDFs.

9   SYSTEMS DYNAMICS (SD) MODELLING

Systems dynamics (SD) was invented by Jay Forrester of the Massachusetts Institute of Technology (MIT). Forrester used SD to study urban dynamics[50] in the 1960s and it has subsequently been successfully used to identify global issues.[51] [52] The SD method is also well suited to analysing underlying structural causal relationships. Furthermore, the SD models that emanate from this method are also useful for advocacy, thereby making both the dynamics and the necessary change visible to decision makers.

---

[50]   Forrester, 1969.

[51]   Papert, S. 1980. *Mindstorms: Children, computers, and powerful ideas.* New York: Basic Books.

[52]   Meadows, D.H., Meadows, D.L., Randers, J. & Behrens III, W.W. 1972. *Limits to growth.* London: Pan Books.

Global issues are also often described as global dynamics. This descriptor leads us directly to the systemic nature of complex dynamics and therefore to the choice of an appropriate identification methodology.

Issues or dynamics do not exist in isolation, and are always embedded in a context of interconnecting forces and causal relationships that hold a specific dynamic or issue in place. It can also be assumed that the level of interconnectedness and therefore the level of complexity also increase over time. An effective and efficient identification methodology therefore needs to enable a systemic view of the world, and needs to lead to action.

A systemic perspective of the world enables its users to look below events and patterns of behaviour to identify structural causes or drivers of specific complex issues. To paraphrase Senge,[53] this perspective enables deeper learning and enables high leverage actions which change the dynamic. The SD method provides a powerful method for identifying as well as mapping complex dynamics. Papert speaks of low threshold, high ceiling learning.[54] By this he means that the method is easy to access for non-specialists but once inside the method there is no limit to the learning that becomes available. The SD method also provides this benefit.

SD was famously used by the Club of Rome team in 1972, as the basis for identifying key global issues and then modelling how long the globe could sustain its growth at the then rates of consumption. This work was published in a best-selling book by Dana Meadows et al. entitled *Limits to Growth*.[55] A sequel to this work was published in 1996, also using SD methodology, by Dana Meadows, Dennis Meadows and others, entitled *Beyond the Limits*.[56] As the latter title reflects, the main thesis of this sequel is that the population on the globe had now overshot its limits.

At an anniversary meeting of the members of the Club of Rome in 2007 in Amsterdam, Dennis Meadows remarked that all of the dynamics identified in the 1972 modelling work, together with their patterns over time reflected in the SD models built at the time, i.e. 1972, had remained valid and were in play at present. This example of robustness over time provides clear evidence and endorsement of the SD method as an effective and efficient methodology.

The SD method is useful for identifying and mapping key causal relationships for a specific issue. The method consists of highlighting key causal relationships. It then uses the powerful SD shorthand to map

---

[53] Senge, 1991

[54] Papert, 1980.

[55] Meadows et al., 1972.

[56] Meadows et al., 1993 Limits to Growth. and Meadows,D.H. 1996 Beyond the Limits

these relationships within the system. This shorthand uses causal loops and causal links to draw attention to key causal relationships in diagrams called causal loop diagrams. A convention of plusses (+) and minuses (-) is used to identify whether two interconnected variables move in relatively the same direction, or in an opposite direction. This provides the mathematical basis for building models and is at this first level a useful, visual map or overview of the key interconnections within a specific issue. Sterman of MIT has provided useful detail on the method for those who are interested.[57]

This first visual map is also very useful when used by a group of decision makers to talk about the causal relationships in a specific dynamic. The causal links usually raise a conversation about the assumptions underpinning the causal relationships between variables. This understanding enables deep learning about assumptions that may be widely held. Assumptions are one of the aspects of structure that are difficult to identify and therefore difficult to influence. Often, assumptions hold specific issues/dynamics firmly, yet invisibly, in place. With this ability to look below the surface into issues, our insights also enable us to identify possible ways to change the dynamics in a sustainable way.

Example: Water Security circa 2008, the approaching global crisis and response options

Now clearly visible to many futurists and others is the convergence of a wide number of resource scarcities, including water,[58] [59] [60]as well as scenarios for catastrophic climate volatility,[61] impending pandemics and species loss, as well as the current economic and financial crisis. All of these systemic dynamics require an aligned, global response. This can only be based on efficient cooperation at scale, resulting in radical global behaviour change. Multilateral bodies such as the United Nations and others were established and strengthened after World War II to provide a forum for gathering leaders to resolve complex interconnected global issues and to avoid a third world war.

However, most dynamics that threaten the existence of humanity are

---

[57] Sterman, J. 2000. *Business dynamics: Systems thinking and modelling for a complex world.* Boston, MA: McGraw Hill Higher Education.

[58] Meadows, 1996 Beyond the Limits

[59] United Nations. 2003. *World Water Development Report (WWDR), Water for the People.* UNESCO Publication ISBN 92-3-103881-8

[60] Foreign Policy in Focus. 2008. FPIF Policy Report: The global water crisis and the coming battle for the right to water, (*In:* Barlow, M. *Blue Covenant.*).

[61] Schwartz, P. & Randall, D. 2003. *An abrupt climate change scenario and its implications for United States national security.* GBN Publication.

initially met with some form of denial, delaying the inevitable moment when humankind must finally take corrective action to re-establish a sustainable balance.

These looming, potentially disruptive, and in some cases existentially threatening, dynamics in the world are the unintended consequences of just four uniquely human attributes.[62] As a species, we started *walking upright*. Bipedal mobility was more efficient. The greater efficiency translated into an energy gain which we directed into *higher population growth*. We started making *tools and artefacts* with which to manipulate our surroundings. Lastly, and more importantly, we *developed a symbolic language and an imagination*.

These attributes, and the unintended consequences of them, have resulted in the unsustainability fix the world is now facing. The latter two have the potential to get us back out of this fix.

These two attributes, if harnessed at scale, could assist us in avoiding possible extinction ourselves and, at best, help us effectively mitigate and deflect some of the dire consequences now bearing down on us. To engage in shifting assumptions and therefore actions at scale, we need to engage methods such as scenario planning and SD modelling that impact on assumptions. The unfortunate truth is that when it comes to shifting behaviour at scale, change does not take place until there is a widespread perception that there is no other way. With time delays to recovery, we could have already passed the point of no return.

Water is a finite resource which we depend on as humanity for our survival. Water security is embedded in a large number of variables (see the figures and tables). However, two variables, namely, population growth and the increase in consumption per person over time, as well as the consumption per sector (see Figure 4) make the decline in security *predetermined* unless a major adjustment in attitude followed by widespread behaviour change take place.

Freshwater is a mere 3% of all water (see Figure 6.5 & 6.6). Of all freshwater, easily available surface water comprises 1% of all freshwater. We use only a small portion of the easily available freshwater and groundwater.[63] There is, therefore, ample room for recovery were we to respond and start using this resource more efficiently.

---

[62] Johanson, D. & Edgar, B. 1996. *From Lucy to Language*. Wits University Press.

[63] Population Information Program. 1998. *Population Report Volume XXXVI, Number 1*, Johns Hopkins School of Public Health.

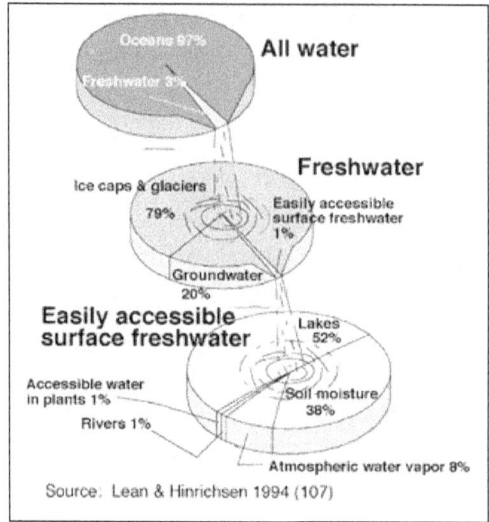

Source: Lean & Hinrichsen 1994 (107)

Figure 6.5 [6.7]: Distribution of the World's Water

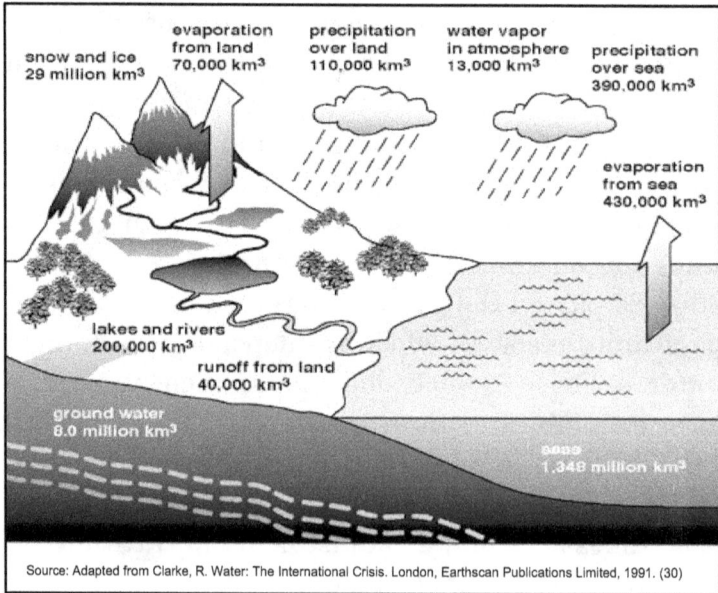

Source: Adapted from Clarke, R. Water: The International Crisis. London, Earthscan Publications Limited, 1991. (30)

Figure 6.6: The Hydrological Cycle

314

Global Annual Water Withdrawal by Sector, 1900–2000

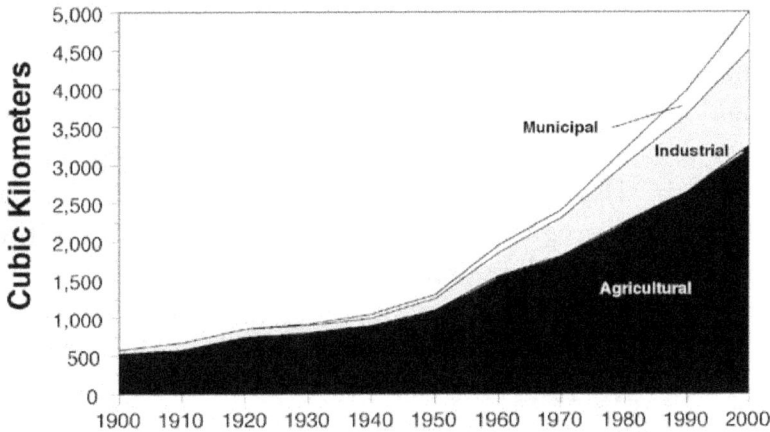

Source: Abramovitz 1996 (1)

Figure 6.7: Rising Water Use

The thesis of this essay is that the impending catastrophic decline in water security will provide the catharsis required to trigger a globally coordinated and aligned response, resulting in a radical change in behaviour.

The approaching water crisis is now well documented by various multilateral organisations such as the UN and others.[64] [65] We know from experience that these dire reports often do not change behaviour at scale or in the timeframe when action is required. Resources such as freshwater, clean air and until recently oil, are widely assumed, it seems from behaviour, to be infinite.

Change in behaviour is facilitated by a shift in assumptions, first at an individual level and then at scale. A widely shared event, because it has traumatised large numbers of people and results in widespread catharsis, will often result in a shift in assumptions. For example, the wars, and the catharsis they create, it seems, have played this role in societal change. It seems that wars, in whatever form, will also be part of this envisaged process of change. The question which is posed by this analysis is, can a catastrophic decline in water security play a key role in enabling a global shift in assumptions and result in action at scale?

The history and chronology of conflict arising from or associated with water security go back to 3000 BCE.[66] This conflicted way of dealing with a threat to water security has continued since then and will probably occur

---

[64] United Nations, 2003.

[65] Foreign Policy in Focus, 2008.

[66] Glieck, P.H. 2008. *Water conflict chronology*, Pacific Institute for Studies in Development, Environment, and Security.

in future. However, this conflict based response cannot continue for much longer without posing an existential threat to humanity.

The signs are already there that a threat to water security compels decision makers to form multilateral organisations to view the dynamic on a regional or river course basis, or eco-regional basis. The ministerial meeting dealing with water security in the Mediterranean region is one such signal.[67] Dealing with water security also inevitably leads to a transnational or eco-regional perspective and avoids the pitfalls of the primacy of national and individual interests.

An overview, at a continental level, of the global water availability versus population size as a percentage of global population[68] provides the following perspective: Asia 36% vs 60%, Africa 11% vs 13%, Europe 8% vs 13%, North and Central America 15% vs 8%, South America 26% vs 6%, and lastly Australia and Oceania 5% vs <1%. Within this picture of the distribution of the global water resources, the number of water-stressed and water-scarce countries (see Figure 6.8) is set to rise from 31 countries with a combined population of 0.46 billion in 1995, to 48 countries with a combined population of 2.8 billion in 2025.

Any decline in water security is interconnected with many far-reaching aspects of society (see Figure 6.9). Note: key variables for (a) to (d) shown in parenthesis. Variables to track closely are marked (*). (a) water use (governance(*), agriculture(*), industry, household use, sanitation(*), etc) (b) environmental impacts (depletion of surface and groundwater, water pollution, land degradation, ecosystem degradation, disruption of the hydrological cycle itself etc), (c) direct human impacts (food shortage(*), water-related illnesses(*), societal and political instability, conflicts over water(*), slowed economic growth, population displacement) and (d) key population dynamics (growth, migration(*), density, distribution, urbanisation, morbidity, mortality(*)).These variables play out across a wide range among the various countries. Because of this, the predetermined lowering of water security will unfold gradually but relentlessly. This gradual unfolding may enable learning and hopefully will also precipitate a global response at scale.

---

[67] Ministerial Conference on Water, 29 October 2008, Jordan Barcelona Process: Union for the Mediterranean, The Official Press Release http://www.medaquaministerial2008.net/press/CP_ENGLISH.pdf-1

[68] United Nations, 2003.

Population in water-scarce and water-stressed countries, 1995-2050

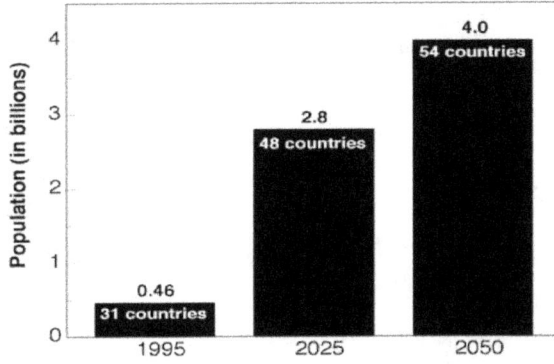

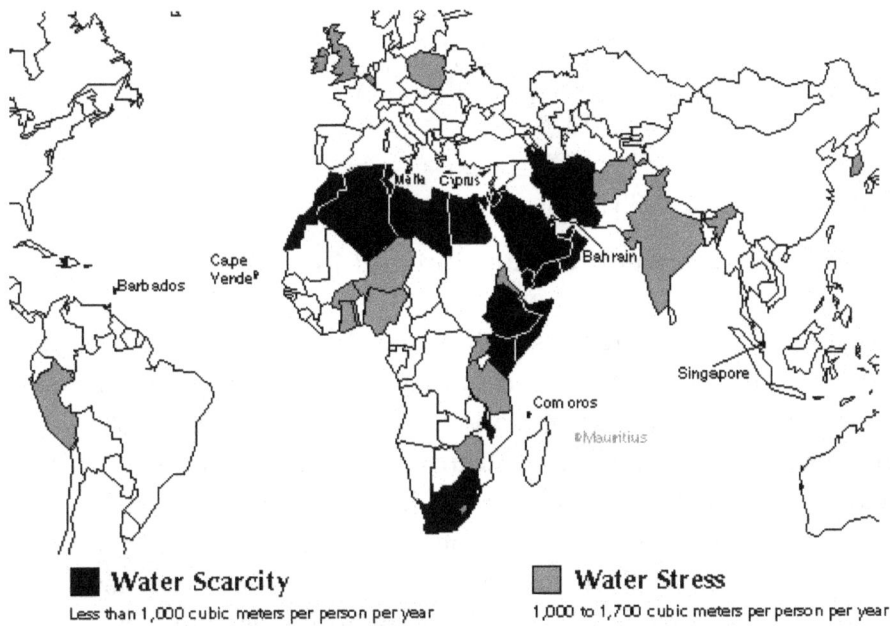

Water Scarcity
Less than 1,000 cubic meters per person per year

Water Stress
1,000 to 1,700 cubic meters per person per year

Source: Gardner-Outlaw & Engelman 1997 (69) and Table 1

Figure 6.8: Water Scarcity & Water Stress

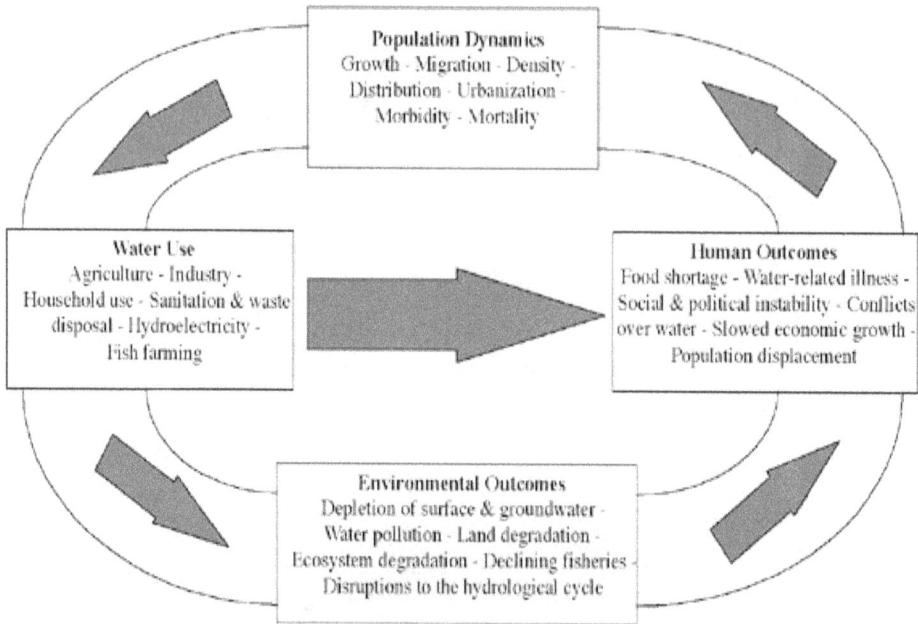

Source: IUCN et al. 1996 (199)

Figure 6.9: Links Between Population and Freshwater

Water is central to our origin as well as our future existence as a species. Any visible decline in water security will probably result in widespread mobilisation to avoid catastrophe and loss of life. The emergent pattern is that the locus of declining water security resides in emergent economies specifically in the southern hemisphere, with a few exceptions such as around the Mediterranean. The way the issue is unfolding will probably enable learning in the organisation for economic cooperation and development (OECD) countries observing the plight of emerging economies. OECD will likely mobilise to prevent compromising their interests.

A decline in water security may be the crisis that enables communities and societies to mobilise their collective intelligence and resources to address the impending water security and other threats. Water security has the potential for being the non-negotiable systemic issue that has to be resolved successfully in order to ensure the survival of the human species. This goal can only be achieved through the mobilisation of human capability at scale.

In the recent past, we have witnessed the decline of multilateral bodies' roles in resolving resource conflicts. Recent resource conflicts in Iraq and elsewhere have all eroded the role of the multilateral bodies' effectiveness. The global multilateral bodies are the natural candidates to mediate the necessary capacity building to respond effectively to a widespread decline in water security. Most of the issues we now face are systemic and will require system-wide, societal mobilisation, resulting in a change of attitudes and widespread cooperation to address them. Examples are climate volatility, HIV/AIDS, water security and viral pandemics.

As a species, our distinctive capabilities have got us into the predicament we find ourselves in now. The possibility of the human species becoming extinct is for the first time being considered seriously. This question can be encountered as the background concern in most of the current debates on climate volatility and species depletion. The two primary human attributes that "caused" these problems are language and imagination. These uniquely human traits are probably the very traits that need to be mobilised to create human capability and capacity at scale.

We are witnessing a groundswell in the importance of skilful conversation and innovation in organisations and the emergent literature on scenario-based strategy, and other approaches to strategy and the resolution of systemic "problems". This may be the seed that enables the evolution of human communities and society in general to survive the emerging discontinuities.

10 GAUGING NOTICEABLE RESULTS IN SCENARIO PLANNING

Many anecdotal claims are made by practitioners regarding their work in scenario-based strategy. These claims have been consolidated in a questionnaire which may serve as a guideline for compiling a post-process report on noticeable results.

10.1 Scenario impact questionnaire (SIQ): Recording noticeable results

Recording and measuring noticeable results during a scenario development assignment constitutes best practice among scenario-based strategy practitioners. The questionnaire has been built up from the anecdotal claims made by leading practitioners. As such it also provides a further guideline for practice. Individual responses may be consolidated and presented statistically to management to protect individual identities and encourage truthful responses.

Private and Confidential: SCENARIO IMPACT QUESTIONNAIRE (SIQ)
Impact of Working with Scenarios and Related Areas
Note: All information will be treated statistically, no individual sets of data will be disclosed.
Write clearly in the space provided.
Name (optional) Date
Level in the organisation
Involvement with scenario building in this organisation. (Please circle as appropriate)

Very involved / Fairly involved / Not involved / Would have liked to be involved

SECTION A: OVERALL IMPACT Please check the appropriate level/scale and illustrate with examples	Strongly agree	Agree somewhat	Disagree somewhat	Disagree strongly
1. Engagement in scenario development has changed the assumptions I hold about how external dynamics work in terms of causal relationships between key variables (drivers) and how this might unfold in the future.	4	3	2	1
Provide examples of the most important changes.				
2. Using scenarios helps me identify areas of risk more clearly and helps me take action (self-correct).	4	3	2	1
Provide examples: (most important)				
3. Using scenarios helps me identify more options and opportunities.	4	3	2	1
Provide examples: (most important)				
4. Working in a cross-function team (forum) helps us build alignment, improve cross-functional teamwork and eliminate wastage.	4	3	2	1
Provide examples: (most important)				

SECTION B: AWARENESS LEVELS To what extent do you personally agree with each of the following statements:	Strongly agree	Agree somewhat	Disagree somewhat	Disagree strongly
1. I notice the dynamics in our different scenarios in the public media	4	3	2	1
2. I look for trigger events as indicators of emerging underlying patterns and dynamics	4	3	2	1
3. A common language and understanding has developed among the people who engage with the scenarios	4	3	2	1
4. I keep track of changes that occur in the marketplace in terms of emerging requirements from customers	4	3	2	1
5. I am alert to competitive activity in the marketplace – actors and positioning	4	3	2	1
6. I keep up to date with important changes in terms of options and opportunities in the market	4	3	2	1
7. I am aware of the opportunities that exist for market growth locally and elsewhere	4	3	2	1
8. I feel that I understand the dynamics of the international market better	4	3	2	1
9. I keep abreast of changes in the economic environment	4	3	2	1
10. I keep abreast of changes in the political environment	4	3	2	1
11. I understand the impact of technology on my sector	4	3	2	1
12. I understand what is required for the sustainability of this sector	4	3	2	1
13. I keep abreast of environmental (green) issues and concerns	4	3	2	1
14. I am aware of my company's environmental policy and record	4	3	2	1
15. I am well informed on the laws and regulations that impact on my business	4	3	2	1
16. I am well informed about the major socioeconomic driving forces in the environment that may impact us	4	3	2	1
17. I am aware of the implications of legislation that encourages diversity	4	3	2	1
18. The interdependency between key variables in the operating environment is now widely understood	4	3	2	1
What is the most significant shift in your awareness levels? Provide examples: (most important)				

SECTION C: LEADERSHIP CAPACITY AND ORGANISATIONAL ALIGNMENT How do you rate your leadership capacity and organisational alignment in terms of each of the following?	Very good	Good	Bad/poor	Very bad/poor
1. The alignment in the thinking of top management so that they act as one (together)	4	3	2	1
2. The clarity of our basic strategic options (create robustness)	4	3	2	1
3. Level of confidence in our decision making	4	3	2	1
4. The length of the horizon on our thinking and strategic planning	4	3	2	1
5. The quality of conversation in the organisation	4	3	2	1
6. The communication and teamwork between sectors/functions within the organisation	4	3	2	1
7. The level of trust in leadership	4	3	2	1
8. Our understanding of the implicit risks in our strategies	4	3	2	1
9. The number of strategic options we are able to identify, open and hold (tolerance for ambiguity)	4	3	2	1
10. Our ability to avoid costly investments in inappropriate strategies or options	4	3	2	1
11. Our ability to communicate with lower-level employees regarding the future operating environments	4	3	2	1
12. The ability of lower-level employees to make decisions that are in alignment with top management	4	3	2	1
13. Our selective monitoring of changes in the operating environment	4	3	2	1
14. The clarity of our thinking regarding the external environment	4	3	2	1
15. Our capacity to act together as an organisation and in the same direction	4	3	2	1
16. Our openness to seeing and facing uncomfortable realities in the environment	4	3	2	1
17. Capacity for learning (openness, lack of arrogance and lack of fear)	4	3	2	1
18. Our ability to take a stand and deal effectively with the reactivity of others	4	3	2	1
19. Role clarity and clear accountability for results.	4	3	2	1
20. The extent to which what the leadership say they believe in is the same as what they actually do	4	3	2	1

SECTION D:

1. What is the single most important uncertainty you still have about how the external environment might unfold in future?

2. What is the single most important internal capacity limit or hindrance that leadership must address?

3. What are the most important external dynamics that you are learning the most about?

4. What are the most important internal dynamics that you are learning about?

5. What are the most significant areas that the scenario work is having an impact on?

6. Any other comment/suggestions you would like to make.

SECTION E: ROLE OF STRATEGY DEVELOPMENT AND EXECUTION	Strongly agree	Agree somewhat	Disagree somewhat	Disagree strongly
1. The time I invested in developing scenarios has given a satisfactory return in terms of my role in this organisation	4	3	2	1
Examples: (most important)				
2. I am more committed to the organisation as a result of engagement in the strategic conversation	4	3	2	1
3. Inclusion in this group has increased my ability to act and lead my team and on projects I participate in.	4	3	2	1
4. I am able to make immediate informed strategic choices which are aligned with other leaders in my organisation	4	3	2	1
5. Participating with leadership from other parts of the organisation eliminates "silo thinking"	4	3	2	1
6. Strategy as an ongoing conversation among executive leadership is essential in dealing effectively with rapid, discontinuous change	4	3	2	1
7. My engagement in scenarios enables me to understand the "why" of decisions and changes in the organisation	4	3	2	1
8. My propensity to leave is lower as a result of my engagement in the scenario building and strategy formulation process	4	3	2	1
9. The cross-functional forum provided me with specific benefits	4	3	2	1
Most important examples of benefits from the cross-functional forum:				

PART IV

Diagnostic Instrument as Feedback and Stimulus for Learning

Contents

CHAPTER 7

A DIAGNOSTIC INSTRUMENT FOR GAUGING CITY GOVERNMENT RESILIENCE

1 THE DIAGNOSTIC INSTRUMENT FOR GAUGING CITY GOVERNMENT RESILIENCE

Building a city government resilience strategy may be viewed as a learning process. Such a process may be facilitated by a quality strategic conversation between city government executive leaders and executive managers. This learning may take place at an individual level, within the executive team or among the members of a forum, consisting of executive leaders and executive managers who link this strategic conversation to the entire organisation.

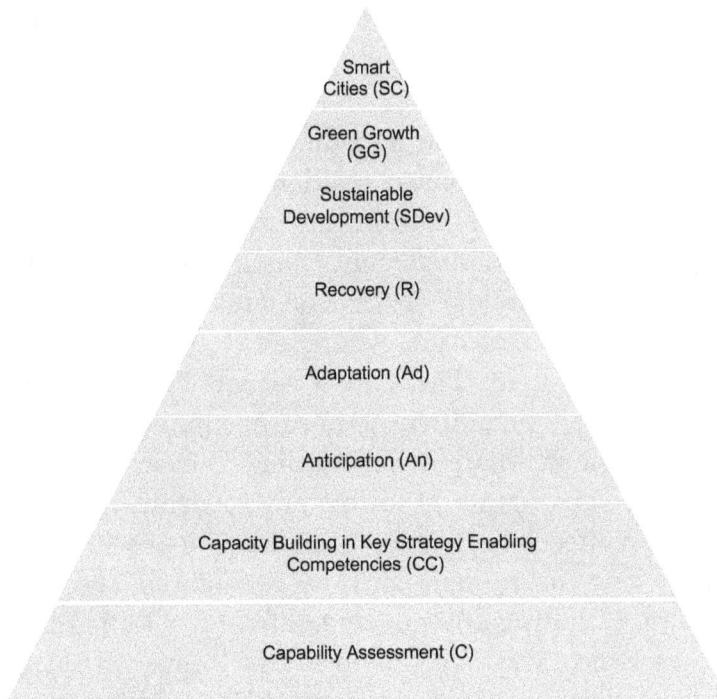

Smart Cities (SC)

Green Growth (GG)

Sustainable Development (SDev)

Recovery (R)

Adaptation (Ad)

Anticipation (An)

Capacity Building in Key Strategy Enabling Competencies (CC)

Capability Assessment (C)

Figure 7.1: The Resilience Strategy Hierarchy (RSH)™ A process framework

This diagnostic instrument has been designed for use by the city government in a facilitated conversation. Its purpose is to stimulate reflection on the factors (and the items within them) and to assist in scoring these factors and items. The associated scores provide a basis for diagnosis for the purposes of improving city government resilience strategy. After instructions for scoring the instrument have been considered, a two-phase process of assessment of city government resilience may be used, facilitated by skilful conversation quality and engagement among executive leadership and executive management. Meta-factors were engaged in completion of the eight factors, followed by considering items within each factor. Greater weight may be given to factors and items where there may be agreement on scores among respondents. Prioritisation and action planning of the remedies for dealing with a lack of resilience will ensure that a process of continuous improvement takes place within a specific city.

Using the Resilience Strategy Hierarchy (RSH)™ A Process Perspective

Scoring using the Resilience Strategy Hierarchy (RSH)™ using a diagnostic process is described below starting with factors and followed by items.

2   FACTORS AND ITEMS FOR GAUGING CITY GOVERNMENT RESILIENCE

A focused strategic conversation on the current reality pertaining to the various factors and items in the instrument, accompanied by associated actions, will result in a more robust resilience strategy.

A quality strategic conversation and engagement among executive leadership and executive management may enable so-called double-loop learning to "retune the minds" of decision makers. Double-loop learning describes a type of conversation where assumptions shift as a result of them being loosely held. Then, in a second learning loop, incoming information is allowed to influence these assumptions. It is envisaged that this diagnostic instrument, when applied by executive leadership and executive management teams in municipal government, will enable the development of an effective city government resilience strategy.

The use of this instrument may be considered successful when it enables learning, including any new insights and actions regarding a city government resilience strategy. Factors and items within factors have been selected based on their leverage for enabling a robust city government resilience strategy. The Green Growth (GG) and Smart Cities (SC) factors have been added based on assumptions about predetermined forces that may have an impact on cities. Accordingly, forces such as climate change and the increased use of technology, which may initially challenge city government resilience, have been considered.

For city government, *raising capability through capacity building* is an essential ingredient and first step in building city government resilience. A regular biannual review of city government capability will result in the capacity to mobilise the factors in the diagnostic instrument.

3   SCORING AND USING THE DIAGNOSTIC INSTRUMENT

The city government resilience diagnostic instrument consists of two levels of assessment and scoring, namely, **factors and items.**

Factors provide an overarching meta-perspective for determining a resilience strategy. They include:

- Capability (C)
- Cross-cutting Competencies (CC)
- Anticipation (An)
- Adaptation (Ad)
- Recovery (R)
- Sustainable Development (SDev)
- Green Growth (GG), and
- Smart Cities (SC)

The second level of assessment and scoring can be found at item level within the factors.

Assessing and scoring factors and items in the diagnostic instrument
Respondents are invited to respond to the descriptive statements for the factors *as a whole*, as the descriptors contain more than one element.

Scoring factors
Score all factors by registering the level of agreement or disagreement on a *descending* Likert scale:

- "Agree Completely": Score 4
- "Agree Somewhat": Score 3
- "Disagree Somewhat": Score 2
- "Disagree Completely": Score 1

Scoring items within factors
All items within factors are also scored as above, except for items in Capability (C) and Cross-cutting competence (CC)

In Capability (C) and Cross-cutting Competence (CC), items are assessed and scored on a four-point *ascending* Likert scale to facilitate the development of competencies:

- "None": Score 0. None or little competence currently exists.
- "Basic/Emergent": Score 1. Guideline: Basic knowledge, skills and

attitudes may exist, and greater proficiency may emerge over time. Comprehensive learning resources need to be identified and engaged.
- "Intermediate/Competent": Score 2. Guideline: An intermediate to competent range in current knowledge, skills and attitudes and overall proficiency exists. Learning resources are known, engaged and being developed.
- "Advanced": Score 3. Guideline: A deep and complete basis in current knowledge, skills and attitudes and commensurate proficiencies exists. Learning resources have been comprehensively mastered and applied.

Note: When questions of clarification arise from technical descriptions and metrics such as "Networked Readiness Index (NRI) or Sendai framework" and "The new urban agenda (Habitat3)" the scorer should indicate a low score for that item.

Factors:

Table 7.1: Factors for gauging city government resilience C, CC, An, Ad, R, SDev, GG, SC

Factors for gauging city government resilience – meta-level. Score each factor as a whole, as a synthesis of its multiple dimensions.	Agree completely	Agree somewhat	Disagree somewhat	Disagree completely
1. Capability (C) Capability may be evidenced by leadership, strategy and service delivery. City government capability may also be summarised as the ability to formulate robust strategy, policy, plans and budgets and execute these on time, on budget and on quality. Regular biannual reviews of capability take place to enable continuous overall improvement in the city government resilience strategy.	4	3	2	1
2. Cross-cutting Competence (CC) Cross-cutting competencies that enable capability. These include essential competencies that support intervening in high leverage points across factors that inform a resilience strategy. City government has built capacity among executive leadership, executive management and middle managers based on competency assessment in teams and individually, which is included in a personal development plan (PDP) as part of their performance contract.	4	3	2	1

Factors for gauging city government resilience – meta-level. Score each factor as a whole, as a synthesis of its multiple dimensions.	Agree completely	Agree somewhat	Disagree somewhat	Disagree completely
3. Anticipation (An) City government anticipates immediate short-term shocks, as well as medium- and long term discontinuities in its contextual environment on a 20- to 25-year planning time horizon. The city engages a state-of-the-art process, methodologies and technologies such as scenario-based strategy and systems dynamics (SD) modelling to shift and broaden assumptions in the minds of executive leadership, executive managers and decision makers. SD modelling may be used to understand key dynamics systemically when building scenarios beyond the ten-year planning horizon. Emergency and risk-management processes are states of the art and in place, regularly practised and ready to be activated. Scenarios are used as a set to stress-test strategies, policies, plans and budgets for robustness across future conditions described in these scenarios.	4	3	2	1
4. Adaptation (Ad) City government absorbs short-term shocks by ensuring that emergency water, food and first aid are readily available. Effective communications and cyber infrastructure to support coordinated adaptation activities have been operationalised. The city has built capabilities and competencies for adapting to shocks that may persist in the medium- and long-term. Leadership is capable of resolving the tensions between performance, action and considered, evidence-based strategic direction along the path of the adaptation process. Leadership takes a stand for policy that will support recovery, sustainable development, green growth and smart cities.	4	3	2	1
5. Recovery (R) City government is capable of springing back to a better position than that prevailing prior to the shock and also improve on it. Established change management infrastructure exists, such as a forum which links to the whole organisation. The forum is building shared vision, a sense of urgency and provides organisation-wide leadership by means of its powerful, inclusive coalition which regularly engages via the forum in strategic conversation. The forum enables the delivery of short-term wins within the city government resilience strategy and has built institutional capability to sustain recovery and embark on sustainable development initiatives. High organisational trust facilitated by quality strategic conversation and regular leadership engagement enables responsiveness, agility and resilience.	4	3	2	1

Factors for gauging city government resilience – meta-level. Score each factor as a whole, as a synthesis of its multiple dimensions.	Agree completely	Agree somewhat	Disagree somewhat	Disagree completely
6. Sustainable Development (SDev) City government complies with the Sustainable Development Goals (SDGs), Paris Agreement 2015 and the Sendai Framework for disaster risk reduction 2015–2030 and is enrolled in the global city mayoral parliament resolutions "the new urban agenda (Habitat3)". It focuses on engagement with a national development plan and municipal mandate for economic development. Small, micro and medium enterprise (SMME) developments are being stimulated. It is invested in community engagement in rights-based sustainable community investment programme (SCIP) development initiatives, including youth in service delivery. National government is engaged in enhancing education and learning quality through teacher development support. The city human resources planning focusses on attracting and nurturing talent.	4	3	2	1
7. Green Growth (GG) City government resilience strategy extends beyond sustainable development, enabling recycling more than 50% of waste using waste as a feedstock into other processes and sectors within the economy. Utilisation of natural resources is improved through beneficiation processes. Continuously measuring and reducing the city carbon footprint through elimination wastage, continuously innovating and identifying areas for improvement of quality of services.	4	3	2	1
8. Smart Cities (SC) City government has invested in the cyber infrastructure to support sensors and connectedness and gauges its networked readiness using the WEF Network Readiness Index (NRI). It emphasises e-governance competencies and technology-enabled coordination and information sharing. It anticipates and leverages disruptions in transportation and energy to enable improved quality of city living. See also the IMD Smart City Index 2019.	4	3	2	1
Subtotal				
Score				
Capability grade %				

Items and indicators:

Table 7.2: Capability (C), Cross-cutting Competencies (CC)

Capability (C) Definition: Strategy, Leadership and Delivery	None	Basic/emergent	Intermediate/competent	Advanced
Capable executive leadership and executive management formulate robust city strategy, policy, plans and budgets and execute these on time, on budget and on quality	0	1	2	3
Leadership by executive leaders and executive managers is exercised by taking a stand, setting direction, motivating people and developing people	0	1	2	3
Scenario-based strategy enables robust, outcomes-focused strategy, evidence-based choices, collaboration and building common purpose	0	1	2	3
Managing performance reviews, shared commitment and sound delivery models, competitive resourcing and innovative delivery structures including continuous improvement processes	0	1	2	3
Organisational routines consisting of regular goal setting and review of service delivery performance and engagement over time to embed a service delivery culture **sub total**	0	1	2	3
Cross-cutting Competencies (CC) Definition: Knowledge, skills and attitudes that cut across organisational processes, departments and divisions	None	Basic/emergent	Intermediate/competent	Advanced
Rule of law: Executive leaders and executive managers and policymakers are knowledgeable and conversant with, and take a stand for, the supremacy of the constitution in city strategies and policies	0	1	2	3
Legislation on local government is known and used as the mandate for local government policy and services	0	1	2	3
Strategy making and execution: Goal setting and regular review within a performance management system (PMS) is an embedded skill across all levels of executive leadership, executive management and middle management, including front line supervisory levels	0	1	2	3

Cross-cutting Competencies (CC) Definition: Knowledge, skills and attitudes that cut across organisational processes, departments and divisions	None	Basic/emergent	Intermediate/competent	Advanced
Strategic conversation and engagement skills are the foundation for performance management, learning and building organisational trust	0	1	2	3
Scenario-based strategy and stress-testing strategy in the scenarios enables double-loop learning	0	1	2	3
Personal development planning (PDP) for executive leadership, executive managers, senior and middle managers is embedded in performance contracts	0	1	2	3
Systems thinking: Systems thinking is used for understanding the contextual environment as well as internal city government dynamics, enabling effective execution of strategy and policy while minimising unintended consequences	0	1	2	3
Systems dynamics (SD) modelling and urban dynamics modelling is used to support scenario-based strategic planning, leadership, decision making and policy making	0	1	2	3
Service delivery quality: Service delivery as a process is citizen centric, structured and innovative, and delivers value-for-money services	0	1	2	3
Service delivery quality is based on elimination of wastage, continuous improvement (Kaizen) and focusses on citizens' quality requirements for services – fit for purpose (water, sanitation, health, housing, transportation and nutrition)	0	1	2	3
Leadership: Competent, servant leadership enables followership and is known for taking a stand for building shared vision, focusing on strategic priorities and shared values. Servant leadership is widespread among executive leadership, executive management middle management and supervisors	0	1	2	3
Revenue management and development: Revenue management processes are structured and effective and ensure that 100% of revenues are billed and 95% or more are collected on time and on budget	0	1	2	3
Investment in a developmental city takes place in communities through, amongst others, rights-based sustainable community investment programmes (SCIP), joint ventures (JVs) and public-private partnerships (PPPs)	0	1	2	3

Cross-cutting Competencies (CC) Definition: Knowledge, skills and attitudes that cut across organisational processes, departments and divisions	None	Basic/emergent	Intermediate/ competent	Advanced
Successful change management: Change management infrastructure has been built in the form of a forum which engages through organisational links to the whole organisation and includes a powerful coalition of leadership which forms critical mass for sustaining and ensuring successful change management	0	1	2	3
Good governance systems: Good governance practice eliminates corruption and wastage and is moving towards 100% clean audits	0	1	2	3
Financial and economic literacy is established and is supported by useful management accounts and management information systems	0	1	2	3
Trust building: Trust building results in greater organisational trust levels which facilitates organisational responsiveness, agility and resilience	0	1	2	3
Stewardship of the commons such as roads, air quality, the physical environment and green spaces is harnessing scientific knowledge, and these are maintained and protected in the service of current citizens and future generations which is seen as a moral responsibility to next generations	0	1	2	3
Recovering from disruptions and improving: Technology-enabled revolutions and disruptions are being actively shaped to enable recovery, improvement and sustainable development	0	1	2	3
Energy disruption knowledge is evidence-based and leveraged in the service of sustainable development	0	1	2	3
Transport disruption knowledge is evidence-based and leveraged in the service of sustainable development	0	1	2	3
Investment in technology infrastructure for enabling smart cities is in progress and is prioritised and gauged using the WEF Networked Readiness Index (NRI)	0	1	2	3
Intercultural competence enables cross-functional collaboration and big teamwork	0	1	2	3
Youth development: Investment in youth development and building appropriate competencies in advance of technology-driven disruptions and job redundancies	0	1	2	3

Cross-cutting Competencies (CC) Definition: Knowledge, skills and attitudes that cut across organisational processes, departments and divisions	None	Basic/emergent	Intermediate/competent	Advanced
National government is engaged in raising the quality of city education by focusing on teacher development and learner-centred teaching	0	1	2	3
Subtotal				
Score				
Cross-cutting competency grade %				

Note: These competencies may be present in the portfolio of executive leadership and executive management or within a forum that builds a resilience strategy. Individuals among these ranks may have personal development plans (PDPs) in place as part of their performance management contracts.

Table 7.3: Anticipation (An)

Anticipation (An) of future shocks and discontinuities in the contextual environment	Agree completely	Agree somewhat	Disagree somewhat	Disagree completely
Emergency reserves are in place such as water, food, energy, medicine, sanitation, law enforcement and communications in sufficient quantities to support affected citizens and communities over initial shocks	4	3	2	1
Emergency preparedness routines and embedded behaviour are in place by regularly practising and rehearsing responses to shocks	4	3	2	1
All gatherings of more than 30 people are recorded and tracked in case these data may be required for enabling emergency evacuation	4	3	2	1
The time focus for strategic planning and policy (future planning time horizons) for executive leadership and executive management levels is 20–25 years into the future	4	3	2	1
Systems dynamics (SD) modelling anticipates key urban dynamics in the future environment in a 20- to 25-year future planning time frame	4	3	2	1
Scenario narratives describing the contextual environment over the next 20–25 years have been developed and are based on concerns among executive leadership, executive management and key stakeholders	4	3	2	1

Anticipation (An) of future shocks and discontinuities in the contextual environment	Agree completely	Agree somewhat	Disagree somewhat	Disagree completely
Scenario narratives are based on deep systemic research into the plausible range of future behaviour of key driving forces (KDFs) described in two-, three- or four relevant, challenging, plausible, internally consistent storylines	4	3	2	1
External remarkable people (RPs) have been engaged to stretch the scenario narratives so that they challenge existing thinking and broaden assumptions in the minds of executive leaders and executive managers	4	3	2	1
Scenarios are used to stress-test strategic planning, proposed policy, draft legislation, business plans and budgets, to ensure robustness in future scenario narratives and to limit unintended consequences	4	3	2	1
Clear policy positions enable economic development, job creation and social transformation based upon national development planning and economic freedom as defined by the Fraser Institute and The Heritage Foundation	4	3	2	1
Subtotal				
Score				
Resilience Grade %				

Table 7.4: Adaptation (Ad)

Adaptation (Ad) to shocks and discontinuities	Agree completely	Agree somewhat	Disagree somewhat	Disagree completely
An inclusive forum has been built as organisational infrastructure to lead, manage and sustain adaptation and organisational change successfully, as a parallel leadership engagement structure without executive authority	4	3	2	1
Inclusive, regular, quality, scheduled strategic conversations among executive leaders and executive managers takes place as the basis of successful change management execution and resistance management	4	3	2	1
A shared vision is being built with a sense of urgency led by a powerful, dominant coalition, which forms critical mass for delivering short-term wins as well as setting and achieving medium- and long-term goals within a city government resilience strategy	4	3	2	1

Adaptation (Ad) to shocks and discontinuities	Agree completely	Agree somewhat	Disagree somewhat	Disagree completely
Identifying and adapting to both future risks as well as opportunities in the environment forms the basis for successful adaptation	4	3	2	1
A high level of trust across the organisation enables responsiveness and agility	4	3	2	1
The rule of law underpins the execution of all policies, planning and engagement with citizens and stakeholders	4	3	2	1
Accountability and authority provide support for decisions and execution across all levels of executive leadership, executive management and supervisors	4	3	2	1
Subtotal				
Resilience Grade%				

Table 7.5: Recovery (R)

Recovery (R) from shocks and discontinuities	Agree completely	Agree somewhat	Disagree somewhat	Disagree completely
Back-to-basics, smart government initiatives build sustainable foundations for economic recovery and a financial platform for recovery and sustainable development	4	3	2	1
Good governance practice is rigorously enforced, and executive leadership and executive management set the example	4	3	2	1
Annual financial audits are moving towards 100% clean audits	4	3	2	1
Community-owned government injects competition into a results-based enterprising government	4	3	2	1
Joint ventures (JVs) and public-private partnerships (PPPs) add capability and are effectively supervised to provide value-for-money service delivery to citizens	4	3	2	1
Subtotal				
Resilience Grade%				

Table 7.6: Sustainable development (SDev)

Sustainable development (SDev)	Agree completely	Agree somewhat	Disagree somewhat	Disagree completely
A national development plan – based on principles of economic freedom as defined by the Fraser Institute and The Heritage Foundation including the rule of law, small efficient government, regulatory efficiency and open markets – forms the basis of the city government resilience strategy and unambiguous policy leadership	4	3	2	1
Rights-based sustainable community investment programmes (SCIP) in informal and formal development communities provide processes for the creation of responsibility, dignity, jobs and wealth	4	3	2	1
The UN Sustainable Development Goals for 2030 (SDGs) and the Paris agreement are integrated into city strategic priorities, goal setting and policy and are regularly reviewed and monitored on a quarterly basis	4	3	2	1
Foreign direct investment (FDI) is attracted from city governments and industrialists, nationally and internationally	4	3	2	1
The national government is engaged in enabling teacher-focused development to raise the quality of learning among selected schools which provide examples to other schools	4	3	2	1
Investment in human capital development and value formation among youth is structured, regulated and effective	4	3	2	1
A human resources strategy attracts top performers from the best schools, enabling investment in talent which is fast-tracked into strategic city government roles	4	3	2	1
Specific communities such as the informal or "invisible" economy and youth are targeted for sustainable community investment programmes (SCIPs)	4	3	2	1
Small, micro and medium enterprises (SMMEs) and entrepreneurs receive institutional support and investment	4	3	2	1
Retention of existing city government talent and attraction of new talent is based on key competencies that enable a resilience strategy and capability	4	3	2	1
Provision of value-for-money delivery of quality services is continuously improved through structured innovation and workforce engagement processes such as Kaizen and total quality management (TQM)	4	3	2	1
Subtotal				
Resilience Grade%				

Table 7.7: Green growth (GG)

Green growth (GG)	Agree completely	Agree somewhat	Disagree somewhat	Disagree completely
Recycling of waste streams is moving towards 50% or higher levels of recycling	4	3	2	1
Building of a circular economy where waste becomes feedstock for the next process or industry informs policy and legislation	4	3	2	1
Understanding, appreciation and support for a green city economy is mobilised and actively promoted	4	3	2	1
Carbon emissions are measured, monitored, minimised and declining	4	3	2	1
Subtotal				
Resilience Grade%				

Table 7.8: Smart Cities (SC)

Smart cities (SC)	Agree completely	Agree somewhat	Disagree somewhat	Disagree completely
The WEF Networked Readiness Index (NRI) is used to assess and gauge the level of enabling infrastructure to support technology-based interconnectedness	4	3	2	1
The Internet of Things (IoT) is pervasive, is used to monitor, coordinate and reduce pollution, promote recycling and is leveraged to raise service delivery quality. IoT powers multiple feedback loops which in turn facilitate city government resilience and self-correction	4	3	2	1
E-governance competence using a competence framework such as the Van der Waldt framework, enables individuals to take responsibility for building of e-governance capacity which in turn enables smart city government	4	3	2	1
Pre-emptive education and retraining mitigates the consequences of transforming work and offsets potentially redundant jobs	4	3	2	1
Energy and transport disruptions are leveraged to accelerate green economics	4	3	2	1
Solar photovoltaic energy powers household energy needs and community needs and is penetrating industrial applications	4	3	2	1

Smart cities (SC)	Agree completely	Agree somewhat	Disagree somewhat	Disagree completely
Autonomous electric vehicles on demand reduces the need for vehicle ownership, roads and parking, reduces emissions and road accidents and frees up highways, also rendering parking space in the city available for alternate use	4	3	2	1
Subtotal				
Resilience Grade%				

4 RECOMMENDATIONS FOR FURTHER RESEARCH

There are numerous areas of scholarly investigation that may benefit the study of city government resilience and support gauging and improving city government resilience. Recommendations for further research are listed below –

- It was specified that reliability and validity testing of the factors and items in this instrument, with a representative sample of executive leaders and executive managers from South African cities, was beyond the scope of this study. This may be undertaken once the instrument has been more extensively used in the field and has stabilised as a result of facilitators and practitioners editing and refining factors and items based on experience with executive leaders and executive managers;
- Developing an index for benchmarking based on the factors and items in this instrument may create a basis for comparison, benchmarking and peer review with a view to continuous improvement of resilience strategies;
- Longitudinal studies to measure the impact of this instrument on city resilience with specific reference to the relative success of organisation development and renewal process approach versus a metric-based so-called balanced scorecard approach;
- Focused studies to establish the relationship in practice between city government resilience and specific factors such as capability assessment, capacity building, anticipation, adaptation, recovery, sustainable development, green growth and smart cities;
- Assessment of building organisational infrastructure for successful organisational change management and a review of high leverage areas for successful organisational change and transformation;
- Studying the role of scenario-based strategy and the use of SD modelling in anticipating discontinuities on a 20- to 25-year planning

time horizon;

- Investigating the role of leadership in general and servant leadership specifically to facilitate city government capability;
- Assessing the improvement and embedding of a service delivery culture through organisation routines including goal setting and review processes as part of city government capability;
- Identifying and analysing the association between the quality of strategic conversations and organisational trust as well as the importance of these organisational dimensions in fostering city government resilience; and
- A comparative analysis between approaching the building of a robust resilience strategy from a rationalist paradigm and from a processual paradigm.

5   CONCLUSION

The global migration into cities supports the rising importance of cities within nation states. Resilient cities and regional towns seem to be on a path to increasingly become the flywheels for national economic development and national resilience. Cities in South Africa that implement an inclusive city government resilience strategy may at the same time address wider issues of government in emerging economies in Africa and elsewhere such as where citizen expectations of government delivery outpace the realities of service delivery. Gauging the current city government resilience strategy may enable pre-emptively developing capability through capacity building of key strategy enabling competencies. Focusing inclusively on city government resilience may include accelerating economic development and the reduction of inequality in cities. A focus on common concerns for building city government resilience may enable community development, supporting a developmental approach to city government and, through this, sustainable economic growth and job creation. City government resilience may be complemented by individual personal and community resilience, and be interconnected with regional resilience, national resilience and international resilience. A capability review of city government may take place on a biannual basis with the purpose of continually improving city government capability. An assessment of the city government resilience strategy may also take place on a biannual basis. Over time, patterns and trends amongst cities for building resilience may be identified and the most effective approaches shared amongst a network of resilient cities in South Africa, regionally and globally.

CHAPTER 8

CONCLUSIONS AND RECOMMENDATIONS

National governments increasingly appear out of touch and slow to respond to shocks and other discontinuities. The reason for this can be found in the work of Elliott Jaques,[1] who posits that the optimal or requisite number of hierarchical levels in an organisation is seven. Jaques has studied, among many other organisations, the military at peace and at war and has pinpointed one of the rare scientific facts in what is called "management science". In a conversation with Jaques during his sojourn at MIT, he described the consequences of organisational hierarchies that are too tall or too shallow – greater or less than the requisite seven levels. He stated that "[w]hen an organisational hierarchy is too tall, that is more than the requisite seven levels, communication from the apex of the organisation to the bottom where members must act on information from the top, takes too long". What are the consequences of this in the military when the hierarchy is too tall one may ask? "People get killed," he says. When one considers the number of levels from central government through provincial government to local government it becomes obvious why national government appears to be out of touch and slow to respond. Self-organising organisational systems move empowerment together with decision making as close as possible to the sources of information at the boundaries of the organisation. To do this effectively, managers and supervisors need specific competencies that enable strategy formulation as well as execution.

Jaques continues: "Alternately, when the hierarchy is too shallow, decision makers at the apex of the hierarchy cannot see far enough ahead to avoid shocks and traps." What happens in the military in battle when the hierarchy is too shallow one may ask? "People get killed," he says once more. In his research, he has concluded that there is a requisite time span for each level in a hierarchy where a decision can be seen as correct or not. He calls this "the time span of discretion". For a city, this time span should ideally be 20- to 25 years ahead, the implication being that the planning time horizon in a city should be 20- to 25 years. Planning time horizons are typically much shorter than this. This short-termism explains the panic and confusion during unexpected shocks.

---

[1]   Jaques, E. 2013. *Requisite organisation: A total system for effective managerial organisation and management leadership for the 21st century.* Orlando, FL: Cason Hall.

1   CITIES AND TOWNS AS HIGH LEVERAGE FOR ECONOMIC GROWTH AND JOB CREATION

According to recent Brookings research,[2] the 300 largest metros globally account for 36% of global employment growth and 67% of global GDP growth. In emerging economies, metros continue to disproportionately drive growth, accounting for 80% from the 60 best performing metropolitan areas out of a total of 300 metros. At the top of the 2014 to 2016 Global Metros Monitor list, Dublin leads the metros that are growing faster than the national economies which they are in, with 21% GDP growth. Pretoria's 3.5% GDP growth on the same list between 2014 to 2016 has more than double the national GDP growth of 1.5% for the same period. This should not be surprising as metros and large towns aggregate dense populations within them where it is easier to communicate, innovate and share resources. In addition, there is currently a large flow of people into cities and towns which, according to futurist Brand,[3] will probably be the defining feature of the 21st century. Extrapolating these GDP figures and population growth in cities and large towns forward 20- to 25 years will see metros and towns playing an increasingly more important role in GDP growth, wealth creation and providing jobs. Resilient cities may be regarded as the flywheels for national momentum for resilience, GDP growth and job creation. Besides this flywheel effect, there is a growing appreciation for the association between economic freedom of choice and wealth creation and creating jobs. Countries with a high level of economic freedom typically have a high level of GDP per capita. The Heritage Foundation in Washington DC, supported by the Canadian Fraser Institute, defines economic freedom as the rule of law including property rights and freedom from corruption, government size including fiscal freedom and government spending, regulatory efficiency which includes business freedom, labour freedom and monetary freedom, and open markets which includes trade freedom, investment freedom and financial freedom (see Figure 4.2, Chapter 4). The Fraser Institute, besides supporting the THF findings, has studied the relationship between conditions of economic freedom and the bottom 10% wage earners, including the poorest of the poor. They have found that they fare best under conditions of relative economic freedom.

In China, special economic zones (SEZs), free from central communist policy interference, are empowered to create conditions for attracting foreign direct investment (FDI) to fund development, wealth creation and

---

[2]   Global Metro Monitor Brookings. 2018. *Global Metro Monitor 2018* Date of Access: 12 January 2019. https://www.brookings.edu/research/global-metro-monitor-2018/

[3]   Brand, S. 2017b. What squatter cities can teach us/TED Talk/TED.com. Https://www.ted.com/talks/stewart_brand_on_squatter_cities Date of access: 8 August 2017.

job creation. SEZs follow a market-based, manufacturing-for-export policy for development. Opening the Chinese economy to market-based policy in SEZs was initiated by Deng Xiaoping and is continued by the current president Xi Jinping in what is referred to as "one country two policies" and "socialism with Chinese characteristics". Resolving the dilemma between centralist communist ideology and market-based manufacturing policy under conditions of economic freedom of choice in this creative way has resulted in the double-digit Chinese GDP growth, sustained over decades. The Chinese SEZs demonstrate the power of economic freedom of choice to create wealth and jobs. South African economic policy also seems stuck on the horns of a similar policy dilemma. A one country two systems approach similar to the Chinese approach could resolve this dilemma. A policy of socialism with African characteristics could provide a creative resolution for this dilemma in South Africa. SEZs in South Africa could combine stakeholder capitalism including freedom of economic choice and principles of Ubuntu in city development to create export-based manufacturing free from centralist policy limits and destructive political interference. This implies that economic recovery and sustained growth should prioritise cities and large towns as SEZs and flywheels to build momentum for national growth, recovery and job creation.

The Resilience Strategy Hierarchy™ offers a framework for developing resilient cities and towns. The most powerful approach for engaging organisational decision makers in leading successful organisational renewal is to use action research also known as survey feedback methodology.[4][5] The survey feedback process consists of starting the process by contracting with the client system to gather data, indicating that the data will be analysed and suitably structured, then feed the results of this data gathering back to the client system together with joint action planning, followed by action. The quality of the process and conversation will influence the quality of the outcome. Developing a resilience strategy should follow the above process. A proposed roadmap should also be based on this process.

This method has the highest probability for successful transformation and renewal. The foundation level in the Resilience Strategy Hierarchy™ is to assess organisational capability. This should be followed by determining capacity-building priorities. Capacity building in cross-cutting competencies is also known as key strategy enabling processes.

[4]   Lewin, K. 1948. *Resolving social conflicts. Selected papers on group dynamics.* New York: Harper & Row.

[5]   Adelman, C. 1993. Kurt Lewin and the origins of action research. *Educational Action Research*, 1(1):7–24, https://doi.org/10.1080/0965079930010102 Date of access 23 February 2020.

This starting point determines the potential for success with all the subsequent levels in the hierarchy up to and including green growth and smart cities. The current popularity and enthusiasm for smart cities has not been matched by expected results at scale. These results will probably not be realised until a capability assessment has been made and investment has been made in capacity building focusing on strategy enabling processes based on developing capability. Smart cities may only be realised when individual behaviour change is considered important and approached from a systemic organisational change perspective. Focusing on tools and techniques and other technologies contained in the 4IR alone will not result in the learning required. Sustaining learning as part of capacity building requires learning at three levels, namely philosophy and worldview, competencies; knowledge, skills and attitudes; and finally tools and techniques. Tools and techniques depend for their successful use on competencies and the philosophy and worldview they are based upon (see Figure 1.3 Chapter 1).

Competent practice should be based on a firm understanding of both theory and practice. Three theoretical domains are considered essential for resilience practice: 1) a systems perspective of organisational dynamics, 2) organisational resilience models, principles and schools of thinking, and 3) modern government.

2   A SYSTEMS PERSPECTIVE OF ORGANISATIONAL DYNAMICS

The evolution of thinking regarding organisations as open systems provides a useful perspective on organisational responsiveness and how this attribute enables resilience. It includes an analysis of the paradigmatic developments, schools of thinking, theoretical principles, theories, and models of organisations. This analysis includes organisational design and development that are directly interconnected with organisational responsiveness and organisational resilience. It also explores the origins and images of organisations, as well as subsystems within organisations. It provides a total systems approach to organisational design and organisation development and identifies so-called "high leverage" components of a systems approach. These high leverage components will allow successful large-scale restructuring of organisations to improve their overall resilience. It has been established here that the process of developing a resilience strategy in a complex, chaotic human activity system, such as a city government organisation, requires adopting a holistic, multidisciplinary, systemic perspective. This may, in turn, require uncovering interdependencies between key variables, as well identifying leverage points within the whole. Leverage points have been pinpointed in optimum areas to raise responsiveness within a whole organisation and, through this, improve resilience. Quality conversations about a truthful perspective on the current reality for specific leverage points may constitute in and of themselves feedback loops, which enable double-loop learning and the adjustment of assumptions, and accordingly lead to greater resilience in an organisation.

3 ORGANISATIONAL RESILIENCE MODELS, PRINCIPLES AND SCHOOLS OF THINKING

Chapter 3 provides a holistic perspective of organisational resilience and sustainable economic growth by means of robust analyses of the paradigmatic developments, schools of thought, theoretical principles, theories and models for organisational resilience. It also entailed a synthesis of the schools of thought such as risk management, long-term sustainability, sustainable development, and green growth. It further provides an analysis of the trends (patterns of behaviour) and factors (systemic structure) that could affect city government resilience. By initially using anticipation, adaptation and recovery (AAR) as the basis for a diagnostic framework, this was extended into a holistic diagnostic instrument.

An organisational resilience strategy may best be achieved within a processual paradigm, enabled by a quality strategic conversation between executive leadership and executive managers. In the context of an inclusive strategy leadership and engagement (SLE) forum, consisting of formal and informal leaders, a powerful coalition can be built that takes ownership of developing and leading a resilience strategy. The diagnostic instrument provides a frame of reference for high leverage areas which may be used to focus this conversation. Diagnosis of current resilience levels and prioritisation should take place and actions decided by the forum, which may be executed with an economy of means. A total quality management (TQM) campaign, as a basis for structured innovation of quality, will ensure continuous improvement of services as well as improvement of government itself. Structured, innovative, continuous improvement and value-for-money approaches in city government will establish a back-to-basics approach which can be extended to setting new standards.

There are emerging predetermined dynamics in the external environment that are relatively certain to have an impact on city government resilience. These include the carrying capacity of the planet, migration to cities, climate volatility, technology convergence, disruptors in transportation and energy, and terror attacks (nuclear and cyber).

These challenges to organisational resilience require that the initial AAR framework be extended to include capability assessment and improvement through capacity building in cross-cutting competencies, aka strategy enabling processes as a prerequisite to AAR factors. These factors enable adapting to shocks, recovering from challenges and then extending from this basis to sustainable development, green growth and smart cities. Smart cities may be enabled by incorporating smart technologies such as sensors offered by the internet of things (IoT) in city government organisations, as well as massively increased portable computing power and storage. In the face of predetermined dynamics, competencies in scenario-based strategy making, SD modelling, organisational trust building and requisite organisational principles are key enablers for ensuring city government responsiveness and, through this, resilience. Urbanisation may require resilient city government organisations to act as the fulcrum for sustainable development projects which enable a developmental state through learning cities and towns. Through greater city government resilience across regions, a critical mass may be built for enabling national resilience and national sustainable development. Resilient cities become flywheels for building and maintaining momentum for national resilience. Servant leadership, openness to learning, trust and an enabling culture, together with routine goal setting and a review of progress, provide the primary platforms for building capability through capacity building for anticipation, adaptation, recovery, sustainable development, green growth and smart cities.

4 MODERN GOVERNMENT

Modern government, according to Fukuyama,[6][7] consists of the rule of law, accountability and capability. The rule of law is usually contained in a widely agreed constitution which embodies the desired results (vision) for society. Serving the constitution serves the best interests of society. In a feudal society, it is exactly the opposite – everybody serves the feudal lords and ownership of property is at the pleasure of the feudal lord. The Magna Carta of 1215, which originated during the reign of King John of England, is acknowledged as the origin of constitutionalism. It was introduced to protect rights in general and property ownership specifically against the shifting power structures of feudal society. If the feudal lord died or was replaced, property ownership was again in question; depending on your

---

[6]   Fukuyama, F. 2011a. *The origins of political order: From pre-human times to the French Revolution*. New York, NY: FSG.

[7]   Fukuyama, F. 2011b. *Political order and political decay: From the Industrial Revolution to the globalisation of democracy*. New York, NY: FSG.

standing with the incoming lord, your property was either secure or at risk. Investments in improvements flourish when future ownership is assured.

Fukuyama states that modern government is also capable. The Australian Public Service Commission[8] describes capability as leadership, strategy and the delivery of services (see Figure 4.1 in Chapter 4). A formal capability assessment process is foundational and should be a regular biannual process. For that reason, it has been included in the city government resilience strategy hierarchy as the first order of business towards creating a robust resilience strategy.

Building a city government resilience strategy should be viewed as a learning process. Such a process may be facilitated by a quality strategic conversation between city government executive leaders and executive managers. This learning may take place at an individual level, within the executive team or among the members of the SLE forum, consisting of executive leaders and executive managers who link this strategic conversation to the entire organisation down to front line supervisors.

The methodology for using the diagnostic instrument is of fundamental importance. An overview of the instructions have therefore been repeated here for convenience. This diagnostic instrument has been designed for use by the city and town government in a facilitated conversation. Its purpose is to stimulate reflection on the factors (and the items within them) and to assist in scoring these factors and items. The associated scores provide a basis for diagnosis for the purposes of improving city government resilience strategy. After instructions for scoring the instrument have been considered, a two-phase process of assessment of city government resilience may be used. Thus meta-factors are engaged in scoring the eight factors first, followed by considering and scoring the items in each factor. Greater weight may be given to factors and items where there may be agreement on scores among respondents. Prioritisation and action planning of the remedies for dealing with a lack of resilience will ensure that a process of continuous improvement takes place within a specific city.

Inner path of a competent resilience practitioner
As a competent resilience practitioner, enabling learning should be foremost in the mind of a practitioner during the design and facilitation processes. Facilitators must develop an internal compass by which to steer through the complexity and group dynamics of developing a robust resilience strategy – making use of the diagnostic instrument and resilience strategy

---

8   Australian Public Service Commission (APSC). 2017a. *Organisational capability.* http://www.apsc.gov.au/about-the-apsc/parliamentary/state-of-the-service/state-of-the-service-2010/chapter-10-organisational-capability Date of access: 19 August 2017.

hierarchy as a basis. All process choices and decisions can and must be guided by this inner sense of priority if resilience practitioners wish to be effective and enable learning. The practitioner must also know the basic principles of adult learning, experiential learning, single-loop and double-loop learning and how to adapt processes to enable and optimise the various modes of learning.

From De Geus's seminal publications, we learn that at individual, organisational and national levels, learning faster than others (competitors) is the ultimate competitive advantage for organisations. Competition and survival of the most competitive is a law of nature. It is the basis on which we evolved as an intelligent species and how all species continue to evolve. Resilience is the ability to spring back and take up a form or shape that existed before the impact or challenge. A resilience strategy is a robust plan of action which anticipates and prepares *in advance* how an organisation will adapt and recover from shocks and discontinuities in the environment.

Often, an internal conversation takes place within the practitioner, which enables them to respond to dynamics in the group they are working with. Contracting with participants initiates any process and, when required, agreement to a set of ground rules for the group if they need firmer, agreed on guidelines for their behaviour during a process. This internal conversation is usually based on acute observation of the process flow, individual participant and group behaviour, intervening where needed to improve interactions and keep the process on track to achieve the agreed end result as contracted. As with servant leadership, facilitators should also be in the service of the group they are engaging, constantly scanning the group for the level of engagement of all members. Practitioners should invite quiet participants into the conversation, intervening where needed and using the conversation quality and engagement (CQE) checklist to enable the conversation quality to remain optimal. Processes should always be inclusive to ensure the widest possible ownership which ensures effective implementation. Practitioners should consistently bring the conversation back to the purpose of developing a robust resilience strategy and, when required, the purpose of specific process components within the broader process.

A competent aircraft pilot only uses their full set of skills during turbulent conditions. A facilitator only actively engages with a group when it is struggling with interpersonal or intrapersonal dynamics that are getting in the way of learning. Interventions should typically involve a "light touch" unless a strong structural intervention is required. The systems iceberg is useful for reflecting on emergent patterns of behaviour while searching for and intervening when needed in structures and processes that will enable and optimise learning. The iceberg is also useful for cutting through dysfunctional patterns of behaviour to address the underlying structures before they become problematic for the group as a whole. For example, an individual who is dominating the group can be drawn back before the group acts to exclude their contribution.

As a competent resilience strategy practitioner, facilitating the scenario-based strategy component is a significant part of the overall process as it is useful for anticipating discontinuities and shocks in the external environment. In the context of scenario-based strategy, the criteria for quality scenarios reflect this emphasis. The quality requirements are *relevance* to the leadership seen as adult learners, *challenging* the existing assumptions, thus influencing them, and *plausibility* based on in-depth systemic analysis and research (see Chapters 5 and 6).

In the process of developing scenarios, there are two key opportunities that provide the richest learning. Firstly, when developing the scenario narratives inclusively with members of the organisation and researching how the key driving forces (KDFs) might unfold; and secondly, when using these scenario narratives to test decisions and policy for robustness (wind-tunnelling). Many large organisations such as Shell International and forward-looking governments such as the government of Singapore have developed and use sets of scenarios to stress-test strategies, policy and decisions for robustness. They have found that by doing this regularly, key dynamics can be selectively observed in the minds of decision makers. They are then able to recognise signs of change earlier than others who have not engaged in this learning. Early recognition as a result of quality scenario work enables decision makers to adapt rapidly and respond in time and in alignment with each other. This is precisely the intent of the founders of scenario-based strategy practice. The scenario method was developed by the founders of the field of scenario-based strategy as a method for shifting and aligning assumptions in the minds of decision makers about how their future contextual environment might unfold.

The Resilience Strategy Hierarchy (RSH)™ consists of foundations at the base as well as levels on which each subsequent level is built in the hierarchy. For example, capability assessment provides the basis for capacity building, which in turn provides the basis for AAR and so forth up the RSH. The instrument to gauge organisational resilience provides the frame of reference for assessing the current level for specific factors and items within the factors for a specific organisation.

5 THE CAPABILITY ASSESSMENT PROCESS

It is important that a capability assessment process takes place on a regular basis, preferably on a biannual basis. Another cornerstone is that a truthful assessment of current capability is made as the starting point. Capability is defined for the public service as strategy, leadership and service delivery (see CIL Questionnaire in Chapter 1). The CIL questionnaire consists of a series of questions for self-completion under the headings, Scenario-based Strategy, Servant Leadership and Service Delivery. It assumes a planning time horizon of 20–25 years for city government executive leadership. It also assumes a specific style of leadership which is in the service of followers. Service delivery and a service culture can be developed by organisational routines that regularly set goals and monitor performance against these goals. Once a capability has been assessed, the capacity that enables capability can be identified, prioritised and executed.

Capacity building priorities

Cross-cutting competencies, aka key strategy enabling processes, can be assessed with the checklist provided in Chapter 1. This checklist can be applied to an intact team or to individuals within a team. Ideally, all individuals, including middle managers and first-line supervisors, should have a PDP which forms part of their performance contract. Personal development will thus be automatically monitored and encouraged during the performance management process. Individual PDPs may be aggregated to identify a priority for an intact team or the organisation as a whole. Executive leadership must provide an example with their PDP to enable the organisation to follow. AAR, as well as subsequent levels in the RSH, depend on organisational capability. Once the organisation has established its foundations with a truthful capability assessment, capacity building adaptation and recovery investment in resilience can be extended to sustainable development, green growth and smart city levels in the RSH hierarchy.

Hierarchical levels in the RSH are Capability Assessment (C), Capacity Building (CC), Anticipation (An), Adaptation (Ad), Recovery (R), Sustainable Development (SDev), Green Growth (GG), Smart Cities (SC). See RSH figure.

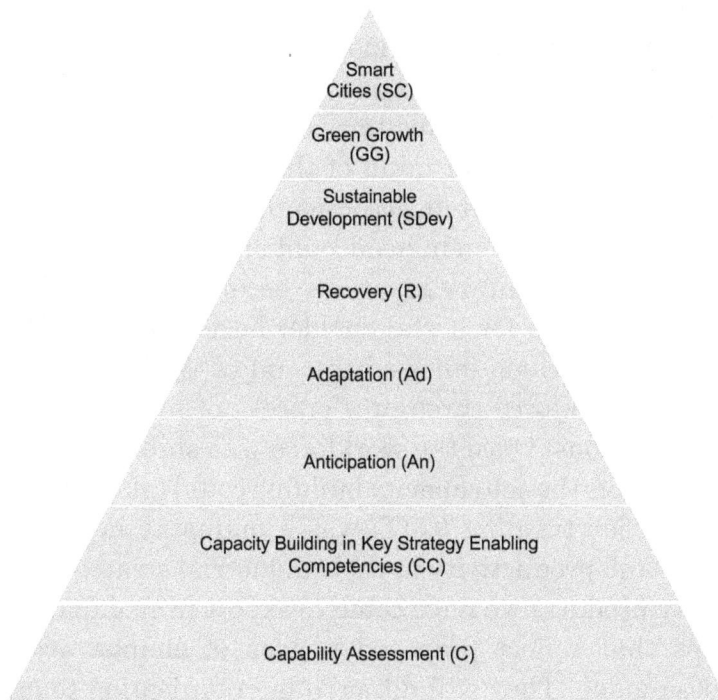

Figure 8.1: The Resilience Strategy Hierarchy (RSH)™ A process framework

Scoring the various levels of the hierarchy truthfully in the Resilience Hierarchy, using the RSH diagnostic instrument, will add precision to the process of establishing a gauge of resilience.

6 PRINCIPLES AND GUIDELINES ENDNOTES

Organisational infrastructure should be built such as a forum for sustainable change leadership, capability assessment, capacity building and the development and management of the resilience strategy. This forum should set aside a regular time, ideally one day per month, to engage the whole organisation in the management of change (see details for structuring this forum in Chapter 1). Membership of the forum should be selected to form a leadership coalition which will guide the organisational renewal process towards building greater organisational resilience. Two essential elements of successful change are to include the whole system in the forum and to create a sense of urgency (see CIL ORCA checklist www.cil.net/learning tools which is based on Kotter's and Endres' descriptions of why change efforts fail). Focusing on high leverage areas for successful organisational renewal involves taking care not to attempt too many priorities in any specific period of time. Raising expectations beyond what can be achieved in the short term is a common problem with managing change, as expectations can always outrun changes. Organisational renewal usually takes longer and requires more resources than the organisation plans and budgets for. Successful renewal and change is also dependent on *both* capability and readiness. Readiness is an intangible which depends on aspirations and the state of mind of the members of an organisation. Organisational renewal is often accompanied by the painful process of reducing headcount. Reduction in headcount should always be a last resort. Natural attrition and voluntary severance accompanied by a fair financial package are first options for a stakeholder-based process. The Japanese industrial revolution, which followed the end of WWII in 1945, consisted of stabilising the workforce through a process of lifetime employment in most large corporations. Once the workforce was stabilised, investment in capability through on-the-job capacity building could take place. Substantial investment in on job training (OJT) was a mainstay in the campaign to improve quality and productivity in their industrial strategy that produced the high quality products we have come to expect from Japan.

Roadmaps that reflect proposed phases of change are useful and always purpose-made. They will differ from organisation to organisation. Ownership of the roadmap by the organisation leaders is always more important than precision. The items included in the roadmap below are offered as examples that may be included in a roadmap for a particular organisational assignment.

7 DEVELOPING A ROADMAP – OPTIONS AND CHOICES

The roadmap example is a starting point from which to agree on useful components and choices on the sequence and priorities with key organisational stakeholders. Practitioners may use these suggestions as the basis for developing an organisation-specific roadmap.

Key ideas have been italicised. **Essential items are in bold**.
Define the organisational system boundaries. For instance, at local government level the municipality is part of provincial and central government. For the purpose of developing a resilience strategy and taking responsibility for the execution of its strategy, it should draw a boundary between itself and the other two levels of government. As a matter of principle, planning should not extend beyond that which is in the remit of the problem owners.

Build organisational infrastructure to sustain the strategic conversation and execute the resilience strategy.

Start by building a shared **desired results (aka vision)** and *at the same time* a **truthful description of the current reality**. Examine the current reality, specifically the following categories: *distinctive competence, assess capability, internal structures and processes that help and hinder formulating a resilience strategy, emerging requirements from stakeholders, other key concerns.*

Understanding the current reality should include **a capability assessment process and priorities for capacity building at individual and team levels**, including in **personal development planning (PDP) integrated with the performance management process**.

Initiate a scenario-based strategy making process with a set of first generation scenarios on a planning time horizon of 20–25 years. *The most consistent question that will emerge for any renewal initiative is the question "Why?" Scenario development answers this question by describing the conditions in the future environment that will confront and shape the organisation. There can also be a natural transition from scenario development and the formation of* **infrastructure for managing renewal by establishing a forum which contains links to the whole organisation.**

Priority areas for early examination may include

* the state of governance in the organisation;
* revenue management and areas of enhancement;
* the elimination of all wastage; and
* engagement in total quality processes to continuously improve the quality of services and product.

Create a shared list of all the sources of wastage in the organisation. This is an effective way of mobilising the workforce and widening ownership for eliminating the greatest sources of wastage first. Once an agreed list has been developed, the Pareto principle can be applied to this list by identifying 20% of the sources of wastage that cause 80% of the wastage. *Engage cross-functional teams in problem solving and action planning* for eliminating specific sources of wastage. Share these solutions in the change management forum and ensure these solutions are applied across the organisation. This engagement can be the start of continuous productivity and quality improvement. Pareto analysis is one of a number of tools for doing this efficiently in the service of raising productivity and the quality of products and services.

Identify the areas of highest leverage for organisational renewal, resilience and transformation (see Table 4.14 in Chapter 4). This prioritisation may be reviewed on an annual basis where no more than four to five priorities are chosen for each annual cycle. Initially, there may be more than four to five priorities, but practitioners should *resist the temptation to include all the priorities as this will dilute the efforts and result in disappointment.*

Create empowered, thinking people throughout the organisation through capacity building and engagement in various group-based processes for the improvement of productivity and quality.

Using a scenario-based strategy process to "Push" decision makers
Contradictions in policy become confusing over time, and sow the seeds of societal change, which eventually result in significant change and renewal. The scenario method has many different applications. Decision scenarios are often used by organisations to test decisions for robustness in future conditions reflected in scenario narratives. Normative scenarios on the other hand can be used to push decision makers in cities and towns in a particular direction. This is best done by describing two starkly different and opposing pathways (scenarios) into the future.

One scenario, call it "Fragile Cities and Towns" describes the depths of the abyss and poor policy choices that go with the descent into the abyss. Once leaders reflect on this abyss, they inevitably choose the opposite positive scenario called here "Antifragile Cities and Towns" which describes a resilient future for cities and towns and the policies that enable that future. The quality of scenarios is important as they form the basis of the strategic conversation. A quality conversation stands the best chance of shifting assumptions in the minds of decision makers, which is the purpose of scenarios. Quality scenarios must be relevant to the concerns of the decision makers. They should challenge existing thinking in order to open the minds of leaders to new and different possibilities. Finally, they must be plausible and stand up to scrutiny. Their plausibility requires deep systemic analysis and research. Scenarios are always specific to the organisation or sector using them. Scenario-based strategy should be a learning process, and the process design and facilitation should be structured to optimise learning. The scenarios described in this chapter have been developed as a starter to stimulate thinking and conversation. They are a starting point for a conversation within city and town government about developing a resilience strategy.

8 A CITY GOVERNMENT SCENARIO STARTER
The following example is offered to potential resilience practitioners as a frame of reference for normative scenarios which "push" participants towards a preferred scenario.

A focusing question to bound the scenario development process:
In an interconnected world a boundary must be set within which the scenarios play out. The purpose of the focusing question is setting this boundary. Scenarios can then be crafted to shed light on the focusing question.

A proposed focusing question:
Which forces in the contextual environment will have an impact on city and town government organisational policies and their resilience strategy? How will these forces enable or inhibit the developmental role of municipalities?

Selected KDFs to start a strategic conversation in cities and towns
Migration to cities and towns, youth dynamics, FDI attractiveness, local service delivery levels, Auditor General interventions, revenue management, government capability, education and employability, energy availability and costs, technology convergence (4IR), climate volatility, water security, food security, econo-political leadership, economic policy uncertainty, youth dynamics, trade union activity and structure, infrastructure build and maintenance, global/regional economic growth, National Health Insurance, HIV/AIDS and silicosis, the economic costs of health and wellness, SoA regional shifts in geopolitics, global dynamics in policy and economics.

9   BLACK SWANS AKA SCENARIO SPOILERS OR WILD CARDS

So-called "black swans"[9] represent the appearance and impact of unanticipated events, analogous to the unexpected appearance of a black swan when white swans are the norm. According to Taleb, they denote an unexpected event or dynamic outside of the general awareness of leaders and executives. He argues that black swans are, by definition, unknowable to most decision makers. Thoughtful decision makers who are accomplished scenario practitioners and who regularly spend time thinking on a 20- to 25-year planning time horizon may be able to identify dynamics that the average decision maker cannot observe or anticipate.

In 2018, van der Merwe[10] identified five unexpected events and dynamics that live outside the awareness of most organisation leaders. If they appeared, they might have a major impact on city government resilience.

---

9   Taleb, N.N. 2007. *The black swan*. London: Penguin.
10   Van der Merwe, L. 2018. City government resilience: Towards a diagnostic instrument. North West University (PhD Thesis).

Black swans, aka scenario spoilers or wild cards, are by definition low probability, high impact events, patterns over time or systemic structural dynamics. Two of these dynamics have already manifested since they were identified in 2018.

The initial list identified is as follows:

- a nuclear detonation on a major metropolis;
- a viral attack on humans similar to the Spanish influenza;
- a prolonged drought over four to five years;
- cyberattacks on ICT infrastructure; and
- an electromagnetic pulse (EMP) caused by a coronal pulse which damages the national electricity generation and distribution capability.[11]

For example, Berkshire Hathaway chief executive, Warren Buffet, stated at his company's 2002 AGM that in his view "a nuclear detonation, on a major metropolis, was now a virtual certainty".[12] Buffett is widely acknowledged by the investment community for his ability to anticipate the future. His view, in this case, may be based on the increasing availability of weapons-grade fissionable material used in nuclear power programmes. Many of these nuclear power programmes are being developed in unstable parts of the world such as Iran, North Korea and Pakistan.

Another example of a black swan, now widely accepted among futurists, is another viral attack on humans similar to the 1918 so-called Spanish flu epidemic. While the occurrence of this dynamic is seen as predetermined, the timing and severity of such a pandemic is unknown and unknowable. Hence, a resilience strategy should take the possibility of such a pandemic into account. The Spanish flu epidemic is estimated to have caused the loss of 20- to 50 million lives worldwide.[13] The SARS-Cov-2 virus which causes Covid-19 was anticipated in 2018 based on scenarios for a virus attack in a major life assurance company in Ireland in 2001. Nevertheless, the Covid-19 outbreak surprised most governments with its disruption across the globe in March 2020. Any organisation doing quality scenario-based planning would have anticipated that a viral attack was predetermined

---

[11]   Van der Merwe, 2018.

[12]   Buffett, W. 2002. *Nuclear attack "virtually a certainty"* https://www.google.co.za/search ?rlz=1C2NHXL_enZA697ZA697&source=hp&q=Berkshire+Hathaway+Chief+Executive %2C+Buffet+nuclear+detonation&oq=Berkshire+Hathaway+Chief+Executive%2C+ Buffet+nuclear+detonation&gs_l=psy-ab.12...3825.14098.0.16754.20.20.0.0.0.0.427 .3611.2-10j1j2.13.0....0...1.1.64.psy-ab..7.10.2553...33i160k1j33i21k1.G8fg_R-uYc0 Date of access: 21 June 2016.

[13]   Influenza pandemic. 2017. *Flu pandemic: Facts & summary.* www.history.com/topics/1918-flu-pandemic *Date of access: 28 August 2017.*

and included this dynamic in its scenarios. Covid-19 has had an impact across the globe and continues to cause major societal disruption and economic damage in countries where lockdown was used as the primary remedy. Much remains to be understood about how the virus spreads and why it manifests in such a wide variety of patterns in different populations worldwide. It appears that few governments have plans for addressing their unlocking and economic recovery. Anticipating these possibilities and examining *what we would do in the event of any of these dynamics* is what a resilience strategy should contain.

SD practitioners are aware that a systemic phenomenon such as climate change may reach thresholds after which the dynamic accelerates or declines rapidly and unexpectedly. Breached thresholds are reflected in the prolonged, unseasonal droughts in the Cape which threatened water security and exposed poor city government resilience strategies. Viral attacks and droughts may be seen as repetitive – the worst may yet lie ahead of us. According to Bohatch,[14] "We should not see the current water crisis in the Cape as a temporary phenomenon that will resolve in a year or two. It's a long-term problem." This conclusion may have implications for other cities in the SoA region. An example of breaching a threshold is reflected in the exponential increase in the number of cyclones in the United States of America.

Cyberattacks are increasing; Wikileaks is an example. Often when hackers break into a database containing confidential information or a financial system which makes payment and financial transfers, it is not in the interests of the owners of these databases to declare the break-in. Because of this, many cyberattacks are kept confidential and remain unreported.

A final example of a black swan event is an EMP or shock caused by an electron shower from the sun in our solar system. An EMP can inflict permanent damage on a country's electrical generation, transmission and distribution system. This would have an impact on cities and towns and their citizens. According to Storm Analysis Consultants in Duluth, Minnesota,[15] an "Electromagnetic shock (EMS) may be caused by a coronal mass ejection from the sun as occurred on 13 March 1989, which had a startling impact on Canada. Within 92 seconds, the resulting geomagnetic storm took down Quebec's electricity grid for nine hours". They posit

14   Bohatch, T. 2017. What's causing Cape Town's water crisis? *Groundup*: https://www. groundup.org.za/article/whats-causing-cape-towns-water-crisis Date of access: 15 November 2017.

15   *Economist*. 2017. The world if 2017: Electromagnetic Shock. http://worldif.economist.com/ article/13526/electromagnetic-shock Date of access: 20 September 2017.

that "it could have been worse,; had it hit the United States of America, the resulting geomagnetic storm would have destroyed a quarter of high voltage transformers". They add that "a prolonged interruption of electricity supply may be life-threatening, removing up to 90% of the population as a result of the prolonged absence of electricity". Storm Analysis Consultants maintain that "future geomagnetic storms are inevitable". They go on to point out that "[a] nuclear blast 40 km above the earth, over the USA, for instance, could also generate an EMS".[16]

If city government resilience is to be robust, there is a need for cities and towns to prepare for these eventualities and others in their resilience strategies.[17] The processes Van der Merwe pinpoints for anticipating disruptive shocks and surprises arriving from the contextual environment are scenario-based strategic planning and its complement SD modelling.

South Africa has been described as one of the most scenario-competent countries because of the ground-breaking contributions of scenario planners such as Clem Sunter, Adam Kahane, Frans Cronje and other scenario-based strategy practitioners. The founders of the scenario-based strategy field, Pierre Wack, Ted Newland, Arie de Geus, Peter Schwartz and others from Shell Group planning, designed scenario-based strategy as a process for influencing the assumptions in the minds of decision makers, thus influencing decision making itself. Besides the impact of Covid-19, we are currently facing an existential threat to humanity from global climate volatility. Neurobiologist Whybrow argues that unless we retune the human mind to adopt sustainable policies, the human population as we know it may not survive.[18] Scenario-based strategy can assist organisational decision makers in this struggle for sustainable policies precisely because it targets shifting the assumptions in the minds of decision makers.

Scenarios, when used in a normative way push decision makers towards a preferred future. This approach played an important role in South Africa, preparing political leaders for the transition to a democracy in 1994. The "high road/low road" scenarios were developed by Clem Sunter in Anglo American Corporation. These scenarios were a by-product of the Future of Gold scenarios which were facilitated by Pierre Wack, founder of the method. In the 1980s and '90s, Sunter's scenarios enabled policymakers to avoid the low road and other unsustainable populist policies often adopted by post-colonial societies in Africa. The high road/low road scenarios, as

---

[16]   *Economist*, 2017.

[17]   Van der Merwe, 2018.

[18]   Whybrow, P.C. 2015. *The well-tuned brain: Neuroscience and the life well-lived.* London: Norton.

well as other corporate and public scenario development in that time frame, assisted in the relatively smooth transition to democracy in South Africa in 1994.

The rise of the importance of cities and towns in a nation-state provides a critical vehicle for ensuring resilience and momentum for national resilience. One of the keys to quality scenario practice is to avoid omitting key dynamics in the scenario narratives. Rigorous analysis can help avoid this (see Rigour Matrix Table 8.1). The categories described below help by enabling analysts to research across an inclusive range of categories which may contain key driving forces.

10 CATEGORIES WITHIN WHICH KEY DRIVING FORCES MAY BE UNCOVERED

Politics, economics, regulation, society, technology, ecology, history (PERSTEH)

Various acronyms exist among practitioners to reflect such categories. *The rule of thumb is to be inclusive.* The first step in scenario development is to identify the natural strategic agenda reflected in the shared concerns among leaders in a particular organisation or sector. This is usually done through one-on-one conversations with organisational leaders. The forces which are reflected in this natural strategic agenda are listed and ranked in a ranking space (see Figure 8.2). This ranking is always an interesting, stimulating strategic conversation amongst organisational leaders as they can engage and test their assumptions and explore other leaders' assumptions. The key to enabling learning in this process is a skilful, learning conversation.[19]

---

[19] Van der Merwe, L., Chermack, T.J., Kulikowich, J. & Yang, B. 2007. Strategic conversation quality and engagement: Assessment of a new measure. *International Journal of Training and Development,* 11(3):214–221.

HIGH

RELATIVE UNCERTAINTY

National Health Insurance

Global dynamics – politics & economics

Infrastructure Build & Maintenance

Economic Policy Uncertainty

Econo-Political Leadership

Government Capability

Revenue Management

Climate volatility

SoA regional shifts, Geo-politics

Global/Regional economic growth

Trade Union Activity & Structure

Education & Employability

Foreign Direct Investment

Water Security

Auditor General Intervention

HIV/AIDS & Silicosis – economic costs, health & wellness

Youth Dynamics

Food Security

Technology convergence

Local service delivery levels

Eskom energy availability & costs

Migration into cities & towns

LOW

RELATIVE IMPACT

HIGH

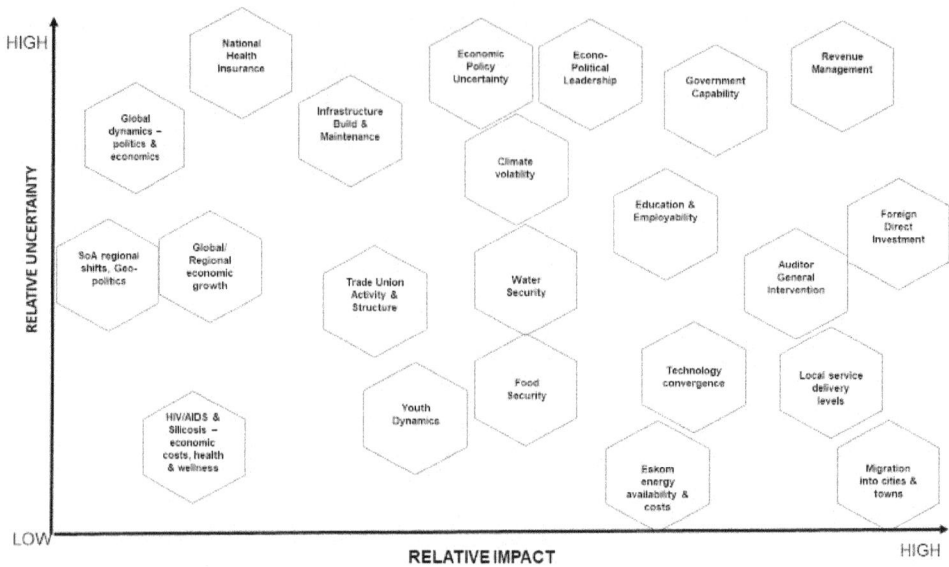

Figure 8.2: Ranking of Key Driving Forces
Note: The KDFs in this ranking space exclude so-called black swans also known as scenario spoilers or wild cards.

In the ranking space, two dimensions are used to rank KDFs – **relative impact** on city and town organisational strategy and **relative uncertainty** about how a specific KDF will play out over the scenario period. Two categories of KDFs emerge from this ranking conversation, namely "predetermined elements" (high impact, high certainty) and key uncertainties (high impact, high uncertainty). These KDFs form the basis for developing scenario narratives. Proto-scenarios listed are a first attempt to provide a frame of reference to develop useful narratives for each scenario.

Many emerging nations seems to be caught on the horns of a specific dilemma. One horn is where individual choice and economic freedom of choice is the energy that drives economic growth, wealth creation, job creation and development. Klaus Schwab calls this inclusive type of capitalism "stakeholder capitalism" as opposed to shareholder capitalism which maximises short-term returns to shareholders. The other horn of the dilemma is where the state owns the means of production and attempts to direct, centrally, through control and coercion, aka socialism and communism. In post-Covid-19 recovery, job creation and economic recovery are the dominant priorities.

In the face of vacillating leadership, the temptation is to address a little of each side of the dilemma. Lopsided thinking favours one horn of a dilemma over the other. Lopsided thinking and action often result from the search for quick fixes and simplistic thinking and populist pressures for specific solutions. In the SoA municipalities as well as the provincial and central government, lopsided thinking has been allowed to emerge, called the National Democratic Revolution (NDR). The NDR is seen by the governing alliance as their historical mission. NDR has, as its goal, socialism first followed by communism within a developmental state.

Evidence that freedom of economic choice is associated with creating wealth and jobs is documented in Chapter 4. The relationship between economic freedom of choice, as defined by the THF, and wealth creation is also set out and is self-explanatory. The Canadian Fraser Institute has studied the conditions under which the bottom 10% of income earners fares best, concluding that this takes place under conditions of economic freedom.

Normative scenarios reflect policy choices in the face of specific dynamics in a scenario called "Antifragile Cities and Towns". Antifragile cities and towns improve resilience under adverse conditions because of policies that enable freedom of economic choice. Policy choices that centrally control economic decisions and the means of production are reflected in the other scenario called "Fragile Cities and Towns". When faced with these polar opposites, rational decision makers naturally gravitate towards the positive Antifragile Cities and Towns scenario and resist policies that create a "Fragile Cities and Towns" scenario.

Antifragile Cities and Towns (strengthen resilience in the face of adversity), and **Fragile Cities and Towns (descending into an un-resilient death spiral)**, represent the two distinctive paths that policy choices may enable over the next 20- to 25 years. These paths are reflected in two proto-scenarios for cities and town as a starting point for strategic conversation.

The concept of "antifragile" properties was first described by Taleb in antifragile things that gain from disorder.[20] He describes antifragility as the property where resilience increases in the face of disruption. He uses the analogy of getting fit through rigorous, painful exercise. The pain or stiffness experienced after exercise is tissue damage to muscles. After initial damage, muscle tissues become stronger through exercise, thus raising fitness. Applying the concept of antifragility to cities and towns describes a response to disruptions affecting them by becoming more resilient. Rigorous application of the RSH described above is aimed at enabling this property. Fragile cities and towns, on the other hand, have a lower capability to withstand disruptions and descend into non-resilience.

---

[20]   Taleb, N.N. 2012. *Antifragile*. New York, NY: Random House.

The RSH naturally leads to antifragile green growth and smart cities. Fragile cities and towns are on a downward trend as a result of poor policy choices, undergoing steady deterioration in the face of KDFs and disruptions.

11 PROTO-SCENARIOS – CITIES AND TOWNS 2020–2040
11.1 Antifragile cities and towns
THE CENTRAL THEME IN THIS SCENARIO: Freedom of choice together with local empowerment is enabled by the developmental application of converging technologies (4IR) which positively engage and enable innovation, economic growth and job creation. Antifragile cities and towns become more resilient and robust in the face of external disruptive forces and are the "flywheels" and build momentum for recovery and national resilience through national development.

KDFs in proto-scenarios
- Migration to cities and towns (rural areas and neighbouring states in the SoA region);
- Young people under the age of 24 years are a significant proportion (48%) of these migratory flows;
- National energy supply unreliable and carbon-dense;
- Relaxation of regulations enable sustainable energy investments;
- FDI attractiveness and flows increase into cities and semi-autonomous SEZs based on the Chinese example;
- City-to-city alliance partnerships, technology exchange and investments;
- FDI growth increases and diversifies;
- Technology convergence (4IR) and disruptions are engaged positively to enhance resilience and build smart cities;
- Revenue management is improved and wastage is reduced;
- Higher education institutions support and partner with city government;
- Auditor General reports, clean audits and Section 139 interventions show a positive trend;
- Service delivery protests in decline;
- Climate volatility threatens water security;
- Support for farming improves food security and food exports.

11.2 Fragile cities and towns
THE CENTRAL THEME IN THIS SCENARIO: Central control, coercion and invasion of personal space are enabled by technology convergence

which creates a toxic, unsustainable co-dependence between citizens and central government; poor policy choices result in economic decline, great inequality, poverty and social instability.

KDFs in proto-scenarios
- Massive migration to cities and towns;
- Young people under the age of 24 years are a significant proportion (48%) of these migratory flows;
- National government dynamics affect provincial and municipal government levels;
- The energy supply unreliable and carbon-dense;
- A total blackout of Eskom requiring a "black start", triggers a number of unintended and unanticipated consequences;
- Expropriation without compensation (EWC) prioritises urban properties with the espoused intent of absorbing the flow of people into urban areas and restitution goals;
- Financial institutions hold property owners affected by EWC accountable for repayment of outstanding debt ;
- Internal factional battles in central and provincial government distract attention from national interests and global competitiveness, and dealing with resilience challenges such as migration, climate volatility, water and food security;
- Auditor General Section 139 interventions increase and become more punitive – decline in the number of clean audits continues leading to collapse in specific municipalities;
- Economic policy uncertainty and ambiguity persists, discouraging investment;
- Technology convergence and disruptions are engaged negatively to control, coerce and invade personal space;
- FDIs decline;
- Borrowings continue to increase to an unsustainable level, threatening the sovereignty;
- A drop in the profitability of Japanese and European Nissan and Renault motor manufacturers impacts local manufacturing. Global competitors in China, India and Thailand fill the void left by local manufacturer departures;
- State-owned enterprises falter and default on debt which draws government-guaranteed debt into the vortex of fragility;
- Ratings downgrade followed by mandatory institutional disinvestment;
- Financial capital and human capital outflows increase;
- Government capability further declines;

- Higher education and employability stagnates;
- Corruption erodes competitiveness and investor confidence;
- Organised labour resists market-based policy and principles of economic freedom of choice;
- Equality of outcome remains the national socioeconomic policy;
- Service delivery protests increase;
- Climate volatility increases the probability of a prolonged drought;
- Water insecurity;
- Food insecurity;
- National Health Insurance launched in spite of insufficient funding;
- Payment of social grants delayed by lack of funds at the national level and dependants panic and mobilise against the government at local and national levels;
- SEZs are compromised and fail to attract FDI to fund manufacturing-for-export markets;
- The World Bank is requested to deal with the liquidity crisis because of its magnitude.;
- Examples of economic policy which create sustainable economic growth such as Vietnam, Costa Rica and others remain ignored by the national government in preference to learning from failed economies such as Zimbabwe and Venezuela.

11.3 Antifragile cities
Policy options:
- Chinese SEZ rules applied including the policy initiated by President Deng Xiaoping of "one country two systems" and socialism with a Chinese character
- A national plan of "socialism with African characteristics" in alignment with the Chinese economic system is initiated locally in selected city and town levels. This resolution enables complete economic freedom to attract FDI for manufacturing and exports based on market-based economic policies in selected zones. One country two systems policies enable economic development and job creation without eroding core Alliance policy contained in the NDR;
- Cities and large regional towns as well as selected coastal areas identified as SEZs in line with Chinese SEZ policy guidelines;
- Revenue management and enhancement to secure efficient collection and budgets for the provision of services;
- Compulsory routine capability assessment processes followed by capacity building and investment in OJT;
- Leadership takes a stand on enabling policies based on the most

reliable surveys of citizens' priorities;
- Rigorous planning and organisational planning routines enable continuous improvement in the quality of service delivery;
- OJT based on PDP rebuilds organisational capability;
- Capacity building focused on key resilience strategy enabling processes (see Chapter 1 Figure 1.2);
- Resilient cities and towns act as economic flywheels and reinforce national resilience;
- Semi-autonomous SEZ enclaves create replicable pockets of sustainable economic growth and wealth;
- Appropriate HIV/AIDS and silicosis policies receive adequate medical support arresting the spread of the virus and compensating sufferers;
- A district-based development model to aggregate scarce competencies and enhance municipal service delivery;
- Metros and rights-based initiatives in specific communities such as unemployed urban youth adopt the Sustainable Community Investment Programme (SCIP) model and institutional infrastructure to sustain its economic benefits.

Scenario narratives must be internally consistent with all the KDFs reflected in both scenarios. The best method for checking this is by using the Rigour Matrix Table. This matrix provides details which may be woven into scenario narratives.

Table 8.1: Scenario KDF Rigour Matrix. A Starter

Key driving force (KDFs)	Antifragile cities and towns	Fragile cities and towns
Migration to cities and towns	Massive migration to cities and towns	Massive migration to cities and towns
Youth dynamics	48% of the population younger than 24 years of age	48% of the population younger than 24 years of age
Local service delivery levels	Quality and costs of local services continually improve	Quality and costs of local services continually decline
Foreign direct investment (FDI)	Grows and is diversified	Declines as a result of ambiguous national policies
Auditor General (AG) interventions	AG Section 139 support more effective. Clean audits increase	AG ignored. Clean audits continue their decline
Revenue management	Collection efficiency, enhancement and management continually improve	Declines affecting budgets available

Key driving force (KDFs)	Antifragile cities and towns	Fragile cities and towns
Government capability	Improves continually with OJT and capacity building	Absent among deployed and continues to decline
Education and employability	Partnerships with leading schools and higher educational institutions to build appropriate competencies and key staff positions	Failure to prepare staff with appropriate competencies for digital economy
Technology convergence (4IR)	Engaged to monitor and continually improve resilience	Engaged to reinforce central control and invasion of personal space
Energy availability and costs	Rapid shift to decarbonise and engage low-cost renewable energy sources together with net metering to enable consumers to add surplus energy to the grid	Continued wastage on vanity installations, corruption, political interference and poor management
Climate volatility	Volatility rising steadily	Volatility rising steadily
Water security	Availability and quality continuously improves with timely investment in and maintenance of infrastructure	Decline of availability and quality with costly disruptions
Food security	Support for farming grows with inclusive job creation and protection of property rights and reduction in farm murders	Neglect and fragmentation create a decline in investment and productivity, degenerating into subsistence farming
Economic policy uncertainty	One country two systems enables socialism with African characteristics	Vacillation, conflict and compromise discourage investment
Special economic zones (SEZs)	Semi-autonomous SEZs based on the Chinese model partner suitable cities and towns to attract FDI and establish manufacturing-for-export markets in a "socialism with African characteristics" frame of reference	SEZs are compromised and linked to centralist ideology and political interference. They fail to attract FDI and promote sustainable economic development and optimise job- and wealth creation
Econo-political leadership as taking a stand	Leaders take an aligned stand against all wastage, combating corruption and crime, creating efficient government services that build trust and social capital	Appeasement of factions and unproductive consensus-seeking. Lack of follow-through erodes confidence in leaders and trust in government

Key driving force (KDFs)	Antifragile cities and towns	Fragile cities and towns
Infrastructure build and maintenance	Timely investment in infrastructure avoids costly emergency maintenance	Diversion of infrastructure funds to short-term vanity projects and public service salaries
Trade union activity and structure	Organised labour partners with leaders to achieve aspirations in the Constitution, create decent jobs, healthcare and relevant education	Ideological inflexibility erodes trust between management and labour
HIV/AIDS & silicosis – economic costs, health & wellness	Social costs of HIV/AIDS and silicosis are met by appropriate private and government healthcare and compensation	Neglect, denial and obfuscation of responsibility for health and wellness institutions
Global and regional economic growth	SoA region enabled by city and town resilience compensates for global economic volatility	Lack of resilience limits the ability to adapt to global and regional volatility
SoA regional geopolitics	One country two systems in SA is emulated by SoA economies creating regional synergies	Influence of failed or corrupt economies in the SoA region forces SoA economies towards the lowest common denominator
Global dynamics – political & economics	The SoA example builds sustainable new dawn in Africa as a whole	SoA region descends into beggar status, losing its sovereignty by reliance on loans to subsidise wastage and bloated public service

Structuring Special Economic Zones (SEZs) to Resolve a Critical Policy Dilemma – Socialism with African Characteristics

The SA socioeconomic policy seems to be impaled on the horns of a dilemma between market-based economic policy and a centrally directed command economy. The productive resolution of dilemmas is sustainable when the resolution takes place by resolving one extreme of the dilemma *through* the other extreme. A constitutional democracy is a resolution of the dilemma between national alignment with desired results (vision) and the engagement of citizens. Alignment is enabled by a prior agreement of the national desired results (vision) determined by citizens, encoded in a Constitution which provides, in turn, the basis for the rule of law and accountability. Accountable and capable government, including local government, provides quality services to citizens. By serving the Constitution leaders, politicians serve citizens and national interests. SEZs clustered within resilient cities and towns, and an official policy of one county two socioeconomic systems would enable the synergies for sustainable economic development hubs and support the developmental state.

Resilient cities and towns, combined with SEZs could provide economic and societal flywheels for sustainable development. Cities and towns are naturally more productive as a result of the proximity of resources and intensified human interaction which enables innovation and the means of production. Most nation states started as city-states. As economic growth in cities and towns, also enabled by inward migration and technology convergence, surges ahead of the national economies they are embedded in, resilient cities and towns could become semi-autonomous economic flywheels that sustain growth in a developmental state.

The final word is that scenarios are meant to be a stimulus for a strategic conversation which enables learning. Hopefully new ideas are generated in this conversation, and assumptions stretched and influenced. A single new idea which is followed by action makes the engagement useful and justified. A colleague once said about the future, rather be approximately right than precisely wrong.

BIBLIOGRAPHY AND RESOURCES FOR PRACTITIONERS

Acemoglu, D. & Robinson, J.A. 2012. *Why nations fail.* New York, NY: Crown Business.

Ackoff, R.L. 1994. Systems thinking and thinking systems. *Systems Dynamics Review,* 10(23):175–188.

Ackoff, R.L. 2016. A lifetime of systems thinking. *Systems Thinker.* https://thesystemsthinker.com/a-lifetime-of-systems-thinking Date of access: 12 June 2017.

Acron, J. & Auracombe, C.J. 2016. A critical analysis of the approach to Local Economic Development (LED) in South Africa. *Administratio Publica,* 24(3):141–165.

Adelman, C. 1993. Kurt Lewin and the origins of action research. *Educational Action Research,* 1(1):7–24, https://doi.org/10.1080/0965079930010102 Date of access: 23 February 2020

Alcock, G.G. 2016. *Kasinomics: African informal economies and the people who inhabit them.* Johannesburg: TMP.

Putnam, R. 1993. *Making democracy work: Civic traditions in modern Italy.* Princeton, NJ: Princeton University Press.

Argyris, C. & Schon, D.A. 1996. *Organizational learning II: Theory, method, and practice.* New York: McGraw Hill.

Argyris, C. 1982. *Reasoning, learning and action individual and organisational.* San Francisco, CA: Jossey-Bass.

Argyris, C. 1992. *On organisation learning.* Cambridge, MA: Blackwell.

Argyris, C. 1993. *Knowledge for action: A guide for overcoming barriers to organisational change.* San Francisco, MA: Jossey-Bass.

Auditor General of South Africa (AG). 2016. *Consolidated General Report on Local Government Audit Outcomes, 2015/16.* Pretoria.

Australian Public Service Commission (APSC). 2017a. *Organisational capability.* http://www.apsc.gov.au/about-the-apsc/parliamentary/state-of-the-service/state-of-the-service-2010/chapter-10-organisational-capability Date of access: 19 August 2017.

Australian Public Service Commission (APSC). 2017b. *Capability assessment.* http://www.apsc.gov.au/priorities/capability-reviews Date of access: 21 September 2017.

Barber, M. 2015. *How to run a government so that citizens benefit and taxpayers don't go crazy.* London: Penguin Random House.

Barber, M., Rodrigues, N. & Artis, E. 2016. *Deliverology in practice.* London: Sage.

Bartlett, J. 2017. Return of the city-state. https://aeon.co/essays/the-end-of-a-world-of-nation-states-may-be-upon-us Date of access: 15 September 2017.

Bass, B.M. & Stogdill, R.M. 1990. *Handbook of leadership: Theory, research and management applications.* 3rd ed. New York, NY: Free Press.

Beckhard, R. & Harris, R.T. 1987. *Organisational transitions: Managing complex change.* 2nd ed. Reading, MA: Adison Wesley.

Bennis, W.G. 1969. *Organisational development: Its nature, origins and prospects.* Reading, MA: Addison Wesley.

Bloomberg Philanthropies. 2014. *Michael Bloomberg Sustainable Cities.* https://www.bloomberg.org/program/environment/sustainable-cities Date of access: 30 March 2016.

Bohatch, T. 2017. What's causing Cape Town's water crisis? *Groundup*: https://www.groundup.org.za/article/whats-causing-cape-towns-water-crisis Date of access: 15 November 2017.

Bohm, D. 1989. *Quantum theory.* London: Dover Publications.

Bohm, D. 2002. *Wholeness and the implicate order.* London: Routledge.

Bohm, D. 2004. *On dialogue.* London: Routledge.

Bolman, L.G. & Deal, T.E. 1997. *Reframing organizations. Artistry, choice and leadership.,* San Francisco, CA: Jossey-Bass.

Bossidy, L., Charan, R. & Burck, C. 2002. *Execution the discipline of getting things done.* New York: Crown Business.

Braes, B. & Brooks, D. 2010. Organisational resilience: A propositional study to understand and identify essential concepts. Paper delivered at the Australia Security and Intelligence Conference organised by Edith Cowan University.

Bragdon, J.H. 2016. *Companies that mimic life: Leaders of emerging corporate renaissance.* London: Greenleaf Publishing.

Brand, S. 1994. *How buildings learn.* New York, NY: Viking.

Brand, S. 2017a. 4 Environmental heresies. TED Talk. https://www.ted.com/talks/stewart_brand_proclais_4_environm Date of access: 4 July 2017.

Brand, S. 2017b. What squatter cities can teach us/TED Talk/TED.com. Https://www.ted.com/talks/stewart_brand_on_squatter_cities Date of access: 8 August 2017.

Braungart, M. & McDonough, W. 2002. *Cradle to cradle: Remaking the way we make things.* London: North Point Press.

Bryman, A. 2012. *Social research methods*. 4th ed. Oxford, UK: Oxford University Press.

Buffett, W. 2002. *Nuclear attack "virtually a certainty"* https://www.google.co.za/search?rlz=1C2NHXL_enZA697ZA697&source=hp&q=Berkshire+Hathaway+Chief+Executive%2C+Buffet+nuclear+detonation&oq=Berkshire+Hathaway+Chief+Executive%2C+Buffet+nuclear+detonation&gs_l=psy-ab.12...3825.14098.0.16754.20.20.0.0.0.0.427.3611.2-10j1j2.13.0....0...1.1.64.psy-ab..7.10.2553...33i160k1j33i21k1. G8fg_R-uYc0 Date of access: 21 June 2016.

Burt, G. & Van der Heijden, K. 2002. Reframing industry boundaries for structural advantage: The role of scenario planning. In G. Ringland (Ed.), *Scenarios in business*. New York: John Wiley, pp. 223–232.

Burt, G. & Van der Heijden, K. 2003. First steps: Towards purposeful activities in scenario thinking and future studies. *Futures 35*(10), 1011–1026.

Business dictionary. 2017. http://www.businessdictionary.com Date of access: 1 August 2017.

Capra, F. & Luisi, P.L. 2016. *The systems view of life*. Cambridge, UK: Cambridge University Press.

Center for Strategic and International Studies (CSIS). 2008. Commission on Cybersecurity for the 44th Presidency. Washington, DC: Centre for Strategic International Studies.

Centre for Development and Enterprise (CDE). 2017. *Youth unemployment: An agenda for action – No country for young people*. Johannesburg: CDE.

Centre for Innovative Leadership (CIL). 1991. *Overview of the life of Ludwig von Bertalanffy: Father of general systems theory*. Issued as part of CIL Executive Education in Systems Thinking for Sustainable Leadership and Transformation (STSLT). http://CIL.net Date of access: 4 August 2017.

Centre for Innovative Leadership (CIL). 1992. *Developing a Strategy, Leadership and Engagement (SLE) Forum*. (Unpublished).

Centre for Innovative Leadership (CIL). 1993. *Manual for executive education: Systems Thinking for Sustainable Leadership and Transformation (STSLT)*. http://www.cil.net Date of access: 13 February 2017.

Centre for Innovative Leadership (CIL). 1995. *Strategic management: Introduction to scenario thinking public workshop*. Rivonia, South Africa: The Centre for Innovative Leadership.

Centre for Innovative Leadership (CIL). 1998. Manuals for managing accountability and performance installation. Shell Europe Oil Products (SEOP). (Unpublished).

Centre for Innovative Leadership (CIL). 2000. United Nations Development Programme (UNDP) Southern Africa Capacity-building initiative (SACI) CIL Competency Profile (Unpublished).

Centre for Innovative Leadership (CIL). 2009. Scenario-based strategy report and capacity building in Eskom. (Unpublished).

Centre for Innovative Leadership (CIL). 2014. The association between organisational trust and conversation quality and engagement for competent leadership. (Unpublished).

Chermack, T.J. 2005. Studying scenario planning: Theory, research suggestions and hypotheses. *Technological Forecasting and Social Change, 72*(1): 59–73.

Chermack, T.J. 2011. *Scenario planning in organisations*. San Francisco, CA: Berrett-Koehler.

Chermack, T.J. & Lynham, S.A. 2002. Definitions and outcome variables of scenario planning. *Human Resource Development Review, 1*(3):366–383.

Chermack, T.J. & Van der Merwe, L. 2003. The role of constructivist learning in scenario planning. *Futures,* 35:445–460.

Chipangura, P., Van Niekerk, D. & Van der Waldt, G. 2017. Disaster risk policy problem framing: insights from societal perceptions in Zimbabwe. *International Journal of Disaster Risk Reduction.* http://dx.doi.org/10.1016/j.ijdrr.2017.02.012 Date of access: 3 March 2017.

Clifton, J. 2011. *The coming job wars*. New York, NY: Gallup Press.

Collyns, N. 2006. In conversation with Napier Collyns and the author.

Concise Oxford Dictionary. 1982. 7th ed. Oxford: Oxford University Press.

Constitution **see** South Africa.

Cronje, F. 2014. *A time traveller's guide to South Africa to our next ten years*. Cape Town: Tafelberg.

Cronje, F. 2017. *A time traveller's guide to South Africa in 2030*. Cape Town: Tafelberg.

Cummings, T.G. & Worley, C.G. 2001. *Organisation development and change*. 6th ed. Cincinnati: South-western College Publishing.

Dallas, M.G. 2014. *What are fractals and why should I care?* https://georgemdallas.wordpress.com/2014/.../what-are-fractals-and-why-should-i-care Date of access: 10 July 2017.

Danoudi, S. 2012. Resilience: A bridging concept or a dead end? *Planning Theory and Practice, 13*(2):229–333.

Davidson, M. 1983. *Uncommon sense: The life and thought of Ludwig von Bertalanffy father of general system theory.* Los Angeles, CA: Tarcher.

De Geus, A. 1988. Planning as learning. *Harvard Business Review,* March–April: 2–6.

De Geus, A. 1997. *The living company.* Boston, MA: Harvard Business School Press.

De Weijer, F. 2013. *Resilience: A Trojan horse for a new way of thinking?* (Discussion Paper 139). European Centre for Development Policy Management. https://ecdpm.org/wp-content/uploads/2013/10/DP-139-Resilience-Trojan-Horse-New-Way-of-Thinking-2013.pdf Date of access: 20 November 2015.

Deming, W.E. 1986. *Out of the crisis.* Cambridge, MA: MIT Press.

Denyer, D. 2017. *Organisational resilience: A summary of academic evidence, business insights, and new thinking.* BSI America and Cranfield School of Management. https://www.bsigroup.com/en-US/Our-services/.../organizational-resilience-research/ Date of access: 22 September 2017.

Dowson, T.A. 1992. *Rock engravings of Southern Africa.* Johannesburg: Witwatersrand University Press.

Drucker, P.F. 1994. *The new realities: In government and politics / In economics and business / in society and worldview.* New York, NY: Harper Business.

Du Pisani, Ed. 2017. *Smuts, van boerseun na wêreldverhoog.* Pretoria: Protea Boekhuis.

Duit, A. 2015. Resilience thinking: Lessons for public administration. *Public Administration*, 1–17. doi:101111/padm.12182

Economic Commission for Africa (ECA). 2014. *Dynamic industrial policy in Africa.* http://www.uneca.org/eca/ Date of access: 4 June 2017.

Economist. 2017. The world if 2017: Electromagnetic Shock. http://worldif.economist.com/article/13526/electromagnetic-shock Date of access: 20 September 2017.

Edmondson, A. & Reynolds, S.S. 2016. *Smart cities? It takes more than a village.* https://www.linkedin.com/pulse/smart-cities-takes-more-than-village-amy-c- Date of access: 20 January 2017.

Endres, J. 2005. *Change management in cities: An international comparison.* Norderstadt: Books on Demand GmbH.

European Parliamentary Research Service (EPRS). 2014a. *Understand waste management.* www.europarl.europa.eu/atyourservice/en/20150201PVL00031 Date of access: 13 September 2017.

European Parliamentary Research Service (EPRS). 2014b. *Understanding waste streams.* Briefing European Parliament. www.

europarl.europa.eu/atyourservice/en/ 20150201PVL00031 Date of access: 14 September 2017.

Eoyang, G. 2001. *Stretching and Folding*. Boston: Systems Thinker Vol 18.

Fabricius, P. 2017. *Peering into a murky crystal ball: Where will Africa be in 2030?* https://issafrica.org/iss-today/peering-into-a-murky-crystal-ball-where-will-africa-be-in-2030?ct= (FFD_February_2017) Date of access: 21 March 2017.

Fioramonti, L. 2015. Water shortages about to put load-shedding in the dark. *Business Day*. http://www.bdlive.co.za/opinion/2015/05/05/water-shortages-about-to-put-load-shedding-in-the-dark Date of access: 5 May 2015.

Flannery, T. 2005. *The weather makers: How man is changing the weather and what that means for life on earth*. New York, NY: Atlantic Monthly Press.

Foreign Policy in Focus. 2008. FPIF Policy Report: The global water crisis and the coming battle for the right to water, *In:* Barlow, M. *Blue Covenant*.

Forrester, J.W. 1961. *Industrial dynamics*. Cambridge, MA: MIT Press.

Forrester, J.W. 1969. *Urban dynamics*. Cambridge, MA: MIT Press.

Forrester, J.W. 1989. *The beginning of systems dynamics*. Cambridge, MA: Sloan School of Management/MIT Press.

Forrester, J.W. 1994. *Learning through systems dynamics as preparation for the 21st century*. Cambridge, MA: Sloan School of Management/ MIT Press.

Foster, K.A. 2007. *A case study approach to understanding regional resilience* (Working paper 2007-08). Berkeley, CA: Institute of Urban and Regional Development, University of California

French, W.L. & Bell, C.H. Jr., 1984. *Organisation development*. 3rd ed. Prentice Hall.

Friedman, E.H. 1985. *Generation to generation: Family process in church and synagogue*. New York, NY: Guildford Press.

Friedman, E.H. 1986. Rabbi, Edwin Friedman [professional conversation]. Spiritual Counselling practise, Bethesda, MD.

Friedman, M. 1980. *Free to choose*. Chicago, IL: Harcourt.

Friedman, M. 2017. *Milton Friedman quotes*. https://www.goodreads.com/author/quotes/5001.Milton_Friedman Date of access: 30 August 2017.

Fukuyama, F. 2011a. *The origins of political order: From pre-human times to the French Revolution*. New York, NY: FSG.

Fukuyama, F. 2011b. *Political order and political decay: From the Industrial Revolution to the globalisation of democracy.* New York, NY: FSG.

Fuller, B. 2017. Buckminster Fuller Institute. www.bfi.org Date of access:16 September 2017.

Geerts, S. 2014. A conceptualization and analysis of the community investment programme with reference to South Africa case studies: Towards a new model. University of South Africa (PhD Thesis).

Georgantzas, N.C. & Acar, W. 1995. *Scenario-driven planning: Learning to manage strategic uncertainty.* Westport, CT: Quorum

Gibson, C.A. & Tarrant, M. 2010. A "conceptual models" approach to organisational resilience. *Australian Journal of Emergency Management, 25*(2):10–15.

Glaeser, E. 2011. *Triumph of the city.* New York, NY: Penguin Press.

Gleick, J. 1988. *Chaos: Making a new science.* New York, NY: Penguin Books.

Glieck, P.H. 2008. *Water conflict chronology*, Pacific Institute for Studies in Development, Environment, and Security.

Global Metro Monitor Brookings. 2018. *Global Metro Monitor 2018* Date of Access: 12 January 2019. https://www.brookings.edu/research/global-metro-monitor-2018/

Global Reporting Initiative (GRI). 2013. *Global Reporting Initiative: G4 Sustainability Reporting Guidelines.* Amsterdam: Global Reporting Initiative.

Good Governance Africa (GGA). 2016. *Government Performance Index.* Johannesburg: GGA.

Good Governance Africa (GGA). 2017. The presidential issue. *The Journal of Good Governance,* (42), July–September. https://gga.org/ Date of access: 10 November 2017.

Greenleaf, R.K. 1964. Greenleaf Centre for Servant Leadership. https://www.greenleaf.org/ Date of access: 7 July 2017.

Greenleaf, R.K. 2002. *Servant leadership: A journey into the nature of legitimate power and greatness.* New York, NY: Paulist Press.

Greffrath, W. & Van der Waldt, G. 2016. Section 139 Interventions in South African local government, 1994-2015. *New Contree,* (75):135–160.

Gunderson, L.H. & Holling, C.S. 2002. *Panarchy: Understanding transformations in human and natural systems.* Washington, DC: Island Press.

Habitat3. 2016a. *The new urban agenda: Key commitments.* https://habitat3.org/the-new-urban-agenda/Florencia Soto

Nino2016-10-26T16:44:36+00:00October 20th, 2016 | Cities, News Date of access: 20 July 2017.

Habitat3. 2016b. *Urban dialogues.* http://habitat3.org/the-new-urban-agenda/preparatory-process/urban-dialogues/ Date of access: 20 July 2017.

Hall, J.M. 1981. *Japan: From prehistory to modern times.* Tokyo: Tuttle.

Harari, Y.N. 2018. 21 Lessons for the 21st Century. Spiegel & Grau.

Harvey, R. 2012. *The Fourth Industrial Revolution: Potential and risks for Africa.* https://theconversation.com/the-fourth-industrial-revolution-potential-and-risks-for-africa-75313?utm_medium=email&utm Date of access: 31 March 2017.

Hausman, D. 2010. *Reforming without hiring or firing: Identity document production, South Africa 2007–2009 Innovations for successful societies.* Princeton, NJ: Princeton University Press.

Hausmann, R. 2014. *Understanding South Africa's poor economic performance.* Johannesburg: Centre for Development and Enterprise (CDE).

Hayek, F.A. 1944. *Road to serfdom.* Chicago, IL: University of Chicago Press.

Heritage Foundation. 2015. *Index of Economic Freedom.* www.heritage.org Date of access: 4 April 2017.

Hersey, F. & Blanchard, K.H. 1969. Life cycle theory of leadership. *Training and Development Journal, 23*(2):22–24.

Herzberg, F. 1987. One more time: How do you motivate employees? *Harvard Business Review,* Sept–Oct:109–120.

Hofstede, G. 1991. *Cultures and organisations: Software of the mind.* New York, NY: McGraw Hill.

Hogg, A. 2015. Nairobi becoming a serious Africa HQ alternate to Johannesburg ask GE. *Biznews.* http://www.biznews.com/rational-perspective/2015/06/04/nairobi-becoming-a-serious-africa-hq-alternative-to-joburg-ask-general-electric/ Date of access: 5 June 2015.

Hogg, A. 2017. *Davos Diary Day 4: Trump's sole attendee, frostbite & Blockchain killed the ...* https://www.biznews.com/wef/davos-2017/2017/01/20/davos-diary-blockchain Date of access: 20 January 2017.

Holling, C.S. 1973. Resilience and stability of ecological systems. *Annual Review of Ecological Systems,* 4:1–23.

Imai, M. 1986. *Kaizen: The key to Japan's competitive success.* New York, NY: Random House.

Independent. 2016. 8 December 2016 edition. https://www.independent.co.uk/environment/sweden-s-recycling-is-so-revolutionary-the-country-has-run-out-of-rubbish-a7462976.html Date of access: 21 March 2017.

Influenza pandemic. 2017. *Flu pandemic: Facts & summary.* www.history.com/topics/1918-flu-pandemic *Date of access: 28 August 2017.*

Institute for Government UK. 2005. Capability reviews: A case study by Panchamia, N. & Thomas, P. London: Institute of Government.

Institute for Risk Management South Africa (IRMSA). 2015. *South Africa Risks Report.* Johannesburg: IRMSA.

Institute for Security Studies (ISS). 2016. *Africa's future is urban.* https://issafrica.org/events/africas-future-is-urban Date of access: 27 April 2017.

Institute of Race Relations (IRR). 2014. *The 80/20 Report: Local government in 80 indicators after 20 years of democracy.* Johannesburg: IRR.

Institute of Race Relations (IRR). 2017a. *The Hope Report.* Johannesburg: IRR.

Institute of Race Relations (IRR). 2017b. *Empowerment for the Economically Disadvantaged (EED).* Johannesburg: IRR.

Institute of Social and Environmental Transition (ISET). 2010. *Planning for urban climate resilience: Framework and examples from the Asian Cities Climate Change Resilience Network ACCCRN.* Climate Resilience in Concept and Practice Working Paper Series. Boulder, CO: ISET.

Intergovernmental Panel on Climate Change (IPCC). 2014. Climate Change 2014. Synthesis Report. Geneva, Switzerland: IPCC.

International Council for Local Environmental Initiatives (ICLEI). 2015. *Resilient Cities Report.* Bonn, Germany: ICLEI.

International Monetary Fund (IMF). 1999. Foreign direct investment in developing countries. *Finance and Development,* 36(1):114–140.

Ishikawa, K. 1985. *What is total quality control? The Japanese way.* London: Prentice Hall.

Jansen, J. 2016. *South Africa's scary new culture of reckless disrespect.* https://www.businesslive.co.za/rdm/lifestyle/2016-12-15-jonathan-jansen-south-africas-scary-new-culture-of-reckless-disrespect/ Date of access: 18 December 2016.

Jaques, E. 1994. Requisite organisation. (Personal Conversation). 23 June, Boston, MIT.

Jaques, E. 2002a. *The life and behavior of living organisms.* Westport, CT: Praeger.

Jaques, E. 2002b. *Social power and the CEO: Leadership and trust in a sustainable free enterprise system.* Westport CT: Quorum Books.

Jaques, E. 2013. *Requisite organisation: A total system for effective managerial organisation and management leadership for the 21st century.* Orlando, FL: Cason Hall.

Jervis, R. 1997. *System effects*. Princeton, NJ: Princeton University Press.

Jewish Virtual Library (JVL). 2017. *The Kibbutz and Moshav: History and overview*. http://www.jewishvirtuallibrary.org/history-and-over-view-of-the-kibbutz-movement Date of access: 4 May 2017.

Jinping, X. 2017. Secure a decisive victory in building a moderately prosperous society in all respects and strive for the great success of socialism with Chinese characteristics for a new era. 19th National Congress of the Communist Party of China. October 18, 2017.

Johanson, D. & Edgar, B. 1996. *From Lucy to Language*. Wits University Press

Johnson, R.W. 2015. *How long will South Africa survive? The looming crisis*. Jeppestown: Jonathan Ball.

JUSE (Union of Japanese Scientists and Engineers). 1983. Japanese Industry Study Tour [personal interviews] 1–25 January, Tokyo.

Kahane, A. 2002. Civic scenarios as a tool for societal change. *Strategy & Leadership,* 30(1):32–37

Kahn, H. & Wiener, A.J. (1967). The next thirty-three years: A framework for speculation. *Daedalus,* 96(3):705–7.

Kaplan, R.S. & Norton, P. 1996. *The balanced scorecard: Translating strategy into action*. Cambridge, MA: Harvard Business Press.

Kast, F.E. & Rosenzweig, J.E. 1973. *Contingency views of organisations and management*. Chicago, IL: Science Research Associates.

Katz, B. & Bradley, J. 2013. *The Metropolitan revolution: How cities and metros are fixing our broken politics and fragile economy*. Washington, DC: The Brookings Institution.

Kearney, A.T. 2017. *2017 AT Kearney Foreign Direct Investment Confidence Index: Glass half full*. https://www.atkearney.com/documents/10192/12116059/2017+FDI+Confidence+Index+-+Glass+Half+-Full.pdf/5dced533-c150-4984-acc9-da561b4d96b4 Date of access: 12 August 2017.

Khoza, R.J. 2012. *Attuned leadership: African humanism as compass*. Johannesburg: Penguin Books.

Kiefer, C. 1986. Leadership in metanoic organisation. (*In* Adams, J.D. (Ed.). *Transforming leadership: From vision to results*.) Alexandria, VA: Miles River Press.

Kilcullen, D., Mills, G. & Trott, W. 2015. *Poles of prosperity or slums of despair: The future of African cities* (Discussion Paper 5). Johannesburg: Brenthurst Foundation.

King IV Report. 2016. *Report on corporate governance for South Africa*. Johannesburg: Institute of Directors (IOD).

Klein, R.J.T., Nicholls, R.J. & Thomalla, F. 2004. *Resilience to natural hazards: How useful is the concept?* (EVA Working Paper No 9). Potsdam, Germany: Potsdam Institute for Climate Impact Research.

Kleiner, A. & Roth, G. 2000. *Oil change.* Oxford: Oxford University Press.

Kleiner, A. 1996. *The age of heretics.* New York, NY: Doubleday.

Kleiner, A. 2003. The man who saw the future. *Strategy and Business,* Spring.

Kolb, D.A. 1984. *Experiential Learning: Experience as the source of learning and development.* Prentice Hall.

Kolb, A. & Kolb, D.A. 2008. Experiential learning theory: A dynamic holistic approach to management learning, education and development. (*In* Armstrong, S.J. & Fukami, C.V. (ed.), *The Sage handbook of management, learning and educational development.*) Thousand Oaks, CA: Sage, pp. 42–68.

Konditi, T. 2015. GE: Rail rehabilitation & infrastructure investment key to Africa growth. *Biznews* http://www.biznews.com/rational-perspective/2015/06/04/nairobi-becoming-a-serious-africa-hq-alternative-to-joburg-ask-general-electric Date of access: 5 June 2015.

Kotter, J. 1995. Leading change: Why transformation efforts fail. *Harvard Business Review,* (March–April):59–67.

Kramer, J.A. 2015. *Lead with humility.* New York, NY: AMAcom.

Kuhn, T. 1996. *The structure of scientific revolution.* 3rd ed. Chicago, IL: University of Chicago.

Kuper, A. 1970. *Kalahari village politics: An African democracy.* London: Cambridge University Press.

Kuznets, J. 2019. Environmental Kuznets Curve. https://www.economicshelp.org/blog/14337/environment/environmental-kuznets-curve/ Date of access: 9 July 2020.

Laloux, F. 2014a. *Reinventing organisations: Summary.* http://www.reinventingorganizations.com/uploads/2/1/9/8/21988088/140305_laloux_reinventing_organizations.pdf Date of access: 11 August 2017

Laloux, F. 2014b. *Reinventing organisations: A guide to creating organisations inspired by the next stage of human consciousness.* Brussels: Nelson Parker.

Laloux, F. 2015. The future of management is teal. *Strategy and Business.* https://www.strategy-business.com/article/00344?gko=10921 Date of access: 17 June 2017.

Lawrence, P. & Lorsch, J.W. 1967. Differentiation and integration in complex organisation. *Administration Science Quarterly,* 1(12):1–30.

Lawrence, P. & Lorsch, J.W. 1986. *Organisational environment.* Boston, MA: Harvard Business School Press.

Lee K.Y. 2000. *From Third World to First*. New York, NY: HarperCollins.

Leong, C.K. 2012. Special economic zones and growth in China and India: an empirical investigation. *Int Econ and Econ Policy,* 10:549–567 (2013). https://doi.org/10.1007/s10368-012-0223-6

Lewin, K. 1948. *Resolving social conflicts. Selected papers on group dynamics.* New York: Harper & Row.

Lewin, K. 1951. *Field theory in social science.* New York: Harper and Row.

Likert, R. 1967. *The human organisation.* New York, NY: McGraw Hill.

Locke, C.A. & Latham, G.P. 1984. *Goal setting: A motivational technique that works!* Englewood Cliffs, NJ: Prentice Hall.

Lynham, S.A. 2002. The general method of theory-building research in applied disciplines. *Advances in Developing Human Resources,* 4(3):221–241.

Malchik, A. 2017. *Who owns the earth? Aeon essays.* https://aeon.co/essays/is-it-time-to-upend-the-idea-that-land-is-private-property Date of access: 14 January 2017.

Mandelbrot, B. 2004. *Fractals and chaos: The Mandelbrot set and beyond.* New York, NY: Springer.

Manning, T. 2002. Strategic conversation as a tool for change. *Strategy & Leadership, 35*(5), 35-38.

Marcos, J. & Macaulay, S. 2008. *Organisation resilience: The key to anticipation, adaptation and recovery.* Cranfield School of Management http://www.som.cranfield.ac.uk/som/dinamic-content/cced/documents/org.pdf Date of access: 26 March 2015.

Masaaki, I. 1986. *Kaizen: The key to Japan's competitive success.* New York, NY: Random House.

Maslow, A. 1954. *Motivation and personality.* New York, NY: Harper.

Masten, A.S. 1999. The promise and perils of resilience research as a guide to preventive interventions (*In* Glantz, M.D. & Johnson, J.L. *ed. Resilience and development: Positive life adaptation.*) New York, NY: Kluwer Academic/Plenum, pp. 251–257.

Maturana, H.R. & Varela, F.J. 1998. *The tree of knowledge: The biological roots of human knowledge.* Boston, MA: Shambala.

Mbonyana, D. 2006. ESKOM Koeberg Nuclear Power Station Accident, Quality Control Circles [personal interview] Eskom Head Office Megawatt Park, Johannesburg.

Meadows, D. 2008. *Thinking in systems.* White River Junction, VT: Chelsea Green.

Meadows, D.H. 1993. *Beyond the limits.* Post Mills, VT: Chelsea Green Publishing.

Meadows, D.H. 1999. *Leverage points: Places to intervene in a system.* Hartland, VT: Chelsea Green.

Meadows, D.H., Meadows, D.L., Randers, J. & Behrens III, W.W. 1972. *Limits to growth.* London: Pan Books.

Meadows, D.H., Randers, J. & Meadows, D.L. 2004. *A synopsis – Limits to growth: The 30 year update.* Post Mills, VT: Chelsea Green.

Meyer, N. & Neethling, J.R. 2016. Perception of business owners on service delivery. *Administratio Publica,* 24(3):52–73.

Michael, D.N. 1973. *Learning to plan and planning to learn.* San Francisco, CA: Jossey-Bass.

Miller, S.L. 1971. The effects of communication training in small groups upon self-disclosure and openness in engaged couples' systems of interaction: A field experiment. (Doctoral Dissertation, University of Minnesota, 1971). Dissertation Abstracts International, 32, 2819A–2820A. (University Microfilms No. 71–28, 263).

Miller, S., Wackman, D. & Nunnally, E.W. 1982. *Straight talk: A new way to get closer to others by saying what you really mea*n. New York: Signet Publishers.

Miller, S.L., Nunnally, E.W. & Wackman, D.B. 1976. A communication training program for couples. Social Casework, 57:9–18.

Mills, G. & Trott, W. 2015. *Poles of prosperity or slums of despair: The future of African cities.* Johannesburg: The Brenthurst Foundation.

Mills, G. 2014. *Why states recover: Changing walking societies to winning nations, from Afghanistan to Zimbabwe.* Johannesburg: Picador Africa.

Ministerial Conference on Water, 29 October 2008, Jordan Barcelona Process: Union for the Mediterranean, The Official Press Release http://www.medaquaministerial2008.net/press/CP_ENGLISH.pdf-1

Mintzberg, H. & Lampel, J., 1998. Reflecting on the strategy process. *Sloan Management Review*, 40(3).

Mintzberg, H. 1979. *The structuring of organisations.* Englewood Cliffs, NJ: Prentice Hall.

Mintzberg, H. 1994. *The rise and fall of strategic planning.* New York, NY: Prentice Hall.

Morgan, G. 1997. *Images of organisations.* London: Sage.

Morgan, G. 1998. *Images of organisations.* The Executive Edition. London: Sage.

Mouton, J. 1996. *Understanding social research.* Pretoria: Van Schaik.

National Planning Commission (NPC). 2012. *National Development Plan 2030: Our future – make it work.* Pretoria: Department of the Presidency.

National School of Governance (NSG). 2017. www.Thensg.gov.za Date of access: 3 March 2017.

National Treasury. 2011. *Local Government Budgets and Expenditure Review*. 10 October. Pretoria: National Treasury.

Nonaka, I. & Takeuchi, H. 1995. *The knowledge creating company*. Oxford: Oxford University Press.

Norris, F.H., Stevens, S.P., Pfefferbaum, B., Wyche, K.F. & Pfefferbaum, R.L. 2008. Community resilience as metaphor, theory, set of capacities and strategy for disaster readiness. *American Journal for Community Psychology,* 41:127–150. Springer Science + Business Media LLC.

Nunnally, E.W. & Moy, C. 1989. *Communication basics for human service professionals*. New York: Sage Publications.

Nunnally, E.W. 1971. Effects of communication training upon interaction awareness and empathic accuracy of engaged couples: A field experiment (Doctoral Dissertation, University of Minnesota, 1971). Dissertation Abstracts International, 32, 4736A. (University Microfilms No. 72–05, 561).

Nunnally, J.C. 1970. *Introduction to psychological measurement*. New York: McGraw Hill.

Orr, D. 2014. Systems thinking and the future of cities. *Solutions,* 5(1):54–61.

Osborne, D. & Gaebler, T. 1992. *Reinventing government: How the entrepreneurial spirit is transforming the public sector*. Reading, MA: Addison-Wesley.

Osborne, D. & Hutchinson, P. 2004. *The price of government: Getting the results we need in an age of permanent fiscal crisis*. New York, NY: Basic Books.

Osborne, D. 1993. Public productivity: Fiscal pressures and productive solutions. *Management Review,* 16(4):349–356.

Oxford Dictionary of Environment and Conservation. 2007. Oxford: Oxford University Press. https://www.oxfordreference.com/ Date of access: 14 October 2017.

Oxford Dictionary of Law Enforcement. 2007. Oxford University Press. https://www.oxfordreference.com/ Date of access: 14 October 2017.

Oxford Dictionary of Sports Science and Medicine. 2009. Oxford: Oxford University Press. https://www.oxfordreference.com/ Date of access: 14 October 2017.

Papert, S. 1980. *Mindstorms: Children, computers, and powerful ideas*. New York: Basic Books.

Porter, M. E. 1998 Competitive Strategy. New York: Free Press.

Population Information Program. 1998. *Population Report Volume XXXVI, Number 1,* Johns Hopkins School of Public Health.

Putnam, R. 1993. *Making democracy work: Civic traditions in modern Italy.* Princeton, NJ: Princeton University Press.

Resilient Organisations. 2015. *Bay of Plenty Lifelines Group Resilience Benchmark Report.* http://www.resorgs.org.nz/. Date of access: 11 June 2015.

Reynolds, N. 2007. A trusteeship for Zimbabwe: Citizens as Mai actors. *EPS Quarterly,* 20(2):1–2.

Rockefeller Foundation. 2015. Cities Resilience Framework. https://www.rockefellerfoundation.org/report/city-resilience-framework Date of access: 31 March 2018.

Rockefeller Foundation. 2017. *100 Resilient Cities Network.* https://www.rockefellerfoundation.org/our-work/initiatives/100-resilient-cities/ Date of access: 15 November 2017.

Rogers, C. & Skinner, B.F. 1956. Some issues concerning the control of human behavior. *Science,* 124(2):1057–1065.

Rogers, C. 1957. The necessary and sufficient conditions of therapeutic personality change. *Journal of Consulting Psychology,* 21(2):95–103.

Rogers, C. 1959. A theory of therapy, personality and interpersonal relationships, as developed in the client-centered framework. *In* S. Koch (ed.), *Psychology: A study of science Vol 3: Formulation of the person and the social context)* New York: McGraw Hill.

Rogers, C. 1961. *On becoming a person.* Boston, MA: Houghton Mifflin.

SACP. 2010. The National Democratic Revolution. The SACP's 1962 proposals for building a national democratic state. http://www.politicsweb.co.za/documents/the-national-democratic-revolution Date of access: 22 June 2017.

Schein, E.H. 1989. *Organisational culture and leadership.* San Francisco, CA: Jossey-Bass.

Schein, E.H. 1996. Three cultures of management: The key to organisational learning. *Sloan Management Review,* 38(1):9–22.

Schumacher, E.F. 1973 Small is beautiful. A study of economics as if people mattered. New York NY: Blond & Briggs.

Schwab, K. 2016a. *Navigating the Fourth Industrial Revolution.* http://www.biznews.com/wef/davos-2016/2016/01/20/klaus-schwab-navigating-the-fourth-industrial-revolution/ Date of access: 23 August 2017.

Schwab, K. 2016b. *The Fourth Industrial Revolution.* Geneva: World Economic Forum.

Schwartz, A-M., Bene, C., Bennett, G., Bozo, D., Hilly, Z., Paul, C., Posala, R., Sibili, S. & Andrew, N. 2011. Vulnerability and resilience of remote rural communities to shocks and global change: Empirical analysis from Solomon Islands. *Global Environmental Change,* 2:1128–1140.

Schwartz, P. & Randall, D. 2003. *An abrupt climate change scenario and its implications for United States national security.* GBN Publication

Schwartz, P. 1991. *The art of the long view.* New York: Doubleday

Schwartz, P., Leyden, P. & Hyatt, J. 1999. *The long boom: A vision for the coming age of prosperity.* Reading, MA: Perseus Books.

Seba, T. 2014. Clean disruption of energy and transportation. https://www.youtube.com/watch?v=2b3ttqYDwF0 Date of access: 9 September 2017.

Seba, T. 2016. Why energy and transportation will be obsolete by 2030. Keynote presentation at the Swedbank Nordic Energy Summit in Oslo, Norway. https://www.youtube.com/watch?v=2b3ttqYDwF0 Date of access: 21 July 2017.

Senge, P.M. 1990. *The fifth discipline: The art and practice of the learning organisation.* London: Random House.

Senge, P.M. 1995. Conversation with Peter Senge

Senge, P.M., Kleiner, A., Roberts, C., Ross, R.B. & Smith, B. 1994. *The fifth discipline fieldbook.* London: Nicholas Brealey.

Senge, P.M., Kleiner, A., Ross, R.B., Roth, G. & Smith, B. 1999. *The dance of change: The challenges to sustaining momentum in learning organisations.* New York, NY: Doubleday Currency.

Sheppard, E. 2010. Adam Smith in Beijing: Lineages of twenty-first century by Giovanni Arrighi. *Clark University,* 86(1):99–101. www.economicgeography.org Date of access: 29 August 2017.

Shockley-Zalabak, P.S., Morreale, S.P. & Hackman, M.Z. 2010. *Building the high-trust organisation.* San Francisco, CA: Jossey-Bass.

Simmie, J. & Martin, R. 2009. The economic resilience of regions: Towards an evolutionary approach. *Cambridge Journal of Regions, Economy and Society,* 1–17 doi:10.1095/cjres029

Smuts, J.C. 1925. *Holism and evolution.* 3rd ed. London: Macmillan.

South Africa. 1993. *The White Paper on Local Government.* Pretoria: Government Printer.

South Africa. 1994. *Public Service Act 1994.* Pretoria: Government Printer.

South Africa. 1996. *Constitution of the Republic of South Africa, 1996.* Pretoria: Government Printer.

South Africa. 1998. The White Paper on Local Government. *Government Gazette* No 30137 of 01 August 2007. Pretoria: Government Printer.

South Africa. Department of the Presidency. 2011. *National Development Plan 2030. Our future – make it work.* Pretoria: Sherino Printers.

South African Cities Network (SACN). 2014. http://sacitiesnetwork.co.za/ Date of access: 10 June 2015.

South African Cities Network (SACN). 2016. *State of South African Cities Report.* Johannesburg: SACN.

StatsSA. 2014. Statistics South Africa http://www.statssa.gov.za/?m=2014&gclid=EAIaIQobChMI2tWHooCj7QIVCU4YCh39xw-PiEAAYASAAEgLiWfD_BwE Date of Access: 23 June 2017.

Stephenson, A., Vargo, J. & Seville, E. 2010. Measuring and comparing organisation resilience in Auckland. *The Australian Journal of Emergency Management,* 25(2):27–32.

Stephenson, K. 2003 *The quantum theory of trust: power, networks and the secret life of organizations.* Prentice Hall.

Stephenson, K. 2005a. *Quantum theory of trust.* New York, NY: Financial Times

Stephenson, K. 2005b. *Trafficking in trust: The art and science of human knowledge networks.* (*In* Coughlin, L., Wingard, E. & Hollihan, K. *ed. Enlightened power*). San Francisco, CA: Jossey-Bass, pp. 242–264.

Sterman, J. 2000. *Business dynamics: Systems thinking and modelling for a complex world.* Boston, MA: McGraw Hill Higher Education.

Steyn, R. 2015. *Smuts unafraid of greatness.* Johannesburg: Jonathan Ball.

Sunningdale Institute. 2007. *Take-off or tail-off? An evolution of the Capability Reviews Programme.* www.nationalschool.gov.uk Date of access: 14 October 2017.

Swanson, R. A. 1997. HRD research: Don't go to work without it! *In* Swanson, R. & Holton, E. (eds.) *Human resource development research handbook.* San Francisco: Berrett-Koehler, pp. 3–20.

Taleb, N.N. 2007. *The black swan.* London: Penguin.

Taleb, N.N. 2012. *Antifragile.* New York, NY: Random House.

Taleb, N.N. 2015. *Few and far between: Black swans and the impossibility of prediction.* http://changethis.com/33.04.FewFar/email Date of access: 10 June 2015.

Tapscott, H.D. 2016. *Blockchain revolution: How the technology behind Bitcoin is changing money, business and the world.* New York, NY: Penguin Random House.

The Heritage Foundation. 2015. *Index of Economic Freedom: Promoting economic opportunity and prosperity.* https://www.heritage.org/index/ Date of access 4 October 2015.

The Tavistock Institute. 2017. www.tavinstitute.org/ Date of access: 10

August 2017.

Torraco, R.J. & Swanson, R.A. 1995. The strategic roles of human resource development. *Human Resource Planning,* 18(4): 3–38.

Trompenaars, F. & Hampden-Turner, C. 1998. *Riding the waves of culture.* 2nd ed. London: Nicholas Brealey.

Turton, A. 2016. *Water pollution and South Africa's poor: Report.* Johannesburg: IRR.

United Kingdom (UK) House of Commons. 2009. *Assessment of the Capability Review Programme: Forty-Fifth Report of Session 2008– 2009.* London: The Stationery Office Limited.

United Nations International Strategy for Disaster Reduction (UNISDR). 2012. *A guidebook to the green economy. Issue 1: Green growth and low carbon development.* Division for Sustainable Development, UNDESA.

United Nations International Strategy for Disaster Reduction (UNISDR). 2012a. *City resilience in Africa: The Ten Essentials Pilot.* http://www. unisdr.org/we/inform/publications/29935 Date of access: 27 October 2015.

United Nations International Strategy for Disaster Reduction (UNISDR). 2012b. How to make cities more resilient: A Handbook for Local Government Leaders. Geneva: UNISDR.

United Nations International Strategy for Disaster Reduction (UNISDR). 2015. Sendai Framework for Disaster Risk Reduction 2015-2030. Geneva: UNISDR.

United Nations International Strategy for Disaster Reduction (UNISDR). 2016a. Strategic Framework 2016-2021. Geneva: UNISDR.

United Nations International Strategy for Disaster Reduction (UNISDR). 2016b. Disaster Risk Reduction Achievement 2016. Geneva: UNISDR.

United Nations. 2003. *World Water Development Report (WWDR), Water for the People.* UNESCO Publication ISBN 92-3-103881-8

Universities of Canterbury/Auckland. 2017. *Resilient Organisations Research Programme.* http://www.resorg.nz/What-is-resilience Date of access: 1 August 2017.

Van Creveld, M. 2008. *The Transformation of War.* Simon and Schuster

Van der Heijden, K. 1996. *Scenarios: The art of strategic conversation.* London: Wiley.

Van der Heijden, K. 1997. *Scenarios, strategies and the strategy process.* The Netherlands: Nijenrode University Press.

Van der Heijden, K., Bradfield, R., Burt, G., Cairns, G., & Wright, G. 2002. *The sixth sense: Accelerating organizational learning with scenarios.* New York: John Wiley.

Van der Merwe, L. 1991. Systems approach to change management: The

Eskom experience. *In* Osler, C. (Ed.) 1991. *Making their future: South African organisations on the move.* Institute for Futures Research: University of Stellenbosch Press, pp. 63–76).

Van der Merwe, L. 1994. Bringing diverse people to common purpose. (*In* Senge, P. et al. (eds.), *The fifth discipline field book.* London: Nicholas Brealey, pp 424–429).

Van der Merwe, L. 2008. Scenario-based strategy in practise: A framework. (*In* Chermack, T. (ed.), *Advances in HRD.)* London: Sage, pp. 216-239).

Van der Merwe, L. 2016a. Lessons from Singapore: Wisdom of invisible markets – social transformation at work. *Biznews,* 28 June 2016. http://www.biznews.com/transformation/2016/06/28/lessons-from-singapore-wisdom-of-invisible-markets-social-transformation-at-work Date of access: 30 June 2016.

Van der Merwe, L. 2016b. *Failing our future: Why SA needs to develop competent teachers at scale.* http://www.biznews.com/thought-leaders/2016/08/12/eating-our-children-why-sa-needs-to-develop-competent-teachers-at-scale/ Date of access: 13 August 2016.

Van der Merwe, L. 2018. City government resilience: Towards a diagnostic instrument. North-West University (PhD Thesis).

Van der Merwe, L., Chermack, T.J., Kulikowich, J. & Yang, B. 2007. Strategic conversation quality and engagement: Assessment of a new measure. *International Journal of Training and Development,* 11(3):214–221.

Van der Waldt, G. & Greffrath, W. 2016. Towards a typology of government interventions in municipalities. *African Journal of Public Affairs,* 9(2):152–165.

Van der Waldt, G. 2004. *Managing performance in the public sector: Concepts, considerations and challenges.* Landsdowne: Juta.

Van der Waldt, G. 2016a. Towards an e-governance competency framework for public service managers: The South African experiment. *African Journal of Public Affairs,* 9(4):114–129.

Van der Waldt, G. 2016b. Towards a typology of government interventions in municipalities. *African Journal of Public Administration,* 9(2):152–165.

Von Bertalanffy, L. 1968. *General systems theory: Foundation development and applications.* New York, NY: George Braziller.

Wack, P. 1985a. Scenarios: Uncharted waters ahead. *Harvard Business Review,* September-October: 73–89.

Wack, P. 1985b. Scenarios: Shooting the rapids. *Harvard Business Review, 63*(6):139–150.

Walker, B., Holling, C.S., Carpenter, S.R. & Kinzig, A. 2004. *Resilience, adaptability and transformability in social-ecological systems.* http://www.ecologyandsociety.org/vol9/iss2/art5 Date of access: 24 October 2017.

Walton, J.S. 2008. Scanning beyond the horizon: Exploring the ontological and epistemological basis for scenario planning. *Advances in HRD.*

Warner Burke, W. 1989. *Organisation development: A normative view.* Reading, MA: Addison Wesley.

Weisbord, M.R. 1992. *Discovering common ground.* San Francisco, CA: Berrett-Koehler.

Wheatley, M.J. 2002. *It's an interconnected world.* Shambhala Sun. http://margaretwheatley.com/wp-content/uploads/2014/12/Its-An-Interconnected-World.pdf Date of access: 3 August 2015.

Whybrow, P.C. 2015. *The well-tuned brain: Neuroscience and the life well-lived.* London: Norton.

Windle, G. 2017. *What is resilience? A review and concept analysis.* Reviews in Clinical Gerontology. Cambridge: Cambridge University Press.

World Economic Forum (WEF). 2015. Survey Report – Deep Shift: Technology tipping points and societal impact. https://search.yahoo.com/ search?p=wef%20survey%20report%20deep%20shiftselect&fr=y-set_chr_cnewtab&type=newtab Date of access: 9 February 2017.

World Economic Forum (WEF). 2016. *The Global Information Technology Report 2016: Innovation in the digital economy.* http://www.org/gitr Date of access: 14 February 2017.

World Economic Forum (WEF). 2017. *Cities, not nation states, will determine our future survival.* https://www.weforum.org/agenda/2017/06/as-nation-states-falter-cities-are-stepping-up Date of access: 19 July 2017.

Yang, B. (2005). Factor analysis methods. (*In* Swanson, R. & Holton, E. (eds.) *Research in organizations.)* San Francisco, CA: Berrett-Koehler, pp. 181–200.

Zondi, S.I. & Reddy, P.S. 2016. The constitutional mandate as participatory instrument for service delivery in South Africa: The Case of Ilembe Municipality. *Administratio Publica,* 24(3):27–51.

INDEX

www.ingramcontent.com/pod-product-compliance
Lightning Source LLC
Chambersburg PA
CBHW080547270326
41929CB00019B/3226